A volume
in
THE DOCUMENTARY HISTORY
of
WESTERN CIVILIZATION

The Century of Louis XIV

The Century of Louis XIV

edited by

OREST AND PATRICIA RANUM

WALKER AND COMPANY

For Helen Haberman

First published in the United States of America
in 1972 by the Walker Publishing Company, Inc.

Published simultaneously in Canada by Fitzhenry &
Whiteside, Limited, Toronto.

Library of Congress Catalog Card Number: 72-80542
ISBN: 0-8027-2031-5
Printed in the United States of America.

Volumes in this series are published in association with Harper & Row, Publishers, Inc., from whom paperback editions are available in Harper Torchbooks.

Contents

Introduction: A Perspective on General European History, 1650–1715

The documents in this volume introduce their readers immediately to the fundamental political, social, and cultural developments of Western European societies in the last half of the seventeenth century. Selections from major philosophical and literary works have been omitted, since these are readily available in complete, inexpensive editions. Sources which have not been republished since the seventeenth or early eighteenth centuries have been preferred, not because they represent something very particular or out of the mainstream of developments, but simply because it is impossible for an entire class to read these works in the rare-book rooms of major university libraries.

Fewer documents have been selected from Eastern European societies, not because they are less important, but because the editors lack the expertise to select and translate them. Futhermore, the interest among both students and their teachers in Western European developments justifies this emphasis. Those materials about Eastern Europe included here, however, serve the important function of illustrating what literate Westerners could know about their Eastern European contemporaries. The siege of Vienna in 1683 is a case in point, for it was an event which captured the interest of many Europeans throughout the Continent.

In the selection of these documents, the focus has been almost entirely on the relationships among Western European societies. Internal developments, except for France, have been sacrificed in favor of presenting the influences of societies upon one another. This is particularly appropriate for the half century of state building and of international war which began in the crises and revolutions of the mid-seventeenth century. Also, every attempt has been made to select documents which had a large reading public in the seventeenth century. Too often the Century of Louis XIV has been viewed by historians only from the perspective of kings, battles, and courts. The increasingly large reading public of the later seventeenth century avidly read about the political, social, and cultural developments of their own day. Their curiosity about themselves permits us to enter their minds and to know directly what they knew about their contemporaries, at least at the level of the educated ruling elites. Furthermore, for nobles, officials, physicians, and merchants, a young man's education continued to include as much as two years of travel abroad. Not all Western European young men who were literate could fulfill this part of their education, to be sure, so they did the next best thing, which was to read voluminously in the published diaries and travel accounts of their contemporaries. What, for example, did the English think or know about French society and culture? This type of question has been too long ignored by historians of the seventeenth century, and for that reason it has been given a special emphasis here through documents selected specifically to reflect cultural and national prejudices.

There are limitations, however, to the presentation of fundamental relationships through the publication of what can be only a handful of documents. The study of changes in population, prices, commercial relationships, and agricultural innovations, all of which has attracted much attention among historians recently, cannot be accomplished without presenting entire series of documents. One will alone is insufficient to establish the social position of a family; hundreds of wills, account books, letters, and other materials are required. Nor would the publication of one bill of lading or credit letter enable us to know whether French commercial developments in the 1670's seriously challenged Dutch and English shipping in the Scandinavian ports. The historical questions which can be answered only by counting or narrating simply do not lend themselves to answers on the basis of a handful of published documents. Here the editors have done what would seem to be the next best thing: to republish analyses of what Europeans *thought* was happening to their societies and economies. In many instances, their assessments were inaccurate, of course; but in themselves these provide insight into the history of political, social, and economic analysis. The last half of the seventeenth century was a period when government officials, members of Parliament, merchants, and scientists sought greater and greater precision in the data which they needed to administer, buy or sell, or speculate. The sciences of politics, economics, and public administration were as yet unborn, but statistical and other factual evidence increasingly became the basis for governmental policies, learned discourse, and coffeehouse talk. Indeed, the spurt in the founding of royal and other academies around 1660 was in part an institutionalizing of this more empirical study of politics, society, nature, and the body at a critical time in the development of scientific methods.

Beneath the level of high politics and ruling elites, however, national, religious, and cultural preoccupations changed very slowly. The name Descartes was probably unknown to 95 per cent of the population in an age often called Cartesian. Among educated Europeans the acceptance of cultural and religious differences as a principle would not appear until the eighteenth century. Central and Northern Europeans may have been more cosmopolitan than those of the South and West, because national identities east and north of the Rhine were less developed. Within the larger states regional particularism remained so strong that Frenchmen, Englishmen, and Spaniards did not have to cross the borders of their kingdoms in order to feel foreign and ill at ease among strange ways and beliefs.

Our knowledge about peasants, artisans, parish priests, and other groups still further down the social ladder is much more limited. Thanks primarily to French historians, statistical information about their average age, number of children, age of marriage, and income has been discovered for certain regions of France.[1] Their researches have opened a frontier in the social history of France, and it is hoped that similar intensive studies will be made for other parts of Europe. But for our purposes the type of statistical knowledge which they develop can scarcely be illustrated by selections from parish registers.

The low rate of literacy among these groups, particularly on the Continent,[2] has meant that they have left virtually no written records of their thought or activities from which selections could be made. Should we then trust the comments of upper-class Europeans on the peasantry and artisans? Literate Europeans were generally content with a quite simplistic literary image of their social

1. Most notably P. Goubert, *Beauvais et le Beauvaisis de 1600 à 1730* (Paris, 1960), and E. Le Roy Ladurie, *Les Paysans de Languedoc* (Paris, 1966).

2. L. Stone, "Literacy and Education in England, 1640–1900," *Past and Present*, 42, 1969.

inferiors; rarely did they take the trouble to record their conversations with persons from these social groups. Letters from lords, ladies, and prominent bourgeois to their domestic servants, even when these were life-long companions, either were not thought to be worth saving or were never written at all. For these reasons historians have turned to more general materials, such as sermons and the *Bibliothèque bleue*, to try to reconstruct the "collective mentality" of these groups.[3] The literature of the barely literate was inexpensive and cheaply bound in blue paper, hence the title *Bibliothèque bleue*. These little books, as well as almanacs and books of devotion, have only recently begun to be seriously researched for the study of popular culture. Their moral precepts, definitions of God and social status, and their portrayal of the world of make-believe suggest a rich and old cultural heritage which extended to the lowest orders of European society and which was also probably quite familiar to bourgeois if not aristocrats. The homogeneity of European society in the seventeenth century, at least on such matters as the belief in a hierarchical social order, is a familiar theme in recent historical works.[4] Selections from the *Bibliothèque bleue* therefore serve the function of illustrating what Frenchmen could have believed in the seventeenth century; but, as is the case with Eastern European developments, the documents chosen here to illustrate the life and thought of groups at the bottom of the social ladder are few in number.

More than half the documents published here deal with French internal affairs. This may seem unfair to historians uninitiated in the historiography of the seventeenth century. But the importance of French cultural developments for the general history of Europe has long been recognized. French fiscal, military, and judicial innovations were probably infrequently copied directly by rulers and ministers of other states, but the impetus for a strong state, reform, and centralization nevertheless came primarily from France. As J. H. Plumb puts it for English officials: "Most practical men of affairs felt a sneaking sympathy for the regime of Louis XIV and Colbert, whose government seemed not only very

3. R. Mandrou, *De la Culture Populaire au 17e et 18e Siècles* (Paris, 1964).

4. Though most specifically for France, England, and Northern Europe, P. Ariès, *Centuries of Childhood* (New York, 1965), P. Laslett, *The World We Have Lost* (London, 1965), and R. Hatton, *Europe in the Age of Louis XIV* (London, 1969).

much more stable than their own but more efficient."[5] The evolution of social structures throughout almost all of Europe favored absolute monarchy[6] and the development of a bureaucratized nobility. In this process of state building, French developments after the revolts of the midcentury served as a model, not only in public administration and social policies but also because these innovations had made French military power preponderant. Other European states faced the choice of either innovating to establish their own massive, totally obedient, standing armies and bureaucracies or facing overwhelming defeat on the battlefield.

Contemporaries, as the documents in this volume illustrate, knew about the relationships between French reforms, her military power, and her expansionist aims in the Rhineland, the Netherlands, and Italy. The aristocratic elites of Europe shared the assumptions of the Sun King, namely that conquest added to the greatness of the state and to the prestige of its sovereign, and that courage in battle was the supreme virtue of nobility. The image of Louis XIV at the head of his obedient army or being honored endlessly in immense palaces appealed to petty princes, noblemen, and men of letters nearly everywhere in Europe. These men of lesser rank, if of equal talent, might respect, envy, or even hate Louis XIV, but their psychological and social involvement with him is incontestable. Thus the principal theme in the general historiography of Europe 1650–1715 is the dialectic between France's solutions to the problems of disorder, heresy, and revolt, her expansionist wars, and the development of other centralized states in a European balance of powers by 1715.

Catching up with France in order to stop her armies involved the overthrow of an oligarchical republic in the Netherlands in 1672, and later the rejection of Catholic Absolutism in the English Glorious Revolution of 1688. In the East, where there had never been a question of adopting republican principles of government, Hapsburg power came increasingly to rest on a more bureaucratically administered Hapsburg state, instead of on Imperial claims in Germany. To the south, the fate of a weakened Spain lay ultimately in the hands of the two superkings, Louis XIV and William III—

5. *The Origins of Political Stability, England, 1675–1725* (Boston, 1967), p. 11.

6. G. M. Clark, *The Seventeenth Century* (Oxford, 1945), pp. 82–97.

for Charles II of Spain had failed to produce an heir. That such a dynastic accident could still count so much in the general struggles for European dominance among states testifies to the elasticity of the institution of monarchy in the seventeenth century. Indeed, while still disguised in medieval trappings, the power of Louis XIV, William III, and Leopold I of Austria was much greater over their subjects than that possessed by their forebears since Roman times.

If multiplied several times, the documents published here would serve quite well for a general history of Europe in the last half of the seventeenth century. What would surprise a contemporary of Louis XIV, of course, would be the absence of accounts of battles, pageants, and religious services; and he might wonder why diplomatic relations have been slighted. The same contemporary of Louis XIV would find the introductions quite baffling. The clues about the significance of a document, as well as its content, will be useful, however, to modern historians. Specialists of the seventeenth century always have in mind the facts and ideas included in these introductions. Whatever the specialist reads, or whatever building or artifact he sees, the "document" stimulates the search for answers to questions which he has been asking, perhaps for years. Beginning historians who have not as yet mastered the historiography of the seventeenth century will find the introductions and glossary particularly helpful; but they may need still more help.

Put another way, the more knowledge a historian brings to the documents, the more knowledge they will impart to him. The historical process is thus one of asking questions as well as of recognition based on factual details. The fashion of learning methodologies in social studies and history encourages clearer thinking and better questioning, but it also unfortunately ignores the important part which recognition plays in research. Indeed, apart from the philological method of learning what words mean in a historical context, the analysis of a document depends much more on recognition of names, dates, places, and institutions than on any other method. The lack of the accumulated factual knowledge which permits historians to recognize specific details in a document, rather than the lack of methodological sophistication, accounts for the difficulty which beginning historians encounter in analyzing documents.

Beginning historians should be asked to look for and to answer specific questions when they are assigned documents to read.

Along with the questions and lectures, J. Stoye's *Europe Unfolding, 1648–1688* (New York, 1969) and R. Hatton's *Europe in the Age of Louis XIV* (New York, 1969) would be particularly helpful, because these very recent works have influenced the editors' choice of documents for this volume. These works give historians a sense of Europe as a whole, of related developments in various societies, and of fundamental political and cultural changes. The scope of the two works is different, and their authors do not agree on all the topics they discuss, but they nevertheless provide excellent frameworks for the general history of Europe in the seventeenth century.

J. B. Wolf's *The Emergence of the Great Powers, 1685–1715* (New York, 1951) sets forth a bold thesis on the relationship between internal developments and warfare to complement Stoye's work very successfully. The shift in focus from Stoye's work to Wolf's reflects not only their interests as historians, but also a shift of priorities among the large European states from internal reforms to decades of war. Indeed the events from the 1680's to 1715—the siege of Vienna, the revocation of the Edict of Nantes, the Glorious Revolution, the Great Northern War, and the War of Spanish Succession—marked a turning point not only in European history but also in the careers of several monarchs. Historians have not lost their fascination for studying the great sovereigns of the late seventeenth century, partly because the duel between states and cultures was personalized in their sovereigns.[7] S. Baxter's *William III* (London, 1966), J. B. Wolf's *Louis XIV* (New York, 1968), and R. Hatton's *Charles XII of Sweden* (London, 1968) demonstrate how historians have gone far beyond the traditional stereotypes of these sovereigns, to create coherent explanations of how each individual's beliefs and foundation of power led him into devastating wars. But despite all the research and writing, there is still much disagreement among historians about the Age of Louis XIV. Yet a historian as remote from us as Voltaire would be able to appreciate the classical qualities of these biographies and probably would compliment their authors for their thoroughness of research.

In translating these documents, care has been taken to remain as

7. More advanced students should read the superb essays by the late Mark Thomson, republished as *William III and Louis XIV*, ed. by R. Hatton and J. S. Bromley (Toronto, 1968).

close to the original French as possible, in an attempt to reflect the often clumsy style of the seventeenth century. The polished wit of La Bruyère was clearly not a talent shared by all Frenchmen. For clarity's sake, interminable sentences have at times been broken into smaller units, a few clauses have been rearranged, and words within brackets replace pronouns which became ambiguous when translated into English. In both the contemporary English and the translated texts, the erratic punctuation and excessive capitalization of the seventeenth century have been modernized. Spelling, however, remains unchanged, as a reminder of the difficulties sometimes encountered while working on old texts. No explanation has been made for personal and place names which, though erratically spelled, are recognizable. Where phonetic variants or copyist's errors stray too far afield, the modern spelling is shown in brackets after the variant's first appearance in the selection. The errors which have crept into the transcriptions, translations, and introductions may not in fact be entirely the fault of the editors, but they nevertheless assume responsibility for them.

Historians traditionally end their seventeenth-century lectures and books in 1713, and not in 1700. The reasons for this tradition are numerous, but the most important ones are the signing of the Peace of Utrecht in 1713 and the death of Louis XIV. After the terrible battles of Blenheim, Ramillies, Oudenarde, and Malplaquet, Europeans would not again witness such high costs in blood and treasure until the Napoleonic campaigns. The decades of internal revolts in the mid-seventeenth century were followed by years of reform, and then large-scale war ending in 1715. To historians all this has seemed a series of related developments, epitomized, of course, by the actions of Louis XIV and France. Born in 1638, succeeding his father on the French throne in 1643, assuming all power for himself after Mazarin's death in 1661, and then ruling until 1715, Louis XIV's was a most remarkable reign in a still very monarchical Europe. The Sun King had sought to become the arbiter of Europe, to assure French commercial and cultural dominance, and later to acquire the entire Spanish inheritance. Thus it was not simply Louis' long reign which accounted for the sense of change felt by contemporaries at his death. Louis had ruled actively himself and had generaled his armies as well as blusteringly informed all literate Europeans that he was the successor to Alexander the Great and Caesar Augustus. No matter how ridiculous this might seem to us in the twentieth century, Louis' actions and claims had great impact on his contemporaries. His top priorities were diplomacy, war, religious orthodoxy, and a culture which would immortalize him; the governing elites, men of faith, and men of letters overwhelmingly shared his priorities, no matter how hostile they were to Louis himself and to French power. Why they shared his views is a question best answered by the documents themselves.

I

Beginnings in War, Revolt, and Misery

The relationship between internal French development and general European history is very clearly observable throughout Louis XIV's long reign. Indeed, there could be no era of isolationism for one of the greatest powers in Europe. This is evident from the immense problems which Louis XIV inherited. When his father died in 1643, France was already at the point of total civil war and complete political disintegration. The costly war which the French had been conducting against Spain since 1635 had already led to large-scale violence and revolt in Spain. The war undermined the political stability of both combatants, while the high taxes needed to pay troops had strained the resources of the peasantry to the breaking point in a period of poor harvests and dire subsistence living. What could an otherwise socially stable population do but attack the tax collectors, pillage records, and burn down the houses of royal officials?

In the desperate attempt to gain revenue for the war, the Crown had also created hundreds of offices and sold them to the highest bidder, undermining the traditional support and loyalty of royal officials. This practice, which severely threatened the wealth and prestige of officials already holding offices, made them unusually responsive to the complaints of the rebellious peasantry and artisans.

And as if this were not trouble enough, the leading aristocrats, some with royal blood in their veins, who held the key provincial military posts and commanded armies, opportunistically sought greater influence in the affairs of state, higher pensions, and increased prestige. In years of peace and relative prosperity, peasants, royal officials, and princes scarcely would have thought of joining to force the Crown to change its policies; but the war and adverse economic conditions raised this to a possibility. The interests of these groups proved to be too divergent, however, and a social revolution failed in France during the Fronde of 1648–1652. But this was a lesson which could be learned only through violence and anarchy.

Yet there could be no simple movement to demand negotiations for peace. Spanish troops in northern France had been a reality in the late 1630's, and Spain represented a real threat to French interests and to those of her Dutch allies. There seemed no solution to the problem so long as Richelieu and Olivares remained willing to risk civil war in an effort to defeat each other. After 1643 a policy of hanging on in grim determination was the only alternative open to the Boy King's councillors, in a war which would last until 1659.

A king who was only five years old, a female regent who was the sister of France's sovereign enemy, and an Italian principal minister during the period 1643–1652 doomed France still further to disorder. Despite all his efforts to reduce the power of the princes and other potential rebels, Richelieu had not, after all, completely succeeded. Even without the enormous burden of the Spanish war, France would have undergone a severe crisis and witnessed violence during the minority of Louis XIV.

In the following documents no attempt has been made to cover the complex series of events which occurred during the minority. But each document represents a major element in the denouement of the political conflict. It is, of course, impossible to define neatly the differences between social and political conflict. That social conflict came to be part of the Fronde is obvious; but if we look at the structure of French society in 1640, and again in 1660, what had changed? The role of the princes as petty kings in their own provinces, each with his own army, had been repudiated. Royal officials too had become more obedient; and as the lot of the peasantry improved, their potential role in the society subsided without a change in their status having occurred. The passion for order which prevailed in the minds of Louis XIV and his ministers, as seen in the documents in Part II, may have been shared by many Frenchmen after the time of troubles at the outset of the reign.

1. Reports of a Provincial Revolt

The civil war known as the Fronde, or "slingshot," did not suddenly erupt in Paris in 1648. Sporadic violent outbursts and rioting were endemic to rural society in the *ancien régime*, but between 1620 and 1648 these incidents occurred with increasing frequency and severity. Some riots were minor, their causes being scarcely more profound than an extended tavern brawl or the arbitrary decision of a local revenue collector. But others, such as the Nu-pied revolt in Normandy in 1639, became a massive insurrection of several thousand persons, and a challenge to royal control of the province.

These revolts have recently been of particular interest to historians.[1] Nineteenth-century historians, apart from A. Feillet[2] and P. Clément,[3] had largely ignored them, but the publication of *Popular Revolts in France from 1623 to 1648* (Moscow, 1945),[4] by Soviet historian Boris Porchnev, changed within France itself the course of scholarship devoted to the first half of the seventeenth century. Instead of seeing these revolts as only a kind of pre-Fronde, and instead of seeing the peasantry as agents of noble or other rebels, Porchnev has linked these rural insurrections to the general development of the absolute state.

SOURCES: "Relation des résolutions prises au Parlement de Thoulouse en conséquence des désordres arrivés à Villefranche," Bibliothèque Nationale, Mss. fr. 23159, fol. 54–55; "Memoire de La Terrière, Intendant en Guyenne sur les souslevemens de Rouergue et ce qui est cause qu'on ne tire pas un teston de l'Eslection dudit pais" (1943), Bibliothèque Nationale, Mss. fr. 15621, fol. 257–258; "Relation de l'Estat présent des souslevemens de Rouergue" (Sept. 14, 1643), Bibliothèque Nationale, Mss. fr. 15621, fol. 247–248; "Plaintes de Charreton . . . ," Bibliothèque Nationale, Ms. fr. 18830, fol. 246.

1. See the general review by J. H. M. Salmon, "Venal Office and Popular Sedition in France," *Past and Present*, 37, 1967.
2. *La Misère pendant la Fronde* (Paris, 1868).
3. As extracted from his edition of Colbert's letters in *Histoire de Colbert* (3d ed., Paris, 1892), I.
4. Available in a German translation published in Leipzig in 1954, and a French translation published in Paris in 1963.

Did the peasantry, as Porchnev states, play a more active and spontaneous role in French political developments than hitherto thought by historians? The conventional historical analysis of the period holds that the primary threat to the Monarchy's ability to govern lay in the princes and the great nobility, who had almost as much power as the king in the provinces they controlled. But Porchnev asserts that fear of the peasantry caused a potential common interest if not an alliance to develop between the nobles and the royal officials. Did the peasants threaten to overthrow the traditional social order?

While not denying that peasants and artisans could and did rebel on their own on occasion, Roland Mousnier[5] has seen them still primarily as groups used by rebels from the upper classes. Is a peasant revolt of political significance if local nobles do not attempt to repress it and if judges condone violence or join in the attack against the Crown? Similarly, Mousnier sees little possibility for an alliance between the nobles and the Crown. The causes of these revolts, as he sees them, lie primarily in the fiscal and bureaucratic changes instituted by Richelieu as devices for increasing royal revenue to pay for armies fighting in Italy, then against the Protestants at La Rochelle, and finally overtly against Spain after 1635.

The following texts illustrate how a royal official, in this instance an intendant, who was also a commissioner, viewed a provincial revolt which broke out in the rugged, isolated region of Villefranche-de-Rouergue, in what is now the department of the Aveyron. Note the role which he attributes to himself, to Governor and Seneschal Noailles, to the troops, the minor courts, and the Parlement of Toulouse. The report of the Parlement's activities subsequent to Charreton's encounter with the rebels on June 2 preceded the main uprisings of the summer; hence it would be fair to conclude that the Crown's ability to rely upon the Parlement to suppress the revolt was limited.

Early in 1643, the *juge-mage*, or lieutenant general, of Villefranche had headed an unsuccessful delegation to Paris concerning a reduction of the *tailles*. Indeed, Charreton later claimed that the rebellion had broken out only upon the *juge-mage's* return, that he had made no efforts to suppress the revolt, and that he had remained in Villefranche with the rebels. On June 3, the *présidial* of Villefranche had delegated Molineri, son-in-law of a member of the Parlement of Toulouse, to represent the rebels before the Parlement. These documents show that Charreton was aware that a group of members of the *présidial* of Villefranche was forming about the *juge-mage* in support of the rebel cause. Its leader was Rainaldi, the *juge-mage's* father-in-law and Charreton's former advocate. Such actions resulted in the interdiction or demotion of certain members of the *présidial* of Villefranche-de-

5. See, in particular, *Peasant Uprising in the 17th Century* (New York, 1971).

Rouergue and of certain consuls, during the months of June and July, creating the problems with the *élus* referred to in these documents. A brief chronology follows:

On June 2, 1643, Intendant Charreton was besieged at Villefranche by 1,200 Croquants, or rebels, armed with pitchforks and scythes, and was forced to issue orders decreasing the amount due for the *tailles*. During July, Governor Noailles, who owned lands near Najac and had connections in the province, was sent by Paris to calm the situation; committed to avoiding the use of force, he brought no troops. By the end of July, Noailles saw he would have to seize the leaders of the rebellion, La Paille, La Fourque, and Petit. Meanwhile, relying on the intendant's and other reports, Mazarin had decided to send troops under Langeron. Without awaiting the arrival of these troops from Paris, Noailles had two of the rebels arrested. In retaliation, the Croquants marched upon Villefranche and besieged Noailles. Langeron arrived in time to rescue him, then liberated Villefranche. In August, Mazarin congratulated Noailles for "calming this little storm" and advised him and Charreton to avoid the use of force. The rebels, expelled from Villefranche, occupied Najac and Saint-Salvadour, from which the royal army later expelled them. Charreton wrote Paris on August 10 that Noailles was too lenient with his old friends and pleaded for the authority to have several rebel leaders chastised as public examples. In September, skirmishing still occurred; the Croquants gained temporary control of a city gate at Villefranche and marauded in the surrounding regions, while their leaders, still at liberty, were attempting to stir up trouble in neighboring provinces. By the end of October 1643 the rebels had sought refuge in the mountain wilderness and the rebellion had been entirely subdued.

These documents leave many questions unanswered, and this chronology is tentative at best, since the history of the revolts in Rouergue is still to be written. But the roles of officials are delineated, at least from one point of view, and the knowledge possessed by Mazarin and Anne of Austria concerning provincial conditions is illustrated. The 1630's and 1640's were crucial in the development of the intendants and commissioners, and these documents demonstrate why the Crown risked great unpopularity by relying on these officials. For further information, see U. Cabrol, "Documents sur les soulèvements des paysans du Bas-Rouergue," *Journal de l'Aveyron,* 1907–1910; and M. Degarne, "La Révolte du Rouergue," *XVIIe Siècle,* 56, 1962.

The manuscripts from which these selections were translated reflect a problem which constantly plagues the researcher: the correct reading of names. In this text those misspellings due to regional pronunciation can be clearly distinguished from those resulting from misreadings by a secretary copying the original memorandas. Note that on several occasions the editors shared his troubles!

Narrative of the Resolutions Made in the Parlement of Toulouse as a Result of the Disorders Which Occurred at Villefranche

On Thursday, June 4, 1643, the Parlement of Toulouse—having been notified of the disorders in Villefranche by the Sieur Molineri, lieutenant general to the *présidial* of the said city [of Villefranche]—although it was a holiday, nevertheless held a sort of meeting of the Parlement to discuss the current events of the time. And it was decided and recorded that all the intendants who had been in their jurisdiction for ten years, and those who worked under them and followed their orders, would be investigated, and that the whole [matter] would be brought by deputies of the said Parlement before the King and our lords of his council.

And it was decided that very humble remonstrances would be made to the King concerning the oppression and the searches which the *peuple* must undergo, for payment of the *taille*, winter quartering of troops, *mainmorte*, *francs-fiefs* [paid by commoners who wished to own a fief], the eighth of the alienated ecclesiastical possessions, verification of notaries, and other [taxes]. And that there would, however, be a postponement in the collection of all the said duties, even of the *tailles*, and generally it was decided that there would be a postponement of the execution of all the edicts and decrees of the Council which had not been carried out during the reign of the late King, until the deputies of every region could express their complaints and request justice from the King now reigning.

That henceforth the *taille* would be collected by a process server alone, and that a complaint would be lodged against those tax receivers who had it collected otherwise, as against extortioners.

That in the event of rebellion in any city or parish because of the *tailles* or otherwise, the Parlement would send commissioners to the spot for the purpose of conducting and completing the trial of seditious persons and rebels.

That the intendants both of Guyenne and of Languedoc would bring their new commissions to the Parlement to be registered there; otherwise they would be forbidden to carry out the functions of their office, and everyone [would be forbidden] to pay attention to their orders, and all process servers, sergeants, or other officers [would be forbidden] to carry them out; the purpose of this article is to bring about modifications in the commissions of the said intendants.

In addition it was also decided that commissioners would be delegated by Villefranche to conduct and complete the trials of rebels, if there were any. . . .

These decisions were made by one part of the Parlement, composed mainly of young members, and were turned in the next day to the bureau, with all the chambers assembled, where there was a great deal of argument. The Parlement met four or five times, and finally one of the more level-headed of the company said that all these decisions would be carried out with the exception of the *taille*, and that they would use it as an excuse for postponing all the other taxes in order to facilitate the payment [of the *taille*].

However the *peuple* of Toulouse and of all the neighboring provinces were caught up by the Parlement's first decision and did not want to hear talk of the *tailles*, all the more so because those who were demanding the postponement of the *taille* had boldly announced in public that if they paid during this first year of our king's reign, it would be useless to hope that during his entire reign he would ever lower it, no matter what promise might be made to the contrary; and consequently that it would be better to die than to pay like that; thus there is neither any parish nor any community which is willing to pay.

This explosion in the Parlement was followed by two or three rebellions, in one of which a *capitoul* [leading municipal official of Toulouse] feared he might be killed by the nursemaid of a councillor in the Parlement.

The *peuple* were stirred up under pretext of the high price of wheat, which is, however, not so scarce nor at such an excessive price, and yet the *peuple* were allowed to steal a boat loaded with wheat in the city without being punished; some shouted boldly that the *tailles* must not be paid, others complained of so many disorders caused by the ambition of the great nobility.

A certain Landes, treasurer of France at Toulouse, brother-in-law of the *juge-mage* [lieutenant general] of the said city, in the middle of a public square of the said city, where there were a great number of persons of quality and of the populace, having become angry with the Sieur Gratareli, treasurer of France at Montauban, concerning the speech about the surcharge on the *tailles*, said that they must not be paid, that the intendants must not be allowed in the province, especially since they were the cause of all the surcharges and were thieves; which the said Gratarely denied; and they came to blows, so that it looked as if there would be another great rebellion there.

At the assembly on Monday, the Sieur de Marmiesse, advocate general in the Parlement, being a creature of Monseigneur the Chancellor [Pierre Séguier], was excluded from the said assembly; and the Sieur de Mambant [Maniban], another advocate general, did not wish to be present, saying that he feared the results of such assemblies. Only the *procureur général* was willing to risk everything, not foreseeing the consequences, since his mind is not one of the most perspicacious.

Monsieur the First President [of the Parlement of Toulouse] is doing everything he can to forestall these disorders, but he is not powerful enough; and it must be considered as given that the Parlement will be carried away and will issue decrees capable of kindling rebellion in all the neighboring provinces.

It should be observed that the councillors [of the Parlement] are great landowners in the province and by the sale of the domain became lords of several communities; those which belong to them are making the worst faces, and they did not even pay the *taille* until the arrival of the intendant who is at Montauban, who forced some of them to pay, and that is why they decided that the *taille* would be collected by a process server, so that they could not be compelled [to pay].

They undertook to abolish the power which the *capitouls* of Toulouse have in the city, all the more so since their authority makes them jealous, and they are the cause of the rebellions which have broken out over the high price of wheat, announcing publicly that it happened through the error of the said *capitouls*. The *peuple* are delegating one of the said *capitouls* named d'Espagny, who is fully instructed both about all the disorders of the said city and about their authors.

Memorandum of [Charreton de] La Terrière, Intendant for Guyenne,
Concerning the Uprising in Rouergue
and Why We No Longer Get a Teston *[12 sous coin]*
from the Élection *of the Said Region*

Similarly, there is not one community which has come to verify the tax rolls.

As of the 16th of this month [only the year 1643 is given] the inhabitants of Villefranche were to bring a thousand écus to the collector's office. The Sieur de Nouailles [François de Noailles, governor of Rouergue] had caused them to believe that once they had paid, their taxes would be abolished, although the sum was not very great and indeed was a very small mark of their obedience, the Sieur Renaldi alone being worth a hundred thousand écus and more. Nevertheless they did not want to meet their obligations, saying that if they paid this sum so promptly they would be believed rich, and thus that no portion of their *tailles* would be lightened. They keep claiming this and say that they have been led to hope for [this reduction].

Petit took up a collection among the rebels in Villefranche so that he would have the means to escape in case he was forced to, and he got up to two hundred pistoles.

The 24th of the said month a lackey of the Sieur Tuillier, treasurer of France at Montauban—who was going from Roddes [Rodez] to Sainct-Anthonin and was passing near Najac, a city in lower Rouergue and consequently rebellious—was attacked by the Croquants of the said city, who searched him and took his papers and his money from him. The said city belongs to the said Sieur de Nouailles, as the intendant stated in previous accounts, and is being stirred up by the rebels of Villefranche, who want to vindicate [their rebellion] by showing that their neighbors are more disobedient than they. The intendant is including the complaint which he received from the said lackey.

A part of the *sénéchaussée* and of the *élection* which is not under restraint is determined not to obey the Council's decrees to have their seat transferred. That is why the intendant—having sent them three ordinances during a period of six weeks or two months that they were to go to Saint-Antonin to attend to their duties—in accordance with orders given him, issued an ordinance by which he commissioned others in their place and forbade them their offices, in view of their disobedience. Nevertheless, if they return within the week, he will reinstate them with His Majesty's good pleasure, although the ordinance was categorical.

The *élus* do not wish to carry out their functions at Saint-Antonin, because this city is at the extremity of the *élection* and is inconvenient; but they fail to take into account that—since in all lower Rouergue only this one city has not rebelled and has not brought weapons to Villefranche to support the league, having as proof of its obedience paid the *taille* while the rest of the *élection* was up in arms—they could not and should not establish elsewhere the seat of the *élection* nor that of the *sénéchaussée.*

The officers of the *sénéchaussée* add to the arguments of the *élus* that they have become *présidiaux-sénéchaux* and that they will obey only when the *présidial* has been reestablished, which is one of the rebels' suggestions, and indeed in Villefranche poems have been written mocking those who obeyed the decree, the gist of which is that they were so cowardly at heart that they allowed themselves to be reduced from a *présidial* to a *sénéchaussée.* These poems are credited to an official under interdiction.

Since the Sieur de Nouailles' departure from Villefranche, they have also sung publicly in the streets of the said city in the local language. "Whatever Monsieur de Nouailles may say, we will not pay any *tailles*, tra-la-la."

From which it is easy to judge that the promised obedience is only lip service and without any results, as the future will clearly show, unless a few troops put in their appearance, with which we can easily quell all the rebels, who have no leader or courageous persons among them.

Upper Rouergue and the county of Roddez are in the same state as before. No one pays and no one obeys there.

The said Sieur de Nouailles convoked the consuls of six or seven communities in an attempt to win them over personally. According to the information which the intendant had sent him in his letter of the 17th of the current month, and realizing that he had been tricked by the rebels of Villefranche, who had not carried out any of their promises, after having received the said letter from the intendant—since the Sieur Renaldi had left him to go visit the Sieur de Campagnac, father-in-law of one of his sons, who had been stabbed twice at Fegeac [Figeac] by some men from Auvergne—he promptly sent a special messenger to look for him and for the *juge-mage*, his son-in-law, and told them that he could see clearly that they had been tricked, but that in the future Villefranche would have no greater enemy than he in calming his anger and resentment. The said *juge-mage* and Renaldy, Bouffart, and Du Puy, who were with him, promised him noticeable results of their blind obedience in a few days. The results of this obedience consist in capturing Petit.

Having learned that some time ago the marshal of Saint-Luc had issued an ordinance granting permission for the nobility of lower Armagnac in Gascony to assemble in order to debate the means of raising the *taille* more conveniently for the *peuple* than it is now being raised by order of the Council, and considering the dangerous consequences of this assembly, the intendant promptly sent a messenger to the said marshal of Saint-Luc to issue an [ordinance] to the contrary, which the said marshal issued at once. And inasmuch as the intendant believed that this would end the matter, he did not notify the Council; nevertheless he was soon notified that despite the marshal of Saint-Luc's last ordinance, the nobility would not give up convoking this assembly, and that lampoons were being distributed and posters displayed in various areas of Gascony, especially in Pardiac; the intendant is enclosing a copy of these in order to show the Council and in order to make it realize clearly that if troops are not sent into the region promptly to punish a few guilty persons, after several assemblies and uprisings some great disorder will ultimately occur, with marked mental debauchery.

Since I wrote the above, a messenger arrived, bringing the edict of the Council dated the 17th of this month, to conduct the trials of the outlaws of Villefranche, along with its orders and instructions concerning the execution of the said edict included in the letter which Monsieur de La Vrillière [secretary of state] wrote to the intendant, which he will promptly carry out and fulfill.

And at the same time one of the consuls of Villefranche also arrived, finally bringing 2,500 livres to the collector's office; and the intendant made it clear that in order to be forgiven, the four tax farms falling due have to be paid by the first two weeks of the coming month, or otherwise they would be subject to the discretion of the troops which His Majesty will send into the province in great number to make them obey.

CHARRETON

Account of the Current State of the Uprisings in Rouergue

The second of this month [September] the Sieur Renaldi [Rainaldy] wrote to the Sieur de Rins, who he believed was with the Count of Nouailles [Noailles] at Caiare [Carjac], where the said Sieur [de Rins] had gone to meet with the Sieur de La Terrière [intendant at Montauban] in order to confer about current happenings, and told him that the rebels of Villefranche, immediately after the Sieur de Nouailles' departure, had become alarmed about the above-mentioned conference and about the rumor circulating concerning the arrival of royal troops to punish them according to the orders of the Sieur de Langeron [*maréchal de camp* and commander of the royal troops]; [and the rebels] had seized one of the gates of the said city and both by this act and by several secret threats had changed matters there in such a way that the said Sieur Renaldi feared that the said Sieur de Nouailles' plans would fare badly. The plan of the said Sieur de Nouailles was to seize the gates, towers, and belfreys of Villefranche in order—with members of his household and several friends who were with him, aided by some influential persons of the said city—to capture those called Petit [a surgeon], La Paille [a mason], and La Fourque [a harness maker], and to place them in the intendant's hands, and by using their punishment as an example, to reestablish the King's authority in the city and its vicinity.

The consuls of Mur de Barrez had shown their obedience by paying everything [that city]owed and by seizing two notorious rebels whom they were keeping in prison to be taken before the said intendant at the first opportunity.

Four days earlier some peasants from the parishes of Saint-André and Saint Salvadour, belonging to the said Sieur Raynaldi, and from La Fouliade near Villefranche, assembled by night totaling about 400, only 111 of whom bore firearms, including ten good fusiliers from Nagac [Najac] and a few soldiers from the vicinity of Nagac and Salvaterre [Sauveterre], all of whom were sleeping with their weapons in their hands; and the next morning they seized the chateau of Salvadour, where they stationed about twenty soldiers to form a garrison which was to be given provisions paid for by the said parishes. The said rebels also tried to take by surprise the chateau of Roumegoux, which belongs to the Marquis of Malante [Malauze], but it is until now still being watched over by his tenant farmers.

It seems that the chief inhabitants of Villefranche are trying to serve the King faithfully, at least according to La Fourque. One of the rebels wrote four days ago to those whom he knew in various places that they should be ready at a moment's notice and that the peasants of a number of parishes some time ago bought guns and prepared themselves to march.

Peasants living along the Lout [Lot] River, at the crossings of Leviniac, Flaniac, Port d'Agres, and others, maintain that they intend to prevent the crossing of the troops under orders of the said Sieur de Langeron which are supposed to arrive.

The regiment of [the Count of] Tavannes, which is stationed at Milhaud [Millau], numbers only 160 men, most of them without shirts and without shoes, and many of them without arms that are in working condition. The inhabitants of the said city of Milhau and those of Compeyre, which is nearby, are at the same time almost all stirred up against the collectors of the *tailles* for the said towns, so that the said collectors have given them up and no longer feel safe there. The consuls of the said Milhau sent a delegation to the said Sieur de Nouailles and presented him with a few rather feeble apologies. The said Sieur ordered that the regiment be lodged in the said city in the homes of the rebels and those who have not paid in full, with the exemption and exception of those who paid; and this [will continue] until the said debtors have entirely paid the assessed sums imposed on the said city by virtue of the King's orders, and in accordance with the assessment list which was verified. Written at Maurs on September 14, 1643.

For two or three days La Paille has been going out from Villefranche to stir up the *peuple* in the direction of Quercy [the region west of Rouergue], and the 3rd of this month when the said intendant passed before the gates of Figeac, the *menu peuple* assembled before the gates of the said city, where the consuls did not dare to appear; and they debated whether they would allow the said intendant to enter, and it was decided that they would not. During this assembly the gates of the said city were open only by wicket doors, at one of which several of the said intendant's entourage, having appeared in order to obtain a meal, were rudely pushed by an inhabitant who was guarding the door and who told them that the consuls had forbidden anyone to be admitted. The next day the said consuls went to see the said intendant to disavow the act and words of the said inhabitant and to tell him that they could not control the *menu peuple*, who had seized upon the pretext and the right to assemble under guise of a syndicate which they had formed by permission of the *Cour des aides* of Cahors. The said consuls promised that, provided we approach the gates of the said city with sufficient troops, they would gain control and would allow the said troops to enter and would bring the *menu peuple* back into order.

Maurs, the said day of September 14, 1643.
CHARRETON [DE LA TERRIÈRE]

Charreton's Complaints about the Parlement of Toulouse

Although the Parlement of Toulouse has on several occasions taken advantage of the privileges granted it by the [Royal] Council in its decree of last May 4, nevertheless, the intendant will be satisfied with showing evidence that it is too daring and scornful toward the edict of the said Council.

By the said edict His Majesty referred the joint trial of Dousset and his accomplices to the intendant and the appeal to the consular and parlementary jurisdictions.

And in order to know the truth about what happened, it will be observed that the said Dousset—in a popular rebellion which occurred in the said city of Figeac—having uttered several seditious statements against the payment of the *tailles* and the King's service, even beaten and insulted the consuls and their liveries, accompanied by a great number of rebels, and which consuls having imprisoned them by order of the said intendant, the Parlement, upon a petition presented by the said Dousset which stated that the said intendant was holding him in an unhealthy prison where he was in danger of his life, ordered that he be taken from the said prison to be placed in another one. And in execution of the said order, a certain

Raissac, process server for the *sénéchaussée* of Figeac, instead of putting him in the prison specified by the said order, let him escape.

Since then, the intendent ordered the said Raissac to bring back the said Dousset, because he allowed him to escape without authorization and even contrary to the Parlement's orders, and if he failed to do so he would be asked to appear in court personally. After several prohibitions, the intendant finally ordered the said Raissac to be punished corporally for having failed to bring back the said Dousset.

The said decree having been carried out by the Sieur Hoqueton [?], the said Raissac appeared before the Parlement and instead of explaining to them the misdemeanor he had committed, and the Parlement's order, he told them that because he had carried out the said order, he had been imprisoned by order of the intendant, and that if that took place, no process server would dare carry out the decrees from the Parlement requesting that someone be released from prison; and moreover that Dousset had obtained a decree from the Council by which the intendants were forbidden to prosecute him, and by which it was ordered that the consuls of Figeac should be summoned before the said Council, upon which and without altering the text or meaning of the Parlement's ordinance, but only [changing] the edict obtained by the said Dousset, of which they even altered the date and the exact sense of the petition, the Parlement ordered that the said Raissac be conducted to the conciergerie of Toulouse and that the proceedings be registered in the records of the said city.

Then the said Raissac was freed and is walking about Figeac, having caused Palue [?] and the consuls for last year for the said Figeac to be called before the Parlement in execution of the said order.

The intendant implores the gentlemen of the Council to consider that since the intendant has had his commission registered before the Parlement of Toulouse, [the Parlement] cannot be unaware that he is empowered to be the sovereign judge of all sorts of crimes, and consequently that it cannot free criminals imprisoned by order of the said intendant, and other unknown [criminals], under these circumstances, except by order of the Council. The affair of Dousset and his accomplices, among whom is the said Raissac, was referred to the said intendant; and hence he demands that by decree of the Council it be stated that the said Raissac shall be conveyed to the prisons of the said city of Figeac, and that the Parlement shall be forbidden to issue decrees or orders to free prisoners who have been imprisoned by order of the intendant.

CHARRETON

2. *The Parlement of Paris and the Fronde*

By the fall of 1648, rebellions and riots in both city and countryside had produced a division of authority in the highest levels of the royal government. One of the highest agencies for the enforcement of the law, the Parlement of Paris, could no longer be relied upon by Anne, the Regent for Louis XIV, to help suppress rebellion. Indeed, the Parlement had responded to public clamor and now found itself in a middle position between Anne, her ministers, and an angry, rebellious population.

Once in a middle position, all the Parlement could hope to do was win enough concessions from the Crown to soothe its more moderate members and the Parisian rebels. The judges were mindful that the concessions which they gained, and even their own role, would be watched not only by the other parlements in the provinces but also by Madrid. Spanish officials gleefully hoped that Omer Talon and his colleagues would make it impossible for France to carry on the war against Spain. Would the French judges behave like the English members of Parliament in these years, and completely dismantle the absolute state?

Omer Talon (1595–1652) was a loyal servant of the Crown, but—at the moment he describes here—his very prestigious court of law was being intimidated by an angry and demanding mob of Parisians. At the same time, some of his own younger colleagues were becoming inflamed by "wild" ideas and demands for still more constitutional concessions from the Crown. The rebellion over high taxes and food had rapidly turned into a grab for power by such princes as Gaston d'Orléans and Condé, and by the Parlement. Thus Talon firmly believed that he had to win enough concessions to keep the moderate judges and Parisians from joining the more radical elements who were beginning to demand still more fundamental changes in the political and social structure of monarchical France.

In the royal declaration itself, the substance of the grievances which had led the men of property and power to join the peasants and the

SOURCE: *Mémoirs relatifs à l'Histoire de France, Mémoires d'Omer Talon,* ed. by Michaud and Poujoulat (Paris, 1857), XXX, 286–297.

peuple in rebellion is dealt with in considerable detail. It was a broad and general attempt to defuse a rebellion and to reverse the absolutist policies of Richelieu and Louis XIII. Note the mixing of constitutional with fiscal issues. The Parlement of Paris, though negotiator between the Crown and the militant Frondeurs, was anything but a disinterested party.

That very day [October 13, 1648] we all went to Saint-Germain a little after two o'clock and were ushered into the Queen's cabinet at three o'clock, where–the First President [Mathieu Molé] having told the Queen of the morning's deliberation and having implored her urgently to have pity on the *peuple* and in words showing great respect but without humility unworthy of his position–the Queen said that we should withdraw and that she would give her reply. And having held an urgent council meeting in one corner of the cabinet, all the deputies from the Parlement being in another one, the Queen called us back and, with the Chancellor [Pierre Séguier] as her spokesman, told us that this delay being created in public affairs was liable to ruin them; that the populace was imagining immense rebates and a sort of liberation from any sort of taxes, during which time they were becoming accustomed to paying nothing; and that as a result with no soldiers, Swiss or French, being paid, [and] no garrisons being maintained, some noteworthy accident might occur in public affairs; that the Queen wished things to be settled as soon as possible; that in order to induce the company* to do so, the Queen was making this effort to grant up to twelve hundred thousand livres' reduction each year on all commodities consumed in the city of Paris, which sum of twelve hundred thousand livres the Queen agrees may be apportioned equally on whatever merchandise the court [of the Parlement] wishes, to bring the most relief to the poor people, but on the condition that this [allocating] be done on the following day, after which time the Queen will tolerate no further deliberations. Such a brief delay shocked those present, [it] being impossible in such a brief time to resolve a matter of this nature, even if everyone were in agreement; so that the First President replied that Her Majesty could blame nothing on the company, which would deliberate

* Talon consistently uses the term *compagnie* to describe the Parlement; though the word can be translated as "group," it seems closer to Talon's thought to call them a "company" or corps.

about the tariffs, and that the Queen having turned over to them up to a certain sum to distribute to the *peuple*, that they had not wanted to issue a decree for the diminution of certain duties on wine, but had thought they might implore the Queen to grant it; that they had thought they should also deliberate about the other goods which are most necessary to life, in order to ask Her Majesty for a reduction on them; which cannot be done by so large a number of persons, and in so short a time.

The Queen having stressed the harm which the assemblies and delays of this nature would do to the King's affairs, [and] Cardinal Mazarin having spoken to one and another privately, the gathering thus dispersed, and we returned to Paris.

On Wednesday, October 14, the First President having recounted what had happened the preceding day at Saint-Germain, the deliberation was begun and lasted until eleven in the morning, when it was recessed until the afternoon; but during this time the hall of the Palace [of Justice] filled with a great number of persons, so that when any of these gentlemen wished to leave the great chamber they found the passageways blocked, the *peuple* grumbling because they had not issued a decree. The presidents urgently wishing to leave, preceded by ushers with their staffs, they encountered rather great difficulty; loud clamors arose against them, and they were extremely harried and mistreated by all those people, who were tavernkeepers, coopers, their valets, their wives, and with them many unknown and shiftless persons, who were demanding justice, threatening and insulting these presidents. All this was announced at Saint-Germain, and in more exaggerated form than it had actually been.

These activities greatly shocked us royal attorneys when we were notified of it, and we resolved that we should act to bring about some order; to do so we resolved to notify the officers of the police to be in the great hall and to station their city guards somewhere in case they were needed. In addition, when we entered the great chamber in the afternoon, we again pointed out to the court the importance of what had happened that morning, and the unhappy consequences which might result; we proposed to them three or four expedients: to bring charges against the authors of the revolt, or to issue a decree forbidding any sorts of persons not having business at the Palace to come there, or to make them leave forcibly, and to arm the bourgeois through the authority of the court; or else to see whether gentle methods were capable of remedying the situation, the disturbance having been created by tavernkeepers who complained of the harshness with which vendors and wine inspectors demanded the duties imposed on them, raising them to whatever sum they pleased; that, upon the complaint by these tavernkeepers, the court provisionally exempted them from a third of the duties levied by these officers; but that they would like their reduction to be fixed and established at a certain sum, so that there would be no further occasions for lawsuits between one another.

Following this remonstrance the court issued a decree by which it ordered that these vendors and inspectors would bring in their certificates to be inspected, and that meanwhile they would not demand more than thirty sous on the hogshead of wine: the terms of which decree having been explained by us to this populace, they were contented, and most of them withdrew.

Then the court worked at continuing the morning's deliberations, upon which followed a decree stating that entry duties on wine would be decreased fifty-eight sous a hogshead, and [the court] also decided that the Queen could be implored to increase the relief she was granting to the *peuple*, instead of twelve hundred thousand livres, up to two million, to be allotted to the commodities most necessary for life; and that to this end the king's advocates would travel to Saint-Germain to make their supplication to the Queen.

Thursday, October 15, we were ordered to the great chamber, where the First President informed us about the court's deliberations. I informed him that we considered it a great honor to carry out the company's orders, but that, not having attended the deliberations, and not knowing the court's thoughts, we needed to be informed, so as not to fail in the mission which had been given us; so the First President told us in detail, and in few words, the court's aim.

In order to carry out this order we went to Saint-Germain, where, having arrived at three o'clock, and having visited the Chancellor, we met Marshal de La Meilleraye, the superintendent [of finances], and having been conducted before Cardinal Mazarin, we found all the minds of these gentlemen very changed, having gotten the idea that we wanted to force from the Queen this rebate of two million, and to postpone the assemblies until the day after

St. Martin's Day [Nov. 12]; and although we assured them to the contrary, they found it hard to believe.

That day, which was the festival of St. Theresa, the Queen had gone to Pontoise to the Carmelite convent, where the Chancellor's sister is mother superior; and the Chancellor's wife gave the Queen and all the princesses a meal; thus the Queen returned to Saint-Germain only after six in the evening, night already being very near. We were immediately ushered into her cabinet, where the entire council was—with the exception of the Duke of Orléans [Gaston, brother of Louis XIII], who had taken medicine, and Marshal de La Meilleraye, who was playing [cards] with him. I said to the Queen: "Madam, we received an order this morning from the gentlemen of the Parlement to have the honor of seeing Your Majesty and making her understand that they deliberated yesterday morning and afternoon on what Your Majesty had told them on this very spot, and that they decided, after having thanked Your Majesty for her kindness in reducing for her subjects a sum of twelve hundred thousand livres a year, to implore her to please increase this relief and be willing to raise it to two million, all the more so because although the sum is great, nevertheless being imposed and apportioned on merchandise, it is insignificant and unnoticeable in retail [prices]. These gentlemen believe, Madam, that beyond this sum Your Majesty meant to abandon the little tariff, which totals two hundred thousand livres; so that it is now only a question of six hundred thousand livres, which sum, if it please Your Majesty to grant them, they mean to apply to the basic commodities necessary for the life of the poor people, and in which sum of two million they include the reduction for the cloven-hoofed animals and yesterday's reduction on wine; which they believed that Your Majesty would not be displeased at their having done, all the more so because they worked within the limits of their power, and because this reduction on wine is included in the sum of two hundred thousand livres which Your Majesty granted them; and in addition they considered this rebate and the publication of it to be necessary to control the *peuple* and to prevent the agitation of their minds, which are already too heated; and they gave us the duty, Madam, of giving Your Majesty to understand that the company intended, once these sums had been apportioned on merchandise, to cease all assemblies, which were held only in order to obtain from Your Majesty some relief for the poor people."

The Queen interrupted us to have us repeat this last part of our speech; and having assured her that the First President had thrice assured us, she commanded us to retire into her chamber while she deliberated; which we did, and spent from seven to nine in the Queen's chamber. A little after nine o'clock we were called back, and the Queen in substance told us that she was granting the sum of two million in consideration of the Parlement's promise to stop all deliberations, and [she] stated for us in writing her intention to make a statement to the Parlement in conformity with the note which she put into my hands, and here is the gist of it:

"The Queen, after having heard from the king's advocates that they had an order from the court of the Parlement to implore Her Majesty to increase the sum of twelve hundred thousand livres which she had granted in reduction on taxes, up to the sum of two million livres, to be apportioned on them, and in consideration of this favor the company had charged them to assure Her Majesty that all deliberations would cease and would be completed on the first day after the allocation of the said sum of two million livres had been completed, and to this end to implore Her Majesty to grant the continuation of the Parlement for several days, Her Majesty recognizing increasingly to what point the continuation of assemblies is prejudicial to the king's service—through the hopes which his enemies gain from it (although unfounded), which serve to make them increasingly stubborn in the war—and desiring to make known that her passion for the relief of the *peuple* makes her forget all sorts of financial needs, no matter how urgent they may be, she willingly grants the sum of two million livres, to be apportioned on the taxes, as the said court of the Parlement will judge most appropriate for the relief of the *peuple*, on the condition that in consideration of this favor all things will remain entirely terminated and finished, and that the assemblies and deliberations will cease at once, without any new ones being formed for this purpose in the future; and so that the said court of the Parlement can deliberate on the current proposition, Her Majesty agrees that it meet again Friday and Saturday; and after Her Majesty has been informed on what the Parlement has decided in conformity to the above, she will willingly grant the time deemed necessary to do the allocating of the said sum of two million livres, and to have the declaration discussed and verified."

The Queen had the goodness to provide us with torches to take us back, with candles to light up the coach, and a police officer and four constabulary guards to escort us, with which equipage we returned to our homes after midnight.

The next morning, Friday, October 16, we went to the Palace [of Justice] early and went to the presidents before the meeting, to notify them in general terms of the success of our mission.

As soon as the chambers had assembled, we were summoned, where I related what had happened at Saint-Germain, and felt obliged to exaggerate the affair and to show the importance of stopping the deliberations at once, because of the advantages which the enemies of the state could gain from them: moreover, that it was necessary to reprimand the audacity of the *peuple*, who had attacked by words and by various outrages the person of the presidents in the great hall of the Palace, which action I considered more rebellious and of greater importance than that of the barricades [of August 27, 1648], because in the first they had as a pretext the liberty of those who had been imprisoned, and there was reason to believe that the Parlement might repress them; but in this second one they insulted royal authority in order to exempt themselves and to acquire freedom from a few taxes, and scorned the image of the magistrates: so that if the riot had become heated, it would have been difficult to put it down. It is a shameful thing, a populace which riots, and which not only goes unpunished but even more gets what it wants through its petulance; and as a result not only gains impunity, but even some sort of reward and satisfaction from its misdeed.

Thus, reporting the Queen's words, as much as I could I urged these gentlemen to cease their assemblies and to deliberate on Friday and Saturday on the remaining propositions, the Queen having told us that the Parlement could take our word as to the continuation of the Parlement; and I told them that the remission of two million was in fact made, provided they would stop all forms of deliberations and discuss the declaration which would bring the matter to a close.

The matter was not debated, but it was decided unanimously that the Queen would be very humbly thanked for the relief she was granting to the *peuple;* that they would immediately proceed to the apportioning of the two million, and that to this end commissioners would meet at the First President's home; which was done that afternoon.

On Saturday, October 17, the officers of the Châtelet and the *prévôt des marchands* were sent for and warned to take in hand the maintenance of order, so that the *peuple* could experience the fruit of the relief which the Queen had given them. After that they read what had been done the preceding day by the commissioners for the apportioning of the two million, which was approved.

Next they debated the article concerning the remission of a quarter of the *taille*, which had been asked of the Queen; and the Queen having wanted to reduce it by one-eighth, she had finally consented to reduce it by a sixth. Having debated this, it was decided that very humble remonstrances would be made to the Queen, to implore her to increase this reduction to a fifth; and to that end we were ordered to go the following day to Saint-Germain to announce it to the Queen.

On Sunday, October 18, we went to Saint-Germain, my colleagues and I, an hour after noon; we visited the Chancellor, who took us to Cardinal Mazarin, where we were for some time, until the Queen sent for us. Near the Queen was her entire council, that is, the Duke of Orléans; Monsieur le Prince [Condé]; the Prince de Conti [Condé's brother]; the Cardinal; Monsieur de Longueville; the Chancellor: Marshal de La Meilleraye, superintendent of finance; and the secretaries of state; Monsieur de Tubeuf [an intendant of finance] even was there, not to give an opinion, but to reply if he was questioned. Nevertheless, in making my report to the court, I did not wish to name those who were present, so as not to have to talk about Cardinal Mazarin, whose name was unpopular, and with whom none of the group had expressed a desire to confer. I said to the Queen: "Madam, following Your Majesty's command, which we received Thursday in this very spot, the following morning we entered the Parlement, where all the chambers had assembled, and told them that it had pleased Your Majesty to grant the *peuple* a remission of up to two million, on condition that all forms of meetings cease and that everything would be reestablished to its former order. This proposition was not a subject of debate, but of public satisfaction, for which it was decided that Your Majesty would be very humbly thanked for her goodness, and that in order to satisfy what she desires, they would immediately begin to work on what remained to be done on this matter; that for that purpose commissioners would assemble in the afternoon to draw up the articles proposed in the Chamber of St. Louis, and to apportion the two million on the most necessary commodities, which was done; and the next morning, the officers of the police having been summoned, they received an order to inform the *peuple* of the relief granted by Your Majesty, and in carrying it out to act so that each one could feel its effect. Then what the commissioners had done having been read and approved, there remained only two items to work out, one concerning the *tailles*, the other the execution of the ordinance of King Louis XI, called the 'article on public safety,' which they thought should be drawn up the same day. And in fact, having urgently worked on the first, they decided that Your Majesty would be very humbly implored to reduce for the *peuple* the fifth of the *taille* on the basis of fifty million; and as for the other article, the hour was so late that they could not debate it, nor set a time for the afternoon, but postponed it until Monday. However, Madam, we are carrying out what it pleased Your Majesty to order us last Thursday: we bring her the record of what happened in the Parlement, which has authorized us, until the time it has the honor of greeting Your Majesty, to express to her its total gratitude, [and] that of the *peuple* of Paris, and of the entire realm, who will bless the King's innocence and Your Majesty's piety, her conduct, and her government. Receive, Madam, please, these few words as a mark of public gratitude and as a witness of the feelings of a group which is the first in obedience and in respect. Excuse, Madam, if you please, the barrenness of our intellect, if we have so few words to thank Your Majesty (great things are expressed in few words); and permit, Madam, that we make you a humble entreaty for the poverty of the poor *peuple*, who are overburdened with all sorts of taxes and levies, for whom the Parlement is interceding and imploring that instead of the sixth they may receive the reduction of a fifth on their taxation, in this unique thought which was left to us in writing by the wisest of all kings, that sovereigns serve on earth, that they are enlightened by the labor and sweat of those who cultivate it, who help it produce fruits, without whom neither princes nor their subjects can live. A strange thing, however, that those who sow and who reap have no bread with which to nourish their families, and that they live wretchedly under the harshness of the taxes which are demanded of them! The Parlement hopes for this favor from Your Majesty's kindness, after which God will bless the *épargne*, for thus is called the treasure of our kings, which must be administered with parsimony and spared more than it has been in the past."

This little speech finished, the Queen told us that we would have to withdraw and that she would make a reply. And indeed we withdrew to the other end of the cabinet, and the Queen held council standing with the princes and ministers who were present; and after having conferred some time together, [they] approached us, and the Chancellor told us that the decision of the Parlement stated that the Queen would be implored to surrender to the *peuple* the fifth of the *taille* on the basis of fifty million total; that her intention was to do so, and that thus she had proposed it to the conference, that is to say, eight million on all the *généralités* subject to the *taille*, with the exception of Orléans, which remission of eight million makes a reduction of one-sixth; and further two million for the *généralité* of Orléans alone, which is so drained that it needs this relief, besides the fact that it is in the neighborhood of Paris, which supplies grain for a part of the nourishment [of Paris], and moreover that this *généralité* being abandoned in regard to the payment of eight million in revenue, if it is not helped it will lose all its value. But indeed the Queen's intention is to remit the fifth of the *taille*, since she is handing ten million of the fifty million over to the *peuple*, being unable to do more in the present state of affairs without an inevitable collapse of the kingdom; which the Queen orders us to explain to the Parlement, and to inform them that she was not lacking in the desire to help all the *peuple*, but that she lacked the power.

The next morning, Monday, October 19, we recounted to the Parlement what we had done at Saint-Germain, and what had been the reply to us there; but in vain, for they ordered that very humble remonstrances be immediately sent to the Queen for the fifth of the *taille*, so that all her subjects might feel its effects equally; and that in regard to the *généralité* of Orléans, the Queen might make them such a special favor as she deemed appropriate, and that in the declaration which would be drawn up by the First President the article would be inserted to that effect.

The afternoon of the same day, the gentlemen were assembled to deliberate concerning the article on public safety, and having given their opinions until after five o'clock, they postponed the reading of the opinions until the next morning.

On Tuesday, October 20, the opinions were reread, and after much argument over the terms, it was finally decided that the King and the Queen would be very humbly implored to grant a declaration stating that all the King's subjects will not be treated criminally, other than by the means included in the ordinances, before their regular judges, and not by selected commissioners; that the ordinance of King Louis XI, of the year . . .* will be carried out, and this [ordinance] being construed that no officer of the sovereign companies or any other [company] will be divested of his charge, nor troubled in the exercise and function of it by *lettres de cachet* or otherwise. Besides this decision, which was to be included in the declaration, there were two other secret ones: one stating that if a *lettre de cachet* to retire [to his country estate, for example] is sent to any officer of the company, that he would be obliged to bring it himself to the company so it may be debated in his presence; the other, that if anyone is imprisoned, his relatives can complain and make a petition to the Parlement, to whatever gentlemen they wish. The same day in the afternoon, the commissioners were assembled at the home of the First President to see and examine the declaration, which was agreed upon.

On Wednesday, October 21, in the morning, it was read and approved in the great chamber, all the chambers having assembled, and then decided that the next day the deputies would go to Saint-Germain to thank the Queen for the two million's remission she had granted; further, that she would be implored to grant the fifth of the *taille*, and to be willing to treat favorably those absent, banished, or imprisoned; and finally that the declaration already prepared would be presented to the Queen, for her command that it be sealed and sent to the Parlement. Several of the gentlemen, and the best part of them, were of the opinion that we should be sent to arrange this accommodation; but the First President wanted to go, and besides the fact that he had made ready to do it, he thought that he would shorten matters and that he would have the authority to carry out what had been decided in the company: this he succeeded in doing in the end.

And indeed, Thursday having come, at one in the afternoon, at Saint-Germain, Monsieur Le Tellier [secretary of state for the army] held two conferences with the First President on the subject of this fifth of the *taille*, during which he could not win over the First President's mind.

We had an audience at half past three; and after the First President had explained in rather precise terms, and advantageous ones

* Talon does not give the date.

for the company, the orders which he had been given, and after he had placed in the Chancellor's hands the plan for the declaration which he had drawn up, the Queen told us that she was going to discuss it and had us retire into the King's chamber, in which we were all given seats so we might rest; and the presidents, who were five in number, went through the railing [about the King's bed] and were seated in the space beside the King's bed.

After an hour of council meeting or thereabouts, the Duke of Orléans, Monsieur le Prince, the Prince de Conti, Monsieur de Longueville, and the Chancellor entered the King's chamber, saying that there were some articles to change in the declaration, which were not in conformity with what had been decided in the consultations. To do this they brought in a table and some seats so we could all sit down, in the same manner in which we had been seated in the other consultations held at the Duke of Orléans', with this sole difference that the Duke of Orléans did not have an armchair, but a simple folding stool, because we were in the King's chamber.* Among the disputed articles, it was not a question of the remission of the fifth of the *taille*, but of two or three other articles which they claimed would make a difference to them of three or four million as a result. The First President defended the articles as they had been written and argued that the disadvantages were not substantial. The Chancellor said that this declaration should have been sent [in advance] in order to be drawn up in a more leisurely manner. The First President replied that it had been drawn up only the preceding day, and that he could have sent it only with the consent of the entire court. The Chancellor replied that he had asked Sainctot to ask him to send it to him. The First President said that he had heard no mention of it; and turning toward the deputies from the Parlement, he said to him: "You see, gentlemen, that I do not have such good connections with Saint-Germain as

* Court etiquette involved precise rules as to who might be seated and the type of chair he might use, based upon his own title and the rank of those present. For example, Gaston d'Orléans, as uncle to the King, was always entitled to an armchair except before the King, when he was restricted to a folding stool. Mazarin, as a cardinal, was obliged to stand in the King's presence, but could sit upon a folding stool before the Queen, Orléans, or the Dauphin. He could sit in an armchair in the presence of princes of the blood, but would have been entitled only to an armless chair had he lived long enough to sit in the presence of Louis' grandchildren. Cf. John B. Wolf, *Louis XIV* (New York, 1968), p. 637.

some give me credit for." Then the Chancellor having complained that since the plan for this declaration had been drawn up for two weeks, read and discussed by the commissioners, he was very angry to have, on the Queen's behalf, no more than a quarter hour to examine it, the First President replied that the declaration had been drawn up according to the decisions of the consultations and according to the deliberations of the company, which the Queen had agreed to; that there was nothing in them that needed changing, and that if the least word was added or deleted, it would be subject to new meetings and deliberations, in which things could be aggravated rather than improved. And after this speech, the Duke of Orléans and the entire group having risen, they told us that they were going to tell the Queen what had just happened; and after a brief quarter hour, the deputies of the Parlement having returned to the cabinet, the Queen told them that she would inform them the following day of her final decision.

We entered the cabinet last; and [as we were] paying our compliments to the Queen, to the effect that she should please not create any difficulties in deciding an affair of this nature, which having been broken off would be difficult to reestablish, the Duke of Orléans, breaking in, told us that the gentlemen of the Parlement showed very great concern for the bourgeois of Paris and for the peasants from the countryside, but they showed little concern for the safety of the state; that there was no money to put the troops into garrison, and that if they were not paid for winter quarters, and if there was no money for new [troop] levies, it would be impossible to make either peace or war. We insisted that if this matter was broken off it would be even more difficult to be hopeful and that the present state of affairs must be taken into consideration. The Queen was marvelously distressed, and worried, and could hardly listen to us; so that, taking leave of her, we spoke to the Cardinal and made him the same entreaty to please end this matter, and promptly; but he replied, with a sorrow he usually manifests, that he considered the kingdom ruined through the impotence we were establishing through this declaration; that Pigneranda, the Spanish plenipotentiary, refused to hear talk of peace and said he had no orders from his master; this could only stem from his knowledge of our affairs and from the hope of divisions among us. We replied that if this matter was broken off, the King's affairs would not be more easy; and thus we separated from him.

It was six o'clock and more when we came out of the château and were led to the captain's quarters, where a big meal had been prepared, which few of the gentlemen ate, each one wishing to leave; this we could do only at ten in the evening.

The council having immediately assembled to learn what reply would be made to the Parlement, the Cardinal said that the matter must not be rushed, but that they must ask for two days in which to examine this declaration, during which Monsieur Le Tellier, secretary of state, would go to Paris to see the First President to deal with some important clauses, change a few words in them, and have removed those which hurt the most. President Tubeuf, first intendant for finances, who is not permitted in the high council but who was present because of the nature of the matter under discussion, said to the Queen that if this matter dragged on longer, it would worsen daily, as had been happening for five months; that a journey by Monsieur Le Tellier to Paris would make his intervention suspect and would provide an occasion to have the clauses of this declaration debated once again, and to bring up new difficulties; that meanwhile things were falling into ruin in the provinces and the *peuple* were becoming accustomed to not paying; that in the explanation and execution of the articles of the declaration there would be ways to protect oneself from the great harm which was feared; that the Queen could make the address not only to the Parlement but to the *Chambre des comptes* and to the *Cour des aides* so that both of these courts could deliberate on it. This proposal was opposed by the Cardinal and by the Duke of Orléans, who disliked giving up and thought that some delay would be more useful; but the rest of those present found this offer very good, and it was followed; and immediately the declaration was signed and sealed, without additions or deletions, and was brought the next morning to the judicial offices at eight in the morning by Sainctot, with letters permitting the Parlement to continue for two days.

These letters we brought the next day, Friday morning, October 23, into the great chamber, with a short preface, to show the company that the Queen was doing it willingly, that she had a complete desire for the relief of the *peuple*, and had no other thought than public tranquillity and the preservation of the state.

The declaration having been read at once with our conclusions, it was decided that the following day it would be read and published, and that to this end there would be a public audience.

At once a petition was brought in which was presented by Madame de Vendôme in the name of her husband and of Monsieur de Beaufort, her son, the first absent outside the kingdom and the other freed from the prison in the woods of Vincennes, where he had been kept prisoner by order of the King for almost five years: the first requested liberty and safety to return to his house; the other requested that his trial be conducted, and to this end he offered to make himself a prisoner in the Conciergerie. Upon this petition, which encountered many difficulties, was inscribed a *Soit montré*.

The difficulties were that Monsieur de Vendôme had left the kingdom without either verbal or written order of the King, and that having done it out of fears that he had conceived, it was unusual to ask for protection against the King; as for Monsieur de Beaufort, he had been made a prisoner by order of the King, and his trial having been begun by *maîtres des requêtes*, the Parlement, to whom the matter had been referred, had corrected the procedure, having ordered that the witnesses be heard once again, after which we had drawn conclusions at the bar, by which we had asked that the said Sieur de Beaufort be heard, and decreed the arrest of his accomplices; this had been done in the great chamber alone, since he was not a duke and peer: so that the petition seemed useless, because his presence in the Conciergerie would put him in a position to obtain justice in the criminal proceedings which had been begun against him.

Declaration of the King bringing settlement on the question of justice, police, finances, and the relief of His Majesty's subjects, verified in Parlement on October 24:

Louis, by the grace of God, King of France and of Navarre, to all present and to come, hail. The love which we bear to our people has obliged us to seek for every means to stop the course of the disorders which are growing to such a degree that it would have been difficult to remedy it later, and since one can recognize by our letters of declaration of last July 31, published in our Parlement in our presence; and having begun to give there the necessary settlements on the distribution of justice, and the order of our finances, and entrusted the remainder to a council which we wished to have assemble, and all the more so since in delaying longer the evils increased daily, to assure the calm of the state and the happiness of our subjects, we, on the advice of the Queen Regent, our very honored lady and mother, and of our very dear and very beloved uncle the Duke of Orléans, of our very dear and very beloved cousin the Prince de Condé, of the other princes, great and notable persons in our council, and of our certain knowledge, full power, and royal authority, have decreed and ordered, decree and order the following:

Firstly,

That although by our declarations of the months of July and August last, the eighth of the *taille* for the present year 1648 had been remitted only upon our subjects in the *pays d'élection*, and for the year 1649, the quarter of the previously deducted charges, nevertheless wishing to increasingly show by deeds how much we wish to bring relief to our aforesaid subjects, we declare that instead of the said eighth remitted for the present year 1648, they will have deducted a fifth on the basis of fifty million, which is the total of all *tailles*, *taillon*, military supplies, quartering of soldiers, and whatever other rights generally included in the certificates for the *taille* and the commission on [these certificates], even the fees for officers, and any other taxes generally; the which fifth totaling ten million will be shared equally by all the *généralités* of the *pays d'élection*, proportionately to the sum which each *généralité* must bear, and which each individual is assessed; so that each individual will have a fifth deducted from his share and assessment, without the other individuals being responsible for the debts of the community, and that no mutual responsibility can be held against them, except in the case of the ordinances, and without the said sum of fifty million being increased during the course of the present year and the following one.

Secondly,

And in order to make known to our said subjects by present actions our passion for their relief, we have remitted for them from taxes which we enjoyed a very substantial sum of our reserve for each year, both on the tax farm [*ferme*] for the entries into our good city of Paris, *aides*, the *cinq grosses fermes*, and on the *gabelles*, beginning from the day and the date of the publication of the present [documents], that is to say, the suppression of the small tariff established by our edict of . . . [*sic*] 1646; reserving the old levies which remain for the eighty thousand livres which the said small tariff totaled, mentioned in the decree of our said court of the Parlement on September 17, 1647. This being done, the treasurers of France in the bureau of finance in Paris will proceed to a new lease on the said farm of the old levies, as we have also annulled and suppressed the right of *maubouge*, consisting of twenty sous on each hogshead of wine entering into the cities and boroughs of our kingdom, and on apple ciders, pear cider, and other brews in the same proportion; and for our city of Paris ten sous only created by the declaration of the month of February 1643, and included in the lease for the *aides*, of which the farmer general created a subfarm of the said ten sous for the farmer of the entries of wine into Paris, established by the said declaration of February 1643, and others following, and on cloven-hoofed animals at forty sous for beef, at five sous each on veal and mutton, twenty sous for cows, and twelve sous on pork, mentioned in the tariff and declaration of the month of November 1640 and of February 25, 1643; duties for trademarks and other taxes on paper and beer, established by the edict of 1634 and the decree of February 16, 1645, and other subsequent declarations, and also the twenty sous' subsidy created by the said declaration of the month of November 1640, established by decree of our council on January 16, 1641, and February 11, 1643; others the twenty sous of Sedan created by a decree of our council of July 13, 1641, and included in our declaration of the month of September 1644; of the sou on the livre both for the said twenty sous' subsidy and the twenty sous of Sedan, and for the ten sous for the right of *maubouge* for entering Paris; of six deniers on the livre on the three sous remaining of the new tariff, to be taken on the hogshead of wine, whose entry is exempted by means of the suppression of the said new tariff, according to the decree of our said court of the 14th of the present month and year; of three livres on each *minot* [approximately 5 pecks] of salt from the Paris granary, and on the *cinq grosses fermes*, from the reevaluation made by decree of our council, in 1647; we very strictly inhibit and forbid our tax farmers, their clerks, and others to increase in the future the said duties and taxes upon penalty of [arrest for] peculation.

Thirdly,

And so that we can also receive the full sum of our revenues, we desire that in the future our tax farms be leased in our council to the highest and last bidder, and proceeded to the adjudication until the light burns out,* after proclamation on the premises, bids and remissions without any fees for entry or in advance, and the farms of the customs levies and other demesnes made by the general treasurers of France in the accustomed manner.

Fourthly,

And to give our officers a reason to continue in the fidelity which they have always shown, we wish and it pleases us that there be in the future no new tax, no reduction in wages, bonds, [or] income on the demesne, no registries and duties transferred and assigned by edicts, nor any offices obtained through inheritance or by reversion, revoked during the four coming years, and after the said time only by virtue of edicts and declarations carefully and duly verified; and if any taxes remain to be paid, we understand that they shall not be collected nor the individuals forced to pay them, and nevertheless that the treasurers of France will only receive three-quarters of their wages for the coming year 1649; the secretaries of the king, two-quarters; the officers of the *élection* two-quarters of their wages and fees, and our subaltern officers of our Parlement, two-quarters of their wages, and of the annual right, without paying us any loan: and if any of the said officers had paid some sum on the said loan, we desire that it be reduced on the quarter denier which is due us on resignation, in case during the period of the said annual right they should dispose of their offices; and as for the officers of our sovereign courts, we desire that the declaration of 1637 be carried out, and nevertheless that all our officers of our sovereign courts be paid three-quarters of their wages during the war only, and once it is over five-quarters.

Fifthly,

In order to assure the payment of the bonds we owe, we desire that the regulation made by the decree of our said court on September 4 last be carried out, and that the tax farmers and successful bidders for our farms pay the principal of these bonds, preferably to the accounts of our treasury, namely, for two-quarters and a half of the income on the salt, clergy, and *aides*, and for two-quarters on the other bonds during the war only; we declare all the gifts of debits for receipts for bonds null, and as of now revoked, and we revoke those which have not been carried out; we desire that the money in the hands of pay clerks, coming from repur-

* Bids remain open so long as the candle burns.

chased bonds, be used each year for the redemption of similar bonds of that nature, to our profit, under the most advantageous conditions possible: to this end the *prévôt des marchands* and the *échevins* of our said city of Paris will draw up a statement each year.

Sixthly,

And in order to preserve the funds of our revenues intact and to use them for expenditures necessary to the state, we very strictly inhibit and forbid the repurchase of bonds due us, or any reimbursement from the public treasury for offices and duties, until publication of the peace treaty, on penalty of the double against those, no matter what their rank or station, who were owners of the said bonds, duties, and new offices, from whom the said bonds, duties, and offices were repurchased and reimbursed since the month of January 1630, [and that they] be constrained to return to us and repay to our treasury the money received by them through the said repurchases and reimbursements, so that contract of constitution may be made in their behalf by the said *prévôt des marchands* and *échevins* at seven and one-seventh per cent, on the same amounts assigned to the said bonds, offices, and duties; and if any reimbursement is found to have been made at five and five-ninths per cent, instead of seven and one-seventh per cent, those who received the said sums will be obliged to pay back the quadruple of the excess they received, and with simple interest, according to the ordinance. We also desire that if any of the said bonds have been created since the month of January 1630, without verified edicts, that they be declared and we declare them as of now null, and for the execution of this, we have sent and send announcement to our said court of the Parlement, to which, to the degree necessary, we delegate total jurisdiction, and we forbid this [jurisdiction] to all other judges.

Seventhly

Wishing also to maintain in their entirety the rights of our demesnes, we order that all acquirers, possessors of [portions of] our demesne alienated by agreement or otherwise, be obliged, within six months from the day of publication of the said documents, to submit to the registry of our said Parlement their letters and contracts to have them verified if necessary; failing which, action will be taken by our said court; we also desire and it pleases us that the sum they claim to have paid be verified in our *Chambre des comptes*, and that in this [sum] nothing be included which was granted them as a gift or gratuity, but only what was actually deposited by them to our profit; and to this end we intend that the list of money received in cash be drawn up before two councillors of our said court whom we will assign to that purpose, so as to see that what was given was entered in payment for the said demesnes.

Eighthly,

And all the more so because the misuse of the said cash sums can cause great injury to our finances, we declare that in the future we will use them only for secret affairs and ones important to our state, and that all gifts, journeys, gratuities, rewards, reimbursements, uses of salaries, and emoluments, purchases, ambassadorial allowances, expenditures for buildings, remissions of interest, of loans, and advances, will no longer be used for them, according to the practice which was followed in the past.

Ninthly,

And in order also to preserve the dignity of our offices, we declare that no judicial and financial offices will be created in the four coming years, and after the said time has expired, only by virtue of correctly and duly verified edicts: and that if some of the formerly created offices remain to be filled, such as alternate, triennial, and quadrennial recorders, or others, and also all offices of the great and small chancelleries of France, and claims created by virtue of edicts not verified in our said court of the Parlement, we desire and it pleases us that they remain revoked and suppressed; to this end the edicts and declarations, and those concerning the rights of the general control of our finances, will be placed in the register of our said court in a month, to be distributed by it as seen proper.

Tenthly,

And in order to see to the safety of the revenues which belong to us, and to preserve the mortgages of creditors, we desire that goods of any nature whatsoever belonging to those who have taken our farms, either contracted with us or taken in part, their securities, partnerships, and interests, and what they have given to their children in behalf of their marriage or otherwise, even the offices they may have received, or which they hold under borrowed names, remain assigned and mortgaged to us, and to all their creditors, and that the separations of chattels between them and their wives, decided since their farms and contracts, will remain null; and that if any acquisitions have been made by them in the name of their wives or others, they will also be assigned to what may be due us, and to their said creditors, despite all customs to the contrary.

Eleventhly,

And before ordering the suppression of the edicts creating officers for the cleaning of our said city of Paris, [officers] for the small seals, notifications, commissioners for the seizure of real property, and controllers of expenditures, we desire that all the edicts, letters patent, contracts for the adjudication of fees stemming from the said edicts, and financial receipts be placed within two months in the hands of our *procureur général*, in our said Parlement, so that by his diligence we may be informed about this by our said court, and see to the relief of our subjects as soon as possible.

Twelfthly,

And in order to provide means to all our subjects who deal with merchandise, to increase their trade within our realm, we have revoked and revoke as of now all the privileges granted individuals to make money on any merchandise whatsoever, leaving all merchants the freedom to act in the future according to the experience which each has been able to gain, with prohibition to trouble those who wish to become involved in the commerce of the said merchandise; as we also forbid all merchants to bring, or to have brought into our realm woolen and silk fabrics manufactured in either England or Holland, and trimmings from Flanders, and laces from Spain, Genoa, Rome, and Venice, to all our subjects to buy them and to use them; on penalty of confiscation and five hundred livres' fine against the offenders.

Thirteenthly,

And also so that our subjects will incur no inconveniences from the passage of soldiers, we desire that the ordinances made by the kings our predecessors, even that of July 29, 1595, verified in our Parlement on September 4 of the said year, and others issued by us concerning the war, be kept and observed; that marching-halts be reestablished and the funds taken from the money of our *tailles* and *taillons*, and left in the hands of the tax collectors to meet as soon as possible those expenditures which are so necessary; that the said soldiers who leave their route be punished according to the severity of the laws of war, lest the leaders, captains, and officers, legally, be made to answer for damages and interest; we enjoin the *prévôts* of our dear and faithful marshals of France to follow the said soldiers, and to order them not to leave their route which has been given them, and to conscientiously report destruction and misdeeds which may have been committed, on pain of having to answer for it in their name.

Fourteenthly,

And in order to make known to posterity the esteem in which we hold our parlements, so that justice may be administered there with the required honor and integrity, we desire that in the future articles 91, 92, 97, 98, and 99 of the ordinance of Blois of the year 1579 be inviolably respected and carried out; to this end, that all affairs which have to do with lawsuits now pending, or which may later be pending, undecided and introduced into our council, be it by removal or otherwise, be sent back, and we send them before the judges who should normally deal with them, without our said council looking into such and similar matters, which we desire to be handled before the regular judges and by appeal to the sovereign courts, according to the edicts and ordinances, without the decrees of the said courts being liable to nullification or rescinding, unless by legal means, which are civil petitions and motions of errors, and by the forms included in the said ordinances, nor the execution of these decrees suspended or delayed by a simple petition presented to the said council. We also desire that no general letters of removal or particular letters of removal by personal instigation be issued, and that the petitions of those who seek the said removals be brought to our council by the gentlemen from the *requêtes* who are in office for that session in order to be judged there according to the edicts, and be granted, the litigants having been heard and the case presented, and not otherwise; that the said removals will be signed by a secretary of state or of finance who has received the letters when the said removals have been discussed; we declare the removals hereafter obtained contrary to the above procedures null in effect and value, and that nevertheless they be disregarded in the preliminary examinations where they were removed; and in order to stop complaints made to us by our subjects concerning the extraordinary commissions created by us earlier, we have revoked and revoke all the said extraordinary commissions, [and] we desire that prosecution be made in each matter before the judges in whose cognizance it is; and the said *maîtres des requêtes* will not be able to instruct the judges in their chambers on matters other than those in their cognizance as granted by [the Parlement's] edicts and ordinances, nor to judge any cases in final appeal, nor supremely, no matter what attributive letters for jurisdictions and transfer may be made to them for the said cases, the whole under penalty of nullification; that the cognizance of cases for which there are letters of state will belong to the judges before whom the cases are pending, the which letters of state will neither be sent nor sealed except in cognizance of cause, after having had the certificate of the general of the army or the governor of the fort, the which certificate will remain attached under the counterseal. That the address of letters of pardon, remission, and absolution will be made only to judges in the jurisdiction in which the crimes have been committed, or to the parlements, and not to the said *maîtres des requêtes*, great council, and *grand prévôt*. That no letters of delay will be sent as a summons, nor letters of revision granted, unless they are addressed to the [judicial] companies to which the cognizance belongs, and that articles 33 of the ordinance of Orléans, 90 and 209 of the said ordinance of Blois, concerning the function of the offices of the said *maîtres des requêtes*, will also inviolably be respected and carried out.

Fifteenthly,

We also desire that none of our subjects whatever their rank or station be in the future treated criminally except in the manner prescribed by the laws of our realm and ordinances, and not by selected commissioners and judges, and that the ordinance of King Louis XI of October 11, 1467, be respected and observed according to its form and tenor; and interpreting and carrying it out, that none of our officers of our sovereign courts and others can be troubled or disturbed in the exercise and function of their offices by *lettres de cachet*, or otherwise, in any manner whatsoever, the whole in conformity to the said ordinances and to their privileges.

So we give and order our dear and faithful councillors, the people holding our said court of the Parlement, *Chambre des comptes*, *Cour des aides* in Paris, that they are to have the present [document] read, published, and registered, and the contents of it respected and observed inviolably point by point according to their form and tenor, without permitting it to be countervened in any way or manner whatsoever; for such is our pleasure; in witness of which we have had our seal affixed to these said [documents].

Issued at Saint-Germain-en-Laye, the twenty-second day of October, the year of Our Lord 1648 and of our reign the sixth.

LOUIS

To the side, "*visa*"; and below, "by the King, the Queen Regent his mother present

DE GUÉNÉGAUD"

And sealed with the great seal in green wax, on ribbons of red and green silk, and again is written:

"Read and published during the audience, and registered in its register, heard, [and] the *procureur général* of the king demanding that they be carried out according to their form and tenor, and copies collated with the original of these [documents] sent to the *bailliages* and *sénéchaussées* of this jurisdiction to be likewise read, published, registered, and carried out by the diligence of the substitutes of the said *procureur général*, who will be held to certify to the court that they have done this within the month. Paris, in the Parlement, October 24, 1648.

Signed, DU TILLET"

Collated with the original by me, councillor, secretary of the king and of his finances.

3. *Mazarin on the Parlement during the Fronde*

In his secret, personal diaries, the *Carnets*, Jules Mazarin (1602–1661) summarized the advice which he gave Queen Anne as she and her councillors reached agreement with the Parlement in October 1648.

SOURCE: Mazarin's *Carnets*, Carnet X, pp. 71 f., 77–78, as quoted in A. Chéruel, *Histoire de France pendant la Minorité de Louis XIV* (Paris: Hachette, 1879), III, 91, 93.

His primary concern is France's international position. And had historians been naïve and believed that the October declaration had been signed by Anne in good faith, Mazarin's words almost prove that the opposite was true from the beginning. Anne violated the terms of the declaration only a few months after it was signed. The Parlement at once presented new demands for concessions.

The fact that the *Carnets* were written for himself alone is very important in any study of Mazarin and the Fronde. These records of the Cardinal's efforts to help the Queen, even to the point of advising that she disparage him in the eyes of the Prince of Condé, have helped historians define Mazarin's great talents as a diplomat and intriguer in the suspicious and violent atmosphere of the French court during the Fronde. The reference to Condé also suggests that Mazarin had all along assessed the princes as the greatest threat to the state. Subsequent events would prove him correct.

. . . Since their view is to bow before the necessity of the time because of the great injuries which could happen to the state if we reach a rupture with the Parlement, which has the *peuple* on its side, at the time when we are in a great war with the Spaniards and are on the eve of ending it if calm were reestablished in the realm, [the Queen] bows before these reasons; but since what is being granted to the Parlement is very unusual and impossible to be kept without abolishing the best part of the royalty, Her Majesty does not intend to carry it out, when the time is convenient to so declare, and to say that she was forced to do it, and that she did it to give peace to the realm, on which Monsieur le Prince [Condé] must agree with her.

. . . The Queen must remember to complain about me especially to Monsieur le Prince, for having become lax, and that such behavior does not increase her affection; that she must take better steps in the future, having recognized in many people that they think longer before doing a disagreeable thing to the Parlement than to the King; that if men fail her, and even the Cardinal, that God will help her and will not permit the bad treatment which she received, both to the authority of the King, while he is in her hands, and to her own person, against which, through the Parlement's malice, the *peuple* spewed out all the infamies imaginable, in private councils and suppers and in assemblies with unheard-of language, God will not permit all that to remain unpunished, and that she could have a minister who was more interested in the offenses concerning her than I have been.

4. *Public Opinion, the Press, and the* Mazarinades

As soon as he came to have dominant influence in the royal councils in 1624, Cardinal Richelieu set about trying to influence French and foreign public opinion. Two methods were available to him at the time. A book or speaker could be censored or suppressed by royal order or by the Sorbonne; the second method was the active sponsorship of writers and speakers who supported his policies. Richelieu never completely abandoned censorship in his efforts to manage public opinion, but he placed much more emphasis on propagating his own views and thus became something of an innovator in the history of propaganda.

While in Cardinal Richelieu's pay, a team of writers, some French, some foreign, scribbled away writing pamphlets on every conceivable controversial matter. His innovation was not so much in sponsoring propagandists—that had been done before—but more in the quantity of writers in his pay and in the large volume of propaganda produced. Historians will never completely know which works were sponsored by the Cardinal and which were not. The highest achievement was the acquisition of a weekly newspaper for his views. After 1631 the *Gazette de France*, published by Théophraste Renaudot, carried news items just as the Cardinal wanted them presented.

Cardinal Mazarin inherited Richelieu's propaganda services upon the latter's death in 1642 and continued to attempt to manage public opinion in the same ways. But Mazarin lacked either the interest in or the sensitivity to public opinion and propaganda which Richelieu had possessed. Pamphlets attacking royal policy went unanswered, censorship was clumsy, and even Renaudot was left without the steady guidance which he needed. This relaxation might not have been significant had it not occurred in a period of increased suffering and taxation resulting from France's war with Spain. In the late 1640's the number of opposition pamphlets began to rise. In 1648–1652 there occurred a fanatical outburst of opposition literature, numbering between four and five thousand pamphlets in Paris alone. Called *Mazarinades*, these attacks

SOURCES: First document found in *Recueil de Diverse pièce* [*sic*] (Columbia Special Collections): "Lettre du Père Michel, Religieux, Hermite de l'ordre de Camaldoli près Grosbois, à Monseigneur le Duc d'Engoulesme sur les cruautez des Mazarinistes en Brie" (Paris, 1649), pp. 9–15, 23–24; second document from *Le Politique Chrestien de S. Germain à la Reyne* (Paris, 1649), pp. 1–8.

on the Cardinal, the Queen Mother, and their policies became a confused outburst of opinions of every sort. Verses, songs, violent *ad hominem* attacks, and replies as well as counterattacks, the *Mazarinades* are a remarkable and unique source of public opinion in seventeenth-century France.

But as yet no historian has succeeded in using them effectively as sources. The thousands of pages of material quickly intimidate all but the most courageous researchers. And yet there are fine collections of *Mazarinades* in the United States at the Newberry Library, the Folger Shakespeare Library, and the Widener Library of Harvard University.

The two selections below illustrate the difficulty of interpreting these texts. Their authors are highly informed about the political and religious issues of the Fronde. But even after the specific purpose of the *Mazarinade* is established, and the persons discussed identified, it remains very difficult to draw any general conclusions from them. Here if anywhere should the techniques of the historians of *mentalités* be tried, the punch card used for themes, fears, and terms, and then perhaps a data bank would yield some results.

Père Michel, the author of the first *Mazarinade*, may well have used a pseudonym. Count Grancey (Raoul Rouxel de Médavy) had been duped by some peasants to ride off in the wrong direction against an army which rode into Thionville with little difficulty and forced Condé to besiege the city in 1643. Grancey's record as an officer in Piedmont, Flanders, and Lorraine had been very good prior to the Fronde. After the revolt he became a marshal of France and governor of Thionville.

The monastic habit which I wear and the religion which I profess, although both foreign, have not robbed me of the feelings of a true Frenchman. Nature obliges me to preserve them, God orders me to, and also orders me to hate the enemies of my country. Your Highness brought me in touch with him by founding a house of our order in this kingdom. You gave us a retreat in which to live in retirement and to await a natural death. Nevertheless we are today in greater danger in the heart of France, five leagues from Paris, under Your Highness' protection, than [we were] in the midst of the bandits of Italy. God gave us weapons against the devil's assault, and these weapons are but a useless protection against foreign troops, chosen from among all the most detestable persons of all nations.

We are hunted in our woods by these tigers more cruel than those of Libya, who never did wrong to the ancient hermit fathers. The innocent color of our habits inspires in them frenzied anger against all candor, and our poverty, which has always assured our safety along the most dangerous paths, causes our blood to be desired by these insatiable beasts, who cannot bear to let anything escape their fury, except that which satisfies their avarice. They commit all manner of profanities in the vicinity of the abbeys of Yerre and Iarcy, and those holy virgins, spouses of Jesus Christ, make compromises daily in order to ensure their honor for twenty-four hours. These sacred vestals, who thought they could guard that eternal fire which they preferred to a legitimate flame [love] which would have given them sure help in the cities in their husbands' arms and in the just worth of their children and of their near ones, are constantly afraid of receiving the opprobrium of this accursed nation which has committed debaucheries and filth which cannot be put into words, in the sacred vessels, and which now has only to commit generally this abominable sacrilege which we have been told has been perpetrated upon a number of individual nuns.

Great God who has protected Paris, do you want the impious to say that you reign only in fortified cities? Do you want the atheists to utter that blasphemy of saying that you were defended by the walls and by the multitude of bourgeois of this great city? [The city] is innocent, 'tis true, it is moreover very just; but it is the cause of all our troubles, because it is unjustly besieged. The countryside is accused of no crime, neither a true one nor even a crime of state; why must it be pillaged, burned, why must those who hope for your protection be unable to find a safe asylum in your houses and in your presence? Women and girls are violated at the foot of your altars, it is said even on the sanctuary. We see, ah, miserable eyes, that you are being trampled under foot. It is no longer the Normans who have invaded France by our rivers; it is not even the pagan Attila, for he showed respect for the bishops and pastors, he believed in a god, since he said he was his scourge; these are Frenchmen, Germans, Italians, Poles, that is to say, Scythians and citizens of Gelonus.

It is true that few Frenchmen are accused of these impieties, it is true that they are being committed for an Italian, and for a cardinal, and that the Queen who upholds them against the just indignation of the people is not a Frenchwoman either. But princes introduced [these impieties] into the midst of the state; and it is a French count who commands them in Brie, who approves of all the abominations and who shares in all the pilfering. It is Count—— [de Grancey], Monseigneur, it is this unhappy Vulcan, and this miserable cripple whose soul is even less straight than his body, and whom God will punish the first as soon as his justice is satisfied with our punishment. He has robbed Lezigny and Panfou, he cut the very paintings from their frames to carry them off, and did not carry off castles and houses solely because they were attached to the earth, but he laid waste to them. He is a man whose crimes have made his name known, and who has created only enemies in his own country, where the baseness of his extraction makes him scorned by the nobles and where the *peuple* detest his violence and his tyrannical temper. One of our fathers knows his origin and has assured us that the name he bears is common, like the blood and the heart of the most common people of ——— [England?], that he has no praiseworthy relatives other than by his mother alone, daughter of a marshal of France [Marshal de Hautemer], who was an atheist, and the chief of those violent ministers who corrupted the morals of the Duke of Alençon and Anjou, brother of Henry III, who urged him to rule by force and by fortifications over the Flemings and the inhabitants of Brabant, who called, received, and declared him their legitimate prince. He [Grancey] attached himself to Monseigneur the Duke of Orléans, who made him *maréchal de camp* and governor of ——— [Montbéliard], and these acts of kindness are proofs that he has done little for His Royal Highness [Orléans] except that, judging him capable of some jealousy over the exploits of Monsieur le Prince [Condé], he countered his plans at the siege of Thionville by granting passage to troops, which entered the city to defend it.

He came to this war against his country with the hope of certain prey; he ruined every place he passed, he besieged Brie-Comte-Robert, which was defended by its governor with every sign of valor and singular generosity. But since the stronghold was no longer tenable, without powerful and immediate help, he had to surrender it by coming to terms. He [Grancey] granted it to avoid the loss of his men and promised to allow the besieged soldiers to leave and to preserve the possessions of the bourgeois and the honor of their wives and their daughters; but he broke this promise, which even the Turks break only rarely, and never without cause. The Parisian soldiers were vilified, . . . then stripped, then killed for the most part, or held captive.

Shall I tell the rest, and if I tell it, where can I find colors black enough? It was the same, Monseigneur, with everything which was promised to the bourgeois, but it was worse than in a city captured by force and carried by assault, where the general if only he was a man, if only he was human, and if only he was not a devil, gave only one, or two, or three hours' time at the most for pillaging. But this pillaging is still going on, and I fear to tell the rest; but I must tell everything, so that everyone will know the cause of the thunder which is grumbling, which is going to fall upon this criminal head, and on those of all his accomplices: as is usual when some storm arises, or there is a downpour, those who are in the open countryside seek the shelter of some tree, and the fewer trees there are, the more people are to be found there; the same was true in the poor town of Brie. The nobles who had no fortified houses, the *laboureurs,* in sum, all the families scattered throughout the countryside, had retreated to Brie. The city surrendered; the women and girls, and among them several gentlemaidens, under the protection of the surrender terms and a gentleman's word, gained the shelter of the churches. This asylum was violated, as if it were not enough that these wild troops had violated the article concerning the pillaging of goods. They forced pastors and priests to open the door of that holy sheepfold to them. These looters and these lechers shared those poor ewes indiscriminately, not even sparing the milk lambs, whom they killed and caused to expire under torments which nature forbids to wild beasts and which they never have practiced. Gentlemaidens of condition fell by lot to the most infamous, who took from them the means of killing themselves and of going to heaven bearing in their bloody hands that holy virginity which the laws of God and of honor oblige them to protect more dearly than their lives, which they are permitted to lose voluntarily only in order to preserve that treasure.

You were there, my God, you who being a man had chased the merchants from the Temple. Why did you, God and man together, not exterminate that accursed race, which showed no more horror than do the demons, nor honor for your Holy Sacrament exposed on the altars? They pushed it off the sanctuary to make room for these wretched victims, they trampled it under foot. You caused the fire from heaven to descend and light the sacrifices of the Jews. Why did you not send your lightning bolt to consume these divine and human hosts, to burn simultaneously these executioners, these still-pure bodies, and the temple which served as the theater of this profanation and which can be purged only by its ashes? The rape of a Roman lady, but a pagan, and who was modest only because of public opinion, caused a legitimate throne to topple; you authorized the establishment of a republic through the just revenge for a crime committed, not by a king, but by his son. A foreign tyrant, who wears less worthily the emblem of a prince of the Church than those who wear the turban, will he be the unpunished cause of the most horrible cruelty which France has ever seen? His ancestors crucified you; is that not enough of your blood and of his individual crimes? And can he do worse to earn a cruel death, since all the torments which Sicily—so ingenious in tortures—could still invent after Phalaris were still too mild, without his provoking your wrath by such strange outrages against you, against your creatures, against your spouses? Did this miserable Ixion have to combine adultery and murder in your own house, and in your own bed? . . .

The *peuple*, who are neither succored nor protected, are imperceptibly losing the respect and love which they owe to the house of their princes. God permitted this in the very house of Solomon. Rehoboam, his son, dominated by bad advice, answered imprudently the just request of his subjects, so that instead of helping them, he made their yoke heavier, so that far from whipping them with ordinary sticks like his father, he added chains and goads. The Holy Scripture observes in precise terms that he made this rough and cruel reply only because he felt an aversion for the Lord, who had hardened him and who had permitted him to be blinded, and this was the same God who gave such tragic results to this frightful query of the tribes, already rebeling in their hearts: "What is the importance of taking so much interest and in showing so much respect for David's posterity? What need is there to attach ourselves so closely to the race of Jesse?" It is His Royal Highness [Orléans], it is the son of Henry the Great, who at present is invoked by this text of the Holy Scripture. It is not up to the King, who is young; it is up to Monsieur the Duke of Orléans to say why we should risk our inheritance to protect a bad minister and to preserve for him an authority which is inseparable from our blood. Is it a fit task for a *fils de France*, and for the first prince of the royal blood, to endanger the Crown in order to defend the son of Pietro Mazarini, a foreigner, hated by the French, condemned by the justice of the kingdom, and by the general voice of her people?

Madam [Anne of Austria, Queen Regent],

Great ruin is bit by bit prepared by great accidents, which are still easy to remedy at the beginning of the malady. But when it has reached a certain degree of malignancy, then the sick person perishes without anyone's being able to help him. Perhaps, Madam, the ills of this state are not incurable, provided we are not incorrigible. But it is quite apparent that they will soon become so if we do not hasten to become reasonable. In order to heal them, we must know them, because there has never been a sure cure for an unknown poison. If the pilots who took Jonah in their boat had been unaware of the cause of the tempest which tormented them, they would not have been able to avoid the shipwreck which threatened them.

Seven years ago, Madam, the prelates of France assembled in a council at Meaux to debate the means of saving France, which was almost attacked by the same symptoms from which it now suffers. The minutes of this assembly show clearly enough that the disorders of that time resembled so closely those of the present that they do not need different remedies. Since people do not tire, said the fathers of this council, of committing sins in this realm, since peace has abandoned us, and since the grace of heaven, which used to come to our aid in our afflictions, seems to have deserted us, since God scorns our tears and our suffering, and since now only justice can punish our crimes, we believe that we ought to offer him tears and sobs, that we ought to think seriously of preserving this monarchy and its prince and of obtaining with all our might, through the help of Jesus, the salvation of the people.

Thus, Madam, spoke these wise prelates of France. And it is thus we believe we should speak to Your Majesty. The true cause of the ills which we have suffered, which we are suffering now and which we ought to fear we shall suffer in the future, is sin which has irritated God: it is injustice which has sown disorder in all the [social] orders of this realm. The remedy is the reestablishment of justice and of good morals in all parts of the state. Two of the greatest kings who ever governed the people of God, Jehoshaphat and Hezekiah, behaved in this way on a similar occasion. They were not content to issue edicts to reform the abuses of their kingdom; but in addition they sent special commissioners of known and incorruptible probity everywhere to have them carried out. They did not withdraw until their holy ordinances had been fully observed. And that produced such an effect that a state which was on the eve of ruin became the most powerful and the most flourishing in the world.

Truly, Madam, there must be something divine and supernatural about our ills: for if they had been born of an ordinary cause, wisdom could have foreseen them and avoided them. Or if it had been able to do neither one nor the other, at least it would have found some expedient to make them cease. But it is very strange how our misfortunes can be seen multiplying, through the same means used to stamp them out. We see that the remedies serve only to irritate the illness. Difficulties of one sort and another have arisen and have become entangled the more we have tried to disentangle them. Our disasters have been great in their cause, they were even more so in their progress, and we are to fear that the consequences will be even more deadly, since it is very difficult to clearly understand them. The ill is indeed extreme when it is equally dangerous to speak of it or to be quiet, when one dares neither diagnose it nor propose the remedy.

But, Madam, because I am speaking as a Christian *politique*, and as one of those most concerned with the happiness of Your Majesty and of the state, and because if there is a danger in speaking, there is an incomparably greater one in remaining silent, and because the number of flatterers equals that of our miseries, you must be told, Madam, with a freedom which our times authorize, which the necessity of the affairs of state demands, which the interest of the King, of you, and of all of France requires, you must be told with more truth than kindness, that when God wishes to take revenge upon a kingdom and scepters, he allows those who administer them to lose their commonsense and reason, and lets them take the night for the day, and the day for the night. When he had decreed and decided upon the destruction of the Kingdom of the Jews, those who governed it used for its defense only those means which would cause it to perish. All its leaders had no more lucidity than just what was needed to rush headlong into the darkness. As a means of salvation they seized everything which could bring about their doom. Wisdom itself served them only for inventing stratagems, to make their misfortune helpless. We do not dare believe, Madam, that God wishes us to act likewise; we are too aware of his mercy and of your piety: but we nevertheless tell Your Majesty that we have seen not without astonishment how many vows and prayers have been useless in disarming God's anger and yours. And in circumstances in which all the reasons in the world make it wished for and hoped for, and at a time when—the tempest only beginning to arise—it was so easy to avert it. We have seen with dread that the best princess in the universe and the best-intentioned one, despite her own inclinations and so many wise remonstrances, has become so severe, toward herself, toward the King her son, toward his kingdom, and toward an entire people, which has cherished her more than sight. And in a situation in which any show of that kindness which is natural in her could work miracles for her own reputation, as well as for that of this Crown. It is not without shuddering that we have reckoned that the innocence and the interests of the monarch whom God has given us have been incapable of averting our calamities, and that bad advice has always won out over good. It is again not without terror that we fear that in the future our ills will have to be treated with remedies which are worse than the illness itself because we failed to apply them when it was necessary, when we could have, and when we should have. Who advised you, Madam, to undertake the ruin of Paris and the stifling of the Parlement? And that at such a time, and under such a pretext, and by such means? And this advice was followed, it was embraced, and they felt obliged to carry it out; it was even thought that it was part of the royal conscience and authority to spare nothing in order for it to succeed. It was in fact made a point of religion and of the state. Savants and the uneducated applauded equally; the iron and fire were used to bring it about.

O judgments of God, how impenetrable you are! But O abysses of our sin, how deep you are, since you thus blind us, since you provoke so strangely the infinity of God's anger upon us! It is indeed now, Madam, that France is proving that it is true, that human prudence is useless to help those whom the justice of God wishes to afflict. What the Holy Spirit says is true through the mouth of a prophet, that those who sin work in vain to make cloth, because they will not be able to cover themselves, and the work of their hands will not be able to clothe them. All they do will evaporate without effect, and even the advice they take to save themselves will help toward making them perish. They shall sow the wind, says Hosea, and they shall only reap the whirlwind.

A great archbishop of Seville once used to say that Spain had to be entirely devastated so that it could be entirely rebuilt. France itself, Madam, had to collapse under the weight of its own disorders so that it would be capable of feeling its illness and of regaining its health. It was necessary that no healthy part of this monarchy remain so that a general reform might be thought of, and so that with everyone demanding it, it could not possibly be refused. It had to fall into a state which would wring tears and sobs, as well as the blood and the lives of so many people; it was necessary that not being able to die other than by its own hand, it had to become serious, to arm itself against itself, in order to execute in a month of fury what its enemies had not been able to do by so many years of war. Bourgeois had to take up arms against bourgeois, friend against friend, brother against brother. In an excess of impetuosity, they had to do destruction which will cost the regrets of more than a century and which will perhaps be irreparable.

And finally after having been the subject of the jealousy of her most cruel adversaries, [France] finally had to become the subject of their compassion. And these misfortunes had to happen to her at a time when she could observe the revolutions in Catalonia, the changes in Portugal, the uprisings in Naples, the assassinations in Constantinople, the horrors in England, the judgments of God upon the crowned heads as well as upon their vassals.

All this had to happen, Madam, to show us by force what we could not be convinced of by reason: that justice and piety are the two pillars of republics, and preserve them to the degree that they are preserved.

The Holy Scripture, which is the book of the true maintenance of order, which your ancestor [Emperor] Charles the Fifth read daily, and which ministers of state should always have both in their hearts and in their hands, says nothing more often than this truth. Never did the people of God fail to be greeted by some noteworthy misfortune when they had committed some notable impiety. Their happiness lasted no longer than their virtue; the end of one was the end of the other. God abandoned them as soon as they abandoned themselves to impiety. And his justice, which had promised them happiness proportionate to their merit, was very exact in sending them chastisements proportionate to their faults.

The Kingdoms of Judah and of Israel were destroyed, like salt thrown into the water, as soon as they destroyed God's service among themselves. All the monarchies of the universe have experienced a similar fate when they have fallen into similar impieties. When the Assyrians were subjugated by their voluptuousness and delights, they were also subjugated by the Chaldeans and the

Medes. As soon as the Babylonian Empire decreased in virtue, it also decreased in power. No sooner had the Persians thrown themselves into debauchery than distress threw itself upon them. The Greeks, Egypt, and Idumaea lost all their prosperity when they lost their piety, and they became the slaves of their enemies as soon as they became slaves of their vices. This is the fulfillment, Madam, of that oracle of the Holy Spirit, which says that crowns pass from one family to another because of injustice, cheating, and deception. All our prophets who have spoken in God's name announced it in that way; all the histories of the world report it likewise. All experiences agree with this truth. A kingdom must of necessity perish when it has allowed justice and piety to perish.

5. *The Fronde of the Princes*

Love of war and courage in hand-to-hand fighting still captured the imagination of the French aristocracy in the seventeenth century. The princes of the blood, most notably Condé, perpetuated the ethos of the aristocratic warrior. And though Condé changed sides very often, his personal power, reputation, and general influence remained considerable until his death in 1686. In 1643 Condé had commanded an army which dealt a decisive defeat to the Spanish at Rocroi; for a time during the Fronde he used his talents as an officer to suppress rebellions against the Crown, then he rebelled and led an army against royal troops. Though he later fought under the Spanish flag against France, Condé ended his career as an enormously influential and popular, if not a very good, general during the personal reign of Louis XIV.

François, Duke of La Rochefoucauld (1613–1680), himself a prince, rebel, and great writer, here recounts the end of the princely Fronde at the battle of the Faubourg Saint-Antoine outside Paris, in 1652. Neither La Rochefoucauld nor Condé was quite able to state clearly what they were fighting for in this period; the endless negotiations and intrigues which transpired among all parties were typical of aristocratic rebellion. Pensions, freedom to travel about, and control over border forts, as well as the right to sit on the Conseil d'en Haut, or High Council, frequently constituted their demands. Still more difficult for subsequent generations to fathom were the terrible disputes over precedence and titles.

The impact of the great nobles was real. They were looked to as

SOURCE: *Mémoires de La Rochefoucauld*, ed. by A. Petitot and Monmerqué (Paris, 1826), LII, 160–173.

natural leaders and defenders by the lower social orders. Wild shouting, the sight of wounded princes, and the confused irresolution of Gaston d'Orléans, the King's uncle, were enough to admit a wild band into the city of Paris. Historians later spoke of Louis XIV's humiliation of the nobility. It was not the entire nobility to which the King addressed himself, but precisely to this group of *grands* which he wished to emasculate and break to the royal will. Note how La Rochefoucauld refers to himself in the third person, a characteristic of the aristocratic writer of memoirs in the seventeenth century.

Monsieur le Prince [Condé] decided to join his troops, fearing that those of the king would charge them along the way. He left Paris with twelve or fifteen horse; and thus exposing himself to an encounter with enemy bands, he joined his army at Linas and took it toward Villejuif to billet. Then it continued to Saint-Cloud, where it stayed a long while, during which time not only was the harvest completely lost, but almost all the houses in the countryside were burned or pillaged. This began to embitter the Parisians, for which Monsieur le Prince would soon feel disastrous repercussions at the battle of Saint-Antoine, which we shall relate.

However, Gaucourt had held secret conferences with the Cardinal [Mazarin], who kept expressing to him his desire for a prompt peace. The principal conditions were agreed upon; but the more he insisted upon the lesser ones, the more they came to believe that he did not want to negotiate. These indecisions gave new strength to all the cabals and lent credibility to all the various rumors being spread. Never had Paris been more agitated, and never had Monsieur le Prince's mind been more divided over deciding for peace or for war. The Spaniards wanted to get him away from Paris in order to prevent a peace; and Madame de Longueville's friends played a part in this plan in order to alienate him from Madame de Châtillon as well. Moreover, Mademoiselle [daughter of the Duke of Orléans] had exactly the same plan as the Spaniards and Madame de Longueville; for on the one hand she wanted war like the Spaniards, in order to have revenge upon the Queen and the Cardinal, who did not want her to marry the King; and on the other she wanted, like Madame de Longueville, to break Monsieur le Prince's liaison with Madame de Châtillon and to have a greater share in his trust and in his esteem. To attain this by the means which would most touch Monsieur le Prince, she raised troops in his name and promised she would supply him with money to raise others. These promises, joined to those of the Spaniards and to the stratagems of Madame de Longueville's friends, caused Monsieur le Prince to forget his thoughts concerning peace. What drove them even further [from his mind] was not only his lack of trust in the court, but also (which I find the most difficult to believe in a person of his quality and merit) his inordinate desire to imitate Monsieur de Lorraine in several aspects of his free and independent fashion of living, and particularly in the way he treated his troops; and he was convinced that if Monsieur de Lorraine, stripped of his states and with far less advantages than his [Condé's], had become so influential through his army and his money, that having qualities infinitely superior to his, he would gain a proportionately more advantageous position and, moreover, in order to attain it, would lead a life entirely consistent with his temperament. This was believed to be the true motive which involved Monsieur le Prince with the Spaniards, and for which he was willing to risk everything which his birth and his services had acquired for him in the realm. He hid this feeling as much as possible and showed the same desire for peace, which was still being negotiated in vain. The court was then at Saint-Denis, and Marshal de La Ferté had joined the king's army with troops he had brought from Lorraine. Those of Monsieur le Prince were weaker than the least of these two corps which opposed him, and they had held until then the post of Saint-Cloud, in order to use the bridge to avoid an unequal battle. But the arrival of Marshal de La Ferté provided the king's troops with a chance to separate and attack Saint-Cloud on both sides by making a pontoon bridge in the direction of Saint-Denis; this made Monsieur le Prince decide to leave Saint-Cloud, with the aim of reaching Charenton and taking up position in this tongue of land at the junction of the Marne and the Seine rivers. He would doubtlessly have made a different decision had he been free to choose; and it would have been safer and easier for him to keep the Seine River on his left, and to go via Meudon and Vaugirard to take up position in the Faubourg Saint-Germain, where he perhaps would not have been attacked, for fear of inducing as a result the Parisians to defend it. But Monsieur the Duke of Orléans would not agree to it, out of fear aroused in him over the occurrence of a battle he could see from the windows of the Luxembourg [Palace], and because he was led to believe that the king's artillery would make continual salvos to dislodge him

[Condé]. Thus, believing in an imaginary peril, the Duke of Orléans exposed Monsieur le Prince's life and fortune to one of the greatest dangers he ever ran.

Therefore he made his troops march at nightfall on July 1, 1652, in order to reach Charenton before those of the king could come up to him. They passed by Cours la Reine and along the outskirts of Paris, from the Porte Saint-Honoré to that of Saint-Antoine, in order to reach the road to Charenton. He wanted to avoid requesting passage through the city, fearing that he would not obtain it and that a refusal at such a time would show his weak position. He also feared that if he obtained it, his troops would spread out into the city and that he would not be able to make them leave if he needed to.

The court was immediately warned of Monsieur le Prince's march, and Monsieur de Turenne left that very hour with all the troops he had in order to follow him and stop him, until Marshal de La Ferté, who had been ordered to cross back over the bridge and march with his men, had had time to join him. The King, however, was taken to [the heights of] Charonne, in order to watch as from the balcony of a theater a military action which, it appeared, would lead to the inevitable defeat of Monsieur le Prince and the end of the civil war, and which was indeed one of the most daring and perilous occasions of that entire war, and the one in which the great and extraordinary qualities of Monsieur le Prince appeared most brilliantly. Fortune herself seemed to become reconciled with him in this encounter, to share in a success in which both sides gave *gloire* to his worth and his conduct; for he was attacked right in the Faubourg Saint-Antoine, where he was able to use the breastworks which the bourgeois had erected there a few days earlier to protect themselves from being pillaged by Monsieur de Lorraine's troops; and there was only this one spot along the entire line of his intended march which had such defenses and where he could prevent himself from being totally defeated. Several squadrons of his rear guard were even charged in the Faubourg Saint-Martin by men whom Monsieur de Turenne had detailed to divert him, and retired in disorder to the breastworks of the Faubourg Saint-Antoine, where battle had begun. He only had the time necessary to do so, and to strengthen with infantry and cavalry all the posts by which he might be attacked. He was forced to put the baggage train of his army on the edge of the Saint-Antoine moat, because it had been refused entry into Paris. Several carts had even been pillaged; and the partisans of the court had arranged so that they could watch from there, as from a neutral spot, the unrolling of this event.

Monsieur le Prince kept near him those of his domestic servants who were present, or persons of quality not having a military command, to a total of thirty or forty.

Monsieur de Turenne laid out his attacks with extreme care and with all the confidence of a man who thinks his victory assured. But when his detail of men was thirty paces from the breastworks, Monsieur le Prince came out with the said squadron and, mingling sword in hand, completely defeated the battalion which had been commanded [to attack him], took officers prisoner, carried off their banners, and withdrew behind his defenses. On another side, the Marquis of Saint-Mégrin attacked the post defended by the Count of Tavannes, the lieutenant general, and by L'Enques, *maréchal de camp*. So great was the resistance that the Marquis of Saint-Mégrin, seeing that his entire infantry was weakening, was carried away by enthusiasm and anger, and advanced toward the king's company of light horse in a narrow street, closed by a barricade, where he was killed with the Marquis of Nantouillet, Le Fouilloux, and several others. Mancini, Cardinal Mazarin's nephew, was wounded there and died a few days later. Attacks continued on all sides with extreme vigor, and Monsieur le Prince charged a second time with the same success as the first. He was everywhere; and in the midst of the shooting and the fighting he gave orders with a clearness of mind which is so rare, and so necessary, in these encounters. Finally the king's troops had forced the last barricade in the street which runs from that of the Cours to Charenton, and which was forty paces beyond a very big square which led into this same street. The Marquis of Navaille had gained control of it and, in order to keep better control of it, had had holes broken into the nearby houses and had placed musketeers everywhere. Monsieur le Prince planned to dislodge them with his infantry and to break through other houses in order to chase them out by greater fire power, which was indeed the decision which should be made. But the Duke of Beaufort, who had not been with Monsieur le Prince at the beginning of the attack, and who felt some jealousy that the Duke of Nemours had been there all the time, urged Monsieur le Prince to have the infantry attack the barricade; and since this infantry was already tired and disheartened, instead of going toward the enemy, it lined up along the houses and was unwilling to advance. At this point, a squadron of troops from Flanders, posted in the street which ended at the corner of this little square on the side of the king's troops, being unable to remain there longer for fear of being cut off when the neighboring houses had been won, returned to the square. The Duke of Beaufort, believing that they were the enemy, proposed to the Dukes of Nemours and La Rochefoucauld, who were just arriving there, to charge them. Thus, being followed by the persons of quality and the volunteers who were there, they pushed toward them and needlessly exposed themselves to the open fire from the barricade and from the houses around the square, having discovered upon approaching this squadron that it was on their side. Seeing at the same time some astonishment among those guarding the barricade, the Dukes of Nemours, Beaufort, and La Rochefoucauld and the Prince of Marsillac* pushed on and forced the king's troops to retreat. They then dismounted and guarded it alone, the infantry being unwilling to follow its orders to reinforce them. Monsieur le Prince stood fast in the street, with those of his followers who had rallied around him. Meanwhile, the enemy, who held all the houses along the street, seeing the barricade guarded by only four men, would undoubtedly have retaken it had Monsieur le Prince's squadron not stopped them. But, having no infantry to prevent them from shooting through the windows, they began to fire in all directions and could aim from head to foot at the backs of those who were holding the barricade. The Duke of Nemours was hit thirteen times in his body or in his weapons, and the Duke of La Rochefoucauld was hit by a musketball which, piercing his face below the eyes, caused him to lose his sight at once: this obliged the Duke of Beaufort and the Prince of Marsillac to withdraw in order to carry off the two wounded men. The enemy advanced to capture them; but Monsieur le Prince also advanced to extricate them and gave them time to mount on horseback. Thus they left to the enemy the post which they had just forced them to leave, and almost everyone who had been with them in the square was killed or wounded. Monsieur le Prince lost that day the Marquis of Flamarins and the Marquis of La Roche-Giffart, the Count of Castres, the Count of

* The author's son.

Bossu, Desfourneaux, La Martinière, La Mothe-Guyonnet, Bercenet, captain of the Duke of La Rochefoucauld's guards, L'Huillière, who was also one of his men, and many others whose names cannot be included here. Finally the number of dead or wounded officers was so great on both sides that it seemed that each side would think more about repairing its losses than about attacking its enemy.

This sort of truce was advantageous to the king's troops, discouraged by so many attacks in which they had been repulsed. During this time, Marshal de La Ferté had marched quickly and was preparing to make a new effort with his fresh and entire army, when the Parisians, who until then had been only spectators at such a great battle, declared themselves in favor of Monsieur le Prince. They had been so forewarned of the treachery of the court and of Cardinal de Retz, and they had been so persuaded to believe that Monsieur le Prince's individual peace had been made without considering their interests, that they had looked upon the beginning of this battle as a comedy which was being played in cooperation with Cardinal Mazarin. The Duke of Orléans even corroborated this conviction by issuing no order in the city to go help Monsieur le Prince; and Cardinal de Retz, who was with him, increased even more the irresolution and anxiety in his mind by finding obstacles to everything he proposed. Moreover, the Porte Saint-Antoine was guarded by a company of bourgeois whose officers, who had been won over to the court, prevented almost equally anyone from entering or leaving the city. In short, everything there was badly arranged for the acceptance of Monsieur le Prince and his troops [into the city], when Mademoiselle, exerting pressure on the mind of Monsieur [the Duke of Orléans], her father, shook him from the lethargy in which Cardinal de Retz was keeping him. She went to bear his orders to the city hall that the bourgeois should be armed. At the same time she ordered the governor of the Bastille to fire his cannons at the king's troops; and returning to the Porte Saint-Antoine, she convinced all the bourgeois not only to receive Monsieur le Prince and his army, but even to go out and skirmish while his troops were retreating. What finally also moved the people in favor of Monsieur le Prince was seeing so many persons of quality being brought in dead or wounded. The Duke of La Rochefoucauld wanted to take advantage of this circumstance for his side; and although his wound made his two eyes almost hang out of his head, he went on horseback from the square where he had been wounded all the way to the Hôtel de Liancourt, in the Faubourg Saint-Germain [on the other side of Paris], exhorting the *peuple* to aid Monsieur le Prince and in the future to understand better the intentions of those who had accused him of double-dealing with the court. That created, for a time, the desired effect; and never was Paris more partisan of Monsieur le Prince than it was then. However, the noise of the cannon of the Bastille aroused two very different sentiments in the mind of Cardinal Mazarin: for first he thought that Paris was declaring itself against Monsieur le Prince, and that he was going to triumph over this city and his enemy; but seeing that to the contrary they were firing on the king's troops, he sent orders to the marshals of France to withdraw the army and return to Saint-Denis. This day of battle may pass as one of the most glorious in the life of Monsieur le Prince: never did his valor and his conduct have more to do with a victory; and it can also be said that never had so many persons of quality caused a smaller number of troops to fight. The banners of the regiments of the Guards, of the Marine, and of Turenne were carried to Notre-Dame [Cathedral], and all the captured officers were allowed to leave on their word of honor.

Nevertheless, negotiations continued. Each faction wanted to make peace or to prevent the others from doing it; Monsieur de Chavigny had to all appearances got back into favor with Monsieur le Prince; and it would be difficult to say what his opinions had been until then, because his natural flightiness constantly aroused in him diametrically opposed views. He would advise that matters be pushed to the extreme every time he had hopes of destroying the Cardinal and returning to the ministry; and he would want them to beg for peace on their knees every time he imagined that his lands would be pillaged or his houses razed. Nonetheless, in this case he was of the opinion, like everyone else, that advantage should be taken of the good feelings of the *peuple*, and that a meeting at the city hall should be proposed to resolve that Monsieur [the Duke of Orléans] be recognized as lieutenant general of the State and Crown of France; that everyone inseparably unite to bring about the Cardinal's exile; that the Duke of Beaufort be given the government of Paris in place of Marshal de L'Hôpital; and that Broussel be established in the office of *prévôt des marchands* instead of Le Febure. But this assembly, in which they believed lay the security of their party, was one of the chief causes of its ruin, through violence aimed at killing all those assembled at the city hall, and it lost for Monsieur le Prince all the advantages which the battle of Saint-Antoine had won him. I cannot say who was the author of such a pernicious plan, for all alike have disavowed it; but in short, while the assembly was being held, they stirred up armed men who came shouting at the doors of the city hall that not only must everything come to pass as Monsieur and Monsieur le Prince wished, but that at that very moment everyone connected with Cardinal Mazarin must be turned over. First it was believed that this noise was only an ordinary result of the *menu peuple*'s impatience; but seeing that the crowd and the tumult were increasing, that the soldiers and even the officers were taking part in the revolt, and that at the same time they had set fire to the doors and shot at the windows, then everyone in the assembly believed himself doomed. Several, in order to escape the fire, exposed themselves to the fury of the *peuple*. Many persons were killed, of all classes and of all political groups; and it was very unjustly believed that Monsieur le Prince had sacrificed his friends in order not to be suspected of having caused his enemies to perish. None of this action was blamed upon the Duke of Orléans: all the hatred fell upon Monsieur le Prince. As for me, I think that both had used Monsieur de Beaufort to frighten those in the assembly who were not on their side, but that indeed neither of them had planned to hurt anyone. They promptly calmed the disorder, but they did not erase the impression they had created in everyone's mind. It was then proposed that a council be created composed of Monsieur, Monsieur le Prince, the Chancellor of France, princes, dukes and peers, marshals of France, and general officers of the party who were in Paris. Two *présidents à mortier* were also to attend on behalf of the Parlement, and the *prévôt des marchands* on behalf of the city, to make a final judgment on everything concerning the war and the administration of the city.

This council increased the discord instead of diminishing it, because of claims over the precedence they were to have in it; and there were, as in the assembly at the city hall, dire results: for the Dukes of Nemours and Beaufort, embittered by their past differences and by their interest in several ladies, quarreled over precedence in the council and finally fought with pistols; and the Duke of Nemours was killed in this fight by the Duke of Beaufort, his brother-in-law. This death aroused the compassion and anguish of all those who knew this prince; the public itself had reason to mourn him, for in addition to his fine and agreeable qualities, he was contributing to peace with all his might; and he and the Duke of La Rochefoucauld had, in order to facilitate its conclusion, renounced the advantage which Monsieur le Prince was to obtain for them through his treaty. But the death of the one and the wounding of the other left the Spaniards and Madame de Longueville's friends all the liberty they desired to involve Monsieur le Prince. They no longer dreaded that their proposals to take him to Flanders would be challenged. They promised him everything he desired; and it seemed that Madame de Châtillon even appeared less lovable to him once he no longer had to fight a rival worthy of him. However, he did not immediately reject the peace proposals; but wishing also to take measures for waging war, he offered the Duke of La Rochefoucauld the same position which the Duke of Nemours had had; and as he could not accept it because of his wound, he then gave it to the Prince of Tarante.

Paris was then more divided than ever: every day the court won over someone in the Parlement and among the *peuple;* the massacre at the city hall had aroused everyone's horror. The army of the princes did not dare to conduct its campaign; its stay in Paris increased the bitterness against Monsieur le Prince; and his affairs had sunk to a lower level than they had ever before been.

6. The French Countryside during Civil War

Raised for suppressing rebellions or fighting in foreign wars, mercenary armies became the scourge of seventeenth-century society and government. The high taxes levied to pay the troops caused rebellions; the troops themselves frequently rebelled or refused to fight because of lack of pay; or, worst of all, entire armies would go on the rampage in the countryside in search of food, women, and booty. When this occurred, as it often did, not even their officers and distinguished commanders were able to maintain military discipline. The civilian population paid the price.

A real and understandable fear of troops prevailed throughout Europe in the seventeenth century. And when rebellions broke out,

SOURCE: *Memoirs of the Sieur de Pontis, faithfully Englished by Charles Cotton* (London, 1693), pp. 279 ff.

despite orders to be lenient and to respect property, both men and officers would often take advantage of their power to "punish" the countryside. Thus the rural houses built by the wealthy in seventeenth-century France could still rightly be called châteaux, for they almost always possessed high walls, moats, and barbed, wrought-iron gates in strategic locations. These were not built to withstand sieges; but in the event of a marauding army in the countryside, the neighboring peasants would still rush to the châteaux with all their belongings in search of protection.

In the memoirs of Louis de Pontis (*c.* 1578–1670), written about the Fronde near Paris, a typical encounter with troops is vividly described. Note how Pontis, known for his courageous service in the armies of Henry IV and Louis XIII, attempts to use his rank and influence with the officers, and their general inability to be certain what the troops will do. Clearly Turenne had some troops which were more obedient than others. The German mercenaries, in suppressing a rebellion in France, soldiered for money and the chance for pillage and booty. Their loyalty to the boy-king Louis XIV was nonexistent.

Madame Saint-Angel had desired me (being a relative) to go do a little business for her estate of Saint-Angel; and there I presently found myself perplexed again with troubles that I never thought to be concerned in any more. For Mareschal Turenne's army, who were guilty of great disorders in their way from Bordeaux, surprised me there so suddenly that I had scarce any time to provide for my own defense. All of the court[yard] of Saint-Angel was immediately full of cattle, and the granaries filled with the wealth of all the inhabitants thereabouts. Apprehending the house was in danger of being plundered, I went to meet the troops upon their march, and to try if I could find any of their generals of my acquaintance at the head of them. The first I met was Marshal Hocquincourt, whom I went and paid my respects to, and told him that being accidentally in the country at Monsieur Saint-Ange's house, who had the honour to be known to him, having succeeded his father in the office of First *Maître d'hôtel* to the Queen; I came most humbly to intreat the favour of him, to take that house into his protection, and secure it from being plundered. Monsieur Hocquincourt replied with an oath, "How should I secure Monsieur St. Angel's house, when I could not secure one of my own, and above twenty more of my friends' and relations' that have been all rifled? There's no such thing as discipline in this army: The souldiers are made with perfect hunger, and are but so many robbers." "Sir," said I, "since they are robbers and hungry wolves, you will not take it ill, I hope, if we defend ourselves, and kill as many of them as we can." He answered me, "Do your best, in God's name, defend yourselves from their violence and rapine; and if you can keep them from plundering St. Angel, do."

But I quickly saw what a folly it would be to pretend to hold out with thirty or forty souldiers against so many troops that might pour in upon the house, and therefore resolved to try some other way for securing the castle. I went to Monsieur Vaubecourt, *maréchal de camp*, who was a friend of mine, and desired his assistance in this difficult point, but he gave me no better satisfaction than Monsieur Hocquincourt. . . .

Just then Monsieur Turenne went by about forty paces off, and knowing me at that distance called me to him and asked me what made me there, raillying [ridiculing] me for my paltry equipage, for in truth I had a rascally horse under me, and not so much as a bridle on him, for I could not come at my own, it being locked up in the castle, the draw-bridge to which I had ordered to be broken down. I answered Monsieur Turenne that I happened to be at Monsieur St. Ange's house, and was much distressed for the passage of his army. He had shewed me great kindness all along, ever since I had the honour to be acquainted with him, and his brother Monsieur Bouillon, at the Prince of Orange's court, who was their uncle, and who (as I observed formerly) was exceeding gracious to me. So he offered me his service immediately, and asked what he could do for me. I told him if he would favour me with three regiments I would post them at three mills hard by, and by that means I should at once save the castle and do the army service, by taking care that they should have a good quantity of meal and bread. Monsieur Turenne embraced my proposal presently. . . . I would set the guards of the army in the most convenient places. I did so very willingly, but first took the regiments of Turenne, Uxelles, and the Marine, and set them about five hundred paces from the castle, to block up the avenues. I chose to keep them at this distance, for fear the very men I set to guard the house should be the first to rob it. Then I went to set the corps de garde for the army, in the places where the enemy might advance; and having appointed five hundred German horse a very forward post, the commander began to swear in his own tongue, and said they perceived I knew where to set them to be knocked on the head. Though I did not understand the language he spoke, yet I easily guessed his meaning, and without taking notice, ordered a thousand foot to sustain those five hundred horse, and three hundred horse more to support them again, with the same number upon both wings, which presently won me the collonel's favour, insomuch that he came and gave me his hand, and proffered to do me any service.

When I had discharged my trust . . . I went back to the castle with an officer, whom with some others I invited to supper. But was told to my great surprize, that the souldiers were come on the backside of the house, and had made a breach already in the wall of the base-court, which they were upon entring at. I was enraged to see that all my measures were broken, and all my care to no purpose, and that the 3 regiments had not begirt the castle quite round, as I gave order they should. In this passion not knowing what to resolve, I took this course at last. I told the officer with me it was to no purpose to undertake the beating off those men with a few firelocks in the castle; and therefore if anything could, authority, and not opposition must do the work. "I know a little back door," said I, "which we must go through and so go straight into the breach. Pray be so kind to follow me, and be pleased to do as you see me do." So through this door we went, and directly to the place where the souldiers had made a large passage, and running upon them with my cane in my hand: "How, rascals," cried I, "what do you think to play the rogue here while the enemy are forcing the quarter?" And so laying on as hard as I could about their pates, and then pushing them with the flat of my sword, we alarmed them so effectively that they never attempted to defend themselves, but to make their escape. . . . Afterwards I sent Monsieur Turenne nine veals for his own table, and made him some other presents in acknowledgement of his civility to me. . . . This was in the time of the second Paris war.

7. *Descartes and the Fronde*

Though not actively engaged in the political turmoil of the Fronde, René Descartes (1596–1650) nevertheless had strong views on the political and international events of his time. Here he makes no distinc-

SOURCE: Letter from Descartes to Brasset, March 31, 1649, in C. Adam and P. Tannery, *Oeuvres de Descartes* (Paris, 1903), V, p. 331.

tion between his own passions for a peaceful resolution of the Fronde and the passions which he defined and discussed in his philosophical works. Does his opposition to the Spanish invasion suggest sympathy with the cause of the Frondeurs?

This letter is addressed to a Monsieur Brasset, who had referred to Queen Christina's invitation to Descartes to join her in the Swedish capital, the "excursion" to which Descartes humorously alludes at the end of this letter.

[March 31, 1649]

The philosophy which I study does not teach me to reject having recourse to passions, and I have as violent ones in wishing for calm and the dissipation of the storms over France as do any of those who are the most involved in them; so you may judge, please, how great is my obligation to you for having taken the trouble to inform me of the good news you have had from [the court at] Saint-Germain. My joy would have been perfect had I not read in the latest gazettes that the Archduke [Leopold William of Austria] is advancing upon Paris, and that he has been allowed to pass as if he were a friend as far as Soissons. That is carrying things to an extreme, to wait for help from those whose chief interest one knows is to prolong our troubles. I pray God that the fortunes of France will overcome the efforts of all those who intend to harm her.

As for the excursion on which I have had the honor of being invited, if it were as short as that from your home to the woods of the Hague, I would quickly be won over; the length of the road merits taking some time for thought before undertaking it; thus, though it is difficult for me to resist a summons from such a fine place, nevertheless I do not think I will leave here for three months more. And I beg you to believe that wherever I go in the world, I will always be as zealously, etc.

II

The Monarch and His Kingdom

The decades of the 1660's and 1670's brought great innovation to France. The rather tentative reforms of Richelieu toward improving internal administration by founding intendancies and administering justice by special commission, as well as Le Tellier's establishment of effective royal control over the army, laid the foundations for a new bureaucratic and monarchical state. The ideological and legal framework for a totally paternalistic state, in which the monarch would and did intervene in every aspect of the lives of his subjects, had existed for centuries. But the machinery of government to make this possible had never come into being. Lack of information about local conditions, particularism which expressed itself in latent and overt hostility to Paris, and the existence of layers of local and traditional public administrations made it exceedingly difficult for the King to make his will law on any specific subject in any specific geographic area. It was one thing to sign eloquent edicts and to send them off to the provinces, and quite another to be assured that they were actually enforced. Resistance to royal authority at every level in the society was as old as the monarchy itself. Seventeenth-century absolutism must be seen as an attempt to break down that resistance and to resist the interests of particular groups in order that the interests of the sovereign and all his subjects might prevail.

No concern was too insignificant for the attention of the King and his officials. Louis XIV saw himself as the seigneur of all his subjects and would overlook no appeals for subsidies to repair church roofs, build hospitals, repair roads, and build bridges, or to settle disputes between conflicting guilds, monastic chapters, and municipal officials. The education of priests, the contents of books, the existence of prostitutes and beggars, plagues, polluted water, and threats posed by heretics were all within the range of concerns which the Crown must attend to and somehow resolve. Often these concerns involved a judicial decision to the prejudice of one individual group, in favor of another; and when the traditional judicial officials were not considered impartial by both parties, an appeal for help was made to the intendants and to the King directly.

Louis believed that he had a special mandate from God to deal with these problems. His actions and decisions, he and the vast majority of his subjects believed, represented and were imbued with the divine will. There were cynics and skeptics, of course, but the fabric of the society remained sustained by this shared belief in the divine protection given French institutions. The sacraments of the Mass, confession, and absolution in which Louis XIV participated daily and regularly throughout his life joined him with his subjects at every level. The character of the ceremonies in the Parlement of Paris, the provincial estates, and guild and confraternity meetings was taken for granted and sustained the traditional corporate quality of French society. As the father of his people, Louis agonized over his "errors" and feared that God was punishing him and his subjects for his failure to do God's bidding. When Bishop Bossuet chided him for his extramarital relations, Louis considered very seriously the possibility that he and his subjects would suffer for *his* weaknesses of the flesh.

At once traditional, paternalistic, and absolute, yet also bureaucratically more centralized and modern, France reached an apogee of power among the European states in the seventeenth century. Her fiscal administration, laws, and public administration would serve as models to less developed societies for at least a century.

Needless to say, not all the problems were solved, and not all the private interests were broken down in favor of some paternalistic public good. But nevertheless the achievement was impressive as the largest and most successful effort thus far to cope with the problems of an entire society according to rationally derived, unifying principles.

Finally, there can be no separation of the royal administration from the personalities of the King and his ministers. The letters of these men, as well as their official documents addressed to both Frenchmen and foreigners, reveal men of power who feel secure in their roles. Under Louis XIII the menace of disgrace was never lifted from even the King's most loyal minister, Cardinal Richelieu. In the reign of the Sun King we find a ruler able to inspire confidence and assurance in the minds of his ministers, generals, and subjects.

8. The Character of the People in the Généralité *of Paris*

Though the following document is dated about 1620, the conceptions of Frenchmen described in it were held to be true during Louis XIV's reign, and even later. Indeed, the conceptions of peoples and regions probably changed very slowly before the development of the popular nationalism which came out of the French Revolution.

Under Colbert these conceptions, as collected by the intendants, served as part of the knowledge which the Controller General sought in order to formulate royal policies. If the response of a particular town toward a new tariff or royal manufacture could be anticipated, then the Crown's policies might have better hope of success and favorable response.

Since we have undertaken to discuss the customs of the whole of France, it will be very appropriate to speak of its capital city, which is Paris, customary residence of our kings and a miniature of the entire realm, as man is of the world. The Parisians are thus of a rather pleasant nature and do not appear as ill-tempered as the inhabitants of several other cities of France. They are nevertheless very easily stirred up, and an engaging man is capable of making a thousand revolt. They are extremely desirous of money, so that there is nothing in the world a Parisian will not undertake to get some. This is true in the case of low-class persons as well as of those of the opposite extreme.

In the past Parisians appeared rather foolish, so much so that they were given the name *badauds* [gapers] by all of France; but today they have become so smartened up that they are even capable of cheating others. It is not that there are not a lot of persons accustomed to seeing nothing and doing nothing, who are still worthy of that title; but no sooner have they set out into the

SOURCE: A. M. de Boislisle (ed.), *Mémoires des Intendants sur l'État des Généralités dressés pour l'Instruction du Duc de Bourgogne* (Paris, 1881), I, 450–454.

world than they become much more difficult to deceive than many others. It is true that I consider that the distrust of all things, which is suggested to them at every turn, because of an infinity of cheats whom one sees in Paris, is the greatest asset they possess.

The women of all sort desire to appear and to be much better dressed than their class allows, whatever the cost may be, and their husbands, who for the greatest part try to please them (the more so as women run everything there), leave no stone unturned in order to satisfy their desire. But the women are commendable in that even the most beautiful, and the most delicate and rich, deign to visit the hospitals, to handle the ulcerated and feverish sick, and to feed and doctor them.

These people are very desirous of learning what new things are happening on all sides, just as Caesar said of our ancestors. They are very fond of all sorts of pastimes and enjoy living pleasurably, being encouraged by the common example of those who frequent the court, most of whom have no better occupation than gambling, laughing, and eating well.

Moreover, the Parisians, who formerly considered every new thing which appeared a marvel, are no longer astonished by anything, so accustomed have they become to seeing strange things. These people are usually suspicious of foreigners who approach them, and because of this, each is on his guard to see that his guests do not go off with what they owe him. It is true that there are many examples of those who have been disappointed through being too courteous, without knowing the persons with whom they were dealing. But if they have recognized you as a man of honor, and if you have lived a long time in their lodging, you will receive more pleasure from them than from anyone else in the world. They have the peculiarity of not stirring from their lodgings at night, no matter what noise they may hear in the street, and although someone is crying out that he is being robbed or murdered: so that a person finding himself among the cloak snatchers should place his sole hope, after God, in his own hands or else in his feet. And what keeps them in their lodgings in this manner is that they have often answered false alarms given by drunkards, or else cries of vagabonds who enjoy stirring up everyone in order to laugh about it later, or of a group of wicked persons who make this noise purposely in order to try to make those they hate come out so they can be assassinated. In conclusion, the people of Paris are of a rather pleasant and pliable temperament, and I believe that they surpass in politeness all the other people to be seen in the rest of France.

Everything in the area around Paris is scarcely different. But I must still add that the peasants are as proud as anywhere else in the world, because of their proximity to the Parlement, and that no one could say a displeasing word to them without their immediately replying in such a way as to almost beg you to lay hands on them: upon which they assemble in order to try to have you punished.

They also have this custom in the entire vicinity of Paris: they milk travelers as much as they can and would take their last denier from them if it were possible. Thus, no matter from which side one approaches Paris, one finds things unbelievably expensive everywhere.

The people around Chartres are amicable, courteous, communicative, and kind to one another, and usually live together in peace; they like foreigners who have agreeable qualities; are given to piety and very attached to the faith of their ancestors; are charitable, give alms, and devote themselves to trade.

Those of the Beauce are of almost the same nature as those of Chartres, and are rather good souls, going in for agriculture and the wheat trade. In many places they are rather sly, because of the rather great number of travelers coming from all directions. The inhabitants of Châteaudun are well-meaning, keen-witted and cunning, and read the meaning behind what you are saying, and are also rather terse. Sometimes they say so little that they do not even listen to one another or allow those who are speaking to finish what they are saying: this is the natural vice of the region.

The citizens of Blois take after the bounty of the soil and the mildness of the air in that region, and are as courteous, pleasant, affable, sprightly, cunning, and witty as possible, thrifty and perpetually busy; they are devoted to God's service, are fond of foreigners, and live agreeably with one another. In a word, the entire region has inhabitants who cannot be excelled in kindness by all the rest of France.

The inhabitants of Vendôme have a mild, pleasant nature, given to extreme politeness, and even born to excel in something, as did Pierre Ronsard, a gentleman of this region, known throughout Europe for his works, which have made him not only the pride of his province but the very ornament of the whole of France.

Those of Orléans and vicinity are rather polite and cultivated and speak in a very agreeable fashion; but they are of a sharp and biting nature, which has won for them the oft-quoted name, the *Guépins* [the wasplike ones]. They are very plucky and help one another very much and devote themselves to trade, which they carry on in many places.

Those around Sens have already shown in the past how plucky they are, as they were the first to decide to accompany Brennus* to Italy. The people there are rather good, and less sly than in many other places, and in this region almost everyone you see is rather religious. And such is also true about the region of Auxerre, the people being of rather good character, but plucky, rebellious, and also fond of trading their produce.

As for the inhabitants of Champagne and Brie, although their neighbors criticize them for being fixed in their opinions, and call them *stubborn*, nevertheless this imperfection is covered over by an infinity of virtues which makes them commendable, because reason makes them control their natural warmth, giving rise to this vice which is assigned to them. They are approachable, quick to please, God-fearing, and not liable to become easily infatuated with new opinions.

9. Louis XIV, the God-Given Child

After more than twenty years of childlessness, Louis XIII and Anne of Austria found themselves parents in 1638. To them and their subjects the birth of Louis XIV was a miracle and a sign that God's special favor on the French Monarchy continued through the ages from Clovis to St. Louis, the ninth to bear the name that the little prince was given at his christening. The boy's godfather was Cardinal Mazarin.

Louis XIV's bookish education may have been neglected, but his training in manners and conduct certainly was not. For the man who would so rarely lose his temper or publicly show any distress or uneasiness, in decade after decade of ruling, this letter from his father to

SOURCE: *Louis XIII d'après sa correspondance avec le Cardinal de Richelieu*, ed. by the Count de Beauchamp (Paris, 1902), pp. 379–380.

* A Celtic chief of the fourth century whose troops sacked Tuscany and Rome.

Richelieu describing the boy's conduct reveals how young Louis XIV was when educated in ceremony and in reverence for his father.

From Saint-Germain [-en-Laye]
this 13th of September 1640

I am writing you this note to tell you that through the ingenuity of Madame de Lansac my son begged my pardon on his knees and played with me for much more than an hour. I gave him some toys to play with. We are the best friends in the world. I pray the good God that this will continue, and that He will give you a long, happy life and perfect health.

LOUIS

10. Louis' Reflections on Kingship

The recent work of scholars has demonstrated that Louis XIV was a more profound thinker about politics than either his admirers or his detractors had suspected. His concern with finding the true, Christian principles upon which to base his policies led him to reflect on the nature of man, the public good, and divine intervention in human affairs. Profound and coherent though his principles were, and despite his diligent efforts to live up to them, Louis' political principles were anything but original. This is to his credit. The Sun King is sometimes disparagingly described as someone who did not keep abreast of his times. But as a head of state who had to negotiate with Leopold of Austria, Innocent XI, or even Queen Anne—to say nothing of some of his most learned subjects in the provincial parlements who insisted on persecuting his subjects for witchcraft—Louis did well to remain firmly attached to the traditional principles of French Absolutism. But on another level, the price for this traditionalism would be high; for did not these same principles which helped him remain a conscientious ruler also lead him to recognize a Stuart pretender at a most undiplomatic time (1701) and to revoke the Edict of Nantes?

Kings are often obliged to do things against their natural inclinations and which wound their natural goodness. They ought to love

SOURCE: "Réflections sur le métier du Roi" (1679), Bibliothèque Nationale, Mss. fr. 1033, fol. 125–130.

making people happy, and they must often chastise and condemn people whom they naturally wish well. The interest of the state must come first. One must overcome one's inclinations and not put oneself into a position of reproaching oneself, in something important, for not having done better because personal interests prevented one from doing so and distorted the views which one should have had for the grandeur, the good, and the power of the state.

Often there are things which cause pain; there are delicate matters which are difficult to straighten out; one's ideas are confused. So long as that is the case, one can remain without deciding; but as soon as one has fixed one's mind on something and believes one sees the best solution, one must take it. This is what has enabled me to succeed often in what I have done. The errors which I have committed and which have caused me infinite troubles have been through obligingness, and through letting myself go along too nonchalantly according to the advice of others.

Nothing is so dangerous as weakness, whatever sort it may be. In order to command others, one must rise above them; and after having heard what comes from all sides, one must determine what must be done by one's own judgment, without worrying, always thinking of ordering or executing nothing which is unworthy of oneself, of one's title, or of the grandeur of the state.

Princes who have good intentions and some knowledge of their affairs—either through experience or through study—and who work diligently to make themselves capable find so many different things by which they can make themselves known that they must take special care and apply themselves universally to everything.

One must guard against oneself, guard against one's inclinations, and ever be on guard against one's own nature. The king's craft is great, noble, and extremely pleasant, when one feels oneself worthy of carrying out everything one sets out to do; but it is not exempt from pain, fatigue, cares. Uncertainty sometimes leads to despair; and when one has passed a reasonable amount of time in examining a matter, one must decide and choose the side believed to be best.

When one keeps the state in mind, one works for oneself. The good of the one makes the *gloire* of the other. When the former is happy, eminent, and powerful, he who is the cause as a result is *glorieux* and consequently must savor more than his subjects, if the two are compared, all of the most agreeable things in life.

When one has been mistaken the fault must be mended as soon as possible, and let no motive prevent it, not even kindness.

In 1671, a minister [Hugues de Lionne] died who held a position as secretary of state, in charge of the Department of Foreign Affairs. He was a capable man, but not without his shortcomings. It was essential to make a good selection for this post, which is very important.* I spent some time thinking about whom I would name to his position; and after having made a careful examination, I found that a man who had served in the embassies for a long time was the one who would fill it best. I sent for him [Arnauld de Pomponne, then ambassador to Sweden]; my choice was approved by everyone, which does not always happen. Upon his return I put him into possession of the office. I knew him only by reputation and by the tasks which I had given him, which he had carried out very well. But the work which I gave him turned out to be too great and too extensive for him. For several years I suffered from his weakness, his obstinacy, and his inattentiveness. He cost me a considerable amount, I did not profit from all the advantages which came my way, and all because of obligingness and kindness. Finally I had to order him to resign, because everything which passed through his hands lost the grandeur and strength which one must have when carrying out the orders of a king of France who is not unfortunate [in his affairs]. Had I made up my mind to send him away sooner, I would have avoided the inconveniences which came to me and I would not have to reproach myself that my obligingness toward him did harm to the state. I have gone into detail to give an example of what I said above.

11. The Body, Its Functions, and Social Behavior

By 1715 some scholars and physicians had rejected the traditional conceptions of the body and its functions as first developed by the ancient Greeks, but the majority of Frenchmen, including Louis XIV, still continued to uphold the old theories and to treat their bodies ac-

SOURCE: *Almanach:* "Les quatre complexions de l'homme selon le calendrier des bergers," as quoted in Robert Mandrou, *De la Culture populaire au 17e et 18e siècles* (Paris: Stock, 1964), pp. 189–194.

cordingly. The perception of the body, moreover, had important implications for social behavior in general. The physical features of a person were thought to be indications of how he would behave in his relationships with others. For social historians the implications of these theories should be important clues to the general patterns of acceptable social behavior. The particular ways in which seventeenth-century Frenchmen perceived one another played an important role in the careers of men and women at every level of society.

Shepherds' Almanac: The Four Complexions of Man

The choleric nature is one of fire, hot and dry, is naturally thin and lank, covetous, extravagant, hasty and unstable, rash, mad, generous, malicious, deceptive, subtle where he applies his judgment. A lion with wine, that is to say, when he has drunk a lot he wishes to dance, to pick a quarrel and to fight; most fond of dressing in a neutral color such as gray.

The sanguine nature is of the air, moist and warm; and so it is generous, fertile, moderate, amiable, of a voluble nature, joyful, singing, laughing, fleshy, high-colored, and gracious. A monkey with wine, that is to say, the more he drinks, the happier he is, draws close to the ladies; naturally likes clothing of a vivid color such as scarlet, violet, and fine colors.

The phlegmatic nature is one of water, cold and damp and thus is sad, pensive, lazy, sluggish, sleepy, animated and clever, with abundant phlegm, tends to spit when he is moved, has a fat face, and is a sheep with wine, that is to say, when he has drunk a lot he seems weaker and more attentive to his work; naturally loves the color green.

The melancholy nature is of the earth, dry and cold, and so it is sad, sluggish, covetous, unproductive, a scandalmonger, suspicious, malicious, and lazy, a pig with wine, that is to say, when he has drunk a lot he desires only to sleep or to doze; naturally likes clothes of black.

Coming to the subject of the visible signs, let us begin with those of the head, but first we warn you that one must beware of all people having a defect in one of their natural members, such as the foot, eye, or any other member, of a person with a limp, and especially of a beardless man, for they are inclined to various vices and evil habits and one must shun them as he would his mortal enemy.

After this the shepherd says that silky hair signifies a piteous and weak person. And those with red hair age readily and lack sense and are not very loyal. If a person has black hair, a good-looking face, and good color, it means he has a true love of justice. Thick hair means that the person loves peace and harmony, and thus is very clever and subtle. If a person has black hair and a red beard it means that he is lecherous, is a slandermonger, is disloyal, and a braggart. Curly blond hair means a laughing, joyous, lecherous, and deceptive man. Black curly hair means a melancholy, lecherous, evil-thinking, and very generous man. Those whose hair hangs down show good sense with uneasiness. A thick head of hair on a woman means she is robust and greedy.

A person with very big eyes is lazy, shameless, disobedient, and thinks he knows more than he does. But when the eyes are average, neither too large nor too small, and neither too black nor too green, the person is exceptionally clever, courteous, and loyal. A person with bloodshot, damaged, and strained eyes shows malice, vengeance, and treason. Those whose eyes are large, with thick and long eyelids, show folly, great deceit, and a bad character. If the eye moves rapidly and has sharp sight, such a person is full of fraud and larceny, and is not very loyal. Those whose eyes are black with little drops in them, shining brightly, are the best and surest, and it means they have good sense and good discretion, and such a person should be loved, for he is full of loyalty and of all other good traits. Those whose eyes glow and sparkle have a big heart and are powerful. Whitish or pulpy eyes mean a person inclined to vice and lechery, who is full of fraud. The shepherds say that when a person looks at them and is as if dumbfounded and also as if ashamed and yet enjoying it, and if in looking at them seems to be sighing and if droplets appear in his eyes, then the shepherds are certain that such a person loves them and desires the well-being, and the honor too, of the one he is looking at; but when someone looks at them by casting his eyes to the side, except by delicacy, such a person is deceptive and is seeking to shame, and such are the people who dishonor ladies, and one must take care to avoid them, for such a look is false, lecherous, and very deceptive.

Those whose eyes are small, russet-colored, and piercing are melancholy, impudent, meditative, and cruel persons. And if a little ruptured vein appears between the eye and the nose of a woman, it means that she is a true virgin, and in the man it means a great subtlety of understanding, and if it is thick and black it means corruption, heat, and melancholy in a woman, and in a man harshness and also lack of sense. But this vein does not always appear. Yellow eyes mean leprosy and a poor physical condition. Likewise, he who has big and long eyelids shows great severity, harsh judgment, and lust. Eyebrows which are thick and joined together over the nose indicate a great degree of malice, cruelty, lust, and envy. He whose eyebrows are thin and long shows a subtle cleverness, reasonable good sense, and loyalty. Those with deep-set eyes and thick brows above as well are scandalmongers, evil-thinkers, who drink too much and prefer to use their cleverness for evil purposes.

Now comes the face. Those whose face is small and short and who have a thin neck and a thin nose, long and slender, are very big-hearted persons, hasty and wrathful. Likewise a nose which is long and prominent by nature means prowess and audacity. Likewise, a short nose signifies hastiness, lewdness, impudence, and that one is enterprising. A hooked nose which goes down as far as the upper lip indicates a malicious, deceptive, disloyal, and very lecherous person. A prominent nose which is fat through the middle means a wise and eloquent man. A nose with large and open nostrils means gluttony and also ire. Likewise, a face which is short and ruddy means a person full of riot, noise, and debate, and of very little loyalty. Likewise, a face which is neither too long nor too short and which has not become too fat and has a good color signifies a true and amiable person, wise and of good intentions, obliging and good-natured and well regulated in all these things. A fat and fleshy face means a discreet and decorous person in everything he does. A face which is small and short and which has a yellow color means a deceitful person, not very loyal, and full of shame. A long and handsome face signifies a deceptive, not very loyal, spiteful, wrathful, and very cruel person.

Those with a large and wide mouth show signs of ire and audacity. The small mouth signifies thoughtful melancholy, a great deal of ruse, and evil thinking. Likewise, he who has thick lips, it is a sign of very great roughness and a lack of sense. Thin lips mean lechers and liars.

After this the shepherds also speak of the teeth and of speech. Teeth which are small and close together signify a person who loves loyally, a person who is lustful and also of a good constitution. Likewise, teeth which are long and big indicate hastiness and ire in a person. Big ears in a person signify foolishness, but he has a good memory. Likewise, small ears signify lust and larceny.

A person with a good voice is often bold, wise, and speaks well with persons. Likewise a medium voice in a person which is neither too glib nor too loud signifies good sense, a good provider, truthfulness, and also uprightness. Likewise, a person who speaks rapidly and who has a weak voice is a person of very great value. A loud voice in a woman is a very bad sign. Likewise, a soft voice signifies a person full of envy, suspicion, and lies. Also, too glib a voice signifies a big heart and great foolishness. Likewise, a loud voice signifies forwardness and ire. A person who moves about when he speaks and whose voice breaks is envious and simple-minded, drunken and very badly brought up. A person who speaks moderately without moving is of great and perfect understanding and of very genteel station, and gives loyal advice.

Likewise, a person with a round face and bleary eyes, and yellow teeth in addition, is a person of little loyalty and is treacherous with foul breath. Likewise, a person who has a long and thin neck is cruel and pitiless, hasty and harebrained. A person with a short neck is full of fraud and cheating and of all forms of wickedness and deceit and malice, and no one should trust such a person. Such is also true for a person with a long and fat neck, signifying gluttony, lechery, strength, and a great amount of lewdness.

A woman who is masculine and has large and angular limbs is by true nature melancholy, fickle, and also lewd. Likewise a person with a large and long belly shows little sense and understanding, is proud and lewd. A person with a small belly and large feet shows good understanding, good and loyal conscience. Likewise a person who has large feet and high and sloping shoulders shows prowess, audacity, forwardness, good sense, and also loyalty. Sharp and broad shoulders signify disloyalty, cheating, deceptiveness, and a person of very bad character.

When the arm is so long that it can reach as far as the knee joint, it signifies valor, generosity, loyalty, honor, good sense, and good understanding. Likewise, when the arm is short, it signifies ignorance and very bad character and a person who likes quarrels, tension, and debates. Likewise, he who has long hands and long thin fingers is subtle and a person who has a strong will and a great desire to know and see several things. Large hands and fat fingers signify strength, forwardness, frivolity, audacity, and a person full of good sense and good understanding.

Those who have light and shiny nails of a good color show good sense and an increase in wealth and in honor. Likewise those who have raised and long nails will have sorrow, tribulation, anguish, and hard work. Those who have short and hooked nails are avaricious, lecherous, proud, and with a heart brimful of sense and malicious malice.

Those with large and flat feet are scurrilous, vigorous, and of little sense and understanding. Those with little and light feet are persons of harsh judgment and little loyalty. Those with short, flat feet are cruel, not very good, and very impolite. A person who takes long and slow steps will greatly prosper in all things. He who takes short and quick steps is superstitious, full of envy, and of ill will. A person with little, flat feet who throws them like a child is audaciously loyal and of good sense, but this person has many diverse thoughts.

The shepherds say: Because there are diverse signs in man and woman which are at times contrary to one another, one must most commonly judge by the facial signs and principally the eyes, for these are the truest and most probable.

And they also say that God has made no creature to live in this world which is wiser than man; for there is not a condition or manner in any animal which is not found in man.

Man is naturally audacious like the lion. Gallant like the ox. Generous like the cock. Avaricious like the dog. Hard and bitter like the stag. Meek like the turtledove. Malicious like the leopard. Intimate like the dove. Hurtful and cheating like the fox. Simple and meek like the lamb. Light and agile like the horse. Slow and woeful like the bear. Costly and precious like the elephant. Vile, lazy like the ass. Rebellious and disobedient like the nightingale. Humble like the pigeon. Cruel and stupid like the ostrich. Profit-making like the ant. Dissolute and vacant like the goat. Spiteful and proud like the pheasant. Calm and mild like the fish. Lustful like the pig. Strong and powerful like the horse. Shrewd like the mouse. Reasonable like the angel. And for this reason he is called the little world; for, such as he is, he shares the condition of all creatures.

12. Saint-Simon's Description of Louis XIV and His Court

In a monarchy the royal court is the key institution of prestige and influence in the society. As their sovereign lord, the king receives and entertains his subjects; the bishops, generals, diplomats, poets, painters, and hangers-on from nearly every station are "honored with the sovereign's presence" and hopeful of some job or pension. The ceremonial is elaborate, every individual knows his place, and the stakes are high in money and in real service to the Crown, as well as in flattery.

Louis de Rouvroy, Duke of Saint-Simon (1675–1755), was the son of a noble who had been honored with a duchy for his ancient fief by Louis XIII and who, as First Gentleman of the Bedchamber, had enjoyed enormous influence over that sovereign. The author of the famous *Mémoires* hoped for as much at the court of Louis XIV but never succeeded in gaining the political influence he considered commensurate with his high social distinction. Saint-Simon's writings are therefore those of a disappointed courtier and influence seeker. His obsession with aristocratic claims to power endeared him little to the Sun King, but it did complement his keen historical intelligence, making him the French court's best contemporary historian. Saint-Simon was more than an observer or journalist. He sought to be accurate, judicious, and even fair. The results are a brilliant analysis of the French elite in the late seventeenth century, recounted chronologically, volume after volume.

A more accurate knowledge of Lous XIV himself, and of his courtiers, may be gained from reading personal correspondence. But what men thought and did privately is only one part of history; Saint-Simon's contribution concerns their public image. We sense that when Saint-Simon, though disappointed, is impressed by the King's manner and bearing, there is every reason to believe that the San King was indeed very impressive in public. By acting the way a king was *supposed* to act according to the ancient public image of kingship, Louis maximized his personal assets to effect his policies at court, in France, and in Europe.

Several things contributed to removing the court permanently from Paris and keeping it without interruption in the country. The

SOURCE: *Mémoires de Saint-Simon*, ed. by A. Chéruel (Paris, 1857), XII, 452–458, 461–471.

troubles during the [King's] minority, for which that city was the great theater, had given the King an aversion for it and also had persuaded him that staying there was dangerous, and that the court's residing elsewhere would make cabals less easy in Paris—owing to the distance between the localities, somewhat removed as they were—and at the same time more difficult to hide since absences would be so easy to observe. He could not forgive Paris for his fugitive departure from that city on the eve of Epiphany 16[49], nor for having let it, in spite of himself, witness his tears over Madame de La Vallière's first withdrawal. The quandary over his mistresses, and the danger of creating great scandals in the midst of a capital so populous and so filled with so many different opinions, had no little part in keeping him at a distance. He felt himself importuned by the crowd of *peuple* there each time he went out, returned, or appeared in the streets; he was no less importuned by another sort of crowd of bourgeois, a crowd which was not likely to go and seek him assiduously farther off.* [Other reasons were] worries, which were no sooner observed than the most intimate of those who were in his employ—old Noailles, Monsieur de Lauzun, and several subordinates—sought favor by their vigilance and were accused of purposely multiplying false warnings, which they had people give them in order to make themselves seem more important and to see the King privately more often; his fondness for walking and hunting, much easier in the country than in Paris, far from forests and lacking in places to walk; [his taste] for buildings which came afterward, and kept gradually growing, did not allow him amusement in a city in which he could not have avoided being the constant center of attention; lastly, the idea of making himself more venerated by escaping from the view of the multitude and from the custom of being seen by it daily. All these considerations made the King settle at Saint-Germain [-en-Laye] soon after the death of his mother the Queen. It was there that he began to attract society by fetes and gallantry, and to make it known that he wished to be seen often.

His love for Madame de La Vallière, which was at first a secret, gave rise to frequent excursions to Versailles, then a little "house of cards," built by Louis XIII, who was annoyed, and his courtiers

* Great numbers of bourgeois and *gens de robe* would appear at all public court functions.

even more so, by having often slept there in a wretched tavern on wheels and in a windmill, exhausted by his long hunts in the forest of Saint-Léger and even farther, a time far removed from these days reserved for his son in which the roads, the speed of the dogs, and the number of hired beaters and hunters on horseback have made hunts so easy and short. This monarch never or very rarely slept at Versailles more than one night, and out of necessity: the King his son [did so] in order to be more alone with his mistress, pleasures unknown to the Just [Louis XIII], to the hero and worthy son of St. Louis who built that little Versailles. These little outings of Louis XIV gradually gave birth to those immense buildings which he built there, and their conveniences for the numerous courtiers, so different from the lodgings of Saint-Germain, [led the King to] transfer his entire residence there shortly before the death of the Queen. There he built countless lodgings, [and] courtiers flattered him in order to request one, while at Saint-Germain almost everyone suffered the inconvenience of living in the town, and the few who were lodged in the château were incredibly crowded.

Frequent fetes, private walks at Versailles, and excursions were means which the King seized upon in order to single out or to mortify [individuals] by naming the persons who should be there each time, and in order to keep each person assiduous and attentive to pleasing him. He sensed that he lacked by far enough favors to distribute in order to create a continuous effect. Therefore he substituted imaginary favors for real ones, through jealousy—little preferences which were shown daily, and one might say at each moment—[and] through his artfulness. The hopes to which these little preferences and these honors gave birth, and the deference which resulted from them—no one was more ingenious than he in unceasingly inventing these sorts of things. Marly, eventually, was of great use to him in this respect; and Trianon, where everyone, as a matter of fact, could go pay court to him, but where ladies had the honor of eating with him and where they were chosen at each meal; the candlestick which he had held for him each evening at bedtime by a courtier whom he wished to honor, and always from among the most worthy of those present, whom he named aloud upon coming out from saying his prayers. The official jerkin was another of these inventions; it was blue, lined with red, with red cuffs and vest, embroidered with a magnificent golden design with a bit of silver, reserved for these clothes. There was only a fixed number of them, which included the King, his family, and the princes of the blood: but the latter, like the rest of the courtiers, obtained one only when one fell vacant. The most distinguished persons at court by themselves or through an influential courtier asked the King for them, and it was an honor to receive one. The secretary of state for the King's household would send a commission for one, and none of them [the secretaries of state] was entitled to have one.* They were conceived for those, a very small number, who were entitled to follow the King on excursions from Saint-Germain to Versailles without being named [on a list], and when that practice ceased, these clothes also ceased to confer any privileges, except that of being worn even when in mourning at court or for one's family, provided the mourning was not deep or that it was near its end, and also at times when it was forbidden to wear gold and silver. I never saw it worn by the King, Monseigneur [the Dauphin], or Monsieur [the King's brother], but very often by the three sons of Monseigneur and by all the other princes; and until the King's death, as soon as one fell vacant, the question arose who among the most notable persons at court would have it, and if a young lord obtained it, it was a great honor. One could never finish enumerating the attention he paid in order to have a great many persons at court, and the various devices of this sort which followed one upon the other as the King advanced in age and as the fetes changed or decreased in number.

Not only was he sensitive to the continual presence of the distinguished, but he was also so for those on lesser levels. He would look to the right and to the left upon rising, upon going to bed, during his meals, while passing through apartments, and in his gardens of Versailles, where only courtiers had the right to follow him; he saw and noticed everyone; no one escaped him, even those who did not even hope to be seen. He very clearly observed to himself the absences of those who were always at court, those of passersby who came there more or less often; he pieced together the general or personal causes of these absences and did not lose the slightest opportunity to act accordingly toward them. It was a demerit for some, and for all those who were the most distin-

* That is, they were reserved for nobles, and no man of the robe, even on the highest level, was eligible for one.

guished, not to make the court their habitual residence, [a demerit] for others to come there rarely, and a sure disgrace for those who never, or almost never, came. When it was a question of something for them: "I do not know him," he would reply proudly; about those who rarely appeared: "He is a man whom I never see," and those sentences were irrevocable. It was another crime not to go to Fontainebleau, which he considered like Versailles, and for certain people not to make a request to go to Marly, some each time, others often, although he did not plan to take them there, some always or others often;* but, if one were in a position to go there at all times, one needed a valid reason to be excused, men and women alike. Above all he could not stand people who enjoyed being in Paris. He could rather easily bear those who liked their country estates; yet even there one had to restrain oneself or to have taken precautions before going to spend more than a short time there. This was not limited to persons in office, nor to close friends, nor to the well-treated, nor to those whom their age or their dignity singled out more than the others. The intended purpose [of their absence] alone sufficed among these habitual courtiers. . . .

Louis XIV carefully trained himself to be well informed about what was happening everywhere, in public places, in private homes, in public encounters, in the secrecy of families or of [amorous] liaisons. Spies and tell tales were countless. They existed in all forms: some who were unaware that their denunciations went as far as [the King], others who knew it; some who wrote him directly by having their letters delivered by routes which he had established for them, and those letters were seen only by him, and always before all other things; and lastly, some others who sometimes spoke to him secretly in his cabinets, by the back passageways. These secret communications broke the necks of an infinity of persons of all social positions, without their ever having been able to discover the cause, often very unjustly, and the King, once warned, never reconsidered, or so rarely that nothing was more [determined]. . . .

No one ever gave more graciously and in doing so increased so greatly the price of his benevolence; no one ever sold more dearly his words, his very smile, even his glances. He made everything

* That is, he never intended to invite some of these suppliants; the others rarely were invited.

precious by discernment and stateliness, to which the rarity and the brevity of his words added much. If he were addressing someone, whether a question or small talk, everyone present looked at him; [being spoken to by Louis XIV] was an honor which was talked about and which always conferred a sort of distinction. Such was also the case for all the attentions and the honors and the preferential treatment which he bestowed according to one's due. Never did he let slip an uncivil word to anyone, and if he had to reprove, reprimand, or correct, which was very rare, it was always in a more or less kind manner, almost never curtly, never in anger, with the exception of the unique adventure of Courtenvaux* . . . although he was not exempt from anger—and sometimes with an air of severity.

Never was a man so naturally polite, nor of a politeness which was so greatly restrained, so increasingly firm, nor which took better notice of age, merit, and rank, both in his replies, when they went beyond the "I shall see," and in his manners. These various levels were clearly marked in his manner of greeting and of receiving bows, when people departed or arrived. He was admirable in the different ways he received salutes at the head of the lines in the army or during troop reviews. But above all nothing equaled him in respect to women. He never passed before the least coif without raising his hat, I mean to a chambermaid, and whom he knew to be one, as often happened at Marly. Before ladies, he removed his hat completely, but to a greater or lesser degree; to titled persons, half off, and held it in the air or near his ear for a few more or less prolonged instants; before lords, real ones, he merely put his hand to his hat; for princes of the blood, he removed it as he did before ladies; if he approached ladies, he put on his hat only after having left them. All this only was true outside; for in the house he never

* Courtenvaux, the debauched eldest son of Louvois, had been dismissed from an important position for incompetence and had been given command of a company of Swiss guards. When his guards were excluded from a certain chamber at Versailles which other Swiss guards could frequent, Courtenvaux, prone to fits of temper, exploded, not realizing that the order had been issued by the King himself. That night at supper he was dressed down publicly by Louis XIV. Saint-Simon claims that the King was angry because Courtenvaux had inadvertently called attention to his secret use of certain Swiss guards to spy upon courtiers.

wore a hat.* His bows, more or less pronounced, but always slight, had an incomparable grace and stateliness, down to his very manner of getting halfway up at the supper table for each seated lady [a princess of the blood, duchess, or foreign princess, the only ones entitled to a seat in the King's presence] who arrived, not for any other, nor for the princes of the blood; but toward the end that tired him greatly, though he never ceased doing it, and the seated ladies avoided entering during his supper once he had begun. It was with the same refinement that he accepted the services* of Monsieur [his brother], of the Duke of Orléans [Monsieur's son], of the princes of the blood; to the latter he showed only slight gratitude, likewise with Monseigneur [the Dauphin] and his sons, out of familiarity; to high officials he displayed an air of kindness and attentiveness. If he were made to wait for something while dressing, he always did so patiently. Punctual to the hours he had established for his entire day; clear and brief precision in his orders. If, in the wretched winter weather when he could not go outside, he happened to go to see Madame de Maintenon a quarter of an hour earlier than he had announced, which almost never happened with him, and if the captain of the guards on duty was not there, he never failed to tell him afterward that it was his own fault for having come early, not that of the captain of the guards for having missed him. Also, with that regularity which never failed, he was served with the greatest exactitude, and this was of infinite convenience for the courtiers.

He treated his valets well, especially those for the interior. It was among them that he felt the most at ease and that he expressed himself the most familiarly, especially with the principal valets. Their friendship and their aversion often had great effects. They were constantly in a position to render good and bad services; they also brought to mind those powerful freedmen of the Roman emperors, to whom the senate and the great men of the empire paid court, and yielded to in a humiliating way. The latter [the valets], throughout this entire reign, were no less reckoned with nor less courted. Even the most powerful ministers humored them openly,

* Elsewhere Saint-Simon explains that Louis XIV did wear a hat for "first audiences with ambassadors, when paying homage to Monsieur de Lorraine, etc."

* "Services" in this instance meant presenting him his shirt in the morning.

and the princes of the blood, even the bastards, to say nothing of all their inferiors, behaved likewise. The offices of first gentlemen of the bedchamber were more than obscured by the first valets, and high offices were worthwhile only to the degree that the valets or the minor, very subaltern officers connected with them of necessity approached the King more or less often. The majority of them were also very insolent, so that one had to know how to avoid it, or to bear it patiently. The King upheld them all, and he sometimes complacently told how, having in his youth sent one of his footmen, I do not know why, with a letter to the Duke of Montbazon, governor of Paris, who was in one of his country houses near that city, [the footman] arrived as Monsieur de Montbazon was sitting down to table, that he had forced this footman to sit down with him and escorted him, when sending him away, as far as the courtyard, because he had come on the King's behalf. Also, he rarely failed to ask his gentlemen-ordinary, when they returned from expressing congratulations or condolences on his behalf to titled persons, men and women, but to no others, how they had been received, and he would have been very displeased if they had not been made to sit down and the men escorted back to the coach.

Nothing matched him at inspections, fetes, and everywhere where an air of gallantry might be assumed owing to the presence of ladies. It has already been said how he had learned it at the court of his mother the Queen and from the Countess of Soissons; the company of his mistresses had made him even more accustomed to it; but always stately, although sometimes with gaiety, and never anything improper or indiscreet in public, but down to the least gesture, his walk, his bearing, his entire countenance, everything was restrained, everything was decent, noble, grand, stately, and always very natural, to which habit and the incomparable and unique superiority of his entire face lent a great facility. Likewise, in serious things, audiences with ambassadors, ceremonies, never was a man so imposing, and one had first to become used to seeing him, if in addressing him one did not wish to risk becoming speechless. His replies upon these occasions were always brief, to the point, complete, and very rarely without something considerate, sometimes even flattering, when the speech deserved it. Also the respect which his presence demanded, wherever he was, required silence, and even a sort of fright.

He greatly loved fresh air and exercise, as much as he could do. He had excelled in dancing, in croquet, in tennis. He was still an admirable rider in his old age. He loved to watch all these things done with grace and skill. To perform well or badly before him was a merit or a demerit. He used to say that one should not get involved in these things which were not necessary if one did not do them well. He dearly loved to shoot, and there was no better marksman than he, nor one so graceful. He insisted upon excellent retriever bitches; he always had seven or eight of them in his rooms and enjoyed feeding them himself so that they would know him. He was also very fond of the stag hunt, but in a calash,* after having broken his arm while hunting at Fontainebleau, shortly after the death of the Queen [Maria Theresa, in 1683]. He would ride alone in a sort of *soufflet* [a small calash], pulled by four small horses, in five or six relays, and he himself drove at top speed, with a skill and an accuracy which the best coachmen lacked, and always the same gracefulness in everything he did. His postilions were children from nine or ten years of age up to fifteen, and he directed them.

In everything he loved splendor, magnificence, profusion. He turned this taste into a maxim for political reasons, and instilled it into his court on all matters. One could please him by throwing oneself into fine food, clothes, retinue, buildings, gambling. These were occasions which enabled him to talk to people. The essence of it was that by this he attempted and succeeded in exhausting everyone by making luxury a virtue, and for certain persons a necessity, and thus he gradually reduced everyone to depending entirely upon his generosity in order to subsist. In this he also found satisfaction for his pride through a court which was superb in all respects, and through a greater confusion which increasingly destroyed natural distinctions. This is an evil which, once introduced, became the internal cancer which is devouring all individuals—because from the court it promptly spread to Paris and into the provinces and the armies, where persons, whatever their position, are considered important only in proportion to the table they lay and their magnificence ever since this unfortunate innovation—which is devouring all individuals, which forces those who are in a position to steal not to restrain themselves from doing so for the

* A light, low-wheeled, open carriage.

most part, in their need to keep up with their expenditures; [a cancer] which is nourished by the confusion of social positions, pride, and even decency, and which by a mad desire to grow keeps constantly increasing, whose consequences are infinite and lead to nothing less than ruin and general upheaval.

Nothing before him ever approached the number and magnificence of his hunting equipage and all his other sorts of equipment. His buildings, who could count them? At the same time, who will not deplore the pride, the capriciousness, the bad taste? He abandoned Saint-Germain and made in Paris no ornament or convenience beyond the Pont Royal, out of pure necessity, for with its incomparable expanse, [Paris] is inferior [in bridges] to many cities in all parts of Europe. When they built the Place Vendôme, it was square. Monsieur de Louvois saw to the completion of the four façades. His intention was to locate there the Royal Library, the Medals [royal collection of medals, cameos, etc.], the Royal Scales, all the academies, and the Great Council, which still holds its sessions in a rented house. The King's first concern, on the day of Louvois' death, was to stop this work and to give orders to create diagonals at the corners of the square, making it proportionally smaller, to locate there nothing which was destined to be there, and to build nothing but houses, as we see it today.

Saint-Germain—a unique site which joins the marvels of the view, the immense level expanse of an adjacent forest, unique also in the beauty of its trees, its terrain, its location, the advantage and the convenience of the springs on this plateau, the admirable attractiveness of the gardens, of the heights and the terraces, which one after the other could so easily be extended as far as one might desire, the charms and the conveniences of the Seine, [and] lastly, a city already built, self-supporting by its location—he abandoned it for Versailles, the saddest and most unattractive of places, with no view, no woods, no water, no soil, because everything there is quicksand or swamp, consequently without fresh air, for the air there cannot be good. He enjoyed tyrannizing nature, defeating it by art and treasures. He built everything there one after the other, without a general plan; the beautiful and the ugly were glued together, the vast and the constricted. His apartment and that of the Queen are the ultimate in inconvenience, with views on the small rooms and on the darkest, most enclosed, most foul-smelling back areas. The gardens, whose magnificence is astonishing, but whose slightest use wearies one, are also in bad taste. One can reach the coolness of the shade only by passing through a vast torrid zone, at the end of which there is no choice, wherever one is, but to climb up and go down again; and with the hill, which is very abrupt, the gardens end. The sharp stone chips there burn one's feet; but without those chips, one would sink here into the sand, or there into the blackest mud. The violence which has been done to nature everywhere repels and disgusts despite oneself. The abundance of the water pumped and collected from all directions makes [the gardens] green, thick, oozy; they give off an unhealthy and discernible humidity, an odor which is even more so. Their effects, of which one must, however, be very tolerant, are incomparable; but the overall result is that one admires and one flees. From the courtyard [the Marble Court], the constricted aspect suffocates one, and these vast wings flee without taking hold. On the garden side, one enjoys the beauty of the whole; but one thinks one is looking at a palace which has been burned, in which the upper story and the roofs are still missing. The chapel which overpowers it, because Mansart wanted to force the King to elevate the whole building by one story, from every direction conveys the sad impression of an immense catafalque. The workmanship [in the chapel] is exquisite in all its forms, the architectural orders are nothing; everything was done for the tribune, because the King scarcely ever went below, and those on the sides are inaccessible, owing to the single passageway which leads to each [tribune]. One could go on forever about the monstrous failings of such an immense and immensely costly palace, with its dependencies, which are even more so: orangery, kitchen gardens, kennels, great and small stables likewise, a prodigious commons; in a word, an entire city where once stood only a very wretched tavern, a windmill, and that little "house of cards" which Louis XIII had built so that he would not have to sleep on the straw, which was only the narrow and low area around the Marble Court, which served as the courtyard, and whose main buildings had only two short and small wings. My father saw it, and slept there many times. Moreover, this Versailles of Louis XIV, this masterpiece which is so ruinous and in such bad taste—and where complete changes in the reflecting basins and thickets have buried so much gold which goes unseen—could not be finished; among so many salons piled one upon the other, there is neither a theater, nor a banquet hall, nor a ballroom, and in front and behind much remains to be done. The parks and the avenues, all planted, cannot live. Wild game must be constantly put in; there are countless ditches four and five leagues in length; and finally the walls, which in their immense circumference enclose as in a little province the saddest and most unsightly country in the world.

Trianon, in this same park and at the city gate of Versailles, was first a porcelain house in which to go snack, enlarged later so one could sleep there, and finally a palace of marble, jasper, and porphyry, with delightful gardens; the [buildings of the] Menagerie, opposite it, on the other side of the crossbar of the canal of Versailles, are all exquisite trifles, and equipped with all sorts of the rarest two- and four-legged beasts; lastly, Clagny, built for Madame de Montespan at her own expense and passed on to the Duke of Maine [a bastard son by Montespan], at the end of Versailles, is a superb château with its fountains, its gardens, its park; aqueducts worthy of the Romans on all sides; neither Asia nor antiquity offer anything so vast, so multiple, so worked over, so superb, so full of the rarest monuments of all centuries, in the most exquisite marbles of all sorts, in bronzes, paintings, sculptures, or so consummate in recent [centuries].

But water was lacking, no matter what they did, and these artistic marvels of fountains dried up, as they still do constantly, despite the foresight of those sealike reservoirs which cost so many millions to build and to lay through the quicksand and the mud. Who would have believed it? This error became the ruination of the infantry. Madame de Maintenon was reigning; . . . Monsieur Louvois was then on good terms with her; we were enjoying a time of peace. He got the idea of diverting the Eure River between Chartres and Maintenon, and of making it come in its entirety to Versailles. Who can say the gold and the men which the obstinate attempt cost over several years, since it was forbidden, under the most severe penalties, in the camp which had been set up there and which was maintained for a very long time, to speak of the sick, especially of the dead, killed by the hard work and even more by the fumes from so much stirred-up earth? How many others took years to recover from that contagion! How many never regained their health for the rest of their lives! And nevertheless, not only individual officers, but colonels, brigadiers, and those general officers who were put to work there had not, no matter who they were, the liberty to leave for a quarter of an hour, nor to personally miss a quarter hour of service on the construction. Finally the war interrupted them in 1688, without the work having since been resumed; all that remain are shapeless monuments which will make eternal this cruel folly.

In the end the King, wearied by the beautiful and the crowded, convinced himself that he sometimes wanted the small and the solitary. He sought in the vicinity of Versailles something to satisfy this new taste. He visited several spots; he climbed over the slopes which reveal Saint-Germain and that vast plain which lies below it, where upon leaving Paris the Seine twists and waters so many important places and fertile areas. He was urged to stop at Luciennes, where Cavoye has since built a house with an enchanting view; but he replied that this favorable spot would ruin it, and that, since he wanted a nothing, he also wanted a location which would not permit him to think of doing anything to it.

He found behind Luciennes a narrow, deep valley with steep sides, inaccessible because of its marshes, with no view, closed in by hills on all sides, extremely cramped, with a mediocre village on the slope of one of these hills, which was called Marly. This enclosure's lack of a view, or any means of having one, made it valuable; the narrowness of the valley where there could be no expansion added a great deal to it. It was as if he were choosing a minister, a favorite, a general in the army. It was a great labor to dry up this sewer for the surrounding area, which threw all its refuse there, and to bring in earth. The hermitage was built. It was only for sleeping in three nights, from Wednesday to Saturday, two or three times a year, with a dozen or more of the most indispensable courtiers in his service. Little by little the hermitage was enlarged; from growth spurt to growth spurt, the hills were cut out to make room and to build, and most of the end hill was carted away in order to give at least a glimpse of a very imperfect view. Finally, in buildings, gardens, fountains, aqueducts, in what is so curious and so well known under the name of the "Machine of Marly" [a pumping system to raise water from the Seine], in parks, in ornamental and dense forests, in statues, in precious furnishings, Marly became what one still sees today, stripped though it is since the King's death: in forests already grown and bushy which were constantly brought as great trees from Compiègne, and from much farther, more than three-fourths of which died, and were immediately replaced; in vast expanses of thick woods and dark alleys, suddenly transformed into immense reflecting basins on which floated gondolas, then returning to forests which did not let the daylight through from the moment they were planted; I am talking about what I saw in six weeks; reflecting basins changed a hundred times; likewise cascades with successive and completely different figures; abodes for carp ornamented with gold leaf and the most exquisite paintings, scarcely finished, altered and renewed in a different fashion by the same masters, and that an infinity of times; that prodigious machine [the Machine of Marly], of which we have just spoken, with its immense aqueducts, its conduits, and its colossal reservoirs, consecrated uniquely to Marly and no longer bringing water to Versailles; it is an understatement to say that Versailles as we saw it did not cost as much as Marly. That if we add to it the costs of those continual outings, which finally became at least equal to the stays at Versailles, often almost as numerous, and at the very end of the King's life his most usual residence, we will not be exaggerating about Marly alone in counting by billions.* Such was the fate of a lair of snakes and carrion, of toads and frogs, uniquely chosen so no money could be spent on it. Such was the King's bad taste in everything, and his arrogant pleasure in forcing nature, which neither the most onerous war nor religious devotion could blunt.

13. Moreri's Description of France

Louis Moreri (1643–1680) was not trying to be original in his *Historical Dictionary* (1674). His articles are therefore extremely useful for discovering the knowledge and conceptions commonly held by literate Frenchmen. This description of France from one of the expanded editions published after Moreri's death was a cliché to the educated French reader in 1700; and precisely for this reason we find it so interesting.

Pride in France, and in the accomplishments of Frenchmen, is one of the principal themes of this work. Note how Moreri seeks to demonstrate that Frenchmen have excelled in every field of learning and

SOURCE: Louis Moreri, *Le Grand Dictionnaire Historique*, "France" (Paris, 1699).

* An exaggeration.

have surpassed the ancients in some. And yet there is pride in provincial achievements as well, for Moreri does not attempt to be logical about whether it was the greatness of a province or the greatness of France in general which produced some particular man of genius. It is safe to conclude that few of his contemporaries would have seen the contradiction in his analysis.

The reverence for the ancients and for the arts and learning in general seen here is a sort of vulgarized humanism. The subtlety of thought found in the few humanists of the sixteenth century is gone, but historical conceptions and the categories used to define greatness remain in less refined form to set the cultural tone of the late seventeenth century.

FRANCE, the most beautiful country, the most powerful kingdom, and the most illustrious monarchy of Europe. I could perhaps justly say, of the world, if I did not fear appearing too biased. But in order to be persuaded that the kingdom of France is the most ancient and most noble of all the states of Christendom, one must only remember that it has existed for nearly thirteen hundred years, and that today it counts a continuous succession of sixty-four kings. . . .

On the Regions and Inhabitants of France

France is situated in such a temperate climate that one must not be astonished that it is a very agreeable place to live, being subject neither to the great cold of Germany and Sweden nor to the extreme heat of Spain and Italy. It lacks none of the ordinary things of life. For it abounds in rains, wines, oils, hemp, salt, saffron, fruits, pastures, cattle, poultry, wild game, and in short everything which is useful or necessary to man. Strabo and Athenaeus make mention of its gold and silver mines, a few veins of which are still to be found, along with iron mines. It also has diverse mineral waters, tar pits, etc. It is asserted that the Emperor Maximilian, reflecting upon the fertility and the advantages of France, said jokingly that if he should happen to become God, the elder of his sons would succeed him, and the second would be king of France. The people are industrious and succeed in everything they undertake. They are lavish and delicate in their eating and in their dress; they like arms and on every occasion show signs of their bravery. All nations admit that the French have a certain characteristic of politeness, honesty, and a free manner which is not found elsewhere, where one usually sees only constraint and anxiety. Sciences and letters are happily cultivated there, and especially at the present time. And so this century has produced more great men there than that of Augustus. On this subject it can be observed that more books are printed in Paris and Lyons than in any other spot in Europe; and that from there they are supplied to Spain and several other kingdoms. In general the people of France are good: the common ones love the great; and since [the people] are martial, they hold warriors and the nobility in esteem; and nevertheless honor the judicial officers. The French are also accused of not being able to bear fatigue, of not liking difficult things, of conquering without difficulty, but of not knowing how to hold on to their conquests; of sometimes being licentious, and too brash; of being fickle, especially in their dress. I will finish this section by the report that Charles V [the Emperor], according to the story, used to say, "that the Italian appears wise and is; the Spaniard appears so and is not; and the Frenchman is so without appearing to be." Various foreigners admit that the moral virtues of the principal regions of Europe are eminently noticeable in some of the French provinces: such as the frankness of Germany, in Picardy; the generosity of Sweden, in Champagne; the diligence of Poland, in Languedoc; the prudence of Italy, in Provence; the gravity of Spain, in Gascony; the fidelity of Switzerland, in the Dauphiné; the subtlety of mind of Greece, in Normandy; the industriousness of Flanders, in Burgundy. The French language was formed from Greek in part, from Romance, and from German. The Romance language was for a long time accepted in France and especially in the provinces beyond the Loire [i.e., south of the Loire], and the name Romance was given to the story about the exploits of the old knights. Public acts were even written in Latin until 1535, when King Francis I ordered that they be written in French. This language is today extremely refined; all the peoples of Europe, and principally those of the North, like it very much, because it is the enemy of the equivocal, of affectation, of obscure terminology, and because its accent is neither too heavy nor too soft.

The Genius of the French

We know that in the founding of this monarchy, the two nations of the Franks and the Gauls intermingled so much that, no longer forming but one people, they imparted to one another their good and their bad qualities: the Franks grew calmer through their dealings with the Gauls, and the latter to the contrary became more ignorant and more boorish. So that from the beginning of the sixth century the politeness, the eloquence, and the erudition which had been admired in Gaul were no longer to be seen in France. The Latin language, which had commonly been spoken in the region, degenerated into the Romance language, that is to say into corrupted Latin. Thus those who wished to set themselves above the other scholars studied the Latin language as a foreign language. They neglected the reading of the ancient historians, orators, poets; and those who had some talents used them only to convert pagans and heretics, and for affairs directly concerned with religion. Philosophers, mathematicians, or doctors famed for their knowledge no longer appeared. As the people of the century showed neither a taste nor an inclination for letters, a great number of priests in France established public schools in their palaces, to take the place of so many illustrious academies ruined by the Goths and the Burgundians. The Benedictines also opened their schools to secular persons; but in them they analyzed only the Holy Scripture, after having imparted a slight knowledge of the Latin language, and taught them to read Greek. Charlemagne realized that the schools of the bishops and of the religious were not enough for learning in France; that is why, having undertaken the reestablishment of the study of the fine arts and of the sciences, he established public schools to teach them and founded the University of Paris, which became the mistress of all Europe and trained most of the great men who appeared in the Latin Church. This prince with all his zeal and his authority could not succeed in making French writers adopt the politeness of the Greeks and the refinement of the Romans, which the Gauls had so long preserved among them. Louis the Debonnaire and Charles the Bald during their reigns strove to make Charlemagne's plan succeed; but they could not prevent barbarism and ignorance from corrupting the following century, which was the tenth century of the Church. Nevertheless several French authors show in their writing that they had good sense, though they did not have refined tastes: and one can observe in their works, which concern religion, an unction which appears to have dried up once they devoted themselves to the style of the Scholastics. Since St. Bernard, and even in his own time, toward the year 1130, studies began to be reestablished with more ardor than ever. But the simplicity and the natural manner of the preceding centuries were replaced by a singular passion for subtleties, and a spirit of chicanery, which appeared chiefly in dialecticism and in peripatetic metaphysics. It seems quite sure that French writers had caught this vice from the Arabs, through communication with the Spanish. Finally in the last two hundred years sciences and letters have again flourished in France, and one can say that the scholars who appeared during the reign of Louis XII went much further than the Gauls who lived at the time of the Greeks or the Romans.

In the sixteenth century, the French especially applied themselves to reading the Doctors [of the Church], to the study of languages, to the humanities, and to philosophy; in the following one, they tried to join politeness to erudition; to develop differentiation of intellects, as well as of things; and to perfect the arts and sciences, without limiting themselves to what the ancients invented. It is not difficult to rid of their false ideas those who imagine that the French are content to brush over the sciences without deepening their knowledge, to have only a slight smattering, and to take on only the superficial shell. For in regard to grammar, the other nations can find among them writers capable in Hebrew of facing up to Genebrard, to Cinq-Mars, to Dacquin [d'Aquin], and to Messers de La Boderie: but they will have trouble finding any which equal Vatable or Ouatable, Mercerus or Le Mercier, Capel, Bochart, and a few others, who can be seen in the author of *La France Orientale*. For Greek, they can present the most able of their nation against Toussains [Toussain], Lambin, Dorat, Goulu, Henri Étienne: but it will not be easy for them to do the same against Budé, Danés, Turnebus, Chrétien, Casaubon, and Monsieur Valois. As for the Latin language, Passerat, Du Cange, and a great number of others have demonstrated that they knew it perfectly. If one considers French translations one will easily notice that there are almost no more books in Greek or in Latin, of even minor importance, which have not been translated into French; and that several of these translations equal or even surpass the most perfect originals of antiquity. France has also produced excellent philologists, and judicious critics, like Pelissier, the two Scaligers, Turnebus, Muret, Saumaise, and a quantity of others of first rank. The French nation still furnishes Latin poets, who make no concessions to foreigners; and as to French poets, we well know that they have the necessary genius, art, and erudition for the heroic poem, but that they excel in the dramatic genre. The French theater has risen so high in the last fifty years that it even seems to be surpassing that of the Romans, to reach the glory of that of the Greeks. In regard to eloquence, there is no doubt that whether in schools, or at the bar, or in the pulpit, there have been excellent orators in France for two centuries, whose reputation has spread afar; Monsieur Le Maître and Monsieur Patru were outstanding in their speeches for the defense, and a quantity of great men in their sermons. Among a great number of French historians one finds several who can legitimately be compared not only with the most illustrious of the moderns of Italy, of Spain, of England, and of Germany, but even with those of first rank among the Greeks and the Romans. Philippe de Commynes is inferior neither to Tacitus, nor to Polybius, nor to Thucydides; Paulus Aemilius is undoubtedly equal to the ancients. And President de Thou and Monsieur Mézeray are justly held in esteem even by foreigners. No one in the world had studied the science of true chronology until the time of Scaliger the son, and of Father Petau. Monsieur Sanson has not only equaled but has also surpassed all geographers who preceded him even in the opinion of the Dutch; and since him, France has produced other excellent geographers, who work to increase the glory which Sanson acquired for his country. French philosophers have finally won out over all foreigners. Gassendi, who wanted only to pass as a restorer of the philosophy of Epicurus and of Democritus, is regarded by his disciples as a man who had many other lights besides them. Descartes, called *the son of Nature par excellence,* is considered by a quantity of great minds as the master of true philosophy. Mathematics have been treated in France with no less success; and one sees in this century a good number of illustrious mathematicians who have gone far beyond the ancients in their new experiments. Fernel was considered as the prince of modern doctors, as Galen was for those of the Middle Ages, and Hippocrates for the ancients. It is the Italians who have revived Roman jurisprudence in the West, but the French have had a good share in it: such as Placentin, who lived at the end of the twelfth century; Pierre de Belleperche, Jean Favre, or Le Fèvre, and a few others; our nation can legitimately claim the glory for having purified that science with the help of letters; for no one doubts that it was to Budé that jurisprudence owes this obligation. And if foreigners have jurisconsults who have equaled the Rebuffes, Corras, Doneau, Fournier, and others like them, they have very few with the strength of Tiraqueau, Duarein [Duaren], Du Moulin, Brisson, Hotman, and a great number of those who have shone in our century; but they still have had no one capable of standing up to Cujas. Finally, the theologians of France have always been reputed to be the leading theologians of the world; and it is a very remarkable thing that foreign princes and even the popes have sometimes bowed to their decisions; not that they thought themselves dependent upon their authority, but because they were persuaded of their merit and of their capabilities, above the theologians of other nations.

We must now consider in particular the different qualities which are attributed to the French according to the diversity of the provinces. They say that the Parisians, the Angevins, the people of Poitou, the Bretons, the people around Bordeaux, those of Toulouse, etc., are usually good jurisconsults: and that comes from the fact that the universities of these cities provide the opportunity and the convenience of studying law. The Picards are praised for a great love of work, which has often made of them good philosophers and doctors; and that opinion has arisen from the fact that Vatable or Outable, native of Gamaches; Ramus or La Ramée, of the Vermandois region; and Charpentier, of Clermont in the Beauvaisis, have excelled in philosophy; [while] Trigaut, Du Bois or Silvius, and Fernel, in the diocese of Amiens; Grevin and Patin, from that of Beauvais; [and] Ruelle from Soissons, etc., have become known in medicine. They are also famed as better geographers than the other peoples of France, because Monsieur Sanson was from Abbeville, and because he was followed not only by his sons, but by Father Briet, by Monsieur Du Val, and others of this same region. Normandy has often produced fine minds and learned men; but those of this province are accused of liking chicanery, and of being a bit too wily, which is a vice peculiar to only a few of them. It is claimed that in Auvergne those who are born in the mountains have fine and discerning intellects; and those who are born in the valleys are usually coarse and stupid. If that were true, Chancellor L'Hôpital, Genebrard, Savaron, Father Sirmond, and Monsieur Pascal would have to have been born in the mountains. It is believed that the Limousin is a region where, the air being rough, no fine minds are produced; however, Muret, who imitated the elegance of Catullus and the eloquence of Cicero, Dorat, and Du Bois or Bosius, who have become famous through the beauty of their genius and by their station, were from that province. Lower Picardy passes for a region whose air is contrary to the refinement of intellects; and nevertheless, Jacques Le Fèvre, who was from Étaples, reestablished in Paris the taste for matters of theology, philosophy, and other sciences. Lambin, who was from Montreuil, had something more refined than is usually gained in studies in a *collège*. Upper and middle Picardy likewise do not have the reputation of producing fine and free minds; however, Abbot Billy, born in upper Picardy, was of a solemnity both refined and solid; and Voiture, born in middle Picardy, surpassed in refined gallantry all the fine wits at the court of France of his day. . . . From this one can conclude that France has always produced in all her provinces minds which have become famous in sciences and letters.

14. Louis XIV, Head of State

In the seventeenth century very few royal sovereigns actually conducted the business of state themselves. They had principal ministers and a bevy of secretaries, favorites or not, to work for them. When Louis XIV announced, after Mazarin's death in 1661, that he would be his own principal minister, few at court believed him. Others before had expressed good intentions, but after a few months of burdensome paper work, sovereigns generally gave in. Not Louis XIV. He relied on his ministers, of course, but he made the ultimate decisions, year after year, and then decade after decade. Europeans interested in politics observed this and felt the weight of the decisions of a single individual on their own states, especially in diplomacy and war. Louis seems to have known that exercising his office himself would maximize his *gloire*, or self-realization, as Most Christian King. On a more mundane level, he may have realized the value of his work in shaping public opinion favorable to him in France and in Europe. Courtiers, clergy, local magnates, and generals—in short, the elites which had so often rebelled in the early and mid-seventeenth century—hated nothing more than the minister-favorite who controlled patronage and shaped royal policies. Louis XIV was influenced, of course, but he was his own man.

SOURCE: *Documents historiques inedits*, ed. by M. Champollon Figeac (Paris, 1843), X^2, 519–525.

The following letters, addressed to Colbert in a period of severe trial, illustrate the *métier du roi* (or king's craft) as Louis conceived of it on the international level.

At Chantilly, this
24th of April, 1671

I was master of myself enough the day before yesterday to conceal from you the distress I felt in hearing a man whom I have showered with benefits like you speak to me in the manner you did. I felt a great deal of friendship for you; it appears in what I have done; I still feel some now, and I believe I am giving you a rather great proof of it in telling you that I restrained myself a single moment for you, and that I did not want to tell you personally what I am writing you, in order not to risk making you displease me further. It is the memory of the services which you have rendered me and my friendship which makes me feel this way; profit by it and do not dare to anger me again, for after I have heard your reasons and those of your colleagues and have decided upon all your claims, I never want to hear speak of them again. See whether the navy does not suit you, whether it is not to your liking; if you would like something else better, speak freely; but once I make my decision, I do not want a single rejoinder. I am telling you my thoughts so that you can work from a sure foundation and so that you will not make any false steps.

At Liancourt, this
26th of April, 1671

Do not think that my friendship is decreasing: that cannot happen while your services continue; but I must direct them as I wish, and believe that I am doing everything for the best. The preference which you fear that I am showing for others should not worry you. I only want to be just and to work for the good of my service. That is what I shall do when you are near me. In the meanwhile, believe that I am unchanged toward you and that my feelings are what you may desire.

At 11 o'clock, Sunday
[September 27, 1671]

I am very sorry that your fever has prevented you from coming here today as I had ordered you. Consider your health and do nothing which can impair it. I am sending you the letters and the report which Lauzun made concerning what that woman said; you will use it as you see fit; but not wishing to make this matter public and only wishing to make her reveal who forced her to do what she did, it seems to me that Monsieur Pussort might question her privately, and after he has reported her answers to me, I shall do what seems appropriate; if you think that more must be done, I give you the liberty to do so.

I still have to tell you that I declared [Arnauld de] Pomponne secretary of state, and that I do not want Berny [son of Lionne, the secretary of state who had just died] to do the job; tell him on my behalf and that I command him to send all the ciphers to Louvois, whom I have put in charge until Pomponne's arrival, as well as all the other papers he will need for background information. If there is some document under seal, you will remove it with the precautions you judge necessary for your protection, and will put it back with the other important papers until the arrival of Pomponne or until I order otherwise.

Have Madame de Pomponne informed of the honor I am paying her husband, under the conditions which you know, which are the position of first squire of the great stable for 300,000 livres which I am granting as part of the price, so that Pomponne will have to give only the remaining 500,000 livres, for which I shall give him a certificate for deductions until I have done something for him which will free him from the debts he will be obliged to incur for this purchase.

LOUIS

In camp, near Muys
the 31st of May 1672

It appeared so important to me for my military reputation to begin my campaign only with something very splendid that I did not deem the attack upon Maestricht sufficient for that; besides there were too many people there to win it in a space of time which would not spoil my other plans.

I considered it to be more advantageous to my plans, and less banal for my *gloire*, to attack simultaneously four forts on the Rhine and to command in person all the four sieges.

I chose for this purpose Rhimberg [Rheinberg], Vesel [Wesel], Burik [Büderich], and Orsoy. I personally took charge of the siege of Rhimberg, as the best fortified, and where I shall be able to visit the works of the other three sieges daily. My brother will see to the details of that of Orsoy; Monsieur le Prince [Condé] to that of Vesel, and Monsieur de Turenne to that of Burick. Monsieur le Prince and Monsieur de Turenne will be posted as of tomorrow before those latter two forts, each on his side; and I shall be before Rhimberg and my brother before Orsoy on June 2.

I do not know precisely how many men are at each fort; but we shall do our best, and if we can succeed there, I hope that no one can complain that I let down public expectations.

At the camp of Rinberg
June 7, [1672]

Remember the bill of exchange for five hundred thousand livres which you were to have sent me, and tell me as soon as possible what you have done about it and where it will be payable in the region of Liège. Although I held tight rein, as much as possible, so that they would create no disorders, so many armies passed through that some disorder could not be prevented. It will cost me 25 thousand écus which will go to the account of you know who, who works miracles both by his zeal and by his assiduousness. Therefore send me a bill of exchange for that amount. I foresee that I shall soon need another, I do not know for how much, in order for Le Lorgne to pass through the electorate. I am warning you only in order to prepare you to send it when I ask for it. It will be necessary, it seems to me, for you to withdraw some money for Delrieux so that he can buy grain in the region of Liège to set up storehouses where I ordered him. After having spoken of things which cause worry, I must tell you that everything is going so well and so precisely here that I hope for complete success in this campaign. The news which I have sent will surprise you. I hope that the other news will be more favorable, and that I shall have no reason to repent the great sums which I have spent. You will see from the accounts which I am writing to the Queen everything that is going on here, and in this letter the assurances which I give you of my confidence in you, of my friendship, and of my satisfaction in your son's conduct, which cannot be better. He reports to me about everything he receives very exactly and very well, and carries out my orders punctually. I believe that you will not be displeased at what I am telling you and at seeing me satisfied with his conduct. I await with great impatience the news of what has happened at sea; I hope that I shall be as lucky there as I am here, and that the Dutch will lose on all sides more than we could imagine or even hope. I almost forgot to tell you that I have seen all the ordinances which the Queen has signed and the decrees which you have sent me. I approve what has been done, and am content with the way in which everything is going.

LOUIS

At the camp of Deinse [Deinze]
Tuesday, August 30, 1672

I thought it was good to show the enemy that they should not group before me. That is why I marched upon them and made them scatter and withdraw. I do not know if they will do something, but I learned that without a doubt their army is very frightened and that they fled for ten leagues, as if I had pushed right up to them. I think that I shall leave Thursday to return to France, and that I shall be at Saint-Germain on the 6th or 7th of next month. Have everything that is to be done prepared so that I shall find it all ready, and tell Dumay to furnish the Queen's chamber and mine in the old château for Tuesday the 6th; for without fail, I shall be there Wednesday at the latest. I am informing Marshal Lamotte's wife to bring my children there the 5th, so that I may find them settled when I arrive. If there is anything to be done for them, do it and take care that they lack nothing, and that everything I command you is done.

In camp before Besançon
April 4 [1674]

I received the letter you wrote me on the 29th and the report which you attached concerning subsidies. I am returning them to you: you will carry out all the articles marked "good" and will do nothing about the others which are crossed out. I am very pleased about what you tell me and to see that what I have ordered you has been carried out. I have undertaken no small affair here; but I hope that my activity and my assiduousness will let me bring it to a happy conclusion.

LOUIS

Joigny
April 23, 1674

I received the letter you wrote me the 22nd, by which I see that you have carried out everything I commanded, for which I am very pleased.

I do not remember what you tell me I told you in parting which surprised you: tell me what it is; for whatever I might have done, I cannot remember it.

I am very pleased that you paid the 5 (or 3?) millions in the time you told me.

I am sending you a proposal which Lafeullade [La Feuillade?] made so you may give me your opinion of it, before I make a decision.

You will give the enclosed letter to my brother.

LOUIS

In camp before Besançon
May 18 [1674]

I carefully read the letter you wrote me about the stamped paper and about the printed legal forms. I find inconveniences in whichever decision we make; but since I trust you entirely, and you know better than anyone what will be the most appropriate, I rely on you, and I order you to do what you think will be the most advantageous for me.

It seems to me that it is important not to show the least weakness, and that changes at a time like this are ill advised, and that we must take care to avoid them. If we could take some middle course, that is to say decrease two-thirds of the tax on paper, under some genuine pretext, and reestablish the legal forms,* setting a price less

* These printed legal forms, established as a source of royal revenue in March 1673, provoked a rebellion in Brittany and had to be withdrawn in some parts of the realm.

than in the past? I am telling you what I am thinking and what seems best to me; but in the end, I finish as I began, relying totally upon you, being sure that you will do what is most advantageous to my service.

I ordered your son a few days ago to tell you that we should consider having tax farmers for the saltworks at Salins. I am sure you have done so.

I am astonished that you have not yet sent me the plans for the house on the rue du Maine; for it seems to me that the [building] season is very advanced.

Tell me the effect which the potted orange trees create at Versailles in their intended place.

Continue having everything repaired. I forgot in passing by Fontainebleau to notify you that I found everything in good condition, except the garden of Diana, which was not planted. I told Petit to tell you it should be completed. That is my intention. I also ordered Seteran to talk to you about something which the inhabitants are requesting, and about the Huguenot clerks I wanted removed. Tell me what you have done about that. There remains only for me to assure you that I am very satisfied with you and with the manner in which your son is conducting himself.

LOUIS

15. *Affection and Rivalry at Court*

The Duke of Maine was one of the many illegitimate children born to Louis XIV and Madame de Montespan. As was the custom, nurses cared for the needs of children at court, while governesses, tutors, and others helped with their education. Françoise d'Aubigné, Marquise of Maintenon (1635–1719), governess of the Duke and future mistress and wife of Louis XIV, here addresses a flattering and clever letter to Madame de Montespan about the progress of her son, who was just short of eight years old. Madame de Maintenon reaches for a special place in Montespan's affections through this son, and at the same time evokes assumptions and myths about greatness prevailing at the court

SOURCE: Laurent Angliviel de La Baumelle, *Lettres de Madame de Maintenon* (Nancy, 1752) I, pp. 121–125.

of Louis XIV. Reading about and discussion of classical heroes, particularly generals, began at a very early age in all the royal nurseries of Europe.

[1677]

Madam, here is the youngest of authors, who has just asked your protection for his works. He would have preferred, before making it public, to have celebrated his eighth birthday; but he was afraid that he would be suspected of ingratitude if he had spent more than seven years without giving you public proof of his gratitude. And indeed, Madam, he owes a part of everything he is to you. Although he was rather fortunate in his birth, and though there are few authors upon whom Heaven looks as favorably as upon him, he admits that your conversation was a great help to him in perfecting in him what Nature began. If he thinks with some degree of accuracy, if he expresses himself with some degree of grace, and if he already knows how to make a rather accurate appraisal of men, these are qualities which he has striven to snatch from you. As for me, Madam, who knows his most secret thoughts, I know with what admiration he listens to you more willingly than to all his books. You will find in the work which I am presenting to you several rather fine deeds of ancient history; but he fears that in the crowd of marvelous events which have occurred in our day, you will not be touched by what he is teaching you about the past centuries. He fears this with all the more reason because he felt the same thing in reading the books. He sometimes finds it strange that men have to learn by heart the authors who are telling us of things so inferior to those which we see with our own eyes. How could he be smitten by the victories of the Greeks and Romans, by everything which Florus and Justin are telling him? His nursemaids have accustomed his ears since the cradle to greater things. [The books] tell him as if it were a prodigious thing of a city which the Greeks captured after ten years [of siege]; he is only seven, and he has already heard Te Deum masses sung in France for the capture of more than a hundred cities. All that, Madam, disgusts him a bit with antiquity; he is naturally proud. I see clearly that he believes he is a member of a fine house; and despite the praises people sing to him about Alexander and Caesar, I do not know whether he would like to be compared with the children of these great men. I am sure that you will not disapprove this little bit of pride he shows, and that you will agree that he is not a poor judge of heroes. But you will also admit that I am not very adept at making presentations, and that, in planning to dedicate a book to you, I could choose no author who would be more agreeable to you nor in whom you would take more interest than in this one. I am, Madam, your very humble and very obedient servant. . . .

16. Planning for the Immortality of Louis XIV

During the first two decades of Louis XIV's personal reign, and into the third, Colbert supervised the bevy of poets, historians, painters, sculptors, and other artists charged with recording and depicting the deeds of the King. This was a task of the utmost seriousness to Colbert, and probably also to Louis himself.

As early as 1662 we find Colbert sending an extensive plan to Jean Chapelain (1594–1674) for advice and approval. One of the founders of the French Academy and accustomed since the days of Richelieu to take his cue from ministers and sovereigns, Chapelain praises and approves what Colbert has sent him. As one of the leading critics of the day, Chapelain's views counted for a great deal; through him it is possible to grasp the assumptions which almost from the beginning lay behind the enormous artistic production of the Century of Louis XIV.

Paris, this 18th of November, 1662

[To Monsieur Colbert]

Sir, the plan which you have paid me the honor of imparting to me is great, noble, and completely worthy of the grandeur of the King, and of the grandeur of your zeal for His Majesty's service and his *gloire*. I have examined it a hundred times, and each time I was more satisfied than the last. Therefore there is no debating, in my opinion, whether the idea should be carried out, and one must only think of the means to do it.

As for the plan about the medals, since it is an invention which the Greeks and Romans used to make eternal the memories of the heroic actions of their princes, their captains, and their emperors, because of the incorruptibility of the metals of which they were

SOURCE: Tamizey de Larroque, *Lettres de Jean Chaplain* (Paris, 1883) pp. 272–277.

composed, especially those of gold and silver, I highly approve of your using them among others to perpetuate the King's [memory], being a method used throughout the centuries for a similar end and very appropriate to royal dignity. But I am uncertain as to the manner, for these medals can be made in the ancient or in the modern style. The ancient was satisfied to mark on the back some figure signifying the act or the event, sometimes without an inscription, but serious and with no witticism. The modern generally has tended to put on the back a design which consists of a figure and a motto, which is a refinement introduced into Europe less than two hundred years ago. Both are beautiful and praiseworthy; but the ancient style, with its gravity, would seem more in keeping with the royal majesty and I would like [the modern] to be used only for compliments and tournaments. In this, however, His Majesty's tastes must be followed, after he has been shown the reasons on both sides.

As to the poetry, Sir, you could conceive of nothing more in keeping with your aim. Of all durable things, it is without doubt the one which best withstands the injuries of time, when good talent is involved. All the most famous tombs, portraits, and statues have foundered upon this reef; even the most exquisite prose works have reached us only in mutilated and crippled form, and only the poetic ones, beginning with Homer, at least the excellent ones, have come down to us. So that whatever your attention brings about that is really good in this sort of writing to celebrate the King's virtues will infallibly be that which will make them immortal.

It is, however, unfortunate that the numerous marvels which His Majesty has already done and which he will do in the future in still greater number according to the direction he takes had the misfortune of not being treated in a narrative poem, because poetry is distinct from history only in its fiction, and the art of this sort of poem absolutely forbids feigning glorious deeds which can be contradicted by those who, like us, have seen the true successes, because that would make the narrative lose credence and consequently would be detrimental to the prince they wished to serve. In compensation, he can be celebrated in panegyrics, which allow fiction, and which are capable of all the sublimity of poetry. And these panegyrics are composed in rhyming couplets, as they are called, in the manner of elegies; as in that of La Picardière for

Queen Marie de Medicis, and that of Gombault for Cardinal Mazarin; or they are in the stanzas of which odes are formed, as Malherbe composed that for Monsieur de Bellegarde, and after him almost all his successors, judging this rhythm and these cadences more agreeable than that of unbroken verse. I am partisan of the latter, although I do not disapprove of the others. Stanzas in Alexandrines, like those of Malherbe on the visit of Henry IV to the Limousin, are also strong enough to praise great deeds. Even sonnets are not inappropriate, if a good craftsman does them, and some by Malherbe and others do justice to their elevated subject matter and do not detract from their loftiness.

I come now to history, Sir, which you have, very correctly, judged to be one of the principal means of preserving the splendor of the King's enterprises and the details of his miracles. But history is like those fruits which are good only when kept for the autumn. If it does not explain the motives behind the things which are recounted, if it is not accompanied by prudent reflections and documents, it is only a simple narrative without strength and without dignity. Thus, making use of histories during the reign of the prince who is their subject cannot be done without exposing to the public the secrets of the government, without giving the enemy the chance to anticipate them or render them useless, and without betraying those who might have liaisons with [the government] which survive only because of secrecy and in the shadow of deep silence. Thus, I believe that if you put history to work for His Majesty in the manner in which it should be written, it should be done only if the work is to be kept hidden until possible disadvantages can no longer prejudice his affairs or those of his allies. If, however, one wanted to overlook this very important consideration, I would still deem it a very difficult thing to carry out. For, to be a good historian, one must be a very upstanding man, have complete knowledge of the goal of the project and of the conduct of the prince who is to be the subject, be informed about the interests of his friends and of his adversaries, possess a knowledge of political theory, understand how a war is conducted, be ignorant neither of chronology nor of geography, be familiar with both the manners and the customs of nations, and have seen and taken notes on the originals of dispatches and treaties, which is not a very common thing. But in addition to all this, and more than all this, he would have to have the genius required for this profession, which so few persons have had in the three thousand years it has existed. It is a natural talent which is a gift of Heaven and which is linked only to a very solid brain and to long years of experience in official positions or at least in the courts.

How many persons of this caliber does one find, to whom one can entrust such a difficult task, and from whom one can expect faultless work? That, Sir, is what bothers me most in considering your so praiseworthy project. For everything which is done without a very accurate plan and without a very consistent coherence is sure not to be good, no matter how brilliant its parts may seem; and all the wit in the world, scattered through a work in which judgment is lacking, only creates a beautiful monster which follows the nature of monsters and which will doubtlessly not survive.

The persons suitable to carry out this task thus being so rare throughout the ages, especially in our age, I find it risky to commission someone, and there is really only you, with all your good qualities, whom I can vouch would be able to succeed at it.

But in order not to leave the King without the praises he deserves both in prose and in verse, I am of the opinion that the best pens should be employed to deal with these miracles in an oratorical fashion by panegyrics similar to those of Pliny the Younger for Trajan, which a great deal many more persons are capable of doing, and for which less qualifications are required. Moreover, I do not think you could find a great number of them, so sterile has this century become in men of letters who are worthwhile, as you have yourself admitted, and so mingled with confusion and bad sense is that which is called [natural] wit and [acquired] learning. I shall not fail, Sir, to propose to you at once all those I know who have the best reputation in this profession, and to examine their capacities with you, both for French and Latin poetry and for prose, be it in our country or abroad.* You will make your decisions according to my sincere reports and will be the supreme

* In a letter of June 1663 Chapelain pointed out these writers to Colbert and requested that they be rewarded, so as to "encourage other pens to write, in the hope of obtaining the same favors." Among the nonrewarded he included "a young man called Racine," who had brought him an ode on the King's convalescence and who reworked his verses according to Chapelain's suggestions. In 1677 Racine and Boileau were named royal historiographers.

judge of them and of me. For I have no claims other than pleasing you and repaying by my obligingness and my candor the kind confidence which it has pleased you to show me concerning your so praiseworthy intentions.

There are indeed, Sir, other laudable ways of spreading and maintaining His Majesty's *gloire*, of which even the ancients have left us illustrious examples which still attract the eyes of the world, such as the pyramids, columns, equestrian statues, colossi, triumphal arches, marble and bronze busts, bas-reliefs, all historical monuments to which we could add our rich tapestry workshops, our fresco paintings, and our engravings, which, though less durable than the others, are still preserved for a long time. But as these sorts of work belong to art forms other than that of the Muses, about which you asked my opinion, I shall simply mention them to you, so that you may judge whether they can become a part of your sublime ideas.

17. *Colbert on the Royal Finances*

Louis XIV regulated the conditions for the rivalry which developed among his ministers. Indeed, by insisting that this rivalry be expressed over major issues of foreign and internal policy, the King made sure that the final decision would be his alone. By 1670, surely, the rivalry between Colbert and Louvois and their relatives and creatures had led to a difference of views on every aspect of French policy. Louvois and Colbert each held the affection and esteem of their sovereign, yet each also wanted to dominate Louis through the policies he offered. Neither Colbert nor Louvois ever quite gave up trying to win the kind of predominance over Louis XIV which Richelieu had enjoyed over Louis XIII.

A decision to make war, of course, laid the foundations for increased power for Louvois, the secretary of state for war. The need for larger armies and the accumulation of matériel meant a massive shift in expenditures which only the controller general of finances—Colbert—could approve. At the same time, Colbert's efforts to reduce taxes, balance the budget, and stimulate the economy were immediately put in jeopardy once a military campaign had been decided on.

SOURCE: "Mémoire au Roi sur les finances" (1670), *Lettres, Instructions et Mémoires de Colbert*, ed. by Pierre Clément (Paris: Imprimerie Nationale, 1870; reprinted 1873), VII, 233–256.

Jean-Baptiste Colbert (1619–1683) defended his policies very ably, as this document testifies, but Louis ultimately decided upon war as a higher priority than the fiscal stability and prosperity of his kingdom. Yet the cost of war to the economy was probably overemphasized by Colbert. The depression of the 1690's, for example, was largely occasioned by the terrible weather which spoiled the crops. Note the definitions of wealth implicit in Colbert's analysis. The inference is that the power of the state is based as much on gold as on armies. Colbert hoped that cuts in the budget would be made in the army's share, thus clipping Louvois' wings. The occasional hints about Louvois indicate that Colbert felt his influence with Louis was threatened. On page 100 we see Louis admonishing Colbert, while still showing great confidence in him, in the year after this document was written.

Colbert's assessment of the financial position of the monarchy is inextricably linked to his view of conditions in the provinces. The great administrator, whom Madame de Sévigné called *le Nord* because of his coldness and efficiency, sought rationally to relate economic conditions to taxation and expenditures. Though he still had to guess about conditions, Colbert was able to base his policies on sounder evidence than any of his predecessors had possessed or even sought. The work of the intendants and important innovations in bureaucratic government enabled Colbert to make his arguments with greater certainty than previous finance ministers.

For a contemporary English understanding of the French fiscal structure, see the work of an anonymous author published in 1692, in Part IV, document 41.

Financial Memorandum to the King

Sire, the present state of Your Majesty's finances has obliged me to study them extensively, to search for the causes of the change I find, and then to present it to Your Majesty, in order that by his great prudence and his insight he may provide those remedies which he deems necessary and appropriate.

Everything which I shall tell Your Majesty on this subject will be based on nine consecutive years' experience in a rather successful administration, and on mathematical and demonstrable truths which cannot be denied, provided that it please Your Majesty to take the time and patience to listen to them carefully.

Your Majesty knows, by evidence based on the accounts of the [Royal] Council and on the results of the loan of the year 1661, that his finances were reduced to 23 million livres in revenue, and that this same year the unavoidable expenditures of the state were met only by further sale of the royal rights to the aforesaid revenue.

Your Majesty knows in addition that within two years the amount increased to 58 million, and again since then to 70 million livres in revenue.

During these nine years, years of great abundance, the general administration was based on this income, and all expenditures which were beneficial and advantageous to the state were made with grandeur and magnificence.

During the course of this year [1670] I find that the abundance which was apparent everywhere has changed for two very compelling reasons, both discernible, but one easy to understand and the other very difficult to fathom.

The first is the increase in expenditures, which are climbing to 75 million, and which consequently exceed revenues by 5 million in peace time.

The other is the general difficulty which the tax farmers and the *receveurs généraux* are having in getting money out of the provinces, the delays in their payments to the royal treasury, and their daily protestations that the enormous poverty which they find in the provinces makes them fear their financial ruin and that they will not be able to keep up the payments of their tax farms and of the general taxes [*tailles*].

This situation can be accepted as all the more truthful since we know clearly through various accounts that poverty is indeed very great in the provinces, and although it may be attributed to the small demand for wheat, it is clearly apparent that some other more powerful cause must have produced this poverty, even though the failure of wheat sales could indeed prevent farm workers from having enough money to pay their *tailles;* but whatever the case may be, when money is in the kingdom the universal desire to make profit from it makes men set it in motion, and it is by this motion that the public treasury finds its share. And thus, there is necessarily some other cause for this poverty than the failure of the wheat market.

I confess that when I first noticed it, my first thought was to cut back the expenditures for the navy, buildings, commerce, and even those repayments of debts which were not absolutely necessary for the good and subsistence of the state, in order to give priority to war expenditures and to those of the royal household and palaces which are absolutely necessary; but after having reflected upon it, I believed it was first necessary to share with Your Majesty all the information which I have assembled in my close examination of this matter, since I noticed this vast change into which we are ready to plunge. To do that, it is necessary to resume the history of finances mentioned above and, before all else, to establish maxims and principles for it.

The king's revenues are incontrovertibly made up of a part of the goods and money which his subjects collect through their labor, by the fruits which they harvest from the earth, and by that which their industry procures for them.

All that the *peuple* can save up is divided into three portions: the first, what they can set aside for their subsistence and for their small savings; the second, for their masters, who are the owners of the lands which they cultivate; and the third, for the king. That is the natural and legitimate order of this distribution. But when authority is at the point where Your Majesty has put it, it is certain that this order changes, and that the *peuple*, who fear and respect this authority, begin by paying their taxes, set aside little for their subsistence, and pay little or nothing to their masters. And since these people must have the wherewithal to pay before they think of meeting their tax obligations, and since these taxes must always be proportionate to the money that each individual may have, the general financial administration must always be watchful and exercise all the care and all Your Majesty's authority in order to attract money into the realm, to spread it throughout the provinces in order to make it easy for the *peuple* to live and pay their taxes. The proof of this truth is so clear and so unshakable that there cannot be the least opposition to it. Here it is:

It has been established that there are always nearly 150 million livres in silver coin circulating in the realm. Of these 150 million, 10 to 12 million are used up every year, either in products of all sorts or by leaving the kingdom for necessary merchandise and commodities which come from foreign countries.

There is always a relationship and a ratio between these 150 million and the money which comes to Your Majesty as his revenue, so that if on the basis of 150 million the revenue increases by 50 million, for example, it is certain that if we could attract 200 million into the realm, Your Majesty's revenues would increase proportionately; just as, to the contrary, if these 150 million were to decrease, revenues would also decrease proportionately.

But there is another ratio peculiar to the provinces, beyond these general ratios of the entire kingdom. For example, the Limousin customarily has one-fortieth of the ready money circulating in the kingdom, and it is on this ratio that it pays 1,500,000 livres to the king each year. But if it happens that in continually paying 1,500,000 livres without the money's returning, the ratio for the province is no longer correct, and the province then has only one-sixtieth of the total money in the realm, it will no longer be capable of paying these 1,500,000 livres, but only one million.

It is true that this decrease of a third, since it does not leave the realm, is to be found in another province, which will through an increase be able to make up the 500,000 livres' decrease; but that is not practical, since this takes place imperceptibly, and since it is impossible to discern the circulation of money from one province into one or several others; but although this change is imperceptible, it is nevertheless very discernible in the province which is losing, for it experiences first very great difficulty in paying its taxes and in two years falls below the level of assessment.

From this discussion we can draw a clear and demonstrative conclusion, that a balanced royal budget and increased revenues for Your Majesty lie in increasing by every means possible the amount of minted silver continually circulating in the realm, and in maintaining in all the provinces the just ratio which they should have.

Three things remain to be examined:

The first, whether there is at present more money in public commerce than during the last twenty or thirty years;

The second, whether the ratio of revenue to this amount has changed;

And the third, the causes of this change.

For the first, we can assert with certainty that there is at present more money in the realm than there has perhaps ever been, but that there is much less in public commerce.

The clear proof that there is more comes from common knowledge which cannot be denied. The same quantity of money which was in Europe in the past is still there, with the exception of a certain amount which has been used up. Every two years a very great amount of it comes from the West Indies. All the kingdoms and states of Europe–Spain, Italy, England, Germany, Sweden, Denmark, Poland, Hungary, Savoy, and Venice–are very poor and in no condition to make any expenditures; we are experiencing no poverty in the realm, and as a result there must necessarily be more money than there has ever been.

It is at the same time easy to perceive that there is less of it than ever before in public commerce. What makes individuals put their money in commerce are the possibilities for profit, so that, when there is less chance to do so, the money also circulates much less.

Before Your Majesty's administration of finances, individuals had three ways of making profit from their money, that is: the enormous sale of royal rights to revenues, loans to businessmen who paid high interest rates, and commerce.

Your Majesty has eliminated the first two, which were easy and convenient, and which were the occasion for profits of more than 30 to 40 million livres; and he worked at strengthening and increasing the third, so that it could have the same effect as the other two. But the uncertainty of private fortunes during the entire period of the *Chambre de justice*, which finished only a year ago, combined with the grandiose plan, which is an undertaking which has always lasted whole centuries in every other state, have until now prevented this great result, so that, being certain that there is more money in the realm, it is likewise certain that there is much less in public commerce.

Having proved this first point, we must pass to the second, which consists of examining the ratios which the king's revenues have always had and can have to that money which is in public commerce.

According to all the treasury accounts from 1630 to 1660, we see that before war was declared in 1635, the expenditures of the state totaled only 20 to 22 million livres. Since 1635, the highest years have risen to only 45 million livres in beneficial and necessary expenditures.

Also, we can say with certainty that during the same period when there were 150 million livres of minted silver in public commerce, the people paid with difficulty 45 million livres for the expenditures of the state, that is to say a third or thereabouts.

But at present it appears by what has just been said that there are no more than 120 million livres in public commerce.

Observing the same ratio, the king's revenues should be only 40 million; but since they are constantly 70 million, we must examine the causes of this and then see whether they can remain in this state or whether they must decrease or increase.

The causes stem from the great obedience and respect which the *peuple* have for the king's wishes which oblige them to make a very great effort to pay their taxes, thus keeping them in the poverty in which they were and in which they have continued to be since the war, which prevents them from paying their masters, that is to say the lords and landowners, whose complaint is all too public and universal throughout the realm.

In order to know whether this condition can continue for long and whether revenues can and must increase or decrease, we can and must certainly say that this state of affairs is too explosive and that it cannot last long, which is clearly proved by the difficulties which the *receveurs généraux* encounter in the *généralités* when collecting the *taille*, the delays in their customary payments and the protestations which they make daily that they cannot make the loans of the *généralités* on the same basis as they made them during recent years, and the assurances which the tax farmers give that their tax farms are beginning to decrease markedly.

We must also add to this difficulty, which is already very great in itself, the excess in expenditures of all sorts, which this year total 75 million livres; so that instead of doing two things which are equally necessary in time of peace—that is: giving the *peuple* substantial and real relief in order to enable them to get back on their feet and to be in a position to bear heavier burdens in time of war, and setting aside some for the urgent needs of the state—it happens that we are extracting from the *peuple* the double of the ratio which has always been employed between the money circulating in public and their taxes, and that expenditures exceed by 5 million livres the usual and enormous revenues of 70 million.

The conclusions which we can easily draw from this situation are that the *peuple* will assuredly succumb, that we must markedly decrease taxes; and the excess in expenditures obliging us to use up in advance the funds of the coming year for current expenses, we will certainly fall back into all the disorders and poverty of the past. We must at present examine in detail whether the general financial administration and the maxims which have been followed may have contributed to reducing them to such a state.

It has been said that the *peuple* paid the double of the ratio which has always existed between the money circulating in public and their taxes, and that there is at present much less of this money; so that, on these two principles, it was necessary to inform Your

Majesty that it was impossible for this to continue, and he would assuredly have decided to decrease the expenditures and to relieve the *peuple*. Although we could easily say that these great consequences to the whole of a great state like this one will be discovered only by very precise research, long experience, and much meditation, and that it is indeed true that this knowledge came only with time, it is still certain that the maxims on which the research was conducted could in time remedy these great problems, and it is this which we must assiduously examine.

From everything that has just been said, the good and the recovery of the *peuple* consist in making what they pay into the public treasury proportionate to the amount of money circulating in commerce.

This ratio has always been 150 million to 45 million. It is currently 120 million to 70 million. Consequently, it is very high; and consequently the *peuple* are sure to descend into great poverty.

We should have done one of two things in order to prevent this trouble: either decrease taxes and expenditures or increase the amount of money in commerce.

For the first, the taxes have been decreased; but the great authority of the king and the great respect which the *peuple* have for his orders has meant that, notwithstanding the great reductions which have been made, that which formerly produced only small revenues has produced a lot; this can be seen clearly through the *tailles* which, on the basis of 56 million in taxes used to produce only 16 million for the public treasury, and at present, on the basis of 32 million, produce 24; and in the tax farms, that of the *gabelles* of France, which used to produce only 1 million, at present produces 13, although Your Majesty has removed the tax on salt and has everywhere decreased the price by a tenth. Thus, we have seen the revenues of the state increase at the same time that the great reductions which Your Majesty granted to his people would seem to have made them decrease; and proportionately to the increase in revenues, the expenditures have similarly increased.

For the second, which consists of three points: increasing the money in public commerce by attracting it from the countries from which it comes, keeping it within the realm and preventing it from leaving, and giving men the means to make a profit with it.

Since in these three points lies the grandeur, the power of the state, and the magnificence of the king through all the expenditures which the great revenues allow him to make—which is all the greater because at the same time it humbles all the neighboring states, since there is only a given quantity of money circulating in all Europe, which is from time to time increased by silver coming from the West Indies—it is certain and demonstrative that if there are only 150 million livres in silver circulating in public, we cannot succeed in increasing it by 20, 30, and 50 million without at the same time taking away the same quantity from neighboring states, which creates that double rise which we have seen increase so markedly during the past several years: one increasing Your Majesty's power and grandeur, the other humbling [the grandeur] of his enemies and those who envy him.

Thus in these three points lie all the work and all the assiduous attention to financial matters since Your Majesty's administration; and—because only commerce and everything which depends upon it can produce this great result, and because it was necessary to introduce it into the realm where neither the whole nor even individuals have ever given their full attention to it, and because it is even in a certain fashion contrary to the character of the nation perhaps nothing could be undertaken of greater difficulty nor more advantageous to Your Majesty's realm, since to this increase in power through money were attached all the great things which he has already done and which he has yet to do during the rest of his life. It is only a question of examining now what this policy was like and the results it produced. To this end, we must see what was done to attract money into the realm and to keep it there; but since, in the natural order of things, one must always preserve before acquiring, we must see by what means the money was leaving the realm and everything that was done to keep it.

The Dutch, the English, and other nations took from the realm wines, liqueurs, vinegar, linen, paper, a certain amount of clothing, and wheat in time of need, so that, of ten parts of commerce, the Dutch nevertheless carried on nine of them. But they brought us fabrics and other merchandise made of wool and hair; sugar, tobacco, and indigo from the American islands; all the spices, drugs [illegible word] in oils, silks, cotton clothes, leathers, and an infinity of other merchandise from the Indies; the same merchandise from the Levant, through commerce with the port cities of the area; all the merchandise necessary for the construction of vessels, such as wood, masts, iron from Sweden and Galicia, copper, tar, iron cannons, hemp, rope, tin and iron, brass, pilots' implements, bolts, iron anchors, and generally everything which served in the construction of vessels and for the navy of both the king and his subjects;

Powder, match, muskets, bullets, lead, pewter, fabrics, serge from London, silk and woolen stockings from England, barracan, damask, camlet, and other fabrics from Flanders, laces from Venice and Holland, and trimmings from Flanders, camlet from Brussels, carpeting from Flanders; oxen and sheep from Germany, leather from every nation, horses from every nation, silken fabrics from Milan, Genoa, and Holland.

All the commerce from port to port, even within the realm, used to be carried on by the same Dutchmen, so that no sea traffic was carried on by the king's subjects.

By all these means and an infinity of others which would be too long to enumerate, the Dutch, English, Hamburgers, and other nations bringing into the realm a much greater quantity of merchandise than that which they carried away, withdrew the surplus in circulating money, which produced both their abundance and the poverty of the realm, and indisputably resulted in their power and our weakness.

We must next examine the means which were employed to change this destiny.

Firstly, in 1662 Your Majesty maintained his right to 50 sols per ton of freight from foreign vessels, which produced such great results that we have seen the number of French vessels increase yearly; and in seven or eight years the Dutch have been practically excluded from port-to-port commerce, which is carried on by the French. The advantages received by the state through the increase in the number of sailors and seamen, through the money which has remained in the realm by this means and an infinity of others, would be too long to enumerate.

At the same time, Your Majesty ordered work done to abolish all the tolls which had long been established on all the rivers of the kingdom, and he began from then on to have an examination made of the rivers which could be rendered navigable, in order to facilitate the descent of commodities and merchandise from inside the realm toward the sea to be transported into foreign lands. Although everything that invites the universal admiration of men was still in disorder in these first years and although the recovery work was a sort of abyss, Your Majesty did not delay in beginning the examination of the tariffs of the *cinq grosses fermes* and scrutinized the fact that the regulation and levying of these sorts of duties concerning commerce had always been done with a great deal of ignorance on the basis of memoranda by tax farmers, who, being solely concerned with their own interests and the increase in the profits from their tax farms while they possessed them, had always overvalued the commodities, merchandise, and manufactured items of the realm which they saw leaving in abundance, and favored the entrance of foreign merchandise and manufactured items, in order to have a greater quantity of them enter, without being concerned about whether money was as a result leaving the realm, for they were indifferent to this as long as their tax farms produced gain for them during the period of their possession.

Finally, after having thoroughly studied this matter, Your Majesty ordered the tariff of 1664, in which the duties are regulated on a completely different principle, that is to say, that all merchandise and manufactured items of the realm were markedly favored and the foreign ones priced out of the market, though not completely; [for] having as yet no established manufactures in the realm, this increase in duties, had it been excessive, would have been a great burden for the *peuple*, because of their need for the aforesaid foreign merchandise and manufactured items; but this change began to provide some means of establishing the same manufactures in the realm; and to this end:

The fabric manufacture of Sedan has been reestablished, and enlarged to 62 from the 12 looms there were then.

The new establishments of Abbeville, Dieppe, Fécamp, and Rouen have been built, in which there are presently more than 200 looms.

The factory for barracan was next established at La Ferté-sous-Jouarre, which is made up of 120 looms;

That of little damasks from Flanders, at Meaux, consisting of 80 looms;

That for carpeting, in the same city, made up of 20 looms;

For camlets, at Amiens and Abbeville, with 120 looms;

Dimities and twills of Bruges and Brussels, at Montmorin, St. Quentin, and Avranches, with 30 looms;

For fine Dutch linens, at Bresle, Louviers, Laval, and other places, with 200 looms;

Serge of London, at Gournay, Auxerre, Autun, and other places, with 300 looms;

English woolen stockings, in the province of Beauce, at Provins, in Picardy, at Sens, Auxerre, Autun, and elsewhere, with a total of 32 cities or towns;

That for tin, in Nivernois;

That for French lace, in 52 cities and towns, in which more than 20,000 workers toil;

The manufacture of brass, or yellow copper, set up in Champagne;

That for camlet of Brussels, in Paris, which will become large and extensive;

Brass wire, in Burgundy;

Gold thread of Milan, at Lyons;

The manufacture of silks called *organzines*, in the same city.

In order to decrease the importation of cattle into the realm, import duties were markedly increased, and at the same time orders were given to prevent the seizure of cattle by the royal tax collector throughout the realm, which caused at the same time a decrease in leather imports.

Looms for silk stockings were established to a total of 100;

The search for saltpeter, and at the same time the manufacture of powder;

That of match;

The establishment of the manufacture of muskets and of weapons of all sorts in Nivernois, and the reestablishment of the same in Forez;

The distribution of stud horses, which has produced and will certainly produce the reestablishment of stud farms and will considerably decrease the importation of foreign horses, if it does not prevent it completely.

And since Your Majesty has wanted to work diligently at reestablishing his naval forces, and since for that it has been necessary to make very great expenditures, since all merchandise, munitions and manufactured items formerly came from Holland and the countries of the North, it has been absolutely necessary to be especially concerned with finding within the realm, or with establishing in it, everything which might be necessary for this great plan.

To this end, the manufacture of tar was established in Médoc, Auvergne, Dauphiné, and Provence;

Iron cannons, in Burgundy, Nivernois, Saintonge, and Périgord;
Large anchors, in Dauphiné, Nivernois, Brittany, and Rochefort:
Sailcloth for the Levant, in Dauphiné;
Coarse muslin, in Auvergne;
All the implements for pilots and others, at Dieppe and La Rochelle;

The cutting of wood suitable for vessels, in Burgundy, Dauphiné, Brittany, Normandy, Poitou, Saintonge, Provence, Guyenne, and the Pyrenees;

Masts, of a sort once unknown in this realm, have been found in Provence, Languedoc, Auvergne, Dauphiné, and in the Pyrenees.

Iron, which was obtained from Sweden and Biscay, is currently manufactured in the realm.

Fine hemp for ropes, which came from Prussia and from Piedmont, is currently obtained in Burgundy, Mâconnais, Bresse, Dauphiné; and markets for it have since been established in Berry and in Auvergne, which always provides money in these provinces and keeps it within the realm.

In a word, everything serving for the construction of vessels is currently established in the realm, so that Your Majesty can get along without foreigners for the navy and will even, in a short time, be able to supply them and gain their money in this fashion. And it is with this same objective of having everything necessary to provide abundantly for his navy and that of his subjects that he is working at the general reform of all the forests in his realm, which, being as carefully preserved as they are at present, will abundantly produce all the wood necessary for this.

In addition, in order to prevent the Dutch from profiting from the American islands [Dutch West Indies], of which they had gained control and from which they had excluded the French, which was worth at least a million in gold to them every year, Your Majesty formed and established the West Indian Company in which he has up until the present invested 4 million livres; but he has also had the satisfaction of having snatched from the Dutch that million in gold which served to nourish and maintain more than 4,000 of their subjects who continually navigated among the islands with more than 200 vessels.

In order to prevent the same Dutchmen from taking more than 10 million out of the realm through all the merchandise they bring from the West Indies and the Levant, Your Majesty formed companies for the same areas, in which he has already invested more than 5 million livres in capital. And in order to decrease the considerable outlay in silver coin which must be sent to the Indies for commerce, he established in the Dauphiné, Lyonnais, Languedoc, Picardy, and Normandy the manufacture of coarse cloth, which has a very big market in that region; and at the same time he made regulations and statutes for improving the said manufactures and their dyes, in order that French fabrics may be preferred over those of foreigners, which at present are very defective [antecedent unclear here].

And then, in order to increase commerce and navigation, which is the source of all abundance, Your Majesty formed the North Company, which is destined to bring to all the northern countries all our commodities and merchandise and to carry from them all those which serve in the construction of vessels for Your Majesty's subjects, before he has everything in his realm which is needed for that. . . . Nevertheless, by all the methods which he is putting into practice, there is reason to hope that his subjects' commerce and navigation will increase in another twenty or thirty years as much, proportionately, as they have during the past seven or eight years. All the abundance of these sorts of merchandise which are produced in the North will pass from Holland, where they have always remained, into the realm, which alone can attract abundance and money, and consequently increase Your Majesty's revenues and his neighbors' poverty.

It is with this in mind that Your Majesty has worked at rendering navigable the Aube, Lot, Tarn, Agout, Drôme, and Baise rivers, and that he has considerably increased [the navigation] of the Seine, Marne, Allier, Garonne, Somme, and other rivers, and that he is having work done with such care and expense to repair his ports, in order to make it more convenient and easy for his subjects' vessels to dock; and it is with this in mind that he is having work done on this great and famous work of the canal connecting the seas [Canal du Languedoc] which has always been the object of the greatest plans of the greatest princes in the world and whose execution has been reserved for Your Majesty. And it is again with this in mind that he has made the ports of Dunkirk and Marseilles free of all duty, one port in the West, the other in the South, in order to draw foreigners to them and to attract all the commerce.

But all these great things and an infinity of others which are in a certain sense innovations, whose execution Your Majesty ordered begun seven or eight years ago, are still in their infancy and can be carried out to perfection only with work and stubborn exertion and can subsist only with the abundance of the state, considerable expenditures always being necessary to support all this great machinery.

It is certain that if the state had always been in the same poverty as in the past, all the assiduous attention and administration of finances would have been employed in meeting its expenses, and none of these ideas, whose first step toward execution requires money, would ever have been born or have been emphasized; but if all these contrivances which have been put into practice have kept money in the realm, which is undoubtedly the case, it is certain that, though they have used up some assets, they have also brought about much greater abundance, since, by the increase in retail sales, there are no years in which it failed to keep 8 or 10 million livres in silver in the realm; so that, if on the one hand it has taken some of the silver supply, it has contributed to increasing revenues by at least four times more than it has taken.

And from all this reasoning an undisputed conclusion can be drawn: in order to expend 40 or 45 million livres yearly—that is to say if all the king's revenues were reduced to that sum—one need not give one's full attention to continuing all these establishments and all the companies; but in order to bring the king's revenues up to the 71 million livres to which they climbed this year, and in order to see that there is as much money in the realm as is needed for the proper ratio of these revenues, so that by this means the *peuple* can in some way get back on their feet, it is absolutely necessary to make the needed expenditures to sustain, increase, and bring to perfection all these great establishments.

To achieve this, there are only two means: one clear, which is to reduce expenditures, so that they do not exceed and are even less than revenues; and the other, rather difficult to understand, which is that of examining whether the expenditures are of a sort which keeps money in the realm and spreads it equally through the provinces in the necessary proportion, all the more so because it would not be sufficient to labor by all these infallible methods to increase the money in the realm, if expenditures were made outside the realm or in such a way that they made it leave in a greater quantity than all these methods successfully put into practice could make it enter.

In order to clearly understand this point, we must enter into the accounts of all the expenditures of the state for the current year, according to the plan which Your Majesty made at the beginning of the year.

All these expenditures totaling 14,132,000 livres are spent in Paris and vicinity, and spread into all the provinces which supply wines, commodities, and merchandise to the aforesaid city.	For the royal houses	9,000,000
	Cash in the king's hands	800,000
	The Bastille	100,000
	Emoluments, salaries, pensions	2,712,000
	Marshals of France and officers	520,000
	Acquittances patent	200,000
	Paving in Paris	200,000
	Small gifts and voyages	600,000
This sum also spreads through Paris, and in part, about 400,000 livres or so, in the Limousin and the Marche.	Buildings	7,000,000
Of this sum, perhaps 4 or 5 million are used for the regiments of the guards, light horses, and some other expenditures within the realm. The surplus in the newly conquered territories.	Extraordinary war expenses, artillery	18,000,000
	Fortification of conquered strongholds	3,000,000
This sum spreads into the provinces of Poitou, Brittany, Guyenne, Picardy, Normandy, Nivernois, Périgord, Auvergne, Berry, Burgundy, Lyonnais, Dauphiné, Aunis, Provence, Languedoc.	Navy	12,000,000

In all the provinces of the realm.	Daily marches	600,000
Idem.	Public works	500,000
Half in Paris and half in the provinces.	Emoluments of governors and garrisons	2,800,000
Alsace, Bordeaux, and Picardy.	Fortification of strongholds within	1,000,000
In all the provinces of the realm.	Commerce and manufactures	500,000
Idem. and particularly in Paris.	Repayment of debts	7,000,000
Foreign countries.	Embassies	500,000
	Swiss leagues	400,000
Court and king's retinue.	Extraordinary expenditures	2,000,000
	Total	69,432,000

By this account, it appears that Paris and the *généralités* of Normandy, Touraine, Nivernois, Châlons, Soissons, Amiens, and Lyons, which particularly serve to nourish the aforesaid city and the court and king's retinue, receive of all the revenues of the state more than .... 29,532,000 livres.

The provinces within the realm	23,000,000
Conquered territories	16,900,000
Total	69,432,000 livres.

It is in examining these three articles that the last demonstrative proof should be found as to whether money leaves the realm more abundantly than it enters.

The first two remain within [the realm] without difficulty. We must examine the third.

This sum is carried into the conquered territories and used for payment of troops and for fortifications.

The territory is open and hemmed in by the lands subject to the Catholic King [of Spain], and neighbor to the Dutch.

The inhabitants all have their habits and their established trade with these two peoples.

The moneys which circulate there are of another coinage and fineness than those of the king; they are not in circulation in the realm and are weaker than those of His Majesty, so that those of France, which are conveyed there, are carried off to greater advantage than in France.

There are no mints in that territory.

The industry and exertion of the Dutch and Flemish to attract money is known.

All these reasons are more than sufficient to prove that this enormous sum of 16 to 17 million leaves the realm yearly and only slightly or never returns. And if only 6 million enter, as half of the 12 million which the Spanish fleets—which come only every two years—bring us, we can draw a sure conclusion that it is the sole and true cause of the enormous decrease in money which is presently to be found in the public commerce of the realm.

We could say, to the contrary, that during the entire time of the last war, money passed in the same manner into the conquered territories, which were the same as those of today, and that this decrease was not noticed; but it is so easy to answer this objection that it does not deserve a reply:

1. The troops were not paid during the summer.
2. They always returned to France for winter quarters.
3. Our territory was not so extensive.
4. The war prevented free trade and traffic with the cities of Spain.
5. The moneys did not circulate there.

These reasons are more than sufficient to prove the difference between the time of the last war and this one.

But besides the fact that this transport of money was in itself very harmful to the state, more opportunities were provided which greatly increased the injury.

If the treasurer of the extraordinary revenues and the one for fortifications had made the carts for it, they would have been obliged to carry the money of the realm there and to display it for the price which was current there; otherwise they would have been criminals. This money could have returned to the realm, although with extreme difficulty, and even the transport out of the realm would have been easy to observe; but to make it easier, more unfathomable, and more disadvantageous to the realm, a contract was made with the banker Sadoc: for the 2 per cent profit which he gives Your Majesty, he provides all the sums necessary for the payment of the troops and for fortifications. He supplies all these sums in currency of the country, upon which he earns 7 to 8 per cent. This gain gives him the means to buy ingots and Spanish reales at 3 and 4 per cent more than they can be bought for Your Majesty's mint, and for more than the goldsmiths can buy them; and when he lacks the silver of the ingots and reales, he sends silver louis and other currency of the realm. He has them all transported to the mints of Ghent, Antwerp, and Brussels, where he has them converted into skillings, rix-dollars, and *jeux de Flandre*, which are weaker in their fineness and their weight than those of Your Majesty, and then he has them returned into the ceded territories to make his payments.

Your Majesty clearly sees that this method is the easiest one in the world to enrich this banker and to take all the money out of the realm and to impoverish it, all the more so since while earning for himself 2 per cent, by sending at least 12 million, he earns 240,000 livres by the same procedure in which the realm loses these 12 million.

This procedure is quite contrary to that which has always been followed in the general financial administration, in which those who directed the administration have always preferred to lose considerably in the exchange rather than to permit the transport of money out of the realm; and in 1645, although Catalonia drew its entire subsistence from Languedoc and although it carried on no trade with Spain, it was considered more advantageous to give the banker Girardin 40 per cent than to permit the transport of liquid assets as had occurred in the past. There is an infinity of other examples of similar policy, and to tell the truth, never was such a disgraceful contract for the whole of the realm made as that one.

It is true that merchants complained about it from the beginning, but their complaints were disregarded, and I remain of the same mind, in good faith, that I did not foresee such great and important consequences, added to the fact that such a large share of the general financial administration being entrusted to the care of another, I made some effort to fool myself and to persuade myself that it would cause no noticeable harm. But when the decrease in the tax farms, the difficulties in collecting the *tailles*, the scarcity of money, and even more the enormous change in the currency exchange, which will be explained below, obliged me to look for the causes; and when I had merchants come, when the principal and most able among them, after my request, only answered me with a smile, saying that I should remember what I had said to them about the contract with Sadoc, I was as if obliged to delve further into this matter and to consider it as the most important cause of this change.

In regard to the currency exchange, Your Majesty recalls that until the beginning of the past year it had increased: so that when one paid 100 écus in Paris, one got 102 and 103 in Amsterdam, which had never before happened. This is what made Van Beuningen utter that loud exclamation in Monsieur de Lionne's home, that nothing could cause more apprehension in all the states of Europe about Your Majesty's power; inasmuch as all the money would necessarily collect in his realm in time and he would by this means become as superior in money as he was in troops. But in the past eighteen months since money has been pouring out of the realm with such facility, the currency exchange became not only equal, but at present we are even losing 4 per cent; so that we must easily fear for ourselves the same harm which the other states were supposed to fear from the good position of the realm in the currency exchange at the time of Van Beuningen's remark.

After all the explanations and clear proofs discussed in this memorandum, there remains only to summarize in a few words the problem, its origins, its effects, and the remedies which can be applied.

The trouble lies in the decrease in the tax farms and in the difficulty in collections which at the same time produced the decrease in revenue. Its origin:

The excess of expenditures,

The exit of money from the realm,

And the disproportion which exists between the taxes which the *peuple* pay and the money circulating in the realm.

Before entering into these two other points in detail, I beg Your Majesty to permit me to tell him that it seems to me that since he has taken over the financial administration, he has undertaken a silver war against all the states of Europe. He has already conquered Spain, Italy, Germany, England, and several others whom he has made very poor and needy, and he has become rich on their spoils, which have given him the means to do so many great things which he has done and is still doing daily. There remains only Holland, who still is fighting with great strength: her northern trade, which brings her so many advantages and so much respect for her naval forces and for her entire navigation; that of the East Indies, which brings her yearly 12 million livres in cash; that of the Near East, which brings her as much; that of the West Indies, which brings her another 3 or 4 million livres; her manufactures, her trade with Cadiz, with Guinea, and an infinity of others in which all her power resides and lies. Your Majesty has formed companies which, like armies, are attacking them everywhere. In the North, the company has already a capital of 1 million and twenty vessels. In Guinea, six French vessels have begun trade there. In the West, Your Majesty has excluded them from all the islands under his authority; and the company which he has formed from now on is providing all the sugar, tobacco, and merchandise which come from there and is beginning to carry some of it into northern Italy and other foreign countries. In the Orient, Your Majesty has twenty vessels; and just now two vessels have safely arrived laden with merchandise worth 2 million, which is a victory worth this same sum in this war. [The Company] of the Near East in like manner has a capital of 12 million livres, with twelve vessels. His manufactures, his canal for the transnavigation of the seas, and so many other new establishments which Your Majesty has created are as many reserve corps which Your Majesty is creating and forming from nothing in order to do their duty in this war, in which Your Majesty sees clearly that he is winning each year some advantage so substantial that the vanquished cannot conceal their losses, which they make public through the continual complaints made through the mouths of all their merchants about the decline of their trade.

This war—which consists solely of mind and industry, and in which the victor's prize should be the spoils of the most powerful republic which has ever existed next to the Romans—cannot end for some time, or to be more accurate, should be one of the principal goals of Your Majesty's efforts during his entire life. Before we can win a full and complete victory, the vessels of the North Company must be increased to at least 400; upon which Your Majesty must observe that without this number of vessels, if one day he were to wage war against the Dutch, the commodities and merchandise produced in the realm, which are Your Majesty's only mines, especially because they bring in 7 or 8 million livres a year, would remain. That is why war against Holland would have been impossible two years ago; at present it is a little easier; but if Your Majesty continues to protect and to assist financially that North Company, in proportion to the amount of help given, the number of its vessels increasing, he will decrease the difficulty of this war, and in time will even make it to his advantage; all the more so because their vessels being excluded by this means, Your Majesty's subjects will be strongly urged to provide ships to carry the merchandise and to follow the vessels of the Company which will show them the way.

In addition, the 80 vessels which carry on trade with the West must be increased to 150; the 6 of Guinea to 30 or 40; the 20 of the Orient to 100; the 12 of the Levant to 60 or 80, and all the other establishments must be enlarged proportionately. And although all these great increases appear extraordinarily difficult, I would dare to assure Your Majesty that he will have less difficulty in succeeding at this than he had in newly forming them and in bringing all the establishments to their present level. It is true that it will take much more time, but I would likewise dare to assure Your Majesty that every year he would see, through certain and unquestionable proofs, the power of the Dutch decrease along with their trade; and that in twelve or thirteen years' time, he will have reduced them to the last extremity, provided that we employ all the aid and all the assiduous attention which are in Your Majesty's power.

The tangible result of the success of all these things would be that in attracting a very great quantity of money into his realm through trade, he would soon succeed in reestablishing that ratio which should exist between the money circulating in commerce and the taxes which are paid by the *peuple;* but he would also increase the one and the other proportionately, so that his revenues would likewise increase and he would put his people into a position to be able to help him more substantially in case of war or some other need.

After having explained all these things, we must pass to the results which the current situation could produce, if not promptly remedied.

It is certain, Sire, that Your Majesty, as king, and the greatest of all the kings who has ever mounted upon the throne, has in his mind and in his very nature a preference for war over all other things, and that the financial administration and everything which relates to it, which consists of dull figures, is not the usual and natural function of kings. Your Majesty thinks of war ten times more than he thinks of his finances, and although—through his assiduous attention, which has until now been unequaled by any king however great—he has understood the importance of it, there is no doubt that all [war expenditures would not only not decrease but would increase]* his thoughts and his attention would tend to turn to war and that he would think of his finances only when extreme need obliged him to do so, and would not amuse himself with predicting these straightened circumstances and with using the necessary expedients early enough to shift it upon his enemies and to recall and strengthen within his realm the abundance which seemed desirous of leaving it.

It is certain, Sire, that the attention which Your Majesty is willing to give to such an important matter, and the reading of this memorandum, should make him clearly understand that one of two decisions must be made: either that of continuing to take from the coming years the 4 or 5 million livres by which expenditures exceed revenues in 1670 or to eliminate all the other expenditures, such as those of the navy, commerce, repayment of debts, and others.

The first expedient, to use money from the coming years, leads without means of support to such certain and prompt ruin that there is no chance that Your Majesty will allow it.

The second interrupts the general economy and financial necessities, and prevents all the great results which the economy should produce, and which have just been explained, especially since these expenditures for the navy, commerce, and repayment of debts are almost the only ones which return to the provinces the money which tax payments have carried off into the king's coffers; and that the repayment of debts has two very important results, one of which is noticeable, which is the increase in revenues; the other, although imperceptible, should produce a great effect with time: it is that those who receive such repayments always seek to profit from their money; and when commerce has made more progress in

* The phrase within brackets was crossed out. [Note by Clément.]

the public mind, all individuals will share in the profit which it will bring.

Here then are the results which the present financial situation can bring: either it will oblige us to dip into the revenues of the coming years; or it will prevent the continuation and execution of all the great plans which have been explained above, especially since to support them we must not only make the same expenditures which have been made up to the present, but even increase them.

And since we must not doubt that Your Majesty wishes to avoid all these bad results, we must proceed to an examination of the remedies.

In order to get out of this year's bad financial situation, we must find in our income the 5 million livres to be used in excess of the revenues and balance the budget; that means that revenues do not exceed expenditures.

For that, it would be necessary for Your Majesty to reduce all expenditures for the coming year to 60 million livres, including 2 million which Monsieur de Louvois told me we can get from Lorraine.

For this purpose, we must decrease the

expenditures for the navy by	2,000,000
for buildings	3,000,000
for repayment of debts	3,000,000
for war	1,000,000
for fortifications, as was said at the beginning of this year	2,000,000
Total	11,000,000

To decrease, as much as possible, the extraordinary expenses of the royal houses, silver, and other expenditures.

We must increase the expenditures of the trade companies by a million livres	1,000,000
Remaining reduction	10,000,000
Out of which amount we must take for the expenditures of 1670	5,000,000
Remaining	5,000,000

which can serve for foreign agreements and to set aside some reserves. And if Your Majesty wished to return his *peuple* to a position of being able to help him substantially in the event of war—if peace lasts a few more years—it would be very necessary to decrease *tailles* again by 2 million, the first, and 2 million, the second. And that tax cut appears to me to be so necessary considering the condition the *peuple* are now in, I deem it impossible that they can subsist, if war begins, without great reductions.

For buildings, if Your Majesty is willing to settle upon a fixed sum for Versailles, to which he will stick closely without going beyond it for any reason whatever, we shall be able to continue work on the Louvre, to begin the Arch of Triumph, the Pyramid, the Observatory, the manufacture of the Gobelins, and generally all Your Majesty's other projects.

To continue to increase the money within the realm, we must necessarily reduce the expenditures for fortifications to a million at the most, as was said at the beginning of this year;

To decrease the number of troops which Your Majesty keeps in the ceded territories, which could perhaps be done by creating some camp for them where they can pass the winter, on the frontiers of the realm; so that all the commodities and merchandise necessary for their upkeep can be conveniently supplied them within the realm, for example in the vicinity of La Fère where there are many prairies, and in the vicinity of Verdun on the Meuse;

To devaluate foreign money in all the breadth of the ceded territories;

To establish a mint at Tournai;

To promptly close the passage open from Saint-Omer to Aire, which prevents the profit which we have always promised from the establishment of custom houses, which consists in carrying the entire commerce of the conquered territories through France;

To break the contract with Sadoc and to leave the care of all remittances to those who administer finances.

To observe that troops sometimes receive triple pay: one which is paid by the guard of the royal treasury to the treasurer of the extraordinary expenditures; another supplied by the inhabitants of the cities in which they are lodged, under pretext of billeting, on the basis of 8, 10, 12, and 15 sols per cavalryman per day; and the other on the basis of the daily marches, when they march.

Lodging of troops ruins all the cities surrounding Paris and considerably decreases the taxes of the *généralité*. It would be very necessary for Your Majesty to either relieve them in part or at least to prevent this double payment under pretext of billeting. In the event that Your Majesty wages war, he could not think of taking more than 6 million livres from the realm through foreign agreements, subsistence for the troops, and other expenditures. In great need, and for a year only, it could be increased by 1 or 2 million at the most.

In this event, it would be necessary to completely eliminate repayment of debts, and to make a considerable decrease in the expenditures for buildings. But Your Majesty must watch carefully that [these emergency funds] are not spent on marches, roads, and assembly places as was the case in 1668, when 3 million livres were spent in three months' time.

I do not know, Sire, whether I am mistaken, but it seems to me that all these things are very easy to carry out. Your Majesty will judge better than I, but I can assure him and I would dare to reply to him that in case he was willing to settle on an amount, without exceeding, for any reason whatsoever, the 60 million livres in the above plan, that is to say, three times as much as Henry IV ever spent,* and a quarter more than Louis XIII, when he was paying for the armies in Germany, Italy, Catalonia, Flanders, and Champagne, I would dare, I say, reply to Your Majesty that he will see the same abundance during his lifetime, and that he will even see it increase yearly while his enemies and those who envy his *gloire* will imperceptibly decline into poverty. But Your Majesty will easily understand that this general plan must not be interrupted, that it cannot succeed if it is not always consistently supported by Your Majesty, and unless it is administered under his orders by one single head, who renders account of both the general and the particular, not only to Your Majesty, but even to all the councils which he may command.

* According to Forbonnais, in 1610 revenues totaled 15,657,700 livres and expenditures 15,697,000 livres. Colbert obviously does not take into account the difference in the value of money in the two periods he compares. [Note by Clément.]

III

National Rivalries, Particularisms, and Prejudices

The sense of European societies and cultures held by her own literate, ruling elites was in the seventeenth century a constantly changing cluster of myths and facts, rumors and ancient prejudices. Largely as a result of increased literacy in Western Europe, an eagerness to visit and know about other European peoples stimulated travel, official reporting, and the publication of travel journals about all aspects of life on the subcontinent. Fascination with exotic habits, dress, food, religion, government, and sexual mores clearly increased in some parts of Europe more rapidly than in others. A study of this development on a European scale has never been made, but if the number of publications is at all a reliable indicator of this curiosity, the Dutch and English far outdistanced other Europeans in openness and curiosity about other societies. This did not mean, of course, that there were no Spaniards curious about the English or the Russians. But the higher rate of literacy, the maritime interests of the wealthy, and the relaxed or ineffective censorship of books probably developed a curiosity about other peoples more rapidly in Western Europe than in any other part of the Continent. At the same time, this increased curiosity was not grounded in sympathy for the foreigner's ways, nor is there any indication that the curious lacked cultural roots of their own and thus were seeking a culture to adopt. The curiosity aroused in Englishmen by the elephant presented to James I, or even that over the first "savages" brought back from the New World, was morbid in many ways and expressed more general psychological and cultural uncertainties. The travel journals of even the most educated Europeans reflect layers of prejudices about foreign peoples and ethnic groups within their own country. Often there are allusions to man's special place in the great chain of being.

The cosmopolitanism of the seventeenth century scarcely went beyond a tiny minority of freethinkers, diplomats, and generals. In the case of the latter groups, beneath the veneer of adopted French manners lurked very real fears of ethnic and religious differentness.

The ethnic and popular cultural history of Western Europeans is still to be written. The manners appropriate to life at court, the literature, philosophy, and art of the upper classes, have been studied in great detail. But beyond the provincial folklore museum and a few pioneering studies, very little has been studied concerning the popular mentality. Historians have in the past written, and will continue to write, of Spanish society or French culture without bothering to note the enormous linguistic and cultural differences subsumed in such general terms. More is known about the national differences, say, between Englishmen and Frenchmen, because of interest in the origins of nationalism; and still more is known about their religious differences. But the links between racial, ethnic, and social conceptions prevalent in the seventeenth century have yet to be studied. To what extent were there racial differences between the Breton peasantry and nobility, for example, and were these in fact perceived? The attitudes of Englishmen toward the Irish seem to have crossed class distinctions, but what about their attitudes toward the Welsh?

Among Western Europeans, the differences still remained important enough that educated Europeans traveling from London to Amsterdam to Paris perceived far more differences than similarities. The impact of non-European cultures had not yet reached the point where the similarities among Europeans would strike persons as being greater than the differences. Of course the members of these societies were nearly all Christians, in some sense, but the varieties of Christianity, to say nothing about Jewish and freethinking minorities, struck Europeans as much more significant. The same was true about the differences in governmental structure, definitions of nobility, and attitudes toward banking and commerce. International competition in trade and armaments, long histories of conflict, and feelings of cultural superiority divided Europeans still further. Thus the size, location, and population, as well as the linguistic, military, and cultural presence of France in

Europe made Louis XIV's subjects and their accomplishments a source of envy, imitation, and contempt. Regardless of the specific consequences of the French impact, it was nevertheless there. But it was in no way monolithic. German learning, for example, had a much greater influence in the Russia of Peter the Great than did French. At the same time, the French continued to have their own inferiority complexes, in art toward the Italians, ancient and modern, and in commerce toward the Dutch.

The travel accounts are at best naïve and fragmentary. They remind readers in the twentieth century of the first reports written by anthropologists of South Sea island cultures, but they are valuable for at least two reasons. What the author reveals about himself and his own particular society, while in a foreign country, helps clarify the general cultural conceptions of Europeans in the seventeenth century. Second, the details which the travelers wrote down, no matter how impressionistic, are in some instances the only surviving evidence about the daily living and habits of lower-class Europeans in regions where literacy was low. To reach beneath the history of literate classes, historians study paintings, engravings, furnishings, clothing, and other artifacts. It is impossible to reproduce such "sources" here, but the following sources sharpen the ability to understand what Western Europeans were learning to do increasingly in the seventeenth century: namely, to look at societies, cultures, and races as different from one another, with no common development since the days of Adam and Eve.

18. A Frenchman Observes Dutch Republican Culture and Politics

Born in Loudun in 1605, Ismaël Bouilliau became an internationally known scholar. He traveled in Italy, the Levant, and Germany, 1645–1647, and in the Netherlands in 1651. Most of the forty volumes of his correspondence still remain unedited.

A close friend of the Dupuy brothers, and a member of the circle of scholars which gathered around them in Paris, Bouilliau reported to

SOURCE: Ismaël Bouilliau to Jacques Dupuy, B. N., Coll. Dupuy, Vol. 18, letter 104. Quoted in: *Archives Historiques, Artistiques, et Litttéraires* (Paris, 1890–91), II, 137–138.

his friend Jacques Dupuy on life and conditions in the Dutch Republic at a critical moment in its history. William II of Orange had just died in 1650, leaving an unborn child, the future William III, as his heir; the provincial republican institutions and the Estates General rapidly strove to remove the centralized powers of the Stadholder, and to make the United Provinces even more of a republic in its form of government.

Bouilliau, writing on the character of republics, makes an analogy between the political history of Italy and the Anglo-Dutch situation. There is little doubt that Bouilliau was a firm monarchist and something of a French patriot.

From Amsterdam
October 14, 1651

I could not write you last Thursday the 12th, of the current month, having been absent from this city from Sunday the 8th until yesterday. Meanwhile we saw North Holland, the cities of Purmerend, Hoorn, and Enkhuizen, and also the beautiful and agreeable city of Alkmaar.

It is in this region that the industriousness of these Batavian gentlemen appears, who have wrested entire regions from the sea and have created such beautiful and such fertile meadows that twice a day they do their vintaging, I mean of milk, to the point that there is one cow which gives two tuns of milk a year, or nearly so. And this region buried in the water is inhabited by peasants, a rather goodly number of whom are rich with three and four tuns* of gold, whose lodgings are clean and decorated with paintings and wainscoting, with a great amount of porcelain, to such a degree that several have more of it in their kitchens than our most collection-loving ladies in their cabinets. Along with these ornaments you see a fine fat bumpkin and a white and blond woman in these houses, populated also by strong children, rosy and very plump.

Then I recalled the deplorable condition of our peasants and our rural areas, which greatly surpass this country in beauty and in bounty, and certainly it was with feeling and regret at seeing that by bad management we were spoiling a fine country, while by wise conduct and good thrift the others rendered such a bad one good, which bears grass as its only fruit. . . .

* A tun equals 40,000 English crowns.

Everyone here is talking about our affairs very disparagingly and to the detriment of the reputation of the state. The little knowledge they have of our affairs and of our genius causes them to make such sinister judgments and makes them more susceptible to believing that [our affairs] are doomed. I will nevertheless not cease hoping that we will see them restored to health, [that] our versatile humor will also lead us to a reunion, just as it led us to disunion.

Some people are announcing here that the poor King of England drowned himself; it is true that there is no news and that we do not know what has happened to him. All the friends of the late Prince of Orange [William II] are very sorry about the downfall of that poor prince. The rigid republicans to the contrary are joyful about it and say that Holland is at present enjoying full liberty. Their opinion is that the interests of the new English republic and of this one are common and linked together. The same thing will happen to them as to the Italian republics, which waged war among themselves and wreaked horrible vengeance. A republic and a kingdom would talk together in peace better than two republics would. The wisest persons view with jealousy and anxiety the frightful power of this English republic. . . .

19. Military Power and Dutch Republicanism

The brilliant John de Witt—who was only twenty-seven in 1653 when he became Grand Pensioner of the United Provinces of the Netherlands—engaged Spinoza, Pieter de la Court (1618–1685), and others to write about the Dutch political situation. The result was a literature on the meaning of republicanism, one volume of which, *The True Interests and Maxims of the Republick of Holland and West Friesland*, became popular and internationally known. The actual Dutch political and social situation was not as P. de la Court described it, for its provincial particularisms and traditions put the United Provinces beyond rational political categorization. But Europeans believed de la Court, the more so because *The True Interests* appeared under the name of de Witt himself.

SOURCE: John de Witt (really by P. de la Court), *The True Interests and Maxims of the Republick of Holland and West Friesland* (London, 1702), pp. 1–6.

The problem of maintaining the republic's defenses without permitting troops and castles to fall under the control of officers favorable to princely claims of the House of Orange persisted until an invasion by Louis XIV's armies led to a riot in 1672 in which de Witt and his brother were assassinated. The United Provinces turned once again to an Orange prince, this time William III, for defense.

That we may not abruptly speak of the true interest and political maxims of Holland and West-Friesland, nor yet surprize the reader with unknown matters, I judge it necessary to begin with a general discourse of the universal and true maxims of all countries, that the reader being enlightened by such reasoning, may the better comprehend the true political maxims of Holland and West-Friesland. And seeing that almost all the people in Europe, as the Spaniards, Italians, French, etc., do express the same by the word interest, I shall often have occasion to use the same likewise here for brevity's sake. Seeing the true interest of all countries consists in the joint welfare of the governors and governed, . . . we are therefore to know that a good government is not that where the well or ill-being of the subjects depends on the virtues or vices of the rulers but (which is worthy of observation) where the well or ill-being of the rulers necessarily follows or depends on the well or ill-being of the subjects. For seeing we must believe that in all societies or assemblies of men, self is always preferred; so all sovereigns or supreme powers will in the first place seek their own advantage in all things tho' to the prejudice of the subject . . . whereby it clearly follows that all wise men, whether monarchs, princes, sovereign lords, or rulers of republicks, are always inclined so to strengthen their country, kingdom, or city that they may defend themselves against the power of any stronger neighbor. . . . Such princes as are wise, and do not trust their power in other men's hands, will not omit to strengthen their dominions against their neighbors as much as possible. But when monarchies or republicks are able enough to do this, and have nothing to fear from their neighboring states or potentates, then they do usually, according to the opportunity put into their hands by the form of their government, take courses quite contrary to the welfare of the subject.

For then it follows as truly from said general maxims of all rulers that the next duty of monarchs, and supreme magistrates, is to take special care that their subjects may not be like generous and meddlesome horses which where they cannot be commanded by the rider, but are too head strong, wanton, and powerful for their master, they reduce, and keep so tame and manageable, as not to refuse the bit and bridle, I mean taxes and obedience. For which end it is highly necessary to prevent the greatness and power of their cities, that they may not out of their own wealth be able to raise and maintain an army in the field, not only to repel all foreign power, but also to make head[way] against their own lord, or expel him. And as little, yea much less may prudent sovereign lords or monarchs permit that their cities, by their strong fortifications, and training their inhabitants to arms, should have an opportunity easily, if they pleased, to discharge and turn off their sovereign. . . . And though Aristotle says that it very well suits an oligarchical state to have their cities under command of a castle, yet this is only true of a great and populous city that hath a prince over it, and not of a city that governs itself, or hath a share in the supreme government; for in such a republick the governor of that citadel would certainly be able to make himself master of that city, and to subjugate or overtop his rulers. . . .

And though weak, voluptuous, dull and sluggish monarchs neglect all these things, yet will not the courtiers who govern in their stead, neglect to seek themselves, and to fill their coffers whether in war or in peace: and thus the subjects' estates being exhausted by rapine, those great and flourishing cities become poor and weak. And to the end that the subject should not be able to hinder or prevent such rapine or revenge themselves, those favorites omit no opportunities to divest those populous cities of all fortifications, provision, ammunition of war, and to hinder the exercising of the commonality in the use of arms. Since it appears from the said maxims, that the publick is not regarded but for the sake of private interest; and consequently that is the best government where the chief rulers and magistrates and likewise all others that serve the public either in country or city, may thereby gain the more power, honor, and benefit, and more safely possess it, whether in peace or war: and this is the reason why commonly we see that all republicks thrive and flourish more in arts, manufactures, traffic, and populousness and strength, than the dominions and cities of monarchs, for where there is liberty there will be riches and people. . . . And therefore I conclude that the inhabitants of Holland, whether rulers or subjects, can receive no greater mischief in their polity, than to be governed by a monarch, or supreme lord: and that on the other side, God can give no greater temporal blessing to a country in our condition, than to introduce and preserve a free commonwealth government.

20. *Affairs of State and Private Interests*

The specific role of key diplomatic officials is often very difficult to discern in the history of relations between states. What were their personal social aspirations and their knowledge of and prejudices about the states with which they were dealing?

A prominent figure in the lower court circles of Ireland and England during Charles II's reign, Sir William Temple (1628–1699) possessed the gift of being able to write down in familiar terms his assumptions and hopes while negotiating alliances and treaties with the Dutch. Sometimes naïve, and occasionally overestimating his own role, Temple nevertheless must be recognized as one of the most important diplomats of his time.

Temple seems to have shared Charles II's passion that the English flag be respected on the high seas and not be dipped in humiliation before that of the French when vessels met. And yet Temple admits that the matter was "an occasion of quarrel" and not significant in itself. The vagueness about Charles's own views on the matter was no accident, since the sovereign did not know precisely what to do or what he himself thought. Contempt for Charles' ministers is barely concealed here, and yet it was on them that Temple depended not only for information about the King's views but for political influence. Temple refused the office of secretary of state several times. Here the venality of the English governmental system is brought out; it seems very much like that of the French government, except for the lower price on the English secretaryship. Was the money the crucial factor in Temple's decision to turn down the office? Though at least forty-five years old when offered the ambassadorship to Spain, he still felt that he had to consult his father before accepting the post.

The articles [of the Peace of Westminster, 1674], being public, need no place here. The two points of greatest difficulty were that of the flag, and the recalling all English troops out of the French service. This last was composed by private engagements to

SOURCE: "Memoires of what passed in Christendom from the War begun 1672 to the Peace concluded 1679," *The Works of Sir William Temple, Bart.* (London, 1814), II, 254–259.

suffer those that were there to wear out without any recruits, and to permit no new ones to go over; but at the same time to give leave for such levies as the States [of Holland] should think fit to make in His Majesty's dominions, both of English and Scots regiments. The other of the flag was carried to all the height His Majesty could wish; and thereby a claim of the Crown, the acknowledgment of its dominion in the narrow seas, allowed by treaty from the most powerful of our neighbours at sea, which had never yet been yielded to by the weakest of them, that I remember, in the whole course of our pretence; and had served hitherto but for an occasion of quarrel, whenever we or they had a mind to it, upon other reasons or conjectures. Nothing, I confess, had ever given me a greater pleasure, in the greatest public affairs I had run through, than this success; as having been a point I ever had at heart, and in my endeavours to gain upon my first negotiations in Holland; but found Monsieur de Witt ever inflexible, though he agreed with me that it would be a rock upon which our firmest alliances would be in danger to strike and to split, whenever other circumstances fell in to make either of the parties content to alter the measures we had entered into upon the Triple Alliance [England, United Provinces, Sweden]. The sum of money given His Majesty by the States, though it was not considerable in itself, and less to the King, by the greatest part of it being applied to the Prince of Orange's satisfaction for his mother's portion that had never been paid; yet it gave the King the whole honour of the peace, as the sum given by the Parliament upon it and the general satisfaction of his people made the ease of it. And thus happily ended our part of a war so fatal to the rest of Christendom in the consequences of it, which no man perhaps now alive will see the end of; and had been begun and carried on as far as it would go, under the ministry of five men who were usually called the *Cabal*, a word unluckily falling out of the five first letters of their names, that is, Clifford, Arlington, Buckingham, Ashley, and Lauderdale. But though the counsels and conduct of these men had begun the war with two unusual strains to the honour of the Crown, in the attack of the Smyrna fleet, and stopping of the Bank; yet it must be allowed them to have succeeded well in the honours they proposed to themselves: Clifford having gained by it the place of High Treasurer, and title of a baron; Ashley the Chancellor's place, and an earldom; Arlington, an earldom, with the Garter; and Lauderdale a dukedom with the

Garter. The Duke of Buckingham, being already possessed of all the honours the Crown could give of that kind, contented himself to make no better a bargain in this matter than he used to do in all others that concerned him; and so pretended no further than commands in the army. And thus, instead of making so great a king as they pretended by this Dutch War and French alliance, they had the honour of making only four great subjects.

After the peace was made, His Majesty's first care was to soften the stroke as much as he could towards France; which was done by representing the necessities of it (that needed no false colours), and at the same time to offer his mediation between the parties remaining still in the war; in case France either desired or accepted it; which took up some time to determine. In the mean while I continued in the posture and thoughts of the private man I was before this revolution, till about a week after the whole conclusion of it, when my Lord Arlington told me how kindly the King took of me both the readiness I had expressed to go over into Holland, and the easiness I shewed upon the failing of that commission, as well as the pains and success in the treaty with the Spanish Ambassador; and, not knowing any thing better he had to give me, he was resolved to send me ambassador extraordinary into Spain; and to that purpose immediately to recall Sir William Godolphin, the ordinary ambassador there, for many reasons that, he said, made it necessary in this conjuncture.

I acknowledged the honour His Majesty intended me, but desired time to give my answer till I had consulted my father upon it, who was then in Ireland, but in the intention of coming suddenly over; however, in a month I undertook to resolve. My Lord Arlington told me he did not expect any demur upon such an offer, which he took to be of the best employment the King had to give, and therefore he had already acquainted the Spanish Ambassador with it, who received it with great joy, and resolved immediately to give part of it to the Court of Madrid; which he was sure was already done, and therefore he would reckon upon it as a thing concluded; though, for the good grace of it to my father, he undertook the King would give me the time I asked to resolve. When I writ to my father upon this subject, he was so violent against my charging myself with this embassy, that I could not find my temper to satisfy him, and upon it was forced to make my excuses to the King. When I did so, His Majesty was pleased to assure me he did not at all take it ill of me; and that, on the contrary, he intended me a better employment; that he was at present engaged for the Secretary's place, upon my Lord Arlington's removal to Chamberlain; but that he resolved the next removal should be to make room for me. This I told my Lord Arlington, who presently said, that he believed I could not refuse the Spanish embassy, but upon design of the Secretary's place; and since I desired it, and the King fell into it of himself, he would play the easiest part in it that he could. He was indeed agreed with Sir Joseph Williamson for 6000 £ and the King had consented that he should enter upon it at his return from Cologne, which was every day expected; but yet he made such a difference between the persons, that he would find some way to avoid it, in case I would lay down the 6000 £. I assured his Lordship I had no such design, nor such a sum of money to lay down while my father enjoyed the estate of the family: that, if I had, I should be very unwilling to pursue it so far as to give his Lordship any strain in a matter already promised and concluded; and therefore desired him to think no further of it. But he was not of opinion I could stick at any thing but the money, and acquainted Mr. Montague and Mr. Sidney, who were friends to us both, with this transaction, and set them upon me to bring it to an issue before the other came over: they both endeavoured it with great instances, and Mr. Montague was so kind as to offer to lend me the money, but I was positive in refusing it; yet at the same time I told my Lord Arlington, that, not to seem humorous in declining the offers he had made me from the King or from himself, I was content they should both know, that, if His Majesty had occasion to send an embassy into Holland upon the peace, I would very willingly serve him there, where I knew the scene so well. So that matter slept for the present.

In the mean while France had thought fit to accept and approve the King's offer of mediation, that of Sweden being ended by the assembly at Cologne breaking up in expostulations and quarrels upon the Emperor's seizing the person of Prince William of Furstemburg, a subject of the Empire, but an instrument of France, as his brother the Bishop of Strasburg had been in all the late designs and invasion of the Crown upon their neighbours. The King told me, that being resolved to offer his mediation to all the confederates, as he had already done to France, and finding I had no mind to engage in either of these employments which had of late been offered me, he was resolved to send me ambassador extraordinary into Holland, to offer his mediation there, as the scene of the confederates' common counsels, and by their means to endeavour the acceptance of it by the rest of the princes concerned in the war: that I knew the place and persons better than any man, and could do him more service, both in this, and continuing all good correspondency between him and the States, which he was resolved to preserve: that I should have the character of ambassador extraordinary, and the same allowance I should have had in Spain. Upon this offer I made no demur, but immediately accepted it, and so my embassy was declared in May 1674.

21. *England Described by an Englishman*

Edward Chamberlayne (1610–1703) was appointed tutor to an illegitimate son of Charles II and later to Prince George of Denmark, husband of the future Queen Anne. His most famous accomplishment, however, was the adaptation of the *Estat Nouveau de la France* (Paris, 1661) into a work about the government and people of England.

An immensely popular work, the *Angliae Notitia, or the Present State of England* appeared in thirty-six editions between 1669 and 1755. Each one differed from the other, usually by the addition of new material rather than by deletion from earlier editions, which in itself suggests that Englishmen probably continued to view their state and society in generally similar terms for about a century. Foreigners consulted it and read it in translation for pleasure.

Not unlike Moreri's description of France, which appeared later, Chamberlayne's *Angliæ Notitia* combines factual information with the history, manners, and prejudices current in England. Even if England was not the way Chamberlayne—or later, his son—described it, Englishmen in large numbers nevertheless wanted to believe it was that way. Like travel journals and other descriptions which became fashionable on the Continent, the *Angliæ Notitia* thus may well have played a role in educating an increasingly literate society about its own culture. And yet the work does not avoid controversial issues. The partisanship is Anglican; the English Revolution is deplored and explained as a conspiracy started by the "enemy." The suggestion that the "enemy

SOURCE: Edward Chamberlayne, *Angliae Notitia, or The Present State of England* (8th ed., London, 1674), I, 3–5, 22–24, 35, 40–42, 44–49, 56, 71–73.

came" evokes foreign origins for Puritanism and rebellion. At the same time, nostalgia for a pure or pristine England, free of divisions and corruption, pervades the work.

England, the better part of the best island in the whole world, anciently with Scotland called Britain and sometimes Albion, was about 800 years after the Incarnation of Christ (by special edict of King Egbert, descended from the Angles, a people of the Lower Saxony, in whose possession the greatest part of this country then was) named Angle, or Englelond, thence by the French Angleterre, by the Germans Engeland, and by the inhabitants, England. . . .

At present England, according to ecclesiastical government, is divided first into 2 provinces or arch-bishopricks, viz. Canterbury and York; these 2 provinces into 26 dioceses, which are again divided into 60 arch-deaconries and those into rural deaneries, and those again into parishes.

According to the temporal government of England, it is divided into 52 counties or shires, and those into hundreds, laths, rapes, or wapentakes (as they are called in some counties) and those again into tythings.

England without Wales is divided into 6 circuits, allotted to the 12 judges to hold assizes twice a year. It is also divided by the king's justices in Eyre of the forest, and by the kings at arms into north and south, that is all counties upon the north and south side of Trent.

There are in England 25 cities, 641 great towns, called market towns, and 9725 parishes. . . .

The air is far more mild and temperate (if not more healthy) than any part of the continent under the same climate.

By reason of the warm vapours of the sea on every side, and the very often winds from the huge western sea, the cold in winter is less sharp than in some parts of France and Italy, which yet are seated more southerly.

By reason of the continental blasts from the sea, the very often interposition of clowds betwixt the sun and the earth and the frequent showers of rain, the heat of summer is less scorching than in some parts of the continent. . . .

It is blessed with a very fertile wholesome soyl, watered abundantly with springs and streams, and in divers parts with great navigable rivers; few barren mountains or craggy rocks, but generally gentle pleasant hills and fruitful valleys apt for grain, grass, or wood. The excellency of the English soyl may be learned (as Varro advised of old) from the complexion of the inhabitants, who therein excel all other nations. . . .

England hath been possessed by five several nations, and coveted by many more, and no wonder so fair and rich a lady should have many lovers, it being a country (as was said of the tree in the midst of Paradise) good for food, pleasant to the eyes, and to be desired. Whereas the high-lands of Scotland, Wales, Biscay, Switzerland and other like countries, continue still in the possession of their aborigines, of the first that laid claim unto them, none since judging it worth their pains to dispossess them. . . .

The English, according to several matters and parts of the kingdom, are governed by several laws, viz. common law, statute law, civil-law, canon-law, forrest law, and martial law, besides particular customs and by-laws. . . .

The common law of England is the common customs of the kingdom, which have by length of time obtained the force of laws: It is called the *lex non scripta* (not but that we have them written in the old Norman dialect, which being nowhere vulgarly used, varies no more than the Latin) but because it cannot be made by charter or by Parliament, for those are always matters of record, whereas customs are always matters of fact, and are no where but in the memory of the people; and of all laws must be the best for the English: for the written laws made in England by kings or privy councillors, as anciently; or by Parliaments, as of later times are imposed upon the subject before any probation or trial, whether they are beneficial to the nation or agreeable to the nature of the people, but customs bind not the people till they have been tried and approved time out of mind. . . .

In two points the Church of England is truly transcendent; first it hath the grand mark of the true church, which most European churches seem to want, and that is charity towards other churches, for it doth not so engross Heaven to its own professors, as to damn all others to Hell. Secondly, it is the great glory of the English Protestant Church that it never resisted authority nor ingaged in rebellion, a praise that makes much to her advantage, in the minds of all those who have read or heard of the dismal and devillish effects of the Holy League in France by papists; of the Holy

Covenant in Scotland, by Puritans, and of the late solemn League and covenant in England, by Presbyterians.

As for the scandal begotten by the late troubles and murder of the late King, which some of the Romish endeavor to throw upon the English Religion, it is sufficiently known that not one person that was a known favorer and practicer of that religion by law established in England, was either a beginner or active prosecutor of that rebellion, or any way an abettor of that horrid murther. . . .

As some years before the late troubles no people of any kingdom in the world enjoyed more freedom from slavery and taxes, so generally none were freer from evil tempers and humors: none more devoutly religious, willingly obedient to the laws, truly loyal to the king, lovingly hospitable to neighbours, ambitiously civil to strangers, or more liberally charitable to the needy.

No kingdom could shew a more valiant prudent nobility, a more learned pious clergy, or a more contented loyal commonalty. The men are generally honest, the wives and women chaste and modest, parents loving, children obedient, husbands kind, masters gentle, and servants faithful. In a word, the English were then according to their native tempers, the best neighbours, best friends, best subjects, and the best Christians in the world.

Good nature was a thing so peculiar to the English nation, and so appropriated by almighty God to them (as a great person observed) that it cannot well be translated into any other language or practiced by any other people.

Amongst these excellent tempers, amongst this goodly wheat, whilst men slept, the enemy came and sowed tares, there sprang up of later years a sort of people, sowre, sullen, suspicious, querulous, censorious, peevish, envious, reserved, narrow-hearted, close-fisted, self-conceited, ignorant, stiff-necked, children of Belial (according to the genuine signification of the word) ever prone to despise dominion, to speak evil of dignities, to gain-say order, rule and authority; who have counted it their honour to contend with kings and governours, and to disquiet the peace of the kingdom, whom no deserts, no clemency could ever oblige, neither oaths or promises bind, breathing nothing but sedition against the establish[ed] government. . . .

These lurking in all quarters of England, had at length with their pestilential breath infected some of the worse natured and worse nurtur'd gentry, divers of the inferiour clergy, most of the tradesmen, and very many of the peasantry, and prevailed so far as not only to spoil the best governed state and ruin the purest and most flourishing church in Christendome, but also to corrupt the minds, the humors, the very natures of so many English; that not withstanding the late restauration of the king and bishops, the incessant joynt endeavors and studies of all our governors to reduce this people to their pristine happiness, yet no man now living can reasonably hope to see in his time the like blessed days again . . . without an utter extirpation of those tares, which yet the clemency and meekness of the Protestant religion seems to forbid. . . .

The English common people antiently were, and at this day are very apt to hearken to prophesies, and to create prodigies; and then to interpret them to their own extravagant conceits. . . .

The English national vices were antiently gluttony and the effects thereof lasciviousness (when they made four meals in a day and most excessive feasting, with great plenty of French wine) when women of professed incontinency were premitted to profer their bodies to all comers, in certain places called stews or stoves, or bathing places; because men were wont to bath themselves there (as still in other countries) before they adresst themselves to venerous acts. But immediately before the late Rebellion . . . no people, unless perhaps the high Germans, were more modest and chast, more true to the marriage bed, whereby was produced a healthy strong race fit for all arts and sciences, for agriculture, for traffick, for war and peace, for navigation, and plantation, &c. . . .

As the English returning from the wars in the Holy Land, brought home the foul disease of leprosie, now almost extinct here, though not yet in our neighbouring countries, so in our fathers' days the English returning from service in the Netherlands, brought with them the foul vice of drunkenness, as besides other testimonies the term carous, from *gar auz*, all out, learnt of the High Dutch there in the same service, so quaffe, &c. This vice of late was more, though at present so much, that some persons and those of quality may not be safely visited in the afternoon, without running the hazard of excessive drinking of healths (whereby in a short time twice as much liquor is consumed as by the Dutch, who sip and prate) and in some places it is esteemed a piece of wit to make a man drunk; for which purpose some swilling insipid trencher buffoon is always at hand. . . .

The sin of buggery brought into England by the Lombards, as appears not only in the word *bugeria*, but also by Rot. Parl. 50 Ed.

3, N 58, is now rarely practiced amongst English, although sometimes discovered amongst aliens in England, and then punished by death without remission.

Impoysonments, so ordinary in Italy, are so abominable amongst English, as 21 H. 8, it was made high treason, though since repealed; after which the punishment for it was to be put alive in a caldron of water, and there boyled to death: at present it is a felony without benefit of clergy.

Stabbing in England is much more seldom than in Italy, the English being easie to be reconciled, to pardon and remit offenses, not apt to seek revenge; the true well bred English have more of inclination of goodness, which the Greeks call philanthropia, than other nations. . . .

Duelling, so common heretofore, is now almost laid aside here as well as in France. . . .

The English since the Reformation are so much given to literature, that all sorts are generally the most knowing people in the world. They have been so much addicted to writing, and especially in their own language, and with so much licence or connivance, that according to the observation of a learned man, there have been during our late troubles and confusions, more good and more bad books printed and published in English than in all the vulgar languages of Europe. . . .

The English tongue [is] at present much refined, exceedingly copious, expressive, and significant. . . .

Of government there can be but three kinds, for either one or more, or all, must have the sovereign power of a nation. If one, then it is monarchy; If more (that is an assembly of choice persons) then it is aristocracy; If all (that is, the General Assembly of the people) then it is a democracy.

Of all the governments the monarchical, as most resembling the divinity, and nearest approaching to perfection, hath ever been esteemed the most excellent. . . . Of monarchies, some are despotical, where the subjects like servants, are at the arbitrary power and will of their sovereign, as the Turks and Barbarians, others political or paternal, where the subjects like children under a father, are governed by equal and just laws consented and sworn unto by the king as is done by all Christian princes at their coronations.

Of paternal monarchies, some are hereditary, where the crown descends either only to heirs male, as in France, hath been long practiced; or to next of blood, as in Spain, England, etc. Others elective, . . . as in Poland, Hungary, and till of late in Denmark and Bohemia. . . .

England is an hereditary paternal monarchy, governed by one supreme independent, and undeposable head, according to known laws and customs of the kingdom. . . .

England is such a monarchy, as that by the necessary subordinate concurrence of the Lords and Commons in the making and repealing all statutes or acts of Parliament, it hath the main advantages of an aristocracy, and of a democracy, and yet free from the disadvantages and evils of either.

It is such a monarchy as by a most admirable temperament affords very much to the industry, liberty, and happiness of the subject, and reserves enough for the majesty and prerogative of any king that will own his people as subjects, not as slaves.

It is a kingdom, that of all the kingdoms of the world, is most like the Kingdom of Jesus Christ, whose yoke is easie, whose burden is light. . . .

London, so called, as some conjecture, from Llongdin, the British word, signifying in the Saxon tongue Shipton, or town of ships; was built, as some write, 1108 years before the birth of Our Savior, that is now 2779 years agoe, in the time of Samuel the Prophet, and about 356 years before the building of Rome.

In the most excellent situation of London, the profound wisdom of our ancestors is very conspicuous and admirable. It is seated in a pleasant ever-green valley, upon a gentle rising bank in an excellent aire, in a wholesome soyl mixed with gravel and sand, upon the famous navigable river Thames. . . .

In this great city, the streets, lanes, and alleys, as they are called, are in number above 500, and yet, some of them above half a measured mile in length; dwelling houses before the late dreadful fire were computed onely within the walls, above 15 thousand. . . .

That the reader may the better guess at the number of inhabitants, or humane souls, within this great city, he must know: that in one year there were computed to be eaten, in London, when it was computed to be less by one-fourth part, 67,500 beefs, ten times as many sheep, besides abundance of calves, lambs, swine, all sorts of poultry, fowl, fish, roots, milk, etc. . . .

Again, the number of inhabitants may be guessed at the burials and births in London, which in ordinary years, when there is no pestilence, amount of late to twenty thousand in a year, three times more than in Amsterdam, and but one 20th part less than in Paris, as may be seen by the bills of these three cities. . . .

22. *Visiting Amsterdam and Vienna*

Edward Browne (1644–1708) was the son of an eminent physician and author, Sir Thomas, who had traveled to France and Italy and had studied medicine at Montpellier, Padua, and in Holland. A staunch royalist, and author of the famous *Religio Medici*, Sir Thomas gave his son an education at Trinity College, Cambridge. After traveling extensively in the 1660's, Edward Browne settled down to become an eminent, wealthy physician and a Fellow of the Royal Society.

The recording of impressions and comparisons in travel journals, while seemingly haphazard and illogical, followed a pattern of its own in the seventeenth century. Travelers almost invariably went to see the same things in cities and expressed curiosity over the peoples and customs most different from their own. Browne's interests as a physician, however, led him to take particular interest in the hospitals and other institutions established for the care of the poor and sick. His curiosity about the number and status of the various Jewish communities on the Continent is not atypical. Earlier travel diaries may already have aroused his interest in these communities, so that he desired to see them himself. Travel literature spawns stereotypes; in Browne's works the English found described what they were already most curious about.

From Haerlem I went to Amsterdam, a city at present for riches, trade, shipping, fair streets, and pleasant habitations, scarce yielding to any other of the world. It is seated upon the River Ye, and hath its name, as 'tis reported, from a castle appertaining long since to the lords of Amstel, to whom this place also belonged: at the beginning, the seat of a few fishermen; but afterwards increasing, it received many priviledges from the counts of Holland, and was made a town or city by the favor of their grants and charters. In

SOURCE: Edward Browne, M.D., *An Account of Several Travels through a Great Part of Germany* (London, 1677), pp. 8–18, 71–76, 79–82, 84–87, 112–116.

the year 1470 it was walled about by a brick-wall, to defend it against the citizens of Utrecht, they having been in great danger to have fallen into their hands, if those of Utrecht had pursued their victories. In few months after also, the whole town was almost reduced to ashes by fire, but by the increase of their traffic they easily overcame these losses, waded through all difficulties, and rendered good services to their counts, and received the honour afterwards from Maximilian the Emperour to have the Imperial crown over their armes, which are three crosses on a pale. . . .

Of late years this city is mightily encreased and encompassed with a new wall, and fortified after the modern way. The new streets are large and uniform: and the whole town being in a low marshy ground, the water is let in through all the considerable streets. The River Amstel passeth through the city, being let in under a handsome well-contrived bridge of eleven arches, which is so built as to make part of the wall and rampart, and is 26 paces broad. The whole town is built upon piles, or high firr-trees, driven down perpendicularly into the earth so thick together, that nothing more can be forced in between them: And by this means they build houses in the sea, and lay foundations strong enough to support the greatest buildings whatsoever, in places where no solid bottom is to be found. But they must needs be at a great expence and labour before they can lay the first stone. And the number of trees required to each foundation is considerable; since for the foundation of one tower or steeple alone, over against the Church of St. Katherine, Mr. J. de Parivall, who wrote *Les Délices de la Hollande*, reckoneth that there was rammed into the ground a forrest, as he calls it, of six thousand and three hundred and thirty-four great trees. About this manner of work, for the fixing their foundations, I saw them employed in divers places, particularly at the East-India-house, and at a place where a Lutheran church was then designed to be built. So that it was not improbably said, *that if a man could see all under this city, he could hardly behold a greater forrest.*

The *Stadthuis*, or Town-house is the noblest building in all these countries. A pile of freestone of a hundred and ten paces in front, being larger than the magnified front of the Church of St. Peter's at Rome, and eighty-one paces deep, or on the sides. The chambers in it, the pictures and statues, are worthy to be seen and admired. The first room on the right hand, or judgement-hall, where the malefactors receive their sentence, is adorned with large statues, hanging down their heads in mournful postures, as if concerned or grieving at what was then pronounced. The floors are of marble; the roofs are richly gilt and painted. Upon the top of all stands Atlas or Columbus, holding a globe upon his shoulder made of copper of about ten foot diameter, which is as large perhaps as any ball or globe whatsoever employed to this ornamental use. That upon St. Peter's at Rome, as having been in it, I judge to be less; as likewise at Florence. The Turkish ornament to the tower of their mosques, is three balls one above another, and an half moon over them, but they are less by far, at least such as I have seen: and by relation from eye-witnesses, the largest of the three noble gilded balls at Morocco are inferiour to this. . . . The Exchange is fair and large, and above it are shops: it is very well frequented, and he that cometh after twelve payeth six stivers.

Divers of their churches are fair: In the New Church the partition with ballisters of brass, and the carved pulpit are noble. In the Old Church the tomb of Van Hulse and Heemskerk are remarkable. Heemskerk did his country services in their first attempts upon India: for the King of Spain having confiscated some of the Hollanders ships, who traded in his dominions, which were then the staple for the India trade. It was resolved by the permission of Prince Maurice [of Nassau] and the States [United Provinces], to set out a fleet of eight ships for the Indies; four of which were to pass by the way of the Atlantick Ocean, and the Cape of Good-hope. And the other four were to search a passage towards the kingdoms of Cathay and China by the North-east, whereby the passage also into those parts might be expected much shorter than that which was known to the Spaniards.

To this intent these four last vessels sailed out of the Texel, June 5, 1594, and returned in September, not being able to proceed by reason of the ice. But upon the relation of the voyage by William Barenson [Willem Barents], there were two other expeditions afterwards to Nova Zembla [Nova Zemlya]; in the last of which they wintered there, and Barenson lost his life. Heemskerk was the chief of the twelve which returned from that cold habitation, where none but bears and foxes could well endure the winter, where he had been twice, and afterwards made two rich voyages into India. Upon whose happy returns the Holland East-India Company was first established, and a prohibition made for any other of that country to trade thither for the space of one and twenty years.

But to proceed to other publick buildings in this country. The *Tuchthuis* or *Raspelhuis*, or house of correction for debauched young men, such as are incorrigible and disobedient to parents or laws, hath at the entrance of the gate two lions bridled, a proper emblem, with this inscription, *Virtutis est domare quae cuncti pavent*. This was formerly a monastery belonging to the nuns of the Order of St. Clare, and converted to this use in 1595. They who are put in, are forced to work and gain their bread with hard labour. I saw those who rasped Brazil [wood], wood flying upon them, and they were all over painted in a beautiful red colour. Which odd sight made me call to mind the phansie of my Lady Marchioness of Newcastle, of a nation wherein the people were of orange-tawny colour, and the king of purple.

They told us that some that were committed to their charge, and not to be brought to work by blows, they placed in a large cistern, and let the water in upon them, placing only a pump by them for their relief, whereby they are forced to labour for their lives, and to free themselves from drowning. One we saw put into a narrow dungeon, and kept from meat. Some are put into this house for a longer time, some for a shorter. It hath been a punishment for such as have drawn their daggers, or offered to stab anyone. And some citizens, though able and rich enough, contrive it so, that when their sons are extravagant and masterless, the officers seize upon them, and carry them into this house, where they are not forced to any hard labour, but kept in till they see sufficient signs of a mending of their life.

This way of correction may seem severe to many, yet is not comparable to that which is said to have been formerly used in Germany. Particularly at Colen [Cologne], in the White Tower, at the north end of the town, near the Rhine; where it is reported, that such youths who were not otherwise to be reclaimed, were in a barbarous manner shut up in the White Tower. The height and thickness of the walls secured them from escaping, or from their complaints being heard. Near the top was placed out of their reach a loaf of bread, the last remedy against starving, which their bold necessity forced them to reach at, they executed their last sentence upon themselves, and miserably brake their own necks.

Somewhat like the *Raspelhuis* is the *Spinhuis*, or house of correction, for the young women who live loosely, are taken in the night, or can give no account of their living. They are put in for a certain time, according as their fault meriteth, and are bound to make lace, sew, or employ their time perpetually in some honest labour.

Those of the better sort are permitted to have chambers apart. In one room I saw about an hundred of them, and some very well dressed and fine, which was an unexpected sight to me, and would sure be more strange to behold in France and England.

The *Weeshuis*, or hospital for children, where there are six hundred orphans carefully looked after, and well educated.

The *Dolhuis*, or a house for such as are delirious, maniacal, or melancholical of both sexes.

The *Gasthuis*, or hospital for the sick, being large, and hath a great revenue.

The *Mannenhuis*, or hospital for old men, and such as are no longer able to labour towards their own support.

Besides all which, there are great sums of mony collected for the poor, so that there is not a beggar to be seen in the streets, and upon all assignations or appointments, and upon many other occasions, whosoever faileth to come at the exact time, forfeiteth more or less to the use of the poor.

The East-India-houses are remarkable, and the great stores of their commodities, cinamon, green-ginger, camphire, pepper, calecuts, indico, etc. The ships are of a great burden: their house was then enlarging, although it was great before; and a perfect town for all trades within it self.

The *Admiralteyt*, or Admiralty where their stores for war and shipping are laid up, is encompassed with water; near to it there lay then 72 men of war. In the house we saw their cables, grapling-irons, pullies, oars, charges for powder, lanthorns for ships, &c. At the entrance of the gate hangeth up a canoe with a man in it, dryed up, so as to be preserved from corruption, and a paddle in his hand: he was enclosed up to the waste in the canoe, in such sort, as the fish-skins, which were the cover to it, being so sewed together that no water could get in, he might keep the sea in the greatest storms without danger. The top of this house, as of divers others also in this city, is a reservatory for rain-water, which they have the more need of because they have little good water hereabouts.

The fairest streets in the town are Harlem-street, the Cingel, Princes Graft, Kaisers Graft, and the new buildings in the island towards Gottenburg. And if they continue to build with freestone, they will still surpass these, which, I'le assure you, are in no small measure beautiful.

I saw a globe to be sold, made by Vingbomes, between six and seven foot diameter, valued at sixteen thousand guldens: the meridian alone, being of brass, cost a thousand guldens. The globe is made of copper-plates excellently well painted, with all the new discoveries in it, as that of Anthony Van Dimons Land [Tasmania] found out 1642 in 42 degrees of southern latitude, and 170 of longitude, those toward the northwest of Japan, and those places both about N.Z. and also in the Tartarian Sea beyond the Streights of Voygats [Vaygach], New-Holland, West-Friesland, Cape d'Hyver, &c. but I have since met with a book which doth somewhat contradict this; entitled *A Voyage into the Northern Countries* by Monsieur Martinière, who went in one of the three ships belonging to the Northern Company of Copenhagen, in the year 1653, and by that means had occasion to converse with the Norwegians, Islanders, Laplanders, Kilops, Borandians, Siberians, Zemblians, and Samojedes, who are neighbors to the Tartars and Tingorses, in his 46 Chapter he expresseth himself after this manner. ["]There having fallen into my hands several geographical charts of sundry eminent and much celebrated authors, I am much amazed to see how they are mistaken in the position of Zembla, which they place much nearer the North Pole than really it is; they divide it likewise by the sea from Greenland, and place it far distant from it, when as indeed these two countries are contiguous, the coasts of Greenland butting upon the coasts of Zembla, so as did not the great quantity of snow, and the violence of the cold render those borders uninhabitable, the passage would be very easie by land from Greenland to Zembla, and from Zembla passing the Pater-noster Mountains to enter into Samojedia from thence into Tartary or Moscovy, as one pleased: But of the truth of this we shall be further informed at the return of Captain Wood.*

["]I was amazed likewise to see they had described the Streight called Voygat, not above ten French leagues in length, whereas it contains above five and thirty Dutch leagues, which is six times as much. Again, they would perswade us that through that streight

* This Englishman tried unsuccessfully to find a northeast passage in 1676 but was wrecked at Nova Zemlya.

our ships might pass into the great Tartarian Ocean, which is a mistake. And although they indeed do affirm that in the time of Prince Maurice of Nassau, a Dutch vessel passed that way into that ocean, yet it is a manifest error, that streight being bounded, as I said before, by the Pater-noster Mountains, which are half a league high, and the tops of them covered with perpetual snow, which never dissolves. And of this I can give a positive testimony, having been myself in that streight under those mountains in the dog-days, which is the hottest time of the year. [”]

From the steeple of the Old Church of Amsterdam, I had a good prospect of the town, and the great number of ships lying upon one side of it, like a wood; and all the towns about it. The roofs of the houses being sharp, it is a most uneven town to be looked upon downward, as it is a handsome one to be looked upon upward; and is not so diverting or pleasing to the sight, as some towns in France or Italy, which have flatter roofs, or else are covered with a fine black slat or ardoise. Upon this, and all other towers of the town, a trumpet is sounded at midnight, and in other parts of the city at six a clock, night and morning. At eleven a clock, the time of going on to the Exchange, there is good musick at the *Stadthuis*, given by the Earl of Leicester. They make good harmony also every hour in playing upon their chimes and bells in most steeples. And there is a musick-house or entertaining-house, where any one is admitted for a stiver, hears most sorts of musick, seeth many good water-works, and divers motions by clock-work, pictures, and other divertisements.

During my stay at Amsterdam, I had the opportunity of seeing divers learned men, and persons of note. Dr. Ruish showed us many curiosities in anatomy, as the skeletons of young children, and foetus's of all ages, neatly set together, and very white, the lymphatick vessels so preserved, as to see the valves in them. A liver excarnated, showing the minute vessels, all shining and clear. The muscles of children dissected and kept from corruption: entire bodies preserved; the face of one was very remarkable, without the least spot or change of colour or alteration of the lineaments, from what might be expected immediately after death: he had then kept it two years, and hoped it would so continue. Dr. Swammerdam shewed us divers of his experiments which he hath set down in his treatise *De Respiratione;* and a very fair collection of insects brought from several countries; a stagg fly of a very great bigness;

an Indian scolopendria, or forty-foot; a fly called Ephemeron, and many other curiosities. Old Glawber the chymist shewed us his laboratory: And we received much civility from Blasius the physick professour who hath wrote a comment upon Veslingius.

The Jews live more handsomly and splendidly here, than in any other place: Their chief synagogue is large, adorned with lamps of brass and silver. We happened to be there at the feast of their New-year; so that their blowing of horns, showting and singing was not omitted: Some of them understand divers languages. I saw one Moses di Pas, a learned young man, and Orobio, a physician of note. And I was sorry to see divers here to profess themselves publickly Jews, who had lived at least reputed Christians, for a long time in other places: One who had been a Franciscan frier thirty years; and another who had been professour some years at Tholouze [Toulouse], and before that physician to the King of Spain. Juda Leo, a Jew, hath taken great pains in making a model of the Temple of Solomon, of Solomon's house, the fort of the Temple, the Tabernackle, the Israelites encamping, and other curiosities. I was present at the circumcision of a child; which is performed by thrusting a probe in between the glans and praeputium, and separating it, or dilating the praeputium, so as the inward skin may be drawn forward as well as the outward; then by applying an instrument joynted like a carpenter's rule, or a sector, the skin is held fast beyond the glans, and with a broad incision-knife, or circumcision-knife, the foreskin is cut close to the instrument; and what remains of skin is immediately put back, the blood stopped with powders, and a plaister applyed; the relations and acquaintance singing all the while, whereby the cries of the infant are less heard.

Leaving Amsterdam, I passed by a peculiar burial place of the Jews, who are not permitted to interr their dead within the walls, by Overskerk, Bamburg, and in six or seven hours arrived at Utrecht, in a boat drawn with horses through artificial cuts of water, which is the way of travelling in Holland, Utrecht, and divers other provinces of the Low Countries.

Vienna, or Wien, which the Turks call Berch, is the chief city of Austria, in the latitude of forty-eight degrees, twenty minutes, not much differing from the latitude of Paris. The old seat of the dukes of Austria, and for a long time of the Emperours of Germany. . . .

It is not seated upon the main stream of the Danube, but by a branch thereof; for the river running through a low country; it is divided into several streams, and maketh many islands. A small river named Wien, runneth by the east part of this city, and entreth the Danube below it, which upon floods doth often much hurt, yet sometimes low and very shallow, so as I have stepped over it; some will have it to give the name unto this country: it divideth part of the suburbs from it, and hath divers bridges over it. For that we may have a distinct apprehension of Vienna, we must consider the city and suburbs thereof, the suburbs are very great, and not without fair houses, gardens, walks, and all accommodations at large.

The city itself is that walled and fortified part, designed not only for convenience of habitation, but also to sustain a siege, or any attack from the Turk, and is now separated from the suburbs by a fair esplanade or open ground, above a musket shot over. The houses near the wall were pulled down since the last fortification in the Turkish war, when they were in some fear that the Turkish forces about Gran and New-heusel [Neuhäusel], would move towards them. It is fortified *a la moderna,* with ten bastions towards the land, and a very deep ditch, into which they can let the Danube: and with two other bastions towards the water, on that part of the river which lieth on the north-side of the town. The bastions are large; upon one of them I saw Count Souches muster a good part of the militia of the city. The ditch is large and very deep, into which although they can let in the river, yet it is commonly kept dry, lest they might incommode their deep cellars. There are two walls, the one old and inward, little considerable at present, built at first with the ransome of our King Richard the First, who in his return from the Holy War, was detained prisoner by the Duke of Austria upon the 20th of December 1192. The Austrians pretending they had received some affront from the King at Joppa, and that he had taken down the ensign and banner of Duke Leopold in a contemptuous way. The other outward of a great breadth, made of earth, and faced with brick, edged with freestone, so well built as to render this city one of the most considerable fortified places in Europe. The Esplanade gently descendeth from the town for three hundred paces; there are very few out-works. . . .

The whole compass, taking in the suburbs, makes a very large circuit, but the city it self, which is walled in, may be about three miles in circumference, and is exceeding populous, as full of people, for the bigness of the place, as most of the great cities. And I could not but take delight to behold so many nations in it, as Turks, Tartars, Graecians, Transylvanians, Sclavonians, Hungarians, Croatians, Spaniards, Italians, French, Germans, Polanders, &c. all in their proper habits. . . .

The city is fairly built of stone, and well paved; many houses are six stories high; they are somewhat flat roofed after the Italian way; the streets are not narrow, but the compass of ground will not admit them to be very broad; and their buildings are remarkable both above and below ground; their cellars are very deep. To satisfie my curiosity, I went into some of them, and found four cellars one under another; they were arched, and had two pairs of stairs to descend into them. Some have an open space in the middle of each roof, to let the air out of one cellar into another, and from the lowest an *adit* or tube unto the top, to let the air in and out from the street, somewhat after the manner of the mines.

Aenaeas Sylvius [Piccolomini, Pope Pius II], about two hundred years since, commending the city of Nurnburg, among other expressions lets fall this: *Cuperent Scotorum Reges tam egregiè quam mediocres Cives Norenbergenses habitare.* The Kings of Scots would be content to dwell so well as the middlest sort of citizens of Nurnburg. I must confess, when I first entered Nurnburg, I was much surprised to see such a noble, large, spruce, rich, and well built city: But Vienna doth also deserve the commendation which he affordeth it: *Ubi Palatia digna Regibus & Templa quae mirari Italia possit.* Where there are palaces fit for kings and churches, which Italy may admire. And this being spoken so long ago, is now better verified of it.

The Imperial Palace is very noble, substantial, and princely furnished, consisting chiefly of two courts; the one very large, the other lesser, wherein the Emperour lodgeth. At the entrance over the gate, are set in capital letters the five vowels, A,E,I,O,U; whereof the phancies of men make various interpretations. That which was told me was this, *Austriae est imperare Orbi Universo;* or, *Alles Erdreich ist Osterreich Unterthan;* i.e., All the world is subject to Austria. Although I could hardly believe this was the first intended meaning. Besides these two courts is another small one, where some of the pages lodge. . . .

The Cathedral Church of St. Stephen, containeth divers monuments of many princes and great persons, and is a large stately building, but somewhat dark by reason of the thick painted glass: not covered with lead, but with tiles of wood, which is the only blemish thereof, yet makes a good show. The steeple and spire are very remarkable, as being high, large, strong, and handsome. On the top or weather-cock-place of the spire stands a cross under a star and half moon, . . . which the people think to be of gold, or at least very well gilded: and in the time of thunder and lightning it looked pale and whitish.

They have an account of how these came first to be set up in this place: that when Solyman [Suleiman] the Magnificent besieged Vienna, perceiving the forces in the city to be obstinate, he had an intent to batter down the steeple about their ears: But some of the bassas and great commanders, advertising him how unprofitable a business it would prove, and withal when he took the city, what an honour it would be unto him to have such a noble pyramid in his dominions: He sent word unto the town, that he was willing to spare the steeple, upon condition that they would set up the moon and star (the Turkish arms) upon the top thereof. They returned answer that they would, if he would send the same unto them, which he did, and they placed it where it standeth. . . .

At one of the doors of the church is a stone placed in the wall, which is generally conceived to be one of the stones wherewith St. Stephen was stoned. It seemed to me some kind of pebble, and is worn and polished by the hands of the people, who when they enter that door, do touch it with their fingers. . . .

The University of Vienna is also remarkable, if we consider the antiquity thereof, the number of scholars, their course of studies, their accommodations, priviledges and advancements. This is said to have been begun by Albertus the Third, above three hundred years past; and their rules, orders, and statutes to have been borrowed from the University of Paris, and the students were distinguished into four divisions or Nations, who besides the general, have their particular rules and officers, and were comprehended under the classis of Austrians, Nations of the Rhine, Hungarians, and Saxons. . . .

These divisions take up all the nations of Europe; and indeed there are students here of many nations: and upon contentions and differences the several classes will hold unto their own, and take parts, and bandy against each other, but will all unite and hold together in differences with towns-men or Jews, which happen sometimes unto a high degree.

They follow here the old beaten way of knowledge: and I met with few who had any good insight in new philosophy; but there are many good philologers, and are well versed in languages, history and antiquity: and there are many learned men either educated here, or come from other parts. . . .

In fine, the University is noble, their advancements considerable, their priviledges great, and they have the power of life and death, from ancient and latter concessions of their dukes and emperours.

But the greatest lustre unto Vienna is the residence of the present Emperour Leopoldus [I], . . . a vertuous, affable, grave, and worthy prince, and seemed to me to live very happily here, in the love and honour of his people, souldiers, and clergy.

His person is grave and graceful; he hath the Austrian lip remarkably, his chin long, which is taken for a good physiognomical mark, and a sign of a constant, placid, and little troubled mind. He is considered to carry in his face the lineaments of four of his predecessours, that is of Rudolphus the First, of Maximilian the First, of Charles the Fifth, and Ferdinand the First. He was very affectionate unto his [late] Empress, who though but young, was a modest, grave princess, had a good aspect, was zealous in her religion, and an enemy unto the Jews. He shewed also great respect and observance unto the Empress Dowager Eleonora, who was a sober and prudent princess, well skilled in all kind of curious works, and delighted sometimes to shoot at deer from a stand, or at other game out of her coach. He was also very loving unto his sisters, beautiful and good ladies; whereof one, the eldest, was since married unto that noble prince, Michael Wisnowitzski [Wisniowiecki], King of Poland.

He speaks four languages, German, Italian, Spanish, and Latin. He is a great countenancer of learned men, and delighteth to read, and when occasion permitteth, will pass some hours at it. The worthy Petrus Lambecius, his library keeper, and who is in great esteem with him, will usually find some books for him which he conceiveth may be acceptable. While I was there he recommended a translation of *Religio Medici** unto him, wherewith the Em-

* By Sir Thomas Browne of Norwich (1605–1682), physician, author, and father of Edward.

perour was exceedingly pleased, and spake very much of it unto Lambecius, insomuch that Lambecius asked me whether I knew the author, he being of my own name, and whether he were living: And when he understood my near relation to him, he became more kind and courteous than ever, and desired me to send him that book in the original English, which he would put into the Emperour's library: and presented me with a neat little Latin book, called *Princeps in Compendio*, written by the Emperour's father, Ferdinandus the Third.

He is also skilful in musick, composeth well, and delighted much in it, both at his palace and the church, which makes so many musicians in Vienna; for no place abounds more with them: and in the evening we seldom failed of musick in the streets, and at our windows: And the Emperour's delight herein makes the churchmen take the greater care to set off their church-musick, for he goeth often to church, and not to one, but divers, especially the best conventual churches: and in his own chappel some of his own compositions are often play'd. He hath also excellent musick in his palace, both vocal and instrumental; and his private chappel is well served, where besides the excellent musick, there are always eight or ten counts, pages to the Emperour, who serve at the altar with white wax torches in their hands; and after the manner of the Italian princes, divers eunuchs to sing.

For his recreations abroad, he delighteth much in hunting; especially of the wild boar in due seasons; I have known him bring home six boars in a morning. Some stout persons, particularly Count Nicholas Serini, would encounter a wild boar alone, but at last he unfortunately perished by one, which hath made others more wary since; and therefore when the boar is at bay, the huntsmen so stand about him, that the Emperour, or other great persons, may more safely make use of their boar-spears upon him.

Surely there are great numbers of them about the country, for they are no unusual or extraordinary dish in the city, though of a delicious and pleasing taste. They feed upon acorns, beech-mast, and chestnuts, upon the spring or sprout of broom, juniper, and shrubs, and upon the roots of fern, and will range into corn fields, and come out of forrests into vineyards. The huntsmen are notably versed and skilful in that game; for though they see it not, they will distinguish a wild from a common swine, and ghess whether that which they hunt be male or female, old or young, large or small, fat or lean; and this they chiefly conjecture from their tread or foot, and the casting their hindfeet out of the track of their forefeet.

The Emperour being so good a huntsman, it is the less wonder that he is esteemed a good horsman. Certain it is, that he hath a very noble stable of horses, procured from all parts, Turkish, Tartarian, Polonia, Transylvanian, Saxon, Bohemian, Hungarian, Naples, &c. and they are well managed; and they ride them to the satisfaction of the beholders. . . .

Though the winter was sharp, yet the advantage of stoves, and lying between two featherbeds, made it tolerable: For they use stoves here as in other parts of Germany, where they lodge and eat in stoves; and great persons have stoves in the church, or such as look into the church. There are stoves also in the publick schools where lectures are read. And this way of lying between two featherbeds, with a neat laced sheet spread over, is more convenient in a cold country, than most others they make use of. For in the common inns in Germany they generally sleep upon straw, and also in Hungary almost every where; and more easterly upon the ground, spreading a carpet or saddle-cloath under them: and more northerly they content themselves with the skins of beasts, bears, elks, or the like; upon which they sleep in the night. Those that sleep lowest are coolest in a stove; those that lye upon tables, benches, or higher, are more exposed to the heat. The citizens of Vienna are well attired, and use furs very much. The women wear a high velvet bonnet, lined and faced therewith. The place seemed to be healthful; but they speak much of the *colica Austriaca*, as an endemial and local disease, very hardly yielding unto good medicines. They speak good German at the court and in the city; but the common and country people seemed to speak grumblingly, and besides their accent, have divers words different from other parts. . . .

Here is no Christian religion permitted but the Roman, and therefore those of the Protestant and Reformed Religion are fain to resort unto Presburg, forty miles off, for which they have some convenience by the Danube, and a coach which goeth every day. . . .

But here are no small number of Jews, who have a distinct habitation assigned them over the water. They have also a street allowed them in the city for the day time, but they must all depart at night beyond the river into the suburbs.

They are much distasted by the citizens and tradesmen, and the scholars agree but ill with them. While I was at Vienna there was a quarrel between them to an high degree. For the scholars assaulted the Jews' town, beat, wounded, and threw divers of them into the river. Divers scholars were wounded, some killed, and also some souldiers who were commanded out to compose the fray: and the Jews' town was guarded many days by the souldiers of the city. This begot such ill blood and complaints, that a good number of the Jews were to be banished at a certain day. The Jews, to ingratiate with the Empress, then with child, presented her with a noble silver cradle, but she would not receive it. And there was great danger of the general banishment of them when I left the city, which was afterwards effected, they being severely prohibited from living, not only at Vienna, but in any part of Austria, where there were formerly whole villages of them, so as they were forced to betake themselves into the dominions of the Turk, unto Venice, into Poland and Bohemia. They being not permitted to dwell in the neighbour countries of Hungary subject to the Emperour, Styria, or Carinthia.

I must confess they seemed useful unto the place for ready accommodation of any thing, either by sale or exchange, but the people looked with an evil eye upon them, as taking away too much of their trade and employment. They also looked upon them as useless in war for defence of the place; and were not without some jealousie that they held correspondence with the Turks, and gave intelligence of their affairs unto them. Yet the souldiery dealt much with them, and captains for the suddain habiting, furnishing, and accommodating of their companies. . . .

There are many Jews in Italy, yet they seem to me to be in greater numbers in Germany. In Amsterdam they are also grown very numerous. At Franckfurt they told me there were seven thousand of them, which seemed scarce credible. At Colen [Cologne] they are in great numbers: at Hamburg not a few. But the greatest number surely is in Prague.

Though they be permitted in many countries, yet divers Christian princes and states have assigned them some mark in their habits, to distinguish them. In Avignon their hats are yellow. In Italy their hats are covered with taffate. In Germany they wear ruffs and gowns with great capes. In Holland I observed no distinction. But the Jews there, most of them having come out of Portugal, there may be some suspicion of them from their complexion.

Lastly, when I considered the old strength of Vienna, consisting of an old wall and a deep ditch, I cannot much wonder that Matthias Corvinus, King of Hungary, took this city. And I must ascribe it, under God, unto the singular valour and resolution of the defendants, that Solyman the Magnificent, with two hundred thousand men, was not able to take it, and though he made large breaches, could never enter it, but lost some thousands at an assault, and departed at last with the loss of a great part of his army. But this place is now in a far better condition, strongly fortified, and able to resist the greatest forces of Turkey. The houses are cleared from the wall; and yet for better security, when I was there, Count Souches advised the Emperour to pull down part of the suburbs upon the other side of the nearest branch of the Danube, lest the Turks might take advantage to play upon the two bastions on that side.

It would be a sad loss for Christendome if this place were in the hands of the Turk; and no man knows where he would rest. If he should begin with this place, and take it, the strong holds of Rab, Komara, and Leopoldstadt would want their support, and soon fall into his possession; and if he were lord of Austria, a great part of Germany would lye bare unto him: and probably it would not be long before he visited Italy, into which country he would then find other ways than by Palma nova.

23. A Frenchman Visits Rome

Jean-Baptiste Colbert (1651–1690), Marquis of Seignelay, son of the great Colbert, toured Italy extensively in 1671 and, like many other educated, upper-class Europeans, made a special effort to appreciate Rome. The accomplishments of the ancients thus became blended with the religious experiences of a French Catholic in the Eternal City at Easter. Clearly some religious practices in Rome seemed strange to him.

This report back to an enthusiastic father who was always pressing his children to try to serve the king as passionately as he did marked the realization of a dream that the elder Colbert might have had for himself: for the great Colbert's love of Rome and all things Roman left

SOURCE: *Lettres, Instructions et Mémoires de Colbert*, ed. by P. Clément (Paris, 1855), III, pt. 2, 229–232.

its mark not only on French administration but on Parisian architecture as well. Seignelay went on to become the principal administrator of the navy which his father had done so much to build.

Rome, Thursday, March 26, 1671.

Having only arrived in Rome yesterday evening, I still was in time to see the ceremonies of Holy Week, which only begin today. Therefore, as soon as I got up, I went to the Vatican, where I was ushered into the chamber where the Pope puts on his pontifical robes, when he is to hold chapel services. It is also in this chamber that the cardinals assemble before the arrival of His Holiness. I remained there about an hour and only left shortly after His Holiness had entered. Then I went into the great chapel of the Vatican where the *Judgement* by Michelangelo is painted.

There I saw the Pope arrive, borne on his *sedia* and on the shoulders of six men. He was followed by the entire College of Cardinals, the senior members of which took their places at his right, the Pope having been seated upon a throne beside the altar and under a dais of white satin embroidered with gold. His ornaments and his miter were also of white moire embroidered in the same manner as the dais; under his feet was a cushion with the same embroidery and in the same color. Immediately to his right and standing were the ambassador of Portugal; that of Venice, Don Gasparo Paluzzi, who had married [the Pope's] niece and who is general of the Church; and Don Angelo his father; High Constable Colonna, whose turn it was to go that day, attending papal ceremonies alternately with the Duke of Bracciano, who is the eldest of the House of Orsini. Below these gentlemen, on the same side and outside the dais, were the ambassadors of Poland and the conservators [municipal officials] of Rome. To the left of His Holiness, next to the altar, were two cardinal-deacons, who served him: one was the Cardinal of Hesse, and the other Cardinal Carlo Barberini. In front of the Pope and a little to his left was seated Cardinal Cibo, who was the dean of the cardinal-priests: he was taking the place of Cardinal Este, who is the true dean [senior member]. After His Holiness had been seated and all the cardinals as well, the Mass was begun, which was celebrated by Cardinal Antonio Barberini. All the steps of the altar were filled with monsignors, who were dressed in violet robes, and with honorary chamberlains in red robes. After the completion of this very long ceremony, the Pope, borne on the shoulders of the same men who had carried him to this place, passed from this chapel by the *Sala Regia* and other apartments, and went to the balcony called the *Loggia*, which is in front of and above the great portal of St. Peter's. When he was on this balcony, attended by all the cardinals, turning toward the people, who had assembled that day in St. Peter's Square, he had someone read the bull, *In coena Domini*, which contains the excommunication which the popes customarily pronounce on Maundy Thursday against heretics and sinners. While this bull is being read, the Pope holds in his hand a lighted torch, which he throws with an execration into St. Peter's Square after the reading, and, a moment afterward, he lifts the excommunication which he has given and offers his benediction to the people, who during the entire ceremony are on their knees. From there, His Holiness passed into the room where he washed the feet of twelve poor people who are dressed in white robes; after which he again came with a few cardinals who were accompanying him to serve dinner to the same poor. This ended, I went to see the sacred college dine in a lower room of the Vatican, where the Pope's nephews entertain them yearly on this day. The afternoon of this same day, I went to St. Peter's, where I remained a rather long time.

Friday, March 27. This morning I went to hear the Passion at Santa Maria Maggiore and to adore the cross. In the afternoon, I went to several churches and remained a rather long while in St. James of the Spaniards, to listen to the music of the *Tenebrae*. In almost all the churches where I went I saw penitents who whip themselves until they bleed, and in such a rough fashion that one cannot look at them without pain. Most of the time it is persons of quality, and especially Spaniards, who perform this sort of devotion; they go alone, their faces covered, accompanied only by some domestic servant or some friend who follows them at a distance to give them wine when they feel faint, which happens rather often. This same afternoon, I went to see the cardinal patron [secretary of the Pope and superintendent of the Papal States] to give him the letter I had for him, and to request an audience with the Pope. This same evening I also went to watch the procession of penitents or flagellated; most of the cardinals were present, and march after the music, which is at the end of all the processions of penitants, which follow one another. Each procession chooses as patron a cardinal, who pays for a portable structure which each boasts is more beautiful than his companion's. It is lighted by a very great number of candles of white wax; each represents something different, but all try to include in the decor the components of the coat of arms of the cardinal who paid for it, and those of the Pope. This structure is made of the lightest possible material available, because men carry it through the processions; so that they may be numerous, each cardinal sends the gentlemen and ecclesiastics of his household, whom they garb as penitents in various colors. The brotherhood sends after it those members whose devotion includes flagellation, and one can easily see 100 or 150 scourged persons after each [structure]; most of them are barefoot and have their backs all bloody and slashed; there are even some who are not content to use the usual whip, who have a whip with a lead ball at the end which first makes a contusion in the place where it touches, then afterward makes a hole there. There were in the procession I watched this evening about 600 scourged persons. What makes this procession appear very lovely is a very great number of candles of white wax which illuminate it; each cardinal also sends his livery and his lesser domestic servants with torches.

Saturday, March 28. This morning I again went to visit several churches, and in the afternoon I went to hear vespers at St. Peter's in order to see the relics which are shown there; they are shown from the balconies which are above the niches which Bernini dug in the pillars which support the dome. No one can see these relics at close hand, under penalty of excommunication, the canons of St. Peter's being the only ones who can climb the stairs leading to these balconies. I again saw today in the same church, in a procession, a brotherhood of penitents who are called the penitents of death, among whom there were several who flagellated themselves before the altar in the same manner as those whom I had seen the previous day; after which, having left St. Peter's, I went to the audience with the Pope, whose feet I kissed; he had me rise, spoke to me for a rather long time with a great deal of kindness, and had those attending me enter, who kissed his feet and received his blessing.

Sunday, March 29, Easter Sunday. I again was at the Vatican to see the chapel service which the Pope conducted there attended by his cardinals, in the same manner as on Maundy Thursday. Cardinal Francesco Barberini celebrated the mass, at the end of which

I went to hear Mass in the Chapel of St. Louis, which is the parish church of the French in Rome. In the afternoon of this same day, I went to see the procession of the Pope, who withdrew from the Vatican to go to Monte Cavallo [the Quirinal], where I strolled for some time and carefully studied these two [classical] marble horses which are opposite Monte Cavallo. They are both alike, and each has beside it a slave who is trying to catch them and who makes them rear; they are in the same position, and it is asserted that two excellent sculptors of their day wanted to make this experiment to see which of the two would do best.

Monday, March 30. I spent this day seeing the Coliseum and a part of the classical ruins around it. The Coliseum is a great building which was built by Vespasian. It is round outside and oval inside. One side is almost completely intact, at least in height. The four orders of architecture can be seen one above the other, beginning with the Doric and finishing with the composite.

From the Coliseum, built by Vespasian, I went to the Arch of Constantine, which was erected in honor of that emperor, after he had defeated Maximus [Maxentius]. As this arch was made hastily and of several pieces brought from various spots, there are very fine bas-reliefs on the top of the structure, which are Trajan's victories; other bas-reliefs which represent hunts, which are also very well done; as to those which are at the bottom, they are very ugly. The entire structure is composed of a great door in the middle and two at the sides. There are four columns on each façade, which are very beautiful; they are fluted and of the Corinthian order.

From this arch of triumph, I went to see what remains of the famous fountain of Meta Sudans, of which only a shapeless mass now can be seen. I went to the Arch of Titus, whose architecture is very lovely; in the bas-relief of this arch are carved the figures of the booty which this emperor brought from the Temple of Jerusalem, and, among others, one can see the golden candlestick and the tablets of the law. From this arch, I then went to that of Septimus Severus. There are some very fine bas-reliefs, but the arch is almost completely buried. . . .

24. *John Locke Observes the Provincial Estates and the French Army*

After the political fall of his employer, the Earl of Shaftesbury, John Locke (1632–1704) left England to travel in France from 1675 to 1679. He met the scientists then living in Paris, toured the French capital much like any other tourist with a university education, and then set off for an extended stay in the South. The time spent in Montpellier, where the university's faculty of medicine was reputed to be one of the best in Europe, was also one of reflection and observation. Like other educated men of his day, Locke kept a journal of his travels. Clearly not for publication, his journal reflects the author's wide interests. The comparison of the English Parliament with the Estates of Languedoc leaves little doubt about Locke's political sympathies.

[Montpellier], [MON.], 13 JAN. [1676]. Several asses and mules loden with green brush wood of evergreen, oake & bays, brought to towne for fuell. Most of their labour don by mules & asses. Between Lyons & Vienne we met people rideing post on asses, & on the road we met severall drivers of mules, some where of we were told have 800 lb. weight upon them, and severall women riding a stride, some with caps & feathers. We met more people travelling between Lyons & Montpellier by much then between Paris & Lyons, where were very few.

This day I also saw a garden where they blanch wax. They begin in March & then I intend to see it. Here were jasmin flowers blown & ready to open.

TUES. 14 JAN. A woman rideing on a pretty sort of [side] saddle made like a pad, pretty high before & behind, & on the far side a thing comeing up on the back of the woman, something like the back of a chair, & made of cloth stuffed with helme [straw] or some such like thing, & fastend to the fore & hindere part of the

SOURCE: John Locke, *Locke's Travels in France, 1675–1679*, ed. by John Lough (Cambridge University Press, 1953), pp. 18–19, 30–31, 254–255.

saddle or pad. The women carrying earth at the gate in litle baskets on their heads, & singing & danceing in their sabots as they returned for new burthens. The wages per day for men 12 s., for women 5 s. at this time of the yeare; in summer, espetially about harvest, 18 s. for men & 7 for women.

WEDNES. 15 JAN. Mr. Puech bying glasse bottles by weight & she apples. The Towne House adornd with false weights, ballances & measures naild upon the outside. The same at Avignion [Avignon].

T[HURS.] 16 JAN. Fair. N.E. Cold.

FRI. 17 JAN. Fair. Frost. N.E. Ice quarter of an inch thick. Women barelegd washing in the litle streame on the north west side. The picture of God the Father over the altar in church.

SAT. 18 JAN. About 9 in the morning I went to the Towne House where the States of Languedock, which were then assembled in this towne, used to sit every day. The room they sit in is a pretty fair roome. At the upper end, in the midle, is a seat higher some what then the rest, where the Duke of Vernule [Henri de Bourbon, Duke of Verneuil], governor of this province, sits when he comes to the assembly, which is but seldome & only upon occasion of proposing some thing to them. At other times Cardinal [Pierre de] Bonzi, who is Archbishop of Narbone, takes that seat which is under a canapey. On the right hand sit the bishops of this province who are 22 besides archbishops; on the left hand the barons, about 25. This seat is high, soe that the floor of it is about a yard higher than the other where the deputies of the towns sit, who are about 44, & of these consists this assembly. About ten they began to drop into the room, where the bishops put on their habits, i.e. putting of[f] their long, black cloaks, they put on upon their cassocks a short surplice, richly laced commonly at the bottom with straight sleeves, & over this a black hood & a square cap. Only one I saw in purple, & the Cardinal was all scarlet except surplice. It is soe orderd that, when the Duke comes, he never is there, soe that he never sits out of the chair. The bell tolls till he comes & then it ceases. When he & the bishops are habited, away they go to Nostre Dame to masse, a church just by, & soe about 11 they returne & begin to sit, & rise again at 12, seldom siting in the afternoon. . . .

[The Cardinal] had a velvet quishon, richly laced with broad silver & gold lace; the bishops had none at all. He also had his book and repeated his office apart very genteelly with an unconcearned look, talking ever[y] now & then, & laughing with the bishops next him. He keeps a very fine mistress in the town, which some of the very papists complain of, and hath some very fine boys in his train.

The best oyle in France is the oyle of Aramont [Aramon], a town in Provence, not far from Avignion.

One ran his sister into the head a litle above the temple in the house where I lay. The father was lately dead & he had but a small legacy.

Bend a bord with 2 holdfasts & then apply fire to it with helme & soe let it stand till cold. This way you may bring it to any shape.

SAT. 8 FEB. This day the Assembly of the States was dissolved, who meet & sit here every winter about 4 months, breaking up usually in the begining of February. The States of this province of Languedock consist of 22 bishops, 24 or 25 barons & about 30 or 35 deputys of towns. They sit as Jan. 18, & have all the solemnity & outward appearance of a Parliament. The King proposes & they debate & resolve about it. Here is all the difference, that they never doe, and some say dare not, refuse whatever the King demands. They gave to the King this year 2,100,000 livres, & for their liberality are promised noe soldiers shall quarter in this country, which yet never the lesse sometimes happens. When soldiers are sent to quarter in Montpellier, as some Switz did here that were going towards Catalonia, the magistrates of the town give them billets & take care according to the billets that their landlords be paid 8 s. per diem for each foot soldier, which is paid by the town, not by the soldiers.

Besides these 2,100,000 given the King for this yeare, they give him also for the *canal* [*du Languedoc*] 300,000 l.; and besides all this they maintein 11,000 men in Catalonia, raisd & paid by this province. These taxes & all publique charges come sometimes to 8, sometimes to 12 per cent. of the yearly value of estates.

The States being resolved to break up today, the ceremony was this. *Te Deum* was sung in the State House &, that being don, the Cardinall with a very good grace gave the benediction, first puting on his cap, & at the later end of the benediction he puld of[f] his cap & made a crosse, first towards the bishops, then towards the nobility, & then strait forwards towards the people [third estate?] who were, all the while the benediction was giveing, on their knees.

Mr. Harvy's man inticed into a shop & there fallen upon by 3 or 4 & beaten for poysoning their dog. A man shot dead by an other in the street some time before, & an other at Lyons when I was there. N. Very fair & warme. . . .

[Paris], WED. JAN. 4 [1679]. The ausne of Paris is 3 fot 8 inches of the Paris foot. Mr. Auzout.

THURS. JAN. 5. This day was the review of the infantry of the Maison du Roy, for soe the horse & foot guards are called. There were 30 companys, if one may recon by their colours, of French & 10 of Swisse, all new habited, both officers & soldiers. The officers of the French gold or for the most part silver imbroidery or lace in blew, & the Swisse officers all gold on red & much the richer.

The French common soliders all in new clothes, the coats & breeches of cloth almost white, red vests laced with counter fait [artificial?] silver, lace under or at least as much of it as was seen before was red cloth, though if one looked farther, one should have found it grafted to linin. Shoulder belt & bandeleirs of buffe leather laced as their vests, red stocking & new shoes. A new hat laced, adorned with a great white, woollen feather, though some were red. A new paire of white gloves with woolen fringe, & a new sword, copper gilt hilt. All which, I'm told, with a coat to were [wear] over it of a grey stuff, cost but 44 livres, which is bated [deducted] out of their pay, out of which, all defalcations being made, there remains for their maintenance 5 s. per diem. The soldiers, as I over tooke them comeing home to Paris, had most of them oiled hat cases too, a part, I suppose, of their furniture [equipment], & coorse, linin buskins after the fashion of the country to save their red stockings.

The Swisse soldiers were habited in red coats & blue britches cut after their fashion, with their points at the knees, & had noe feathers. The pike men of both had back & breast [plates], but the Swisse had also head peices which the French had not. For the Swisse the King pays each captain for him self & all the men in his company 18 livre per mensem, which is all their pay, but the captain's profit lies in this, that he agrees with his officers as he can per mensum & soe with the soldiers, who have some 9, some 14 £ per mensem & soe between as they can agree.

The French colours were in a feild azure sprinkled with flower-delys or a crosse argent charged at every end with a crown or. Thus they were all but one, which was azure 4 crowns or. The Swisse colours were a crosse argent, the 4 cantons, filld with stropes of yellow, azure & red, wavy, all pointing to the center of the crosse.

As the King passed at the head of the line as they stood drawn up, the officers at the heads of their companys & regiments in armer with pikes in their hands saluted him with their pikes & then with their hats, & he very courteously put of[f] his hat to them again, & soe he did again when, he takeing his stand, they marchd all before him. He passed twise a long the whole front of them forwards & backwards, first by himself, the Dauphin etc., accompanying him, & then with the Queen, he rideing along by her coach side.

The serjeants complaining that their pay would not reach to make them soe fine as was required, i.e. scarlet or red coats with true gold galoon, to make them amends for it, they were alowed to take more on their quarters.

The French for excuseing from quarters make they pay 24 ecus, the Swisse but £ 18.

FRID. JAN. 6. The observation of Lent at Paris is come almost to noe thing. Meat is openly to be had in the shambles [slaughter-houses] & a dispensation commonly to be had from the curat without any more adoe, & people of sense laugh at it, & in Italy it self for 20 s. a dispensation is certainly to be had.

The best edition of the French Bible is that in folio of Elzevir in 2 vols., but the notes are not very good. The best notes are those of Diodati & his Italian Bible is very good. Mr. Justel.

The best edition of Fra Paolo's *History of the Council of Trent* is the Italian one printed at London. This is the originall. ib.

MOND. JAN. 16. A tun of gold is 40,000 crowns. . . .

25. *Pufendorf's Description of Sweden*

Several prominent philosophers and poets served as historiographers for various kings in the late seventeenth century. In return for titles and pensions, the historiographer wrote or at least worked at the history of his patron's dynasty, realm, or reign in order to immortalize him and increase his prestige. Dryden in England, Racine and Boileau in France, Leibniž in Hanover, and Pufendorf in Sweden and later briefly in Brandenburg-Prussia, all wrote history for pensions. Some had a deep sense of loyalty and affection for the sovereigns they wrote about, others had little.

Though himself a German, we find no evidence that Samuel Pufendorf (1632–1694) found it particularly difficult to accept the patronage of Charles XI of Sweden. The honor and opportunities at a royal court were much greater than those at an electoral house in Germany. The Swedish House of Vasa had been attracting much attention ever since Gustavus Adolphus' dramatic invasion of Germany during the Thirty Years' War. The great Descartes had, after all, accepted the patronage of a Vasa queen and had died in Stockholm. And from the viewpoint of the constitution of the Holy Roman Empire, Sweden was in some sense a German state after 1648, owing to her holdings in Pomerania; Pufendorf saw Sweden as a counterweight to Hapsburg preponderance in German affairs.

Curiosity about Sweden increased in all the European courts as a consequence of her increasing power. This English translation of Pufendorf's history of Sweden (1685), which appeared in 1702, was thus very timely. Charles XII, the young, fearless, and heroic King of the Swedes, had defeated the Russians under Peter the Great at Narva in the fall of 1700. The duel for hegemony in Northern Europe fascinated other Europeans, not only because an account of a resounding battle was considered good reading, but also because the Russo-Swedish war affected English, Dutch, and French commerce as well as the course of the War of Spanish Succession.

It remains now to touch upon the constitution of the kingdom, pursuant to the method we have all along observ'd in describing the other states of Europe.

SOURCE: S. Pufendorf, *The Compleat History of Sweden, Faithfully Translated from the Original High-Dutch and carefully continued down to this present year* (London, 1702), pp. 610–616, 618–624.

As for the Swedish and Gothic nations, I may safely saw [*sic*], that they were ever reputed very warlike; they always had the character of a people that are not afraid of their skin, or annoy'd by the smell of gun-powder. Their bodies are very robust, which qualifies 'em for the enduring of fatigue and the other inconveniencies of war. They are equally capable of serve on horseback or on foot; and prove very good marines when once accustom'd to the sea. But after all, the militia of Sweden was in former times but in a sorry condition; for upon the breaking out of any war, they made use of none to make head against the enemy but the peasants, excepting the king's cavalry, which was not numerous, and consisted of some gentlemen. In those times, stratagems and intrigues were not so much follow'd as at present. But of late years, under the government of the Gustavus's, the Swedish troops became better and better every day. For K[ing] Gustavus and his successors employ'd first foreign officers and soldiers, especially English and German, to discipline and regulate the militia; and even to fight upon an important expedition, in order to spare the blood of their subjects, and prevent the dispeopling of the nation. But since the reign of Gustavus Adolphus, the nation has improv'd their military knowledge to that perfection, that at this day the Swedish armies have no need of the assistance of foreigners, unless it be to enlarge their number; of which the present King [Charles XII] has given shining and glorious proofs to the whole world. However, when I speak of foreigners, I do not include, under that denomination, the inhabitants of Esthonia and Livonia, the gentry of that country being as often honour'd with military posts as the Swedish; for in effect they have no other profession but that of arms. The kingdom is indifferently well peopled: but the number of its inhabitants is not so overgrown as that it should commence a war purely to be rid of a part of the number, and give the remainder an opportunity of subsisting, as some have imagin'd; for the arable ground in Sweden bears a very good proportion to the number of the inhabitants. Nay, on the other hand, the great levies made in some provinces during the late wars have visibly lessen'd the number of the people, especially in Finland; tho' indeed, that loss may be quickly made up by peace and the good order that is now observ'd for keeping up the troops. Besides, some alledge that the paucity of the inhabitants of Finland was partly occasion'd by this, that a great many peasants and their retainers have privately remov'd to Muscovy, and fix'd their residence upon grounds belonging to convents, where they might live at their ease. Now, considering the present state of Sweden, one cannot easily conceive how the Swedes could form the ancient colonies in the north parts of Europe, when they sallied out in swarms and overran other countries like an inundation, without draining the source they came from: this, I say, we cannot well account for, unless we alledge that the first adventurers coming from Sweden were join'd by several other nations through which they pass'd, and so enlarg'd their number, as a rolling snowball does its bulk. Besides, 'tis possible, that before the establishment of Christianity, the unaccountable multitudes might proceed from poligamy, which was customary among the ancient Goths; especially considering that in that country the men are very proper for generation. Further, 'tis to be observ'd, that Sweden is not in the same circumstances with the other states of Europe, where populous cities are so frequent, that the citizens make the bulk of the nation; for in Sweden, 'tis only the peasants that, properly speaking, are the inhabitants of the country; and out of them are rais'd all the land and sea soldiers. In effect, the Swedish boors are in a better and freer condition than those of other kingdoms; insomuch that they assist at the assemblies of the States, to give their consent to the laying on of the taxes upon the people; tho' indeed, they are justly excluded from the management of state affairs. All these considerations are plain evidence that their prosperity ought to be much regarded, not only for the sake of agriculture, but for the defence of the kingdom.

As for the customs of the Swedes, and their domestick way of living; 'tis observ'd that they have commonly a certain sort of gravity, not unbecoming when 'tis once temper'd by a correspondence with other nations. They have a natural itch to make a great appearance; by which means, many of 'em ruine their families, by living beyond their incomes. They are very well vers'd in the art of dissimulation; and extreamly jealous and distrustful. Some observe, that they are very invidious, insomuch that one Swede does not commonly love to see another thrive. In general, the Swedes have a good opinion of themselves, and of all that relates to them; but are very apt to contemn others. As for sciences, arts, and trades, they are inclinable enough to learn the first elements of 'em; but few of 'em have the patience to sound things to the bottom, and perfect themselves in the art to which they apply themselves; not to mention, that many of 'em are apt to imagine themselves masters of a science, before they are got half-way in the due progress. Forasmuch, as this nation has but little inclination for mechanick trades, and even slights 'em; 'tis observ'd that they are not qualified for manufactures, especially such as require ingenuity and industry. The Finlanders differ from the Swedes both in their language and customes; and become very good soldiers when they are put in good order: they are a rustick, stiff, opiniative people, but extreamly laborious; and upon that score, are more proper for fatigue and downright labour than for such work as requires ingenuity and dexterity.

As for the land of Sweden, 'tis of a vast extent; but a great part of it is nothing but woods, lakes, and pools: in several places it presents us with prodigious rocks; so that foreigners look upon it as a horrid, disagreeable country, in comparison with theirs. But after all, if we take a narrow view of it, we shall find that it produces very good commodities, and is not so very disagreeable. For when one travels into the heart of the country, he finds that Sweden has a quite different aspect from what it has at Stockholm and among the rocks upon the sea-side. In the middle of the country there are a great many very fertile and pleasant cantons: besides, the woods and forrests are not only necessary for keeping off the cold of the winter, but very useful for preparing the metals they dig out of the mines. The lakes are plentifully stor'd with fish; and afford both profit and pleasure to the inhabitants, inasmuch as upon them they transport every thing as well as themselves from one place to another. As for those lakes that do not admit of that conveniency, the defect is made up by the sledges in winter, which are an admirable conveniency for those who have a mind to travel, or transport goods. And in effect, the boors commonly make use of it for every thing. These advantages considerably allay the inconveniencies of the winter; besides the incomparable sweetness of their summer, and the late nights, which continue for almost three months together, are an equal ballance for what others boast in their southern climate. When the years are not altogether barren, the ground produces corn enough for the subsistence of the inhabitants; so that they have no occasion to import any from abroad, for one province's plenty supplies the scarcity of another. The cattle are numerous enough; and the vast number of lakes in the inland parts of the country, as well as the coasts of the Baltick-Sea and its gulphs, afford such plenty of fish, as is very serviceable in subsisting the nation. Further, this kingdom is well stock'd with copper and iron mines, which in goodness, surpass all the mines that are in any other country; and supply all other nations with those metals. The places where they dig these metals and work 'em, are naturally form'd for that use by reason of the numerous woods and rivers, without which they could never prepare such great quantities. There are mines in Saalberg in Westmania, which produce an indifferent store of silver. Finland affords great quantities of pitch and tar, as Dahl and Wermeland [Vermland] have great plenty of shipmasts. The whole country abounds in all sorts of fowls.

The kings of Gustavus's family enlarg'd the Kingdom of Sweden above one half, by annexing to it several fair and well situated provinces; particularly part of Carelia compris'd under the fief of Kexholm, the provinces of Ingermania, Esthonia, Livonia, and the Island of Oesel [Osel]. The first of these provinces defends Finland as a barrier from the invasion of the Muscovites, and the rest are very fertile in producing grain; and their situation very convenient and advantageous, in regard they lie so near the Baltick Sea. The most considerable city in all Livonia is Riga, which reaps great advantage by the River Duna, by which it exports its commodities, and secures to itself a commerce with Muscovy, Lithuania, and part of Courland. On the other side of the country, the ancient limits of Sweden were lately enlarg'd by the conquest of Jempterland [Jemtland] and Heredachlen [Herjedal] on this side the northern mountains, and Schonen, and the provinces of Halland and Blekingia [Blekinge] towards the Sound. Besides the intrinsick value of these provinces, they are of inestimable worth to the Swedes, for they cover the whole body of the kingdom, which would otherwise be expos'd on the Danish side for above fifty leagues together. But tho' all these provinces lie conveniently of Sweden, and Livonia being at once a bulwark, and capable to receive seasonable succour; yet we cannot say the same of Pomeren [Pomerania] and the Dutchy of Bremen, which lie at a great distance from Sweden; and being sever'd from it by the whole breadth of the Baltick, and very hard to be defended. For this reason, some have doubted whether those provinces are of any great importance to the Crown of Sweden, especially considering that Sweden is every year at more charge in keeping them than their revenues amount to. And towards the end of the German War, when the satisfaction due to the Swedes was treated of, several

Swedish senators were of the opinion that they should not accept of any territories in Germany, partly because the keeping of them would be a great charge, and partly because they might give umbrage to the neighbouring states, and so occasion many inconveniencies. However, those who were of the contrary opinion had very forcible reasons for the not neglecting of that opportunity, of annexing these provinces to the Crown of Sweden. For 'tis evident that as long as the Swedes are masters of Wismar, and have a firm footing in Pomeren, they need never fear an invasion from the German side: besides, when they make levies in the Empire, these countries are very convenient for the rendevouz of the troops. To which I must add, that in case of a rupture with Denmark, they may be very serviceable for the attacking of Denmark on the side of Germany. And as 'tis not to be disputed that the Swedes can never be secure without knowing who are their neighbours on the other side of the Baltick; so 'tis every way their interest to have a footing there, and observe what passes. Besides, if these provinces be govern'd as they ought to be, they may, in time, become capable to stand by themselves. But let that be as it will, the charge of keeping them is as weak a reason for the quitting of such outworks, as the advantage of sowing beans and corn would be for the pulling down of the bastions and horn-works of any place. The Swedes have already been twice masters of Prussia; and by the right of war, they might very well have kept it to themselves, as the Poles did formerly when they took it from the Knights of the Teutonick Order. But this occasion'd so much envy, and rais'd so many enemies to Sweden, that they were oblig'd to quit that conquest. To conclude, we ought not to think always of conquest, or to be too eager in mastering countries that lie conveniently for us; because others may do the same by us. Besides, 'tis a vertue to keep well what we have got; for too large conquests serve only to weaken the foundation of the state, as well as the nation it self. . . .

From what has been said, 'tis plain that the property of this state consists chiefly in the promoting the trade of the iron and copper that they take from their mines. For this purpose the North-Sea and the Baltick are very serviceable. But the security of the kingdom depends upon its armies by sea and land. The late King [Charles XI] much augmented both his infantry and cavalry; and put all his troops upon a better foot than ever they were before.

Sweden had this advantage beyond other nations, that it can maintain a vast body of troops without any great charge to the Crown; for the infantry live with the peasants, and the cavalry, for the most part, subsist upon the farms that belong to the Crown; for the incomes of these farms are allotted to 'em instead of pay. So that the kingdom is always ready to send a puissant army into the field. Beyond the land forces, there's a necessity Sweden should always be provided with a good fleet; and accordingly, ever since the conclusion of the last war, care has been taken to put the fleet into good order. Hitherto, the men of war us'd commonly to ride before Stockholm within the king's view, in the safest harbour of the kingdom. But in regard that the fleet is chiefly to be imploy'd against Denmark; that it cannot put to sea from that place till the middle of April, at which time, the ice that lies among the rocks in the mouth of the harbour begins to dissolve; that they have a great many turnings and tackings before they come at full sea, and even then are at a great distance from Denmark. Upon these considerations, I say, a new haven is now built with infinite charge at Bleckingia where the ships can get out in a little time, and where they live very near to Denmark, Pomeren, and Wismar. Besides all this, Sweden has this further advantage, that she can put a stop to her enemy's progress in her provinces in Germany, which serve them for outworks, or advanc'd guards; and to which they always transmit succours by their fleet. Upon the whole, the Swedes can cover the body of their kingdom from the invasion of their enemies; for towards Norway 'tis defended by high inaccessible mountains, and supposing a party of their enemies should make an irruption into Dalia and Wermeland, the most they could do would be the burning of some country farms; and besides, if they did not retire very speedily, they would quickly forget the way they came. Farther, upon the frontiers of Norway, they are defended by the Weener-Sea, the great Elbe which takes its rise there, and the strong forts of Bahuus Marstrand and Gothenburg. On the other side, the coast of Sweden and Finland, upon the Baltick Sea, is so well guarded, partly by the steep rocks, and partly by an infinity of ittle [*sic*] isles, that no enemy would offer to come near 'em; not to mention that a descent upon Sweden, while the Swedish fleet is in good order, would be a very hazardous attempt. 'Tis true, an enemy may land in Schonen, but then they must first defeat the Swedish fleet, and after that, master some place of strength for a retreat, the execution of which would be extream difficult. And after all, the invader may rest assur'd that all the forces of Sweden would speedily give him a meeting.

It now remains to take a view of Sweden's neighbours, and consider what good or harm she may expect from 'em. In the first place we must observe that Sweden joyns to Muscovy on the east. In former times the Swedes had frequent differences with that state. For Finland, in particular was much expos'd and always upon the alarm, by reason of the frequent irruptions of the Muscovites, before the retaking the fortresses of Kexholm and Noteburg together with the town of Narva, which serve for good ramparts to cover that province, and by which the Swedes have now cut off their communication with the Baltick-Sea. But the Muscovites have forgot that considerable loss more easily, since they have establish'd a commerce by Archangel. The Muscovites have formerly had this peculiar quality, that they stood firmly to their contracts and seals, as much as to their kissing of the Cross, provided they met with equal fidelity from those they treated with; for since the perpetual peace between them and the Swedes in 1627, they always preserv'd the peace; excepting, that in the year 1656, being seduc'd by the Emperor, they broke their alliance with Sweden, but soon after repented of the breach: tho' they commonly made some complaints in their embassies to the Court of Sweden, yet they were but triffling things, and easily adjusted. So that the Swedes had no reason to be apprehensive of being attack'd by the Muscovites, unless they gave occasion to it themselves; especially, considering that they frankly own themselves inferiour to the Swedes in the knowledge of war and consequently are convinc'd they'll get nothing by attacking 'em; however, last summer we have seen the Muscovite, contrary to his solemn promise the year before, break suddenly with Sweden, and besiege Narva with a very numerous army, but the brave young King has so entirely defeated him, that 'twill be scarce possible for him ever to make head to any prejudice of Sweden these many years, or indeed to recover the overthrow he has met with. On the other hand, the K[ing] of Sweden has no reason to desire the enlarging of his conquests in Muscovy, since he can not keep 'em without a great charge, and he would always be in danger of losing 'em, in regard that the Muscovites differ altogether from Swedes, in their language, religion, and customs. However, Sweden was never fond of entring in any alliance with 'em, by reason that they are naturally a nice, scrupulous, opinionative people; they always contented themselves with living in peace with 'em. So that all the advantage that the Swedes can expect from the Muscovites is that of fearing no trouble from that side. And, indeed, they are secure enough there, and they may justly account the Muscovites good and useful neighbours in time of peace.

In former times the Swedes liv'd for the most part in a good understanding with Poland. The Muscovites being their common enemy, oblig'd 'em to unite, and that so strictly, that when the antient royal family was extinct, they sent to Sweden for a new king. But this election was so far from confirming the amity between the two states, that it gave rise to a mortal hatred between 'em, upon the Republick of Poland's offering to intermeddle in a difference between the Swedes and their king; by which the Swedes had an opportunity of conquering all Livonia, and carrying the war as far as Prussia. Nay, the Poles having always shewn a great deal of arrogance and contempt of the Swedish nation, inflam'd the matter so far, that K. Charles Gustavus, whose election they had protested against, was oblig'd to give 'em to know that they ought to be cautious of provoking the men of spirit and resolution too much. At last the difference was adjusted by a great effusion of blood in Poland, which the Poles might easily have prevented. This stumbling block being took out of the way, there remain'd no reason against the perpetual friendship and union of these two nations; for there was no consideration of interest that cou'd move the one to wage war with the other; the Poles having made an absolute cession of Livonia, in the favour of Sweden, and Sweden having drop'd all pretensions to Prussia. Nay, on the contrary, they might reciprocally do great services to one another in case of necessity. But we now see the K[ing] of Poland begin an unjust and dishonourable war with the Swedes, without any reason; or so much as pretence for it, the Republick disowning any engagement or concern in it; but the martial young King has so confounded all his designs, and so entirely routed his armies wherever he met 'em, that he has almost dispirited him, and if his genius pushes him forward, Poland it self may be in danger of being overrun.

Sweden had always a great correspondence with the Empire, by reason of the trade carried on there by the Hans-towns, with which the Swedes have had frequent differences upon the account of their offering to interpose in divisions of Sweden. But afterwards, when all the old quarrels were quite forgot, the ambition and tyranical designs of the Emperor Ferdinand the Second, and his partiality to the Poles, forc'd K. Gustavus Adolphus to carry his arms into Germany, in order to revenge the injuries he had receiv'd, and to provide for the security of his own kingdom. For in effect, Sweden had been in great danger if the Imperialists had got footing on the coast of the Baltick, and been capable to put the neighbouring kingdoms under the yoke of their dominion. But after a war of 18 years' standing, the Swedes, by the force of their arms, brought things to that pass, that the states of the Empire recover'd their former priviliges, and the Protestant religion was establish'd in Germany, and for satisfaction to the Swedes, they got two provinces in Germany, with the same right and privileges that the other states of the Empire are posses'd of: and by this means, Sweden is interess'd in the affairs of Germany, not only as a neighbour, but as a member of the Empire. The interest of Sweden, with respect to Germany, consists, in general, in the Empire's continuing in the same state that 'tis now in, without being subjected to any one soveraign whatsoever. For questionless, if any soveraign should once have subdued all the other states of the Empire, he would not fail to dislodge the Swedes of their possessions in Germany, and ever give 'em trouble at home, after he has made himself master of the coast of the Baltick. However, the most important point that the Swedes have to manage in Germany is to oblige all the parties to a punctual observation of the Peace of Westphalia, which is favourable to all the states of the Empire in general, and particularly to the Protestants. If the Emperour in conjunction with the Catholick princes should offer to violate that peace, and strip Sweden of the advantages 'tis possessed of; the only game that Sweden would have to play would be the having recourse to those who are interess'd in the preservation of it. But as long as they make no infringment upon the Peace of Westphalia, Sweden has no reason to mean 'em ill. And on the other hand, they ought to carry it so with the K[ing] of Sweden, as not to give him any provocation to joyn with those who only project for their ruin. Among the Protestant princes and soveraignties, the Elector of Brandenburg, in particularl [*sic*], was much dissatisfied with that treaty of peace, by reason that to satisfie the Swedes part of Pomeren was adjudg'd to them, which would otherwise have fallen to that prince. By this means he lost the conveniency accruing from that part of Pomeren in its relation to his other provinces; besides, it plants a powerful and dangerous enemy just by him. And 'tis this that obliges him always to maintain a great number of troops, and to burden his people with heavy taxes. But after all, the Swedes may justly alledge, that if they had not display'd their arms in Germany, both the House of Brandenburg, and the other Protestant families, had been reduc'd to a miserable condition, and Pomeren had by this time been under another soveraign. In a word, all the world must own that the Swedes had a great deal of reason to demand satisfaction, especially, if we consider how the Electors of Bavaria and Saxony had plaid their game with the Emperor, whose vassals they call'd themselves. Now a satisfaction being due to the Swedes, there was a necessity of allotting 'em such territories as lay conveniently for a communication with Sweden. Besides, the loss that the House of Brandenburg sustain'd by the cession of these lands was made up by an equivalent of almost thrice the value, without which they would find great difficulty in keeping up a correspondence with their country of Cleves. Nay, further, the King of Prussia has so much the less reason to be alarm'd at the neighbourhood of the Swedes, in that, if we consider the matter narrowly, 'tis not the interest of the Swedes to enlarge their possessions in Germany beyond what they have already, even tho' it were with the consent of the proprietors. Moreover, the Protestants of Germany being morally assured, that sooner, or later they will be disturb'd upon the account of religion, according to all the rules of reason, and equity, they ought to forget a particular interest of so little importance, for the good of the common cause, and seriously to consider what a powerful support they may expect from Sweden in such a conjuncture. In fine, I cannot see what assurance the King of Prussia can have that some body or other would not form some pretensions to the equivalent adjudg'd to him, in case Sweden should lose Pomeren. As for what is between the Crown of Sweden and the House of Lunenburg, both of 'em have particular reasons obliging 'em to a mutual union and good understanding; the one in order to preserve the Dutchy of Bremen, and the other upon the apprenhension of his powerful neighbours, name, the King of Denmark, the King of Prussia, and the Bishop of Munster, in opposition to whom Sweden may do him great services in case of necessity.

'Tis observable, that Sweden and Denmark could never come to an accommodation, to the infinite prejudice of both these states. For, to speak the truth, if these two nations could but live in a good understanding, they might not only be very secure in the peninsula of Scandinavia, but likewise despise all the attacks of their enemies. But the Swedes complain that in former times the Danes always endeavoured to bring them under the Danish yoak, and that they have upon all occasions joyn'd with their enemies, and incessantly oppos'd their prosperity and rising. 'Tis true, the Danes are the most capable to annoy the Swedes, in that Denmark is situated so inconveniently for them that they can not only penetrate into the heart of Sweden, but likewise disturb their trade, or, at least, hinder them to trade with Swedish ships; insomuch, that the Swedes are forc'd, upon that score, to make use of Dutch and English. However, Sweden is at present so far free of those inconveniencies, that Denmark does not now border upon 'em for so long a tract of ground as formerly; and that 'tis now much easier for 'em to oppose the irruptions of the Danes. But on the other hand, Sweden can never find their account in attempting any new conquests upon Denmark; for the other Protestants of Europe will never suffer the Danes to undergo any considerable loss; for they are well pleas'd to see the two Northern Crowns divided at that rate, so that one of 'em cannot make himself absolute master of the Sound. All these considerations are sufficient evidence that Denmark ought to rest assur'd of the friendship of the Swedes, and to make this serious reflection, that in their wars one with another, all they get is only the mutual consumption of their strength. But after all, as reasons of this nature can never amount to a certain security; so 'tis importantly the interest of the Swedes, that the frontiers of Denmark should continue as they are now; and that they should keep up a good understanding with the princes, and free cities of the Empire, who are capable to thwart the King of Denmark's designs. To all which I must add; that Sweden ought to undertake nothing of great importance abroad, without being well secur'd upon the Danish side.

From the time of K[ing] Gustavus, the first of that name, Sweden has been in good terms with France; but they never found the effects of their friendship with that Crown till Gustavus Adolphus gave proof of his valour and capacity in Prussia. After that, France began to encourage him to oppose the House of Austria; and, indeed, his enterprize has been so sucessful that one may justly say that the arms of Sweden have been the greatest instrument in wasting the power of that house, and throwing the ballance of Europe upon the French side. 'Tis very true that the Swedes had some assistance from France; but, at the same time, that kingdom thwarted their designs on several occasions, and watchfully oppos'd their becoming great; and, at least, took care to put it self in such a condition as to be able, for the future, to shake 'em off at pleasure. So that the only view that France had in making that alliance with Sweden was the reducing of the overgrown power of the House of Austria. But now that France is arriv'd at so high a degree of power that it huffs all the states of Europe, and pretends to prescribe 'em laws, Sweden is oblig'd in consideration of the publick good, which consists in preserving the ballance of Europe, not to assist France in the vast designs that she forms every day; especially if she offers to over turn the Empire and the States of Holland, and at the same time to sink the Protestant religion. But after all, the Swedes have no just reason to declare first against France, while there are others, who being more in danger than they, or, at least, equally concern'd, would stand out, or oppose the good intention of the Swedes, in favour of the common cause, and so Sweden would only be repaid with ingratitude and losses. In effect, the situation of Sweden does not allow her to be first in the game. Besides, if that party should be unkind to Sweden, 'tis very probably, that the antient friends of the Swedes would open a door to 'em, as being sufficiently convinc'd what that nation can do under the conduct of a valiant and wise prince, supported by any tolerable measure of succour.

Since Holland assum'd the form of a republick, they have always kept up a friendly correspondence with Sweden; partly out of a regard to the House of Austria, which they look'd upon as the common enemy of the two states, and partly because the Danes laid too heavy duty upon the ships in the Sound. But after Holland had put it self in such a condition, that they were no further apprehensive of Spain, or Denmark, and at the same time, perceiv'd that the Swedes begun to meddle in the way of trade, their friendship became cool; and the Dutch have pursu'd all expedients to oppose the growing power of Sweden, lest the Swedish grandure should prove prejudicial to the advancement of their trade. So that the present friendship between Sweden and Holland is chiefly grounded on this foundation, that the Swedes would not tamely see the Dutch ruin'd, because their maritime forces would be a considerable addition to another power, which, after that, would not fail to prescrible [*sic*] laws to all others in the Baltick with reference to trade; and that the Dutch are equally oblig'd to prevent the K[ing] of Denmark's having too great advantages over Sweden, for fear the Danes should become absolute masters of the Sound and the Baltick-Sea.

Sweden has no occasion to mind England so much as the Dutch; for the English think to keep of their trade in the Baltick by their interest with Denmark, without taking any notice of Sweden in the matter, and imagine that they can easily be without their alliance. So that these two states may expect reciprocal ceremonies one from another.

The Swedes look upon Spain as a branch of the House of Austria, and upon that view, their behaviour to that Crown is regulated by their circumstances with the Emperor. Indeed, in the last wars of Germany, the Swedes would never declare open war against Spain, for fear their vessels should suffer thereby in the Western-Seas. Besides, Sweden is still interess'd in the persecution of the Spanish Netherlands, lest the loss of these should carry Holland along with 'em; if it were not for that, Sweden has no reason to care who are masters of Brussels, or Antwerp.

To conclude, the friendship establish'd between the Swedes and the Portuguese is founded upon their mutual commerce, which is equally advantageous to 'em both. But those too [*sic*] states can do no great service to one another, by reason of their lying so remote and distant.

26. National Prejudices

Cardinal Jacques Du Perron (1556–1618) had a reputation years after his death for his eloquence as a preacher and his success as a diplomat and courtier. His works served as models for young clerics and others who sought favor, especially since his own rise from being merely the son of a physician to the rank of bishop and cardinal made him a quite remarkable social climber. Moreover, his abjuration of Protestantism

SOURCE: *Perroniana Sive Excerpta ex Ore Cardinalis Perronii* (Geneva, 1669), pp. 9, 114.

and his willingness to try to convert others made him the darling of preachers at the Valois court. Later he gave religious instruction to Henry IV and was publicly reputed to have been responsible for that king's "conversion."

The following collection of bons mots is said to have been excerpted from Du Perron's works, but the fact that the place and date of publication are given as Geneva, 1669, makes one suspicious. Throughout the seventeenth century, and especially during the Fronde, pamphlets appeared which were attributed to public figures but which were in fact apocryphal. Whether Du Perron's views or not, these comments on national characteristics in the reign of Louis XIV illustrate the level of feeling and prejudice in that era.

The most envious and the most brutal nation, in my opinion, is the German one, enemy of all foreigners; they have wits of beer and porcelain stoves, as envious as possible; this is why things are going so badly in Hungary, for they are jealous of foreigners and are grieved when they do well, and they do nothing for them. If a Frenchman or an Italian is alone, they kill him, that is sure. Now the English are much more polite, the nobility very civilized; there are some fine wits. The Poles are a genteel people, they like the French, and are witty; the Germans hold a great grudge against them. . . .

The Spaniards say aptly that to eat and build one must only set oneself to doing it. A Spaniard going through the fields found a Gascon [from southwest France], with whom he struck up a friendship, put him behind him on the saddle, and wanted to loan him his coat to wear, which the Gascon several times refused; a little later the Gascon wanted to get off the horse and to go on foot, and so he asked the Spaniard if he could wear his coat; the Spaniard said: "Señor Gascon, you have thought it over, and so have I; you shall not have it." Spaniards forget neither insults nor enemies, nor friends either. The King of Spain has never pardoned an infidelity, and has always punished traitors very severely. He has also liberally rewarded those who serve him well and faithfully. Fifty Spaniards will not be as insolent in a foreign country as four Frenchmen. . . . Spaniards are brave soldiers and are of completely different worth than the French. They have their well-organized militia and discipline among themselves; they thus accomplish more than all the nations of the world; it is not merely today that the Spaniards have this advantage; I was astonished at reading in Titus Livius that in Hannibal's army, which was composed of a great multitude of men, 600 Spaniards composed the army's main strength. . . . The Spaniards have another thing; it is that they all have honor, and that even the least important Spaniard believes that Spain is the monarchy of the entire world. . . . It was also a great treachery and a shameful thing for France forever, to have allied with the Turk against the King of Spain, and recently, why did the King of Spain expel the Moors from Spain if not because we were negotiating with them?

27. *Moscow and the Muscovites*

Augustus von Mayerberg's account of his visit to Moscow in the 1670's has been a very popular source of knowledge for Western Europeans interested in czarist Russia. After the Latin publication in about 1679, there appeared a French edition in 1688, a German edition in 1827, and still another French edition in 1858. The following is from the French edition published in Leyden in 1688.

Mayerberg states that he is a councillor of the Imperial Aulic Chamber and ambassador of Emperor Leopold to Czar Alexis, Grand Duke of Muscovy. Note that though he is German, his interests and observations seem to vary little from the sort which E. Browne made in Mayerberg's native land.

We were well informed that the Muscovites, none of whom the czar permits to leave his state nor to study abroad, and who consequently have no knowledge of other kingdoms, prize their nation above all others; and that out of a prejudice to which they hold tenaciously they exalt themselves above everyone and prefer the power and majesty of their czar to the strength and grandeur of all kings and all emperors: that by thus fancying themselves excellent, they scorn foreigners so much, as being much beneath them, that if they have to receive on their master's behalf the ambassadors of some monarch, they even dare to ask them, as something constantly due them, to descend from a coach or horse first, and to put on their hat first. . . .

SOURCE: Baron Augustus von Mayerberg, *Voyage en Moscovie d'un Ambassadeur, Conseiller de la Chambre Impériale* (Leyden, 1688), pp. 56–57; 60; 124; 144–145.

The Muscovites' usual manner of living, even for illustrious personages, never goes beyond the boundaries of frugality. On a long and narrow table, covered with a coarse linen tablecloth, are placed a bottle of vinegar, a pepper box, and a saltcellar. Each person seated there is given some bread and a spoon, but not always, and as for plates, napkins, knives, and forks, they are given only to persons of quality. Next the courses are brought in one after the other, the same dish multiplied, however, according to the number present. Now the dishes used in the homes of almost all the great [nobles] and other richer folk are of pewter and, through the negligence of the valets, nauseatingly black. The meal begins with brandy. The first course is a chunk of cold boiled beef, seasoned with vinegar and raw onions, and next they bring in the other courses, either boiled, roasted, or others, served with a sauce in which there is a quantity of garlic and onions, of which the Muscovites are very fond. None of the delicacy of the science of cooking can be seen, it being banished from all of Muscovy. . . .

The Muscovites from the cradle are so given to duplicity that as a result sincerity can never be found in their words: so that having been raised in that manner, they continually support their lies by new lies, with such impudence that no matter how sure you may be of the falseness of what they are saying, you still remain in doubt as to what you should believe. If they are incontrovertibly caught in a lie, they do not blush, but act as if they had been surprised in the midst of some good deed, and they smile. The ambassadors of foreign princes should expect no greater sincerity from the czar's ministers.

And to tell the truth, the feminine sex is not venerated among the Muscovites, as it is among the majority of the nations of Europe. No one in that country demeans man's position to the point of speaking to ladies on his knees. No one teaches [women] to become proud to the point of insolence through the adoration of their charms, continued over several years; and not to listen to the entreaties of those who seek them out. . . .

Siberia, which first was made dependent by Ivan [the Terrible], son of Basil, and afterward was entirely subjugated by his son, includes a very vast region, famous for being the place to where the Muscovites banish the innocent and the guilty alike.

28. Christopher Wren's Visit to France

Instead of keeping a journal, Christopher Wren (1632–1723) made or purchased sketches of the principal buildings and other works of art which pleased him during his single brief visit to France in 1665. These sketches and his correspondence from the Continent have been lost; but a single letter survives in a family publication, to record some of his impressions of construction and buildings in the French capital. In 1665 Wren had not yet decided to abandon his career as an astronomer, but his interest in architecture was already evident in his enthusiasm for the great Giovanni Lorenzo Bernini. The plans which Wren so greatly admired were probably Bernini's first ones for the addition to the Louvre, designs which Colbert refused. Wren's visit to Paris at this turning point in his life influenced his future work, especially his unrealized plans for the rebuilding of London after the Great Fire.

. . . I have busied myself in surveying the most esteem'd fabricks of Paris, and the country round; the Louvre for a while was my daily object, where no less than a thousand hands are constantly employ'd in the works; some laying mighty foundations, some in raising the stories, columns, entablements, etc., with vast stones, by great and useful engines; others in carving, inlaying of marbles, plaistering, painting, gilding, etc. Which altogether make a school of architecture, the best probably at this day in Europe. The College of the Four Nations is usually admir'd, but the artist hath purposely set it ill-favouredly, that he might show his wit in struggling with an inconvenient situation–An academy of painters, sculptors, architects, and the other chief artificers of the Louvre, meet every first and last Saturday of the month. Mons. Colbert, Surintendant, comes to the works of the Louvre, every Wednesday, and, if business hinders not, Thursday. The workmen are

SOURCE: Stephen Wren, *Parentalia, or Memoirs of the Family of the Wrens* (London, 1750), pp. 261–263. See Margaret Whinney, "Sir Christopher Wren's Visit to Paris," *Gazette des Beaux Arts*, LI (1958), 229–242, which explains background of and details in the letter.

paid every Sunday duly. Mons. Abbé Charles introduc'd me to the acquaintance of Bernini, who shew'd me his designs of the Louvre, and of the King's statue.—Abbé Bruno keeps the curious rarities of the Duke of Orlean's library, well fill'd with excellent intaglio's, medals, books of plants, and fowles in miniature. Abbé Burdelo keeps an academy at his house of philosophy every Monday afternoon. —But I must not think to describe Paris, and the numerous observables there, in the compass of a short letter—The King's houses I could not miss: Fontainbleau has a stately wilderness and vastness suitable to the desert it stands in. The antique mass of the Castle of St. Germains, and the hanging-gardens are delightfully surprising, (I mean to any man of judgment) for the pleasures below vanish away in the breath that is spent in ascending. The Palace, or if you please, the Cabinet of Versailles call'd me twice to view it: the mixtures of brick, stone, blue tile and gold make it look like a rich livery: not an inch within is but crowded with little curiosities of ornaments: the women, as they make here the language and fashions, and meddle with politicks and philosophy, so they sway also in architecture; works of filgrand, and little knacks are in great vogue; but building certainly ought to have the attribute of eternal, and therefore the only thing uncapable of new fashions. The masculine furniture of Palais Mazarine pleas'd me much better, where there is a great and noble collection of antique statues and bustos, (many of prophyry) good basso-relievos; excellent pictures of the great masters, fine Arras [tapestries], true mosaicks, besides pierre de rapport in compartiments, and pavements; vases of porcelain painted by Raphael, and infinite other rarities; the best of which now furnish the glorious appartment of the Queen Mother in the Louvre, which I saw many times. —After the incomparable villas of Vaux [le Vicomte] and Maisons, I shall but name Ruel [Rueil], Courances, Chilly, Essoane [Essones], St. Maur, St. Mandé, Issy, Meudon, Rincy [le Raincy], Chantilly, Verneul [Verneuil], Lioncour [Liancourt], all which, and I might add many others, I have survey'd; and that I might not lose the impressions of them, I shall bring you almost all France in paper, which I found by some or other ready design'd to my hand, in which I have spent both labour and some money. Bernini's design of the Louvre I would have given my skin for, but the old reserv'd Italian gave me but a few minutes view; it was five little designs in paper, for which he hath received as many thousand pistoles; I had only time to copy it in my fancy and memory; I shall be able by discourse, and a crayon, to give you a tolerable account of it. I have purchased a great deal of taille-douce [copper-plate engravings], that I might give our countrymen examples of ornaments and grotesks, in which the Italians themselves confess the French to excell.

I hope I shall give you a very good account of all the best artists of France; my business now is to pry into trades and arts, I put myself into all shapes to humour them; tis a comedy to me, and tho' sometimes expenceful, I am loth yet to leave it. Of the most noted artisans within my knowledge or acquaintance I send you only this general detail, and shall inlarge on their respective characters and works at another time. . . .

29. The Plight of Spain as Observed by a Spanish Official

Careful to announce and justify his anonymity on political grounds, the author of this political program sought to influence directly the head of state, Marie Anne of Austria, the Queen Regent of Spain for her son Charles II, from 1665 to 1676. Note how he finds Spain's major problems to be within Spain herself; moral decay, corruption, and the collapse of rules of dress as marks of status are refrains common to many "reformers" in Europe in the last half of the seventeenth century.

The present state of this monarchy and the recent changes that have occurred within it have inspired many to write different papers in order to demonstrate that they all can perceive, conjecture upon, and speak widely about these questions. I have had the same goal in writing this paper which I intend to place at the royal feet of Your Majesty and which I will excuse myself from signing for many reasons.

The first because the principal motive I have had in writing this

SOURCE: "The Political Program of an Anonymous *Arbitrista*" [political projector], Archivo Histórico Nacional, Colección Jesuitas (Loyola) 11–4–416 (antiqua). This text was provided and translated by Professor Richard Kagan of Indiana University.

has been to propose to Your Majesty many aspects of different things that need to be remedied in this monarchy, advancing also solutions which appear suitable to me, and speaking about all of this to Your Majesty with clarity and truthfulness while exposing some other things that may not have arrived at your attention since the ministers who have the obligation to do this, to present things clearly to Your Majesty, and to speak clearly without deceit, paying attention only to the royal service of Your Majesty and no other ends or purposes, but this is not customarily their style; it is necessary for the subject who wishes to do this and to speak frankly to Your Majesty to disguise himself.

The second because having to speak in this manner is sure to earn me many enemies. . . .

The third and last reason that I have to excuse myself from signing this is the following: my principal purpose in writing this paper is not the hope of being rewarded for it (as *arbitristas* usually are), even though the solutions I propose may be of considerable utility, because I only desire and solicit the interest of serving Your Majesty and that of encouraging, if it is possible, those who make decisions regarding improvements in the lot of your subjects. I assure Your Majesty that such improvements are very necessary, because this monarchy has reached the unhappiest condition that is believable, and it is in the most decayed and prostrate condition that ever has been seen until today.

I experience this, Señora, every day, because the occupation of my office brings me to many places in which I see and recognize necessities and miseries that until these times were never seen or heard of; towns that only a few years ago had one thousand *vecinos* [heads of families] do not have five hundred today, and in those that had five hundred there are scarcely signs of one hundred. In all these places there are innumerable persons and families that pass one or two days without eating, and others who merely eat herbs that they have gathered in the countryside as well as other types of sustenance never heard of or used before; and this, Señora, is not rumor or wild fancy, but something that Your Majesty can easily recognize and see.

Because if a poor day laborer (I use him as an example, but I ignore many widows, old people, and other persons who cannot work . . .) who does not have one real in his pocket nor any more than what he earns from his own labor, for which he earns . . .

after being fed that day by his employer, 2½ reales (which is the most the employer can give, because, with the food, what is being spent on the laborer surpasses eight reales; this is quite considerable, and the landlords cannot give more because crops are scarce and taxes heavy). And the laborer has three, four, or more [children], and his wife; and since bread generally costs about 12 to 13 cuartos, and he must spend something on the other things which he needs to live, not to mention the taxes that are levied because it is necessary for all of Your Majesty's subjects to help others with something. How is it possible for them to live and to work?* And therefore, it is certain, Señora, that there have been many deaths and illnesses everywhere this year, and everyone has assured me that these have been caused by mere want. La Mancha,† Señora, has been depopulated and many families have emigrated to Madrid, where there have now gathered more poor people than have ever been seen. La Alcarria‡ is deserted, prostrate, and poor; parents cannot help their children, nor brothers their brothers, even though they are watching them die. And in places where poor people were never seen, today they roam about in great gangs. The rest of the province of Toledo is in the same condition, and if it was not for that pastor and prelate (the Cardinal Pascual de Aragon) who gives so many lavish and repeated alms and helps with so many necessities, it is certain that one would see misfortunes never imagined, but since it is not possible to help everyone, many are experiencing these misfortunes already.

And consequently, Señora, today most of the kingdom is in this same state of affairs, and I only wish that it were possible for Your Majesty to visit your kingdom so that you could see these conditions first hand and feel sympathy for them; but because of the continuous business of monarchs and other reasons, it is not possible for rulers to do it in person as the priest Chaquin [Jachin?], being great governor or viceroy of Judea, once did; but they have to do it through their prime ministers. But it is a great disgrace that

* This confused exchange of cash implies that a laborer spent more than two-thirds of his daily income on bread alone, leaving only one-third for other necessities and taxes; in other words, of the 68 maravedis (1 real = 34 maravedis) earned daily, approximately 50 mrs. (1 cuarto = 4 mrs.) went for bread.

† The portion of New Castile to the southeast of Madrid between the towns of Cuenca and Albacete made famous by the travels of Don Quixote.

‡ An area northeast of Madrid around the town of Guadalajara.

the ministers too are ignorant of these things because it is now customary for them, having spent all of their early life pleasantly and without working in a university or college, to arrive young at the leading posts in this monarchy and government. And there they are only exposed to excessive luxuries, salaries, and gifts from the kings and Your Majesty; only the submission and praise of everyone, to demand and to receive all they desire, without having to suffer the least bit of adversity or hard work; and thus it seems to them that everyone else lives in the same way, and they never come to feel sympathy for the poor.

To resolve this, Señora, it is necessary that prime ministers should be trained by first passing through inferior posts and occupations, governing only villages and getting to know provinces and districts, their products, wealth, and possibilities, though this is not done this way at present, but today everyone gets ahead by negotiation and many unworthy men obtain the offices and posts. This plan would mean that no one could rise to a district or appellate court or royal council without having had four different posts, at least three years in each, or having practiced twelve years as a lawyer. With this, Señora, there will be great ministers because they will have much experience, and this is of great advantage in any case, and they will arrive at the higher posts with intelligence, maturity, knowledge, and skill in handling business. And the towns will also be better governed, because I assure Your Majesty that this too involves much reform, since there are at present many incapable, insufficient, and unworthy ministers in these posts, and others of much corruption and ambition, with the result that great evils and inconveniences are happening every day. These pass by without correction, because in the inspections that follow their terms in office, they know it is a well-known and current practice to negotiate with the inspectors, the tax collectors and scribes, who judge the performance of each office by the money the officeholder gives them. By this step, the officeholders circumvent the testimonies of the witnesses with ease and facility. And there are few times when someone wishes to pursue the case and to spend his money in a higher tribunal where it is usually ignored if the case is not very important, and the evils remain without remedy or punishment. . . .

The sins of dishonesty, Señora, are without number, because there is scarcely any place that does not practice this with many public concubinages, and it has reached the point that the shamelessness of this vice is so great that one is considered of less worth if he does not have a mistress on his account, nor is a gentleman believed to be a gentleman, or a grandee a grandee, if they do not have this particular amusement. At this court there are so many of these illicit friendships, and they have been going on for so long, that no one really tries to punish them, and if some lower minister tries to appear that he wishes to correct something of this sin, he does it only to place the mantle of justice upon the particular interest which he solicits, and afterward he becomes quiet, leaving the cause of God in worse condition than before. And if they actually punish something of this sin, it is two misfortunate hussies who, because they are poorly dressed, are easy to disgrace and carry off to the women's prison. This of course is very just, but it would be just as well to carry off many better-dressed women who are often the most obstinate, most scandalous sinners, and of greater prejudice to the Republic, but these for explanations that are neither just nor well investigated (because when God intervenes he does not pay attention to human respects), their lewdness, impudence, and little fear of God are tolerated. But if the majority of ministers (at least among the lesser ones, and God willing the higher ones are few) are compromised by this sin and obstinate diversion, how can they punish it in others with objectivity and honesty?

And the time has come that the fear of punishment is regarded so lightly that even some ministers of God, the priests, walk about the streets as pimps, flirting with the strumpets, accompanying and talking freely and easily with them while taking pride in their own gallantry, their gowns lifted, kicking their silk stockings in the air, their mustaches ironed in place. I attribute this to the fact that their superior does not know of their behavior, because if he did, I am sure that he would punish it rigorously and as is just.

The thefts, Señora, that happen every day are many, but I do not see any great care in investigating or punishing them. Oaths are much more common, despite the laws published against them. Murders are very frequent and done with much skill and daring; it may be that this fearlessness is based on the fact that people are not afraid of killing and that there are pardons for murderers. . . . Interest rates, Señora, are very exorbitant, and there are those who earn 100 per cent interest and even more, and all this is permitted.

The respect for the Church is completely lost, and setting aside what happens on the nights of Christmas and Holy Saturday (when excessive shamelessness takes advantage of these times of so much devotion in order to enjoy the opportunity of sinning), in many places each holiday implies gathering around the churches as if they were lewd fairgrounds where public displays of merchandise are set up and trading is carried on. And even before this is finished, God permitting, they go into the temples to look about and to talk during the sacrifices. This is such a dissonant thing that even the gentiles hated it, and the Romans rigorously punished those who spoke in their temples, without exception, for which the Senate deprived two consuls of their offices. . . .

But in Spain, Señora, where we see so pure a faith and so true a religion, the respect for the churches is gone. One will rarely see a man genuflect down to the floor before that sovereign and divine Señor, nor bend both knees to hear Mass, when they now bend both in the private drawing rooms in order to give something to a woman (a shameful thing). And I believe, Señora, that in the drawing rooms and private visits (never was this customary or permitted before), respect for God and modesty before him have been impudently ignored, because after using them for what I have already said, it is certain that they do not congregate in churches except to assemble families and to make note of all the vacant places of others, and to wear new and extraordinary dresses in order to destroy the husbands, because they have scarcely put on a new one when it is obligatory to throw it into a corner, even though it is still new, because a new one is being worn, and the same happens to this one as happened to the last. In the drawing rooms they also regard as a ridiculous thing and often joke about the saying, when the lights enter: "Praised be the Blessed Sacrament," and it is become such a fashion at the court not to say this (probably more say it in Constantinople) that it is all they can do to reach the absurd extremes of courtly behavior. . . .

Moreover, Señora, one can impose measure and moderation in the clothing that today any person, according to his whims, wears, thus allowing the most wretched official to don more silks than a titled nobleman of Castile and to compete in his costume with the most honored gentlemen. It is just, Señora, that in any republic or kingdom there are hierarchies and distinctions between persons so that they all do not have to mix together with complete equality.

Why must one allow the lowliest little official to wear the best raw silk stockings he can find; he could wear silk plush; or sleeves of the best satin and a beaver hat, to be mistaken for a grandee of the first class in such a way that you do not know him or be certain of who he is? Therefore, Your Majesty must order that no official of any type nor their wives or children may go about dressed in black and with ruffs, nor waste any type of silk, gold, or siver. And similarly one could erect another hierarchy of persons, such as wardens, scribes, solicitors, accountants, and perhaps other persons, and all classes of servants . . . and their wives and children, and that all of these be prohibited from wearing silks and all types of gold and silver, and from going about dressed in black and with ruffs, allowing these to wear woven clothes, coarse and rough woolens, serges, and other types of textiles, permitting them also to wear silk ruffs and stockings that are not made of raw silk. . . .

In this respect, Señora, one can continue making distinctions of persons according to the quality of their estates and occupations, issuing a law with heavy fines for those who go against it, and enforcing these fines with more rigor than those of previous laws. . . .

From this reform it follows . . . that merchants and craftsmen will sell any merchandise and produce any order at prices more moderate than those of today; because there will be fewer persons who will buy these goods since officials will have to spend less on their families. . . .

Señora, one can also reform the abundance of coaches that have been introduced to this court and other regions, and which now proliferate in great numbers. This particularly prized item is also permitted to all classes of persons, in a manner that today the silversmith, merchant, tavernkeeper, oil vendor, rag dealer, and other men of this station have them. And these "little" people insult many men of worth who, because of their bad luck, go about on foot, stepping in the mud along the streets, and this situation vexes and exasperates many people. Because who cannot lose his sense of judgment upon seeing a rag dealer dressed in silk plush in a coach playing lightly with the terms: "Stop, go, to the Prado, to the Comedy"; calling to the lackey at every step, wishing that he had a coach with tassels and garnished with nails, not even distinguishing himself from a grandee, and if one can distinguish himself in something it is to go about more luxuriously than the rag dealer. The insignificant little marquis and many affected women do this, and it is said that they do not eat more than chocolate for breakfast and that this is very good (and I am not astonished, because those who eat a lot of meat will have indigestion as they walk about), and wish to drink only snow on Christmas, not because it is cold then, but because this is something that gentlemen and grandees do. And to resolve this, it would be just and reasonable that the rag dealer and all others dress and act in a way that corresponds to their rank and does not belie their offices and occupations, leaving the finery, ostentation, splendor, chocolate, and the coach and other expenses of this type for gentlemen, titled nobles, and grandees and many other persons who, by their offices and by their blood, alone deserve to carry themselves with this splendor and magnificence.

On the other hand, it is insufferable to see a woman who two years ago was only a barmaid and did not even know how to ride in a coach now go about in a way that it seems that while traveling, even slowly, the shocks and swayings of the coach will throw her outside. Or another woman, the daughter of a tavern- or shopkeeper, who today is the wife of a secretary (I say secretary, because all scribes are now secretaries) or an accountant, made into so much of a lady and great figure, who says that the air of the fans of Spain reddens the face, and that it is neither so healthy nor so cool as that coming from the fans of France. That the little muff which costs 200 reales warms one much better than the one which is worth less (and I say this is untrue, because 50 doubloons warm more and make the body feel better than all the animal skins in the world); and that the chocolate that has not been made at home cannot be drunk and that it also makes one's chilblains worse; and that one could not possibly go out of the house except in a coach or sedan chair, and she will stop going to Mass for a year if she does not have one, even though the church is just opposite her house, because of which she will want a chapel of her own. And this too needs much reform, because I believe the tavernkeepers have their own chapels already, each desiring to have the Mass recited alongside his bed, with scorn for holy things. . . .

I made this digression, Señora, because I did not wish to omit something so badly in need of change; and I return to say that coaches are fine for ecclesiastics and for women who justly merit them, and one must not even permit coaches for the grandees, since they have grown so accustomed to this vice, relaxation, and comfortable life that there is scarcely a noble who knows how to ride a horse; and horses are being used only by those who cannot afford to maintain a coach. But this solution may appear too harsh, and we will be content that some type of partial reform be made in regards to the grandees and that absolute reform be enacted with the other classes of persons; it could all be done in the following manner:

That cardinals, archbishops, ambassadors, grandees of Spain, viceroys, the President of the Royal Council, the Inquisitor General (and other types of persons if you wish) only be allowed to have a coach with four mules . . . , two coachmen, and four lackeys, because this is more than enough and it is sufficient for ostentation and magnificence. That each of these persons can have no more than two coaches, and two teams of mules, but not two sets of lackeys, and their wives be allowed to go about in a sedan chair. That bishops, sons of grandees, titled nobles, presidents of the other councils, councillors of Castile, and generals of the armies and navy (and others if you wish) can have coaches with four mules, . . . only one coachman and two lackeys; they should also be able to have two coaches and eight mules, another coachman, but no more lackeys, and their wives may go about in sedan chairs as well. And the rest of the councillors, royal magistrates, members of the military orders, royal secretaries, aldermen of Madrid, gentlemen who—although they do not belong to the military orders—have incomes of at least 3,000 ducats, representatives to the Cortes, and if there are other persons who appear worthy, can have a coach but only with two mules and one lackey, but they should not be able to have more than three mules, nor can their wives go about in a sedan chair because the coach is enough. And other classes of persons must be prohibited from having a coach with the threat of heavy fines, and these rules must be strictly enforced.

From this follow, Señora, great advantages because, besides, as I have just said, not having as much equality as one sees today so that we will be able to distinguish between persons in order to respect them as each deserves, there will be far fewer mules pulling coaches and many more occupied in labor . . . , something that is rare today because the price of mules has recently risen from 500 reales each to 2,000 reales, and for many higher prices are even asked; as a result, it is rare that a laborer has the money to buy them. . . . And making this reform, because one can rid the court of more than 3,000 mules, it is unavoidable that this animal will be able to be bought more easily, and this will also be useful for the people who will retain their license to have coaches, and consequently, it is certain that mules will be put to work more. . . . Likewise, one will rid the court of more than 1,000 lackeys who today do not serve as anything more than loafers, and since many are old, they cannot work and they fall into worse things; and it will be better if these are employed in other jobs and in working and cultivating the soil instead of only riding up one street and down another, standing behind dishonest hussies. . . .

I recognize, Señora, that you will make an objection, saying that what I have proposed in the preceding paragraphs is against the magnificence, ostentation, and splendor that are necessary for a court so grand and which is seen by everybody, including foreigners of many nations, and that by this display they are made to understand and realize the greatness and power of its monarch; and that therefore it would be faulty *raison d'état* to remove the splendor from the court and to strip it of so much gallantry and show. To which I reply that although *raison d'état* must prevail, it should be only in the court, and not in the rest of the cities and towns of this kingdom; there one can put into force the reforms to which I have referred. But one does not even have to make this excuse at the court, Señora. Because the first goal—and [the goal] to which one has principally to attend—is to mend abuses, correct unjustified novelties, and moderate excessive and superfluous expenses, basing all upon reason and justice, giving and permitting to each person only what he deserves. There is no more *raison d'état*, Señora, than this, and what matters most is to preserve a wealthy kingdom and prosperous subjects so that in times of difficulty they can help Your Majesty to resist and punish your enemies (and this is not done with finery, coaches, and vanity).

It is only a little more than a century ago, Señora, that coaches were first introduced into Spain. In the time of the Catholic Kings, Don Fernando and Doña Isabel, they were unheard of, and in that of the Emperor Charles V they were only begun to be used, and there were never more fortunate nor more happy events and victories in Spain. And it is not by a lack of coaches and superfluous dress that courts stop being great, well known, and celebrated in all nations; your predecessors in those times knew that, and the Spaniards were the most feared of all . . . it was a plan of the foreigners and enemies who, envious of our glories, introduced coaches to Spain (because it is certain they came from outside the kingdom) in order to corrupt and amuse us with them. These coaches have not served nor do they serve today for anything more than to make men effeminate, to make them weak, lazy, and fat, not knowing any longer how to take a step without a coach.

Neither in those happy times did Spain waste its money on chocolate, and now it is so common that it is considered everywhere as an essential food. Madrid alone spends more than three million ducats on it, and in the rest of the kingdom at least another three million are spent. It is necessary to realize that more than nine million ducats are now spent on something that is not a necessity and that not so many years ago we did without. And thus I often say that all the taxes that Your Majesty levies upon your subjects should be heaped upon chocolate as well as tobacco, because they are two superfluous things and very excessive expenses, and in not having them there will be no want except two vices less. And thus one could place on each pound of cacao that enters Spain a half-ducat tax and on each pound of tobacco two ducats or more; because the users of chocolate have the excuse that in the final analysis it is very tasty and of some benefit, but tobacco has no such excuse, because it is only a vice and a great waste, of much harm to its users, and of no taste. And when as a result of these very excessive taxes there will no longer be any more of these goods nor anyone to buy them, we will be saved from two vices. And even if they remain afterward, those who still wish to preserve them will pay dearly. . . .

I request Your Majesty not to submit this paper to the Juntas,* because if that is done it is certain it will be condemned to be burned, since it is predictable that the Juntas have many individuals interested in not enforcing what is presented in it. And we have the experience that of all the ways and means that have been proposed and submitted to the Juntas, none have been well regarded or put into force, because there is always some member of the Juntas who speaks against them for personal interests or for reasons which seem important to him. And therefore, I suggest that Your Majesty discuss this paper with a wise, saintly individual who has experience and practice in all these matters. . . . And if with this wise, dis-

* Subcommittees of the regular royal councils.

interested advice, loyal to the service of Your Majesty and the universal good of this monarchy, the paper appears to be useful and convenient to enforce, Your Majesty can do it with the firmness, vigor, and resolution that is necessary in these cases. . . . And if this paper is all or in part of service to Your Majesty and to the good of your subjects, and it seems worthwhile, Your Majesty can have it printed, because I did not dare. . . . And thus I submit to Your Majesty the manuscript, in Madrid, 20th of April of 1669.

Placed at the royal feet of Your Majesty, and although unworthy, I kiss them one thousand times. The author of this paper.

30. A French View of Spain and the Spanish

Born in the little town of Vayrac in the Dordogne Valley (Quercy) of southwestern France, the obscure Jean de Vayrac has left little trace in history except through his written works. His birth and death dates are not given by the standard contemporary and modern biographical dictionaries, but it is known that he wrote several works in the decade just before and after Louis XIV's death, and that he may have been an abbot in Cahors.

Interest in Spain and in the Spaniards had been greatly stimulated by the War of Spanish Succession, and Vayrac's book is an effort to satisfy that interest. A French prince, Philip, was after all now King of Spain. While Frenchmen struggled to pay for a long and costly war ostensibly fought over the Spanish Crown, their curiosity about the prize is quite understandable.

What is more difficult, however, is to determine to what extent Vayrac gives only a fashionable stereotype. Whether his information about Spain is accurate or not makes little difference here, since he supplied knowledge of the Spanish to his countrymen and to others who could read French. The fashion of analysis or conceptualization of a people was certainly not new or uniquely French, which probably makes the work all the more valuable to the general historian because it may be "typical."

On the Genius and Manners of the Spaniards

The Spaniards have respectable virtues and condemnable faults, like all other peoples. They have a lofty and penetrating mind,

SOURCE: Abbé Jean de Vayrac, *État Présent de l'Espagne* (Paris, 1718), I, pt. 1, 36–37, 39–40, 53–57, 62–63, 69–70, 77–78.

very apt for the most elevated branches of learning; but unfortunately this mind is not cultivated by a good education, so that generally one does not find as many men of learning there as in France and in a few other countries with noted schools and famous academies to instruct the youth. In spite of all this, one nonetheless finds men of profound erudition according to the nation's taste. This taste consists in being particularly attached to the study of philosophy, scholastic theology, medicine, jurisprudence, and poetry, but in a very different manner from us; for in regard to philosophy, they are such slaves to the opinions of the ancients that nothing is capable of making them embrace those of the moderns; nor in regard to medicine either. Aristotle, Duns Scotis, and Saint Thomas [Aquinas] are such infallible oracles according to them that whoever might get it into his head not to follow one of the three in a servile fashion could not aspire to the rank of a good philosopher; and if a doctor did not swear by Hippocrates, Galen, or Avicenna, the sick persons he sent to the other world would not believe they had died in a proper fashion. . . .

If, from their inclination in learning, we move to their other good qualities, we shall find that they are clever, adroit, wise, secretive, fond of mysteries, patient in adversity, ardent in their undertakings, faithful in carrying them out, slow in making up their mind, but solid in their deliberations. They are generous, fond of luxury, munificent, officious, charitable, good friends, sensitive on points of honor, sincere in their friendships, gentle and agreeable in conversation, serious in speeches, enemies of slander, sober in eating, and so far removed from the spirit of debauchery that if a man of distinction were once in his life drunk, he would ruin his reputation for the rest of his days; so that among those who are above the commoners it is more shameful in Spain to enter a cabaret than it is in France to enter a place of ill repute. . . .

Spaniards are naturally very devout, and if one observes that they are a bit too fond of the external forms of devotion, the blame must be laid upon their pastors, who do not strive enough to show them what true piety is. . . . They show such a fervent devotion for the Holy Virgin that—in their excessive zeal—they do not notice that in their pious ignorance they often render to the Mother a worship which is only due the Son. They show such deep veneration for the Holy See that in order not to have the least disagreement with the Pope, they do whatever he wishes and receive everything he sends their way with a truly filial submission: rosaries, statues, Agnus Dei, jubilees, indulgences, and generally everything coming from the hand of the Sovereign Pontiff is sacred to them, and woe be to anyone who dares advance the least argument against his infallibility; if he were denounced, he could count on being thrown into the dungeons of the Inquisition and on being condemned before it as a heretic.

They show an edifying respect for priests and monks, with the distinction that, in paying homage to the one and the other, they seem to suppose that holiness resides only in the person of the former, and that it spreads to the very habits of the monk, to the point that they only kiss the former's hand, and that they kiss the latter's sleeve, to which they sincerely believe great indulgences are attached. I have seen some [monks] so patronized that their entire sleeve was all torn, and all full of filth formed by the breath of those who kissed it. I do not claim to absolutely condemn this practice, since there is a good principle behind it, which is to honor God in his servants; but it often degenerates into a pious mummery.

They show scarcely less respect for women than for priests and monks. One might say that [women] are veritable idols on whom they lavish their incense. Whatever reasons they might have for complaining about [ladies], they are never permitted to say anything shocking to them; those who are proud of being mundane place one knee on the ground when approaching them, kissing their hand, and only rising after having been asked to do so. Their deference for pregnant ladies is so great that when [such a lady] sees a jewel and expresses a desire to have it, they are obliged to give it to her; and unfortunately for them, the ladies are very prone to this sort of craving. . . .

Such are most of the virtues I could observe during the ten years I lived among the Spaniards, and I have tried to paint them in their most natural colors, without permitting any flattery in the portrait I have painted. But since only God is exempt from faults, one must not be surprised if these peoples are subject to a few which counterbalance these virtues.

One of the greatest I have noticed is holding too high an opinion of themselves, and too much scorn for other nations, which makes them believe that in order to be someone important, one must be born a Spaniard; so that when they deal with some foreigner, they assume a superior air which reaches the point of arrogance.

All the other peoples of Europe try to correct the defects in their customs and in their manners by adopting what is good in those of other nations; so that parents take pains to send their children on voyages, in order that by a serious study of the maxims of foreigners they may rid themselves of overly strong prejudices in favor of their own country; but the Spaniards believe they would be degrading themselves in behaving this way. Slaves of their habits, they are the first to praise them, and are always ready to condemn those of other nations. . . .

In every country of the world, jealousy is a condemnable passion, which brings those subject to it to excesses which have unfortunate results and which often trouble the serenity of their lives. But in Spain it is not a passion, it is a fury which has no limits, no moderation. The greatest crimes do not frighten a jealous person who has resolved to take vengeance upon the one who is the cause of his jealously: he counts as nothing the life of his neighbor, be it his friend, his relative, or even his own wife. . . .

One must agree that Spain is the best country in the world and that it would produce immense riches if it were well cultivated; but unfortunately, those who by their social position would seem destined only to till the soil or to work in the vineyards would consider it degrading to devote themselves to agriculture. Their sloth being equaled only by their foolish vanity, even the least peasant has his genealogy all prepared and tries to persuade everyone that he is a direct descendent of one of the ancient Goths who helped Pelaez the Austurian to expel the Moors from old Castille. Infatuated by this fantasy, they are unwilling to risk *dérogeance* from their social standing, and would rather groan under the overwhelming weight of their poverty than to clear their fields, which would lie fallow if foreigners [from other provinces] did not come to cultivate them. There are only a few inhabitants of the mountains of Galicia who come down into the two Castiles to harvest the wheat for the Castilians, when the rye harvest, which is almost the only thing harvested in their region, is not abundant. But when abundance returns to their region, they no longer think of the Castilians, as if they had never even existed; so that these idolaters, in their sloth and their ridiculous vanity, lack for bread although their land is producing a great deal of wheat, because they will not deign to collect it. . . .

I could tell of an infinity of other faults which are attributed to the Spanish, but as they are common with those of a quantity of other nations, . . . I shall simply say that the people there are dirty, insolent, drunken, and proud to excess, that a certain spirit of hyperbole reigns equally among the common people and among the great when speaking of their prowess, of their social position, or of their religious devotion, of which the majority of them make a great show, as our social climbers do of a superbly braid-trimmed suit or of a very quick team.

By everything I have just said, the reader can understand the difference between the manners and the genius of the Spaniards and the French. What I have observed to be common to the two nations is that the youth there are as dissolute as in France, the doctors are as great charlatans, the monks as much intriguers, the police as rascally, the procurators as greedy, the judges as susceptible to the *tibi dabo*, the prostitutes as clever, and the mistresses as unfaithful to their lovers.

When I speak of all these faults, I do not mean that all Spaniards have them; these are failings of the nation in general, faults from which an infinite number of persons are free, and who are the first to condemn the others for them. And to sum it up in a word, if a fair comparison is made between the virtues and the vices which can be attributed to them, the virtues would greatly win out over the vices; this cannot be said of many other nations.

31. Paris Observed by an Englishman in 1698

Born into a family of physicians, Martin Lister (1638–1712) made his first extended visit to France in 1663 after taking an M.A. at Cambridge. By the time of his third visit in 1698, Lister possessed enough knowledge of the country and its language to enable him to observe much more than the stereotyped characteristics which Englishmen from John Fortescue to Arthur Young usually found in Frenchmen.

Lister accompanied William Bentinck, the Earl of Portland, as his physician when the latter was sent by William III to negotiate with Louis XIV a settlement of the Spanish inheritance. Lister had plenty of time to observe everything from the eating habits to the buildings

SOURCE: Dr. Martin Lister, *A Journey to Paris in the Year 1698* (3d ed., London, 1699), pp. 6–19, 20–29, 148–155, 158–163, 166–172, 178, 206–209, 221–225.

of the Parisians. The curiosity and passion for observation seen in Lister, as well as in other physicians of his age, may have been sharpened by his training in medicine.

Though I had much spare time the six months I staid in that city, yet the rudeness of the winter season kept me in for some time. Again, I believe I did not see the tithe of what deserves to be seen, and well considered; because for many things I wanted relish, particularly for painting and building; however I viewed the city in all its parts, and made the round of it; took several prospects of it at a distance, which when well thought on, I must needs confess it to be one of the most beautiful and magnificent in Europe, and in which a traveller might find novelties enough for six months for daily entertainment, at least in and about this noble city. To give therefore a strict and general idea of it, and not to enter far into the vain disputes of the number of inhabitants, or its bigness, compared to London; sure I am, the standing crowd was so great, when My Lord Ambassador [Bentinck, Earl of Portland] made his entry, that our people were startled at it, and were ready the next day to give up the question, had they not well considered the great curiosity of the Parisians, who are much more delighted in fine shows than the people of London, and so were well near all got into the way of the cavalcade. One thing was an evident argument of this humour, that there were some hundreds of coaches of persons of the best quality, even some bishops and lords, which I saw, who had placed themselves in a file to line the streets, and had had the patience to have so remained for some hours.

'Tis also most certain, that for the quantity of ground possessed by the common people, this city is much more populous than any part of London; here are from four to five and to ten menages, or distinct families in many houses; but this is to be understood of certain places of trade. This difference betwixt the two cities also is true, that here the palaces and convents have eat up the peoples' dwellings, and crouded them excessively together, and possessed themselves of far the greatest part of the ground; whereas in London the contrary may be observed, that the people have destroyed the palaces, and placed themselves upon the foundations of them, and forced the nobility to live in squares or streets in a sort of community: but this they have done very honestly, having fairly purchased them.

The views also which it gives upon the river are admirable: that of the Pont-neuf downwards to the Tuilleries, or upwards from the Pont-Royal; and in some other places, as from Pont St. Bernard, the Grève, &c. The River Seine which passes through the midst of the city, is all nobly bank'd or key'd with large free-stone; and incloses in the heart of the city two islands, which causes many fine bridges to be built to pass over them. One of these islands, called l'Isle de Palais [Ile de la Cité], was all Paris for some ages.

The houses are built of hewen stone intirely, or whited over with plaister; some indeed in the beginning of this age are of brick with free-stone, as the Place Royal [Place des Vosges], Place Dauphin[e], &c. but that is wholly left off now; and the white plaister is in some few places only coloured after the fashion of brick, as part of the Abbey of St. Germain [des Prés]. The houses every where are high and stately; the churches numerous, but not very big; the towers and steeples are but few in proportion to the churches, yet that noble way of steeple, the domes or cupolas, have a marvellous effect in prospect; though they are not many, as that of Val de Grace, des Invalides, College Mazarin [Institut], de l'Assumption, the Grand-Jesuits [St. Paul-St. Louis], La Sorbonne, and some few others.

All the houses of persons of distinction are built with porte-cochères, that is, wide gates to drive in a coach, and consequently have courts within; and mostly remises to set them up. There are reckoned above 700 of these great gates; and very many of these are after the most noble patterns of ancient architecture.

The lower windows of all houses are grated with strong bars of iron; which must be a vast expence.

As the houses are magnificent without, so the finishing within side and furniture answer in riches and neatness; as hangings of rich tapestry, raised with gold and silver threads, crimson damask and velvet beds, or of gold and silver tissue. Cabinets and bureau's, of ivory inlaid with tortoishell, and gold and silver plates, in a hundred different manners; branches and candlesticks of crystal; but above all, most rare pictures. The gildings, carvings and paintings of the roofs are admirable.

These things are in this city, and the country about, to such a variety and excess, that you can come into no private house of a man of substance, but you see something of them; and they are observed frequently to ruine themselves in these expences. Every one that has any thing to spare, covets to have some good picture or sculpture of the best artist: the like in the ornaments of their gardens, so that it is incredible what pleasure that vast quantity of fine things give the curious stranger. Here as soon as ever a man gets any thing by fortune or inheritance, he lays it out in some such way as now named.

Yet after all, many utensils and conveniences of life are wanting here, which we in England have. This makes me remember what Monsieur Justell, a Parisian, formerly told me here, that he had made a catalogue of near threescore things of this nature which they wanted in Paris.

The pavement of the streets is all of square stone, of about eight or ten inches thick; that is, as deep in the ground as they are broad on top; the gutters shallow, and laid round without edges, which makes the coaches glide easily over them.

Every stone costs six-pence before it is layed in the pavement; so that the charge hath been very great to have so vast a city paved with them, and also all the roads that lead to it for some leagues together.

This pavement is not slippery from the nature of the stone, which is a sort of course and very hard sand-stone. There is plenty of this very stone in the north of England; and of it those little narrow causeys are made in the West-Riding of Yorkshire, where strangers are afraid, but the natives will freely gallop on them.

However it must needs be said, the streets are very narrow, and the passengers a-foot no ways secur'd from the hurry and danger of coaches, which always passing the streets with an air of haste, and a full trot upon broad flat stones, betwixt high and large resounding houses, makes a sort of musick which should seem very agreeable to the Parisians.

The royal palaces are surprisingly stately: as the Louvre and Tuilleries, Palais Luxembourg, Palais Royal.

The convents are great, and numerous, and well-built: as Val de Grace, St. Germains, St. Victor, St. Genevieve, the Grand-Jesuits, &c.

The squares are few in Paris, but very beautiful: as the Place Royal, Place [des] Victoir[es], Place Dauphine, none of the largest, except the Place Vendosme, not yet finish'd.

The city gates are very magnificent, and mostly new, as erected in the honour of this king: that of St. Dennis, St. Bernard, St. Antoine, St. Honor[é], des Conferences.

The gardens within the walls, open to the publick, are vastly great, and very beautiful as the Tuilleries, Palais Royal, Luxembourg, the Royal Physick Garden, of the Arsenal, and many belonging to convents, the Carthusians, Celestins, St. Victor, St. Genevieve, &c.

But that which makes the dwelling in this city very diverting for people of quality, is the facility of going out with their coaches into the fields, on every side; it lying round, and the avenues to it so well paved, and the places of airing so clean, open or shady, as you please, or the season of the year and time of the day require: as the Cour de la Reyne, Bois de Bologne, Bois de Vincennes, les Sables de Vaugerarde [Vaugirard], &c. . . .

To begin with the coaches, which are very numerous here, and very fine in gilding; but there are but few, and those only of the great nobility, which are large, and have two seats or funds. But what they want in the largeness, beauty, and neatness of ours in London, they have infinitely in the easiness of carriage, and the ready turning in the narrowest streets. For this purpose they are all crane-neck'd and the wheels before very low, not above two foot and a half diameter; which makes them easie to get into, and brings down the coachbox low, that you have a much better prospect out of the foremost glass; our high-seated coachmen being ever in the point of view. Again, they are most, even fiacres or hackneys, hung with double springs at the four corners, which insensibly break all jolts. This I never was so sensible of, as after having practised the Paris coaches for four months, I once rid in the easiest chariot of My Lord's, which came from England; but not a jolt but what affected a man; so as to be tired more in one hour in that, than in six in these.

Besides the great number of coaches of the gentry, here are also coaches *de remise*, by the month; which are very well gilt, neat harness, and good horses; and these all strangers hire by the day or month, at about three crowns English a day. 'Tis this sort that spoils the hacknes and chairs, which here are the most nasty and miserable voiture that can be; and yet near as dear again as in London, and but very few of them neither.

Yet there is one more in this city, which I was willing to omit, as thinking it at first sight scandalous, and a very jest; it being a wretched business in so magnificent a city; and that is, the *vinegrette*, a coach on two wheels, dragg'd by a man, and push'd behind by a woman or boy, or both.

Besides those, for quick travelling there are a great number of post-chaises for a single person; and *roullions* for two persons; these are on two wheels only, and have each their double springs to make them very easie. They run very swiftly: both the horses pull, but one only is in the thilles. The coach-man mounts the *roullion;* but for the chaise, he only mounts the side horse. I think neither of these are in use in England, but might be introduced to good purpose.

As for their recreations and walks, there are no people more fond of coming together to see and to be seen. This conversation without-doors takes up a great part of their time: and for this purpose, the Cour de la Reyne is frequented by all people of quality. It is a treble walk of trees of a great length, near the riverside, the middle walk having above double the breadth to the two side ones; and will hold eight files of coaches, and in the middle a great open circle to turn, with fine gates at both ends. Those that would have better and freer air, go further, and drive into the Bois de Bologne, others out of other parts of the town to Bois de Vincennes, scarce any side amiss. In like manner these persons light and walk in the Tuilleries, Luxembourg, and other gardens, belonging to the Crown and princes (all which are very spacious) and are made convenient, with many seats for the entertainment of all people, the lacquies and mob excepted. But of this more hereafter.

No sort of people make a better figure in the town than the bishops, who have very splendid equipages, and variety of fine liveries, being most of them men of great families, and preferred as such, learning not being so necessary a qualification for those dignities, as with us; though there are some of them very deserving and learned men. I say, they are most noblemen, or the younger sons of the best families. This indeed is for the honour of the Church; but whether it be for the good of learning and piety is doubtful. They may be patrons, but there are but few examples of erudition among them. 'Tis to be wish'd, that they exceeded others in merit, as they do in birth.

The abbots here are numerous from all parts of the kingdom.

They make a considerable figure, as being a gentile sort of clergy, and the most learned; at least were so from the time of Cardinal Richelieu, who preferred men of the greatest learning and parts to these posts, and that very frankly, and without their knowing it before-hand, much less solliciting him for it. He took a sure way, peculiar to himself, to enquire out privately men of desert, and took his own time to prefer them. This filled the Kingdom of France with learned men, and gave great encouragement to study; whereof France yet has some feeling.

'Tis pretty to observe, how the King disciplines this great city, by small instances of obedience. He caused them to take down all their signs at once, and not to advance them above a foot or two from the wall, nor to exceed such a small measure of a square; which was readily done; so that the signs obscure not the streets at all, and make little or no figure, as tho' there were none, being placed very high, and little.

There are great number of *hostels* in Paris, by which word is meant publick inns, where lodgings are lett; and also the noblemen and gentlemen's houses are so called, mostly with titles over the gate in letters of gold on a black marble. This seems, as it were to denote that they came at first to Paris as strangers only, and inn'd publickly; but at length built them inns or houses of their own. 'Tis certain, a great and wealthy city cannot be without people of quality; nor such a court as that of France without the daily inspection of what such people do. But whether the country can spare them or not, I question. The people of England seem to have less manners, and less religion, where the gentry have left them wholly to themselves; and the taxes raised with more difficulty, inequality, and injustice, than when the landlords live upon the desmaines.

It may very well be, that Paris is in a manner a new city within this forty years. 'Tis certain since this king came to the crown, 'tis so much altered for the better, that 'tis quite another thing; and if it be true what the workmen told me, that a common house built of rough stone and plaistered over, would not last above twenty-five years, the greatest part of the city has been lately rebuilt. In this age certainly most of the great hostels are built, or re-edified; in like manner the convents, the bridges and churches, the gates of the city; and the great alteration of the streets, the keys upon the river, the pavements; all these have had great additions, or are quite new.

In the river amongst the bridges, both above and below, are a vast number of boats, of wood, hay, charcoal, corn and wine, and other commodities. But when a sudden thaw comes, they are often in danger of being split and crusht to pieces upon the bridges; which also are sometimes damaged by them. There have been great losses to the owners of such boats and goods. . . .

Amongst the living objects to be seen in the streets of Paris, the counsellors and chief officers of the Courts of Justice make a great figure; they and their wives have their trains carried up; so there are abundance to be seen walking about the streets in this manner. 'Tis for this that places of that nature sell so well. A man that has a right to qualifie a wife with this honour, shall command fortune; and the carrying a great velvet cushion to church is such another business. The place of a lawyer is valued a third part dearer for this.

Here are also daily to be seen in the streets great variety of monks, in strange unusual habits to us Englishmen: these make an odd figure, and furnish well a picture. I cannot but pity the mistaken zeal of these poor men; that put themselves into religion, as they call it, and renounce the world, and submit themselves to most severe rules of living and diet; some of the orders are decently enough cloathed, as the Jesuits, the Fathers of the Oratory, &c. but most are very particular and obsolete in their dress, as being the rustick habit of old times, without linnen, or ornaments of the present age.

As to their meager diet, it is much against Nature, and the improved diet of mankind. The Mosaic Law provided much better for Jews, a chosen people; that was instituted for cleanliness and health. Now for the Christian Law, though it commands humility and patience under sufferings, and mortification and abstinence from sinful lusts and pleasures; yet by no means a distinct food, but liberty to eat any thing whatsoever, much less nastiness; and the Papists themselves in other things are of this mind; for their churches are clean, pompously adorned and perfumed. 'Tis enough, if we chance to suffer persecution, to endure it with patience, and all the miserable circumstances that attend it; but wantonly to persecute our selves, is to do violence to Christianity, and to put our selves in a worse state than the Jews were; for to choose the worst of food, which is sowre herbs and fish, and such like trash; and to lie worse, always rough, in course and nasty woollen frocks, upon boards; to go bare-foot in a cold country, to deny themselves the comforts of this life, and the conversation of men: this, I say, is to hazard our healths, to renounce the greatest blessings of this life, and in a manner to destroy our selves. These men, I say, cannot but be in the main chagrin, and therefore as they are out of humour with the world, so they must in time be weary of such slavish and fruitless devotion, which is not attended with an active life.

The great multitude of poor wretches in all parts of the city is such that a man in a coach, a-foot, in the shop, is not able to do any business for the numbers and importunities of beggars; and to hear their miseries is very lamentable; and if you give to one, you immediately bring a whole swarm upon you. These, I say, are true monks, if you will, of God Almightie's making, offering you their prayers for a farthing, that find the evil of the day sufficient for the day, and that the miseries of this life are not to be courted, or made a mock of. These worship, much against their will, all rich men, and make saints of the rest of mankind for a morsel of bread.

But let these men alone with their mistaken zeal: it is certainly God's good Providence which offers all things in this world. And the flesh-eaters will ever defend themselves, if not beat the Lenten men: good and wholsom food, and plenty of it, gives men naturally great courage. Again, a nation will sooner be peopled by the free marriage of all sorts of people, than by the additional stealth of a few starved monks, supposing them at any time to break their vow. This limiting of marriage to a certain people only, is a deduction and an abatement of mankind, not less in a Papist country than a constant war. Again, this lessens also the number of God's worshippers, instead of multiplying them as the stars in the firmament, or the sand upon the sea shoar; these men wilfully cut off their posterity, and reduce God's congregation for the future.

There is very little noise in this city of publick cries of things to be sold, or any disturbance from pamphlets and hawkers. One thing I wondered at, that I heard of nothing lost, nor any publick advertisements, till I was shewed printed papers upon the corners of streets, wherein were in great letters, "One Two, Five; Ten to Fifty Louises [louis d'or] to be got;" and then underneath an account of what was lost. This sure is a good and quiet way; for by this means, without noise, you often find your goods again, every body that has found them repairing in a day or two to such places. The *Gazettes* come out but once a week, and but a few people buy them.

'Tis difficult and dangerous to vend a libel here. While we were in town, a certain person gave a bundle of them to a blind man, a beggar of the Hospital of the Quinzevint, telling him he might get five pence for every penny; he went to Nostredame [Cathedral], and cried them up in the service time, "*La Vie & Miracles de l'Evesq*[*ue*] *de Reims.*" This was a trick that was play'd the Archbishop, as it was thought, by the Jesuits, with whom he has had a great contest about Molina's the Spanish J[esuit] doctrines. The libel went off at any rate, when the first buyers had read the title further, and found they were against the present Archbishop [Louis de Noailles], Duke and first Peer of France.

The streets are lighted alike all the winter long, as well when the moon shines, as at other times of the month; which I remember the rather, because of the impertinent usage of our people at London, to take away the lights for half of the month, as though the moon was certain to shine and light the streets, and that there could be no cloudy weather in winter. The lanthorns here hang down in the very middle of all the streets, about twenty paces distance, and twenty foot high. They are made of a square of glass about two foot deep, covered with a broad plate of iron; and the rope that lets them down is secured and lockt up in an iron funnel and little trunk fastned into the wall of the house. These lanthorns have candles of four in the pound in them, which last burning till after midnight.

As to these lights, if any man break them, he is forthwith sent to the gallies; and there were three young gentlemen of good families, who were in prison for having done it in a frolick, and could not be released thence in some months; and that not without the diligent application of good friends at court.

The lights at Paris for five months in the year only, cost near 50,000 l. sterling. This way of lighting the streets is in use also in some other cities in France. The King is said to have raised a large tax by it. In the preface to the tax it is said, that considering the great danger his subjects were in, in walking the streets in the dark, from thieves, and the breaking their necks by falls, he for such a sum of money did grant this priviledge, that they might hang out lanthorns in this manner.

I have said that the avenues to the city, and all the streets, are paved with a very hard sand-stone, about eight inches square; so they have a great care to keep them clean; in winter, for example, upon the melting of the ice, by a heavy drag with a horse, which makes a quick riddance and cleaning the gutters; so that in a day's time all parts of the town are to admiration clean and neat again to walk on.

I could heartily wish their summer cleanliness was as great; it is certainly as necessary to keep so populous a city sweet; but I know no machine sufficient, but what would empty it of the people too; all the threats and inscriptions upon the walls are to little purpose. The dust in London in summer is oftentimes, if a wind blow, very troublesome, if not intolerable; in Paris there is much less of it, and the reason is, the flat stones require little sand to set them fast, whereas our small pebles, not coming together, require a vast quantity to lay them fast in paving.

But from the people in the streets, to the dead ornaments there. There are an infinite number of busto's or heads of the Grand Monarque every where put up by the common people; but the noble and intire statues are but few, considering the obsequious humour and capacity of the people to perform.

That in the Place Victoir is a-foot in brass, all over gilt, with *Victoirie*, that is, a vast winged woman close behind his back, holding forth a laural crown over the King's head, with one foot upon a globe. There are great exceptions taken at the gilding by artists; and, indeed, the shining seems to spoil the features, and give I know not what confusion; it had better have been all of gold brassed over; which would have given its true lights and shaddows, and suffered the eye to judge of the proportions. But that which I like not in this, is the great woman perpetually at the King's back; which is a sort of embarras, and instead of giving victory, seems to tire him with her company. The Roman Victory was a little puppit in the Emperour's hand, which he could dispose of at pleasure. This woman is enough to give a man a surfeit.

The other are statues of three of the last kings of France, in brass a horse-back.

That on the Pont-neuf is of Henry the Fourth in his armour bare-headed, and habited as the mode of that time was.

The other of Lewis the Thirteenth in the Palace [Place]-Royal, armed also after the mode of the age, and his plume of feathers on his headpiece.

The third is of this present King, Louis the Fourteenth, and designed for the Place Vendosme. This colossus of brass is yet in the very place where it was cast; it is surprisingly great, being 22 foot high, the foot of the King 26 inches in length, and all the proportions of him and the horse suitable. There was 100,000 pound weight of metal melted, but it took not up above 80,000 pounds; it was all cast at once, horse and man. Mons. Girardon told me, he wrought diligently, and with almost daily application at the model 8 years, and there were two years more spent in the moulding, and furnaces, and casting of it. The King is in the habit of a Roman emperor, without stirrups or saddle, and on his head a French large periwig, à-la-mode. Whence this great liberty of sculpture arises, I am much to seek.

'Tis true, that in building precisely to follow the ancient manner and simplicity is very commendable, because all those orders were founded upon good principles in mathematicks: but the cloathing of an emperor was not more, than the weak fancy of the people. For *Louis le Grand* to be thus dressed up at the head of his army now a-days would be very comical. What need other emblems, when truth may be had; as though the present age need be ashamed of their modes, or that the *statua equestris* of Henry the Fourth or Louis the Thirteenth were the less to be valued for being done in the true dress of their times. It seems to me to be the effect of mistaken flattery; but if regarded only as a piece of meer art, it is methinks very unbecoming, and has no graceful air with it. . . .

The diet of the Parisians consists chiefly of bread and herbs; it is here, as with us, finer and courser. But the common bread or *pain de Gonesse*, which is brought twice a week into Paris from a village so called, is purely white, and firm, and light, and made altogether with leaven; mostly in three pound loaves, and 3 d. a pound. That which is bak'd in Paris is courser and much worse.

As for the *fine manchet*, or French bread as we call it, I cannot much commend it; it is of late, since the quantity of beer that is brewed in Paris, often so bitter, that it is not to be eaten, and we far exceed them now in this particular in London.

The grey salt of France (which there at table, is altogether in every thing made use of) is incomparably better and more wholsom than our white salt. This I the rather mention, because it seems not yet to enter fully into the consideration and knowledge of our people; who are nice in this particular to a fault. But I must take leave to tell them, that our salt causes thirst, and spoils every thing that is pretended to be preserved by it, be it fish or flesh. For whether boiled from the inland salt-pits, or the sea-water, it is little less than quicklime, and burns and reeses all it touches; so that 'tis pity to see so much good fish as is caught upon the northern line of coast, particularly the cod and ling, and herring, now of little value, which were formerly the most esteemed commodities of England. . . .

In Lent the common people feed much on white kidney beans, and white or pale lentils, of which there are great provisions made in all the markets, and to be had ready boiled. I was well pleased with this lentil; which is a sort of pulse we have none of in England. There are two sorts of white lentils sold here; one small one from Burgundy, by the cut of Briare; and another bigger, as broad again from Chartres; a third also much larger, is sometimes to be had from Languedoc. Those excepted our seed shops far exceed theirs, and consequently our gardens, in the pulse-kind for variety; both pea and bean.

The roots differ much from ours. There are here no round turneps, but all long ones, and small; but excellently well tasted, and are of a much greater use, being proper for soups also; for which purpose ours are too strong. We have indeed, of late got them into England; but our gardners understand not the managing of them. They sow them here late after midsummer; and at Martinmas [Nov. 11] or sooner, before the frost begin, they dig them up, cut off the tops, and put them into sand in their cellars, where they will keep good till after Easter; nay, till Whitsuntide. Whereas if the frost take them they are quite spoilt; and that piece of ill husbandry makes them to be despised here; having lost their taste, and they soon grow sticky in the ground. The sandy plains of Vaugerard near Paris are famous for this sort of most excellent root. After the same manner they keep their carrots.

After we had been two or three days' journey in France, we found no other turneps, but the *navet;* and still the nearer Paris the better. These, as I said, are small long turneps, not bigger than a knife-hast, and most excellent in soupes, and with boiled and stewed mutton. I think it very strange, that the seed should so much improve in England, as to produce roots of the same kind six or ten tim[e]s as big as there; for I make no question but the long turneps of late only in our markets are the same.

The potato are scarce to be found in their markets, which are so great a relief to the people of England, and very nourishing and wholsome roots; but there are store of Jerusalem artichokes.

They delight not so much in cabbage as I expected, at least in the season while we were there, from December to midsummer. I never saw in all the markets once sprouts, that is the tender shoots of cabbages; nor in their publick gardens any reserves of old stalks. The red cabbage is esteemed here, and the Savoy.

But to make amends for this, they abound in vast quantities of large red onions and garlick. And the long and sweet white onion of Languedoc are to be had also here. Also leeks, rockamboy [rocambole], and shallots are here in great use.

It has been observed that the northern people of Europe much delight in cabbage, as the Russes, Poles, Germans, &c. 'Tis certain, the cabbage thrives best in cold countreys, and is naturally a northern plant, and the keel [kale] is to be found wild upon the maritime rocks, as I have seen it at Whitby, and the cold ripens it, and makes it more tender and palatable.

The southern people are pleased with the onion kind, for the same reason, for that the great heats meliorate them but give a rankness to the cabbage. The leeks are here much smaller, than with us; but to recompence this, they are blancht here with more care and art, and are three times as long in the white part, which is by sinking them early so deep in mellow earth. There is no plant of the onion kind so hardy as this, and so proper for the cold mountains, witness the use the Welsh have made of them from all ages; and indeed it is excellent against spitting of blood, and all diseases of the throat and lungs.

Though the lettice be the great and universal sallet, yet I did not find they came near our people, for the largeness and hardness of them; indeed, about a week before we left Paris, the long Roman lettuce filled their markets, which was incomparable, and I think beyond our Silesian.

April and May the markets were served with vast quantities of white beets, an herb rarely used with us, and never that I know of in that manner for soups. The leaves grow long and large, and are tied up, as we do our Silesian or Roman lettice to blanch, and then cut by the root. The stalks are very broad and tender, and they only are used, stript of the green leaves. They cook those stalks in different manners.

The asparagus here are in great plenty, but for the first month they were very bitter and unpleasant; from whence that proceeded, I cannot guess; afterwards I did not much perceive it.

They are so great lovers of sorrel that I have seen whole acres of it planted in the fields; and they are to be commended for it; for nothing is more wholesome, and it is good to supply the place of lemons, against the scurvy, or any ill habit of the body.

But after all, the French delight in nothing so much as mushroomes; for which they have daily, and all the winter long, store of fresh and new gathered in the markets. This surprised me; nor could I guess where they had them, till I found they raised them on hot beds in their gardens. . . .

This city is well served with carp, of which there is an incredible quantity spent in the Lent. They are not large, and I think are the better for it, but they are very clean of mud, and well tasted.

They have a particular way of bringing fresh oysters to town, which I never saw with us: to put them up in straw baskets of a peck, suppose, cut from the shell, and without the liquor. They are thus very good for stewing, and all other manner of dressing.

There is such plenty of macreuse, a sort of sea ducks, in the markets all Lent, that I admire where they got so many; but these are reckoned and esteemed as fish, and therefore they take them with great industry. They have a rank fishy taste, yet for want of other flesh were very welcome. I remember we had at our treat at the King's charge at Versailles a macreuse pye near two foot diameter, for it was in Lent; which being high seasoned, did go down very well with rare Burgundy. There is a better argument in Leewenhoeke for birds participating something of the nature of fish, though their blood is hot, than any the Council of Trent could think of, and that is, that the globuli of the blood of birds are oval, as those of fishes are; but this will take in all the bird kind; which also in time those gentlemen may think fit to grant.

As for their flesh, mutton and beef if they are good in their kind, they come little short of ours, I cannot say they exceed them. But their veal is not to be compared with ours, being red and course; and I believe no country in Europe understands the management of that sort of food like the English. . . .

I cannot but take notice here of a great prejudice the French lie under, in relation to our flesh. 'Tis generally said amongst them that our meat in England will not make so strong broth, as the French, by a third part. If they say not so salt and savoury, and strong tasted, I agree with them; and yet the French meat is never the better. For first their meat is mostly leaner and more dry, and (which is all in all in this matter of soups) is long kept, before it be spent, which gives it a higher and salter taste; for as meat rots, it becomes more urinous and salt. Now our people by custom covet the freshest meat, and cannot indure the least tendency to putrefaction; and we have good reason to do so, because our air is twice as moist as theirs, which does often cause in the keeping of meat a mustiness, which is intolerable to all mankind. Whereas the air of France being so much drier, keeping of meat not only makes it tender, but improves the taste. So that could we secure our meat, in keeping it from that unsavoury quality, it would far outdo the French meat, because much more juicy.

I don't remember I eat of above two sorts of flesh, but what we have as good or better in England, and that was of the wild pigs, and the red-legg'd partridge. Of these last I eat at St. Clou[d], taken thereabouts; as to bigness, they are much degenerated from those in Languedoc, and less; but far excel the grey partridge in taste.

As for their fruits, our journey was in the worst time of the year, from December to midsummer, so that we had little save winter fruits; some few *Bons Chritiens* we tasted, not much better than ours, but something freer of stones. The Virguleus pears were admirable, but to our sorrow they did not last long after our arrival.

The Kentish pippin, as we call it, was here excellent; but two other sorts of apples stock the markets. The winter Calvil or Queening, which though a tender and soft apple, yet continued good till after Easter. Also the *pome d'apis*, which is served here for shew, more than use; being a small flat apple, very beautiful, very red on one side, and pale or white on the other, and may serve the French ladies at their toilets for a pattern to paint by. However this tender apple was not contemptible after Whitsontide; and, which is its property, it never smells ill, though the ladies keep it (as sometimes they do) about them.

I never met with any thing peculiar in their sweet meats, but a marmalade of orange flowers; which indeed was admirable. 'Twas made with those flowers, the juice of lemons, and fine sugar.

The wines about Paris are very small, yet good in their kind; those *de Surene* are excellent some years; but in all the taverns they have a way to make them into the fashion of a Champagne and Burgundy.

The tax upon wines is now so great that whereas before the war they drank them at retail at 5 d. the quart, they now sell them at 15 d. the quart, and dearer, which has enhansed the rates of all commodities and workmen's wages; and also has caused many thousand private families to lay in wines in their cellars at the cheapest hand, which used to have none before.

The wines of Burgundy and Champagne are most valued; and indeed, not without reason; for they are light and easie upon the stomach, and give little disturbance to the brain, if drawn from the hogshead, or loose bottled after their fashion. . . .

Besides wines, there is no feasting without the drinking at the de[s]sert all sorts of strong waters, particularly *ratafia*'s; which is a sort of cherry-brandy made with peach and apricock stones, highly piquant and of a most agreeable flavour.

The pungent and acrimonious quality of these and such like kernels was not unknown to the ancients, and very poisonous to some animals. Dioscorides tells us a paste made of the kernels of bitter almonds will throw hens into convulsions, and immediately ill them. Birds have but little brain, and so are the stronglier affectede with this volatil venom. Not unlike effects 'tis possible *ratafia* may have in some tender and more delicate constitution, and weak and feeble brains, and may be one cause of so many sudden deaths, as have been observed of late.

Vattee is a sort of perfumed strong-water from Provence, made (as it is pretended) of muscat wine distilled with citron pills and orange flowers.

Fenoulliet de l'Isle de Ree is valued much, 'tis much like our anniseed water.

I must not forget the plain *eau de vie*, or Nant[e]s brandy; which was formerly the morning's draught of (*crocheteurs*) porters only; but is now valued very much, as one of the best spirits of wine in Europe, and yet it is made of a poor, thin, and half-ripe sowrish white-wine of Brittany. 'Tis worth enquiry what the reason of this should be, that so lean and sowre a wine should yield so palatable a liquor, far beyond any the most ripe and oily wines of Languedoc, Spain, or Italy. I take it to be the due mixture of an acid and oil; which acid is much wanting in the ripe wines. This therefore is a sort of natural punch. And for the same reason, I make no doubt, but our grapes of the growth of England, as unripe as most of them are, if pressed and fermented in any quantity would in like manner yield excellent brandy.

These and many more sorts of strong-waters and strong wines, both of France, and Italy, and Spain, are wont to be brought in, at the latter end of the desert in all great feasts, and they drink freely of them: which custom is new; when I was formerly in France I remember nothing of it. But it is the long war that has introduced them; the nobility and gentry suffering much in those tedious campagnes, applied themselves to these liquors to support the difficulties and fatigues of weather and watchings; and at their return to Paris, introduced them to their tables. Sure I am, the Parisians, both men and women, are strangely altered in their constitutions and habit of body; from lean and slender, they are become fat and corpulent, the women especially: which, in my opinion, can proceed from nothing so much as the daily drinking strong liquors.

Add to these drinks the daily use of coffee with sugar, tea and chocolate, which now is as much in use in private houses in Paris, as with us in London: and these sugar'd liquors also add considerably to their corpulency.

I must not forget that amongst the drinks that are in use in Paris, sider from Normandy is one. The best I drank of that kind, was of the colour of claret, reddish or brown: the apple that it was made of was called *frequins.* which is round and yellow, but so bitter that it is not to be eaten; and yet the sider that is made of it is as sweet as any new wine. It keeps many years good, and mends of its colour and taste. I drank it often at a private house of a Norman gentleman, of whose growth it was; otherwise, if I had not been assured to the contrary, I could not have believed but that it had been mixt with sugar.

There are also very many publick coffee-houses, where tea also and chocolate may be had, and all the strong-waters and wine above-mentioned; and innumerable ale-houses. I wonder at the great change of this sober nation in this particular; but luxury, like a whirlpool, draws into it the extravagancies of other people.

'Twas necessity from the badness of water, and the want of wine, either naturally, as in a great part of Persia and the Indies; or from their religion, as in Turkey, that put men upon the invention of those liquors of coffee and tea: chocolate, indeed, was found out by the poor starv'd Indians, as ale was with us. But what else but a wanton luxury could dispose these people, who abound in excellent wines, the most cordial and generous of drinks, to ape the necessity of others?

Mighty things indeed are said of these drinks, according to the humour and fancy of the drinkers. I rather believe they are permitted by God's Providence for the lessening the number of mankind by shortning life, as a sort of silent plague. Those that plead for chocolate, say it gives them a good stomach, if taken two hours before dinner. Right; who doubts it? You say you are much more hungry, having drunk chocolate, than you had been if you had drunk none; that is, your stomach is faint, craving, and feels hollow and empty, and you cannot stay long for your dinner. Things that pass thus soon out of the stomach, I suspect, are little welcome there, and Nature makes haste to get shut of them. There are many things of this sort, which impose upon us by procuring a false hunger.

The wild Indians, and some of our people, no doubt digest it; but our pampered bodies can make little of it; and it proves to most tender consitutions perfect physick, at least to the stomach, by cleansing that into the guts; but that wears it out, and decays Nature.

It is very remarkable with what greediness the Spaniards drink it, and how often a day, five times says Gage, at least. The women drank it in the churches, and the disorder could scarce be remedied. This shews how little it nourishes.

The old Romans did better with their luxury; they took their tea and chocolate after a full meal, and every man was his own cook in that case. Caesar resolved to be free, and eat and drink heartily; that is, to excess, with Tully; and for this purpose Cicero tells his friend Atticus, that before he lay down to table, *Emeticen agebat*, which I construe, he prepared for himself his chocolate and tea; something to make a quick riddance of what they eat and drank, some way or other.

There are two sorts of water which they drink at Paris: water of the River Seine, which runs through the town; and the water brought in by the aqueduct of Arcueil; which, by the bye, is one of the most magnificent buildings in and about Paris, and worth going to see. This noble canal of hewn stone conveys the water fifteen miles to Paris.

The river water is very pernicious to all strangers, not the French excepted, that come from any distance, but not to the natives of Paris, causing looseness, and sometimes dysenteries. I am apt to think the many ponds and lakes that are let into it to supply the sluces upon the Canal de Briare are in part the cause of it. But those who are careful of themselves purifie it by filling their cisterns with sand, and letting it sink through it; which way clears it, and makes it very cool and palatable.

Monsieur Geofrys hath this caution about the waters of the River Seine (having as a mark of the magistracy he bore, a pipe laid into his court) that he drinks them drained through a great body of sand; that is three foot at least of fine sand in a large cistern. And it is by this means that they drink clear and cool, and no doubt are much more wholsom. The cisterns at Venice are made after this manner; which Sir George Wheeler in his travels hath very particularly well described. . . .

I cannot say that our being Protestants gave us any great trouble in conversation; and even in meeting the Host, which we frequently did, whether a foot, or in coaches, we had no affront put upon us that I know of. Yet in the main, as to religion, I could observe there was a great difference in the tempers of the French nation, from what they were some years ago. Indeed, in the nobility and men of learning I did not much take notice of it; for their genteel manners hid it: but in most of the inferiour people it was most manifest: I mean a certain air of fierceness towards all Protestants, and a scorn and contempt of us. If this humour of bigotry continue, which undoubtedly ow[e]s its beginning from the late persecution which they have made of their brethren and neighbours, and trade not be opened, to take off, by conversation, this growing evil, they will soon distinguish themselves by a new and odious character, and become the common scandal of Europe, as they were once the darling people and school of good breeding. . . .

As to the Palace of Versailles, (which is yet some miles further within the mountainous country, not unlike Black-Heath or Tunbridge) 'tis without dispute the most magnificent of any in Europe. Yet what of it was first built, and much admired thirty years ago, is now no longer relisht. However this king intends to rebuilt it where it is faulty. 'Tis, as I said, plac'd in a very ungrateful soil, without earth proper for herbs, or water; but he hath brought that to it in abundance, and made the ground too to be fruitful.

There are books writ to describe this famous palace in every part; to which I refer the reader. The way to it is new, and in some places the mountains are cut down forty foot, so that now you enjoy it a mile in prospect, before you come to it; it opens and closes in three courts, the more remotest, narrow and narrower; which is a fault; and is, as I was told, designed to be pulled down, and made into one noble large square court of the same order of building as that magnificent front is which looks upon the gardens. The gilded tiles and roof have a marvellous effect in prospect. The splanade towards the gardens and parterres are the noblest things that can be seen, vastly great, with a very large basin of water in the middle, low walled round with white marble, on which are placed a great number of incomparable brazen vasa, and large brass figures *couchant*, of the best masters in sculpture; it were endless to tell all the furniture of these gardens, of marble statues, and vasa of brass and marble; the multitude of fountains, and those wide canals like seas running in a streight line from the bottom of the gardens, as far as the eye can reach.

In a word, these gardens are a country laid out into alleys and walks, groves of trees, canals and fountains, and every where, more especially the chief walks, adorned with ancient and modern statues and vasa innumerable.

May the 17th the waters were ordered to play for the diversion of the English gentlemen. The playing of the spouts of water, thrown up into the air, is here diversified after a thousand fashions. The *Théâtre des eaux* and the Triumphal Arch are the most famous pieces. But in the groves of the left hand, you have Aesop's Fables, in so many pieces of water-works, here and there in winding-alleys. This might have been said to be done *in usum Delphini.* 'Tis pretty to see the owl wash'd by all the birds; the monky hugging her young one, till it spouts out water with a full throat, and open mouth, &c.

The Orangery, or conservatory for tubs of winter greens, is what corresponds to the greatness of the rest. 'Tis a stupendious half square of under-ground vaults, like the naves of so many churches put together, of exquisite workmanship in hewn stone, well lighted and open to the south sun. It contains 3000 cases of greens; whereof near 2000 are orange-trees, and many hundreds of them are as big as generally they naturally grow in the earth. Hence amongst them are some which are said to be in cases from the time of Francis the First.

They did not think fitting to put them out this year till the latter end of May; and indeed the oleanders, laurels, lentiscus's [mastic trees] and most other greens, had suffered miserably.

In the *Pottagerie* (which is part of these gardens, and hath its magnificence also) there are 700 cases of figs, besides wall-fruit of all other kinds. By all the gardens in and about Paris, I perceived they are very fond of this fruit. . . .

After all, it must be said that this magnificence, and the number of these palaces and gardens, are the best and most commendable effect of arbitrary government. If these expences were not in time of peace, what would be this king's riches, and the extream poverty of the people? For it is said that every three years, some say much oftner, he has all the wealth of the nation in his coffers; so that there is a necessity he should have as extravagant and incredible ways of expending it, that it may have its due circulation amongst the people.

But when this vast wealth and power is turned to the disturbance and destruction of mankind, it is terrible; and yet it hath its use too: we and all Europe have been taught, by the industry of this great king, mighty improvements in war; so that Europe has been these twelve years an over-match for the Turk; and we for France by the continuation of the war. The forty millions sterling which the late war hath and will cost England, before all is paid, was well bestowed if it had been for no other end than to teach us the full use and practice of war; and in that point to equal us with our neighbours.

It was observ'd by Polybius of the Romans that wherever they met with an enemy that had better weapons than themselves, they changed with them; this docility gained them the empire of the world. On the contrary, those late Eastern tyrants have despised learning, and consequently must submit to the more refined valour of Europe. I say, the effects of arbitrary government, both in war and peace, are stupendious.

The Roman emperors, because absolute lords of the people, far out-did the commonwealth in magnificent buildings, both publick and private. Augustus left Rome a marble city, which he found of brick only. Nero burnt it and rebuilt it, and a golden palace for himself, like a city. Vespasian and Titus built amphitheatres and baths far surpassing any buildings now upon the face of the earth; in one of which 120,000 persons might see and hear, and be seated with more convenience than upon our stages. [H]Adrian visited most parts of the world, on purpose to build cities. Trajan had his name on every wall, which he either restored, or built. His pillar and bridge over the Danube are stupendious monuments of his expences.

The Aegyptian kings built them monuments, wherein they slaved their whole nation, and which are the wonders of the world to this day, the obelisks I mean, and pyramids.

The Asiatick emperors of China and Japan have outdone the Europeans in this kind of immense buildings, as the wall in China, the cut rivers and sluces and bridges there. In Japan the buildings are no less incredibly great.

Of this absolute dominion we have examples even in those two American empires, of Mexico and Peru. In this last, meer Nature forc'd impossibilities without art, tools, or science. The Cusco fortress was a master-piece, where stones were laid upon stones, which no engine of ours could carry, or raise up; or tools better pollish, and fit together; where a country near as big as all Europe was turned into a garden, and cultivated better than Versailles, and water-works brought to play and overspread some thousands of miles, where it never rains. This was the only arbitrary government well applied to the good of mankind I ever met with in history; where roads and store-houses of food and raiment were the guides, and numbred the miles for the travellers, and the whole Empire turned into an useful and intelligible map.

As for the Turks, Persians, and Mogul, the whole empire is intended solely for the pleasure of one man; and here even tyranny it self is foully abused.

Yet I should be loth to see them in any kind exemplified in England. In our happy island we see such palaces and gardens as are for the health and ease of man only; and what they want in magnificence, they have in neatness. There is not such a thing as a gravel walk in or about Paris, nor a roller of any sort; when it rains the Tuilleries are shut up, and one walks in dirt some days after. The grass-plots, or, as they call them, bowling-greens, are as ill kept: they clip them and beat them with flat beaters as they do their walks. This puts me in mind of what I saw in the garden of the Prince of Condé in Paris; where there was a grassy circle of about four foot wide, round one of the fountains in the middle of the garden; to keep this down and make it of a finer turf, the gardner had teathered two black lambs, and two white kids, at equal distances, which fed upon it. Whatever the effect was, I thought it look'd pretty enough; and the little animals were as ornamental as the grass.

All the paintings and prints made of late years of the King make him look very old; which in my mind is not so; for he is plump in the face, and is well coloured, and seems healthy, and eats and drinks heartily, which I saw him do. This is certainly injury to him, and possibly in complaisance to the Dauphin, or worse. This is the meanest compliment I have known the French guilty of towards their prince; for there are every where expressions of another nature all over Paris. See the *Description of Paris*, where they are collected and at large. The Romans under Augustus, (the first absolute master of that people, as this king is of the French) had upon this subject from the people a much finer thought and wish, "*De nostris annis tibi Jupiter augeat annos.*". . .

32. *Pett's Comparative Religion, Politics, and Economics*

Though extremely naïve and unsystematic, Sir Peter Pett's (1630–1699) *Discourse on the Growth of England* . . . reflected a willingness to examine any and all possible causes of social and economic change. Pett became Advocate General for Ireland and an author of numerous tracts and books, after having been schooled at St. Paul's, London, then Sydney Sussex College, Cambridge, and finally All Souls, Oxford. Though one of the original fellows of the Royal Society when it was founded in 1663, Pett was later expelled.

Pett's familiarity with many of the works written about Continental countries and his willingness to test theories by trying to find pertinent facts wherever possible reflect a quite remarkable detachment from any specific ideological or religious position dominant in his own time. But his unwillingness to go deeper into any problem or to challenge the sources which he quotes reminds us of the other sources, no matter how partisan, which appeared during the seventeenth century.

They who unjustly cry out of the constitution of the Church of England, for interrupting the trade of the kingdom, would be loud enough in their complaints of *omnia comesta à belo* under Popery.

He who knows not that the revenue of the King now depends in a manner solely upon trade, and that trade depends on populous-

SOURCE: Sir Peter Pett, *A Discourse of the Growth of England in Populousness and Trade* . . . (London, 1689), pp. 104–107, 119–120, 248–249.

ness, and that the encouragement of people to live under any government is that great thing call'd property in their estates, religion, and laws, and that therefore anything that calls itself religion, that goes to exterminate above a hundred and fifty persons for every one it leaves (for so the proportion between Non-Papists and Papists by the bishop's survey made about the year 1676, was return'd to be) and to call them hereticks, and which makes their goods and life *ipso facto* a forfeit of the law, will not *ipso facto* exterminate trade, is fitter for the galleys or a trading voyage to the Anticyrae, than for any discourse of trade and commerce.

Your Lordship hath in your travels sufficiently seen it long since exemplified, that the Protestant countries for the quantity of ground exceed the Popish in trade, and numbers of people, and that thus the Protestant Hanse towns have eclipsed their Roman Catholick neighbours, and Amsterdam, Antwerp, and the United Provinces, Flanders, and that in Flanders where the ecclesiasticks are proprietors of seven parts of ten of the whole country, levies of men and money for the defence thereof have been made with so much slowness and difficulty, and been so inconsiderable as not to have secured themselves against invaders.

Nor did the ecclesiasticks there think it worth their while to strain themselves in contributions to resist an invader who is of their own religion (the which made the French King's victories there flie like lightning) more than our over-rich English regulars did oppose William the Conqueror, when he came here under the Pope's banner. And thus were they here, and in Flanders are like wenns in the body which draw to themselves much nourishment and are of great trouble and no use, and thus ridiculous is it that so over great a part of the property of the land should be linked to persons who are no way linked to the interest of the country, more than professed gamesters and empyrics and soldiers of fortune, and are no more damnified by Popish invaders than fishes of the sea are by earth-quakes.

But on the other hand in the United Provinces, how easily and soon are vast taxes raised when their all is at stake, & to what a prodigious encrease of the numbers of their people have they attained since the Reformation? Insomuch that the author of a political discourse of the *Interest of Holland* printed in Dutch in the year 1697, and licensed by John de Witt and by Van Beaumont, makes the people in the province of Holland to be 2 millions and

400 thousand, and so likewise doth Pellenis in his *Learned Notes on Klockius Aerario*, p. 300, and there cites that book of the interest of Holland, when as [whereas] Gerard Malynes in his *Lex Mercatoria* makes the people in Flanders in the year 1622 to have consisted of a hundred and forty thousand families, and he reckoning each of them one with an other at 5 persons, makes the total of the people in Flanders to have then amounted but to seven hundred thousand souls.

And yet as that author of the *Interest of Holland* saith, the province of Holland can hardly make 400 thousand profitable acres or *morgens* of land, down and heath not put in, and that the 8th part of the inhabitants of Holland cannot be nourished with what is growing there: but tells us what prodigious granaries they there have, and that Amsterdam that in the year 1571 was about 200 *morgens* or acres of land, was in the year 1650 enlarged to 600 *morgens* or acres of land in circumference, and to have in it three hundred thousand souls.

And the *Defence of the Zelanders' Choice*, printed in the year 1673, mentions Aitsmas Liere to have reckon'd the publick incomes of Holland alone in the year 1643 to have amounted to 1100 thousand pounds sterling; and the author of the *Interest of Holland* saith that in one year in a time of peace, viz. in the year 1664, the inhabitants of Holland did over and above the customes and other domains of the earls or States of Holland pay towards the publick charge as follows, *viz.*

To the States of Holland, 11 millions of gilders
To the Admiralty of the Maze, 472,898 gilders
To the Admiralty of Amsterdam, 2 millions of gilders
To the Admiralty of the Northern Quarter, 200 thousand gilders

Which comes to in all about 14 hundred, 87 thousand pounds sterling. How meanly do the atchievements of Venice, and their efforts to aggrandize their republick, compared with Holland's shew in story, for the quantity of years many times doubled since the Dutch threw off the yoke of the Papacy! History hath recorded the longevity of the Venetian government as it has of Methusalem, of whom we read, not of any great thing he said, or did, or attempted; but a few days of the short life of Alexander, in the ballance of same weighs down the 999 years of the other.

The very religion of Popery makes the Venetians more narrow in their principles, and even in their rules of traffick than are the inhabitants of Protestant countries. The Popish religion doth hamper its devout professors as to trading with hereticks, and holding communication with such as are *ipso jure* & *ipso facto* excommunicated, and giving any quarentine to men said to be infected with heresie, insomuch that we are told in D'Ossat's *Letters*, Part 2d, that the Republick of Venice would not suffer the ambassador of Henry the 4th to them, because they did not know his master to be reconciled to the See of Rome.

And Bodin de Rep. [Jean Bodin, in *Six Books of the Republic*] says that the number of the inhabitants of Venice was taken Anno 1555, and was then in all but one hundred and eighty thousand and four hundred and forty.

Sir William Temple in the 5th Chapter of his *Observations on the United Provinces*, makes one of the great causes of the first revolt in the Low-Countries to be the oppression of men's consciences, or persecution in their liberties, estates, and lives on the pretence of religion; and it may be truly said that by their buying the truth at the rate of such high taxes as they now pay, and not selling it either to France or Spain, they have been no losers; for many good artists and wealthy fugitives have brought their persons and families and estates to them for shelter, from the storm of Papal persecution, and daily continue so to do; insomuch that the author of *The Zelanders' Choice* in Sect. 3 observes that of late years some of the wise men of the Reformed Religion in France, being fearful of its being there utterly supplanted, have required their children by their last will and testament to leave France and settle themselves in the United Provinces: and in so doing, they bestowed rich legacies on Holland, each head of any new comer being judged to add at a medium 3 £ per year to the riches of the state.

The late great accession of Protestant strangers to Amsterdam, hath caused many new houses to be there built, and hath raised the rents of the old ones a 5th part, whereas they are sunk a 4th in Cheapside in London.

'Tis there that men of every nation under Heaven, Parthians, and Arabians, Jews, Papists, Calvinists, Lutherans, and the Christians of the subdivisions of all sects do hear men speak in their own language, and what they think most musical to them, the wonderful works of God.

Nor are the enemies to Monarchy to ascribe the flourishing state of Holland to its former throwing the power of the State-holder, and Captain General out of the ballance of their government. Their breaking down the banks of his authority, introduced the sudden inundation of the French power among them, that they had else been more secured against than the assaults of the ocean, and not have so perfectly forgot the art and nature of defensive war in their frontiers: and thô it may seem plausible that an animal, supposed to have most heads, will have most brains, and that republicks are more apprehensive of their true interest than other governments, yet to the reproach of such politicks it appear'd that when the regnant faction in Holland were no more headed by a Captain General or State-holder, and had thrown the poise of his power out of the scales, they grew so vain, as thô they had no capital ships, yet to becôme aggressors in a naval war against England, that had ships enow [enough] of that kind to affright the world, and of which war the result was the abolishing their great navigation to England, from whence their forced frequenting of our harbours still occasions their exporting more of our commodities than we import of theirs. But this by the way.

However so vast yet is their navigation, and the number of their mariners that thô we need them not for our carriers, both Spain and France do: and to which kingdoms they have and probably will for some ages to come, have the honour and profit to be carriers, how much soever France is or seems to be fear'd by us: and thus that book of the *Interest of Holland* tells us, *viz.* that the French have very few ships and marriners of their own, so that almost all their traffick for Holland (some few English ships of trade excepted) is driven by Dutch ships, and that when any goods are transported from one French haven to another, they are laden on board Dutch vessels, and that as to Spain, that it hath so few marriners and ships that since the peace between them and Holland, they have used to hire Dutch ships to sail to the Indies.

And therefore when I consider what that ingenious author hath thus discoursed, and that Sir W. P. in a manuscript discourse in the year 167½ [*sic*], hath calculated the number of the total of the seamen, who are subjects of France to be 15,000, and that a great and fatal diminution of the number of them since happen'd in the year 1678, by so many of their then perishing under D'Estre [d'Estrées] in the West Indies, and that as the author of *Britannia languens* saith, "The Dutch have at least 10 times as many seamen as the English," I shall venture to conclude that more than all the millions of mankind now living will be dissolved to ashes before (humanly speaking) it will be possible for France to over-ballance either the Dutch or English at sea, and whoever they are that pretend to fear the contrary, I think they do but pretend to fear it.

But at once to return to the consideration of the gain Holland hath from fresh *advenae* [arrivals], and to take my leave of it, all old trades being there fully improved, such newcomers are forced to dig up a new soile of trade and industry, as I may call it, for their subsistance; and thus at the charge of their experiments the country is enriched: and many new artists there bring with them their old experimented arts, and thus 'tis known that an English-man from Yarmouth coming to be an inhabitant among them, taught them the rich *arcanum* [secret] of the fishing trade: and since they disused to pray to dead saints in the way of Popery, they have found living saints praying to them to be admitted to live with them, and have not only had the honour to entertain saints, but "by being not forgetful to entertain strangers, they have unawares entertain'd angels" (as the Scripture expression is) and such who have proved *tutelar* ones to their country and religion.

No marvel therefore if the learned divine, the author of the *Defence of the Zelanders' Choice*, doth there so pathetically pronounce his opinion, that if ever the Protestant religion shall leave Holland, that country may be called Icabod, i.e., "the glory is departed from it."

And here I should be injurious to the political energy of the Reformation in England, if I should not observe how vastly it has contributed to the encrease of the value of our land, and the number of the people and the extent of our commerce, and indeed of commerce it self.

It was not long before the Reformation that the kings and people of England maintained themselves chiefly by sheperdry, and the kings and people of France by tillage, and their great improvement in manufacture, bears date but from Harry the 4th's time. The great scene of merchandizing was not open'd in Europe till about 6 or 7 hundred years ago, and till then none were there worthy the names of merchants except some few in the republicks of Italy, who lived in the Mediterranean parts trading with the Indian caravans in the Levant, or driving some inland trade, and then and some hundreds of years afterward, the nations in the worst soil of Europe being the greatest breeders, and having superfluity of nothing but people, had no invention for living but by being murderers and by the boysterous trade of fighting their way into better quarters: and during that dark and iron age that produced herds of men void of knowledge, there was nothing in humane conversation or discourse valuable; and in our European world it was scarce worth men a few steps to gain one another's acquaintance: but on the gradual increase of knowledge there, men found a readier way at once with delight and profit to exchange notions and commodities of traffick, and the Protestant religion at last drawing up the curtain that kept all things obscure on that stage of the world, men being better taught the knowledge of the God of Nature and of Nature it self, were grown worth one another's knowledge, and were for the surprising brightness of their intellectual talents gazed on by the wondring world, like in machines, gods coming down out of clouds, and it was worthy of the bounty of Heaven, then to spread on the earth the commerce of men and the medium of commerce too, and to allow them to converse together with more splendor by the donative of the American mines when the dawn of the knowledge a little before that of the Reformation had rendered them conversable creatures, and fit for the interviews of one another: and shortly afterwards by a mighty encrease of navigation, many did pass to and fro, and knowledge was more and more encreased. . . .

We are told by the observator on the Bills of Mortality* that anxiety of mind hinders breeding, and from sharp anxieties of divers kinds hath the Protestant religion rescued English minds, and from their former daily yariness for their daily bread, and their fears of being arbitrarily dispossest of it. What princes (as I may say) are the English infantry, and even the boors of Holland to the peasants of France, who with chains on do propagate their species,

* In an earlier reference to this work, Pett comments: "The thanks of the Age are due to the observator on the Bills of Mortality, for those solid and rational calculations he hath brought to light, relating to the numbers of our people" (p. 112).

and servitude it self? And what pity was it that commerce which with its infant smiles cheer'd our isle in the reign of Edward the 6th, was almost frighted away from it by the frowns and arbitrary practices of Queen Mary; and that after that Edward the 6th consulting the advancement of our trade had legally suppressed the Corporation of Merchant-Strangers, and null'd their monopoly; Queen Mary endeavour'd the suppression of our native merchants, and that too by illegal impositions. It is not denyable that in the fourth year of her reign she did lay an impost upon our cloth: and one who had been a judge of the realm, and who had no spight to her story, mentioning it in his book call'd *The Rights of the People Concerning Impositions*, saith there, "This religious prince [i.e., Mary] inviron'd with infinite troubles in the Church and Commonwealth, and impovrish'd by her devotion in renouncing the profits of the Church lands that were in the Crown, was the first that made digression from the steps of her worthy progenitors, in putting on the imposition without assent of Parliament:" and the same author on pag. 91 mentions another unjust imposition of hers on Gascoyn [Bordeaux] wines.

And her expulsion of the Dutch Church and their pastors from London, and her canselling of the legal priviledges that Edward the 6th (for himself, his heirs and successors) gave them and other strangers by his letters patents, was an arbitrary blow given to the trade of the kingdom in general, and of that city in particulars; the copy of her proclamation for the expelling them is printed in Fox,* in which they are stiled, "A multitude of evil disposed persons being born out of Her Highness's Dominions in other sundry nations, flying from the obeysance of the princes and rulers, under whom they be born, some for heresie, some for murther, treason, robbery," and are further represented as such, "whose secret practices have not fail'd to stir His Highness's subjects to a rebellion against God and Her Grace, &c." But secret traitors they were found by the realm, and secret they were left by it. Two of them were John a Lasco, uncle to the King of Poland, and Peter Martyr, that were thus sent out of the realm with *sanbenitos* [sackcloth] on: and so far were our Popish ancestors from hospitality to strangers, and thereby unawares entertaining angels, that they

* John Foxe (1516–1587), author of the famous *Book of Martyrs*.

made devils of them, and as such used them: and to make amends to the multitude of forraign artists for the gold they brought here, they had the dirt of shams thrown at them by a proclamation.

And as if not only the biting, but the very barking of mad doggs had power to make others mad, she grew so enraged by the books of heresie and sedition, printed in forraign parts and here imported, that she publish'd a proclamation printed likewise in Fox, wherein she declared to all her subjects that, "Whoever shall after the proclaiming hereof be found to have any of the said wicked and seditions books, or finding them do not forthwith burn the same without shewing or reading the same, shall in that case be reputed and taken for a rebel, and shall without delay be executed for the offence according to the order of martial law."

But nothing can palliate the arbitrariness of Queen Mary's proclamation, for the exercising of martial law, but that she thought her reign a time of war, and perhaps not altogether improperly; for that hereticks have the title of hostes given them by Popish masters of ceremonies.

There was another reason that induced Queen Mary to use the arbitrary power that her Popish predecessors did not, and that is this: the people of England in the days of Popery were like to the three fools in Lipsius, that being ty'd together by a twine thread, went whining about the house, and consenting that they who would unty the knots of it should have what money from them they pleas'd: and thus were our foolish ancestors innodated with Papal censures, and the priests did but arbitrarily ask and have their rewards to absolve them. But that Queen finding that the Reformation begun had proved physick to cure those idiots of their dull stupidity, she therefore supposed that the fools who before were held by the twine thread, must then be bound to the good behaviour with chains. . . .

As to the former unconcernedness of France in preserving or encreasing the numbers of its people, there is an observation of Sir Thomas Culpeper, Knight, in his *Discourse* about usury where he saith, France "tho so good a soyle lies half of it waste, the natives even loathing their own country, and burdening all the habitable world with their beggarly colonies, one third of the lacqueys and valets in Europe being French men." Witness Dr. Heylin who tells us, that "once at Madrid they banished them all as dangerous for their numbers, finding the French servants in that town alone to exceed thirty thousand, so just and natural is it for oppression to disarm it self."

But I have already mentioned it that the present great French monarch, not more renowned for his *armaforis* then his *consilium domi*, and his able counsellors there, doth by accurate measure, study the encrease of his people, and 'tis very remarkable that in the *Code Loüys* which he published in April 1667, he made some ordinances with great care for the registring the christenings and marriages and burials in each parish in his realm, as appears by title 20, article 8, 9, 10, 11, 12, 13, 14, there from p. 107 to 112, and with much more exactness then the Bills of Mortality in our metropolis are ordered, and the which that great prince thought worthy to be enjoyned in his Code of Laws, having perhaps been informed by his ministers that many political inferences as to the knowing the numbers of people and their encrease in any state are to be made from the Bills of Mortality, on the occasion of some such published about 3 years before by the observator on the Bills of Mortality in England, and where thô many are apt to think that the registring of the births of people was first used and invented by [Thomas] Cromwell, in Harry the 8th's time; yet is the thing as old as the ancient times of the Romans. . . .

But what was worthy of the French King's providing for the stability of his throne, he further ordered an exact registry to be took of the numbers of his half subjects, I mean the regulars and seculars [clergy] by the following articles there, namely the 15th, 16th, 17th in that title.

Mr. Samuel Pepys, the great treasurer of naval and maritime knowledge, and of that great variety of the learning which we call *recondita eruditio*, having communicated to me the sight of a paper mentioning that in the whole number of men in the realm of Spain, long since when by secret survey, there were returned a 11 hundred and 25 thousand and 3 hundred and 90 men, (and which secret survey I suppose was made some time before the year 1588) I observed that the number of the regular and seculary clergy was not included in that survey.

But I think the numbring of the many regulars there who (no doubt) so often say in their hearts, *Nos numerus sumus* &c, had been of as much importance to the government, as the numbering of the lay-men, and for the number of which the *Code Loüys* hath as aforesaid so carefully provided, and thereby made the prudence of this French King's *Code* outweight Justinian's, and hath discovered to the world the acuteness of his understanding, to be not inferior to that of his sword. And the expences of the Crown being under the government of this monarch so very much greater than in his father's time, have necessarily occasioned such an exact knowledge of the numbers and wealth of his realm, as hath provided him his strong sinews for war.

33. Language and Particularism

In the seventeenth century, thousands of different dialects and languages separated the European peoples into groups and identities much smaller than the areas delineated by present national and linguistic boundaries. Dialects often extended only to a valley or a few villages, or to one major town and its *contado;* some languages were more like constellations of dialects, while Provençal, Welsh, Flemish, Breton, and Catalan flourished in entire provinces or small kingdoms.

The history of the relationship between European languages and cultural-political identities has received decreased attention from historians since the decline in studies of nationalism after World War II. But the recent interest in popular culture, in the thought and ways of living of the millions of predominantly illiterate peasants, artisans, and others nearly at the level of economic subsistence in the seventeenth century, will inevitably lead to a revival of studies in the history of language in general.

The preface to Thomas Jones's dictionary of Welsh and English contains many interesting clues to the conception which at least one "Briton" had of the relationship of a minority culture and language to a more powerful nation. By evoking the historical "Brittains," Jones accepts a measure of unity for the island (excluding Ireland?), but he was clearly worried about the corruption of and loss of Welsh. For that purpose he prepared his dictionary. With the decline of Welsh, Jones felt that other particularisms and customs would be lost as well.

To languages as well as dominions (with all other things under the sun) there is an appointed time; they have had their infancy, foundations and beginning, their growth and increase in purity and

SOURCE: Thomas Jones, *The British Language in its Lustre, or a copious Dictionary of Welsh & English* (London, 1688), Preface.

perfection; as also in spreading and propagation: their state of consistency; and their old age, declinings and decayes.

And thus it pleased the Almighty to deal with us, the Brittains; for these many ages hath eclipsed our power, and corrupted our language, and almost blotted us out of the Books of Records: We know that we are, and that we had a beginning; but if we take it upon us to manifest our geneology, we shall be opposed by variety of opinions, and authors; yea and are ready to quarrel amongst ourselves about our pedigree: certainly the greatness of our sins was the cause of our confusion; yet let us be contented, and make it our business to study the performance of our duty towards God and man; and shew our obedience and loyalty to those princes and powers which God was pleased to set over us.

We are now as happy as any subjects in the three kingdoms, and want nothing but the perfection of our original tongue, and for that want, we may thank ourselves: we had not known the want of it, had we kept it when we had it. We have made too much use of new fashions (in our speaking) to retain our mother tongue, which might before now extirpate our antiquity, had not some faithful lovers of our language planted small pillars of this nature to support it in times past.

IV

The Battle for Europe

Louis XIV never hoped to conquer the entire European land mass, nor did he seek to impose French culture on the peoples who came under his power. His aims were clearly more modest than those of the more national conquerors seen in Europe since Napoleon, but they were nevertheless grandiose for the seventeenth century. Only the Hapsburgs had previously sent soldiers all over Europe for such high stakes; Louis XIV was the heir to Philip II of Spain and Emperor Ferdinand II in more than blood.

In studying French foreign policy of the seventeenth century, attention to minute details should never be permitted to blot out the long-range objectives. Indeed, these objectives remained remarkably constant and easy to recognize. After Richelieu had gained complete control of foreign policy in 1630, his objectives soon became the recognition of the House of Bourbon as the highest, most honored, and most powerful in Europe. The details were then put simply: defend all the "rights" of that house in Italy, Flanders, and the Rhineland, as well as insist that all lesser powers more or less become satellites of France. The Sun King, who learned more from Richelieu's great pupil, Cardinal Mazarin, than he realized, would have found little to add to these forthright but ominous objectives. Along with them came a high degree of persistence and downright stubbornness, for not even the frightful weaknesses created by the Fronde forced Mazarin to bow to the Spanish Hapsburgs. This stubbornness of purpose in aggrandizing the House of Bourbon would persist as long as Louis XIV breathed. What the Sun King added, however, was a kind of bombast in French foreign policy. Neither Richelieu nor Mazarin, nor even Lionne, Louis' first foreign minister, would lecture Europe and issue ultimatums to her other sovereigns in the way Louis did after 1666. This bombast resulted as much from previous success as from the changed character of public opinion in court and in city circles. Yet at Louis XIV's zenith, his conduct is reminiscent of Emperor Ferdinand in 1629, for in reaching for too much each laid the foundations for his own setbacks. The important thing to note is that in substance the objectives of French foreign policy would have changed very little had Richelieu still been in control in 1680, or Mazarin in 1715. This continuity is remarkable, and there is considerable evidence to suggest that astute observers and sovereigns throughout Europe recognized this.

The second aspect of the question is whether Louis XIV himself differed markedly in character from the other European sovereigns he combated. That the battle for Europe was seen in some respects as a personal duel, first between Leopold and Louis, and later between Louis and William III, owes its origins to propagandists who presented the war in that way. In seeking spectacular victories, especially in the 1680's and 1690's, Louis and William themselves seem quite aware of the battle as a duel in which each sought to humble the other so that he would have to sue for peace. The result was the recognition that, as a king, Louis was really not different from other kings, except that he seemed to be more powerful. Had Emperor Leopold been King of France, would the battle for Europe have been much different? The same might be asked for the Swedish, the Spanish, and even the last Stuart King. Again the German princes seemed to differ from Louis XIV in power and not in conduct. Only William III may have conceived of kingship and Europe in terms radically different from those of his peers, but even here the similarities were probably greater than William's Dutch and English subjects ever realized.

It would be interesting to attempt to measure statistically what Louis XIV thought about most, less, and least, hour after hour, day after day, and year after year in his long reign. What would be the percentage of thought about diplomacy and war, internal affairs, his own salvation, the court, his mistresses, and the future? Were it possible to measure the mental preoccupations of Louis XIV, and then compare them with those of William III, Emperor Leopold, and Charles XII of Sweden, among others, historians could determine roughly the priorities of the state, at least as sovereigns conceived of them. But we will never know what was going on in Louis' mind as he walked through the gardens of Versailles, listened to sermons (a brief moment of calm reflection in the day?), hunted, or otherwise diverted himself. Nor will we know the content of the nightmares which increasingly afflicted him later in life; and unlike psychoanalysts, confessors did not write down the details told them by those who sought their help. But one thing is clear: Louis worked hard at the business of state. If we measured only the number of hours spent with ministers in discussing reports, drafts of letters, appointments, and so on, we would probably find that none of his contemporary sovereigns, nor anyone since Philip II of Spain, spent so much time on affairs of state. At the same time, it is evident that Louis did not spend so much time governing because he was slow to understand affairs. It was rather his passion, even his compulsion, to do his *devoir* which made him work, for in the seventeenth century men and women of every rank had a specific sense of what their roll was. Louis' was to govern, and he took this seriously.

As with other sovereigns, however, diplomacy and war, not internal politics, remained Louis XIV's central preoccupation. A famine here, a quarrel among judges there, deficits, ecclesiastical disputes were all worthy of the King's attention; but at times they seemed no more important to him than hiring workers to finish the gardens at Marly or commissioning the history of his reign. Only Europe, and France's place in it, as well as the status of the House of Bourbon and the fate of French diplomats, warships, and armies transcended the lesser occupations and commanded the unrelenting attention of the Sun King.

Together the European sovereigns shared common conceptions of prestige and power. These bore traditional names, and men in the seventeenth century probably did not realize how greatly these measurements had actually changed. "Lands," or *pays*, by tradition, had meant feudal holdings, revenues from customs, and so on; but after 1648 they came to be considered as part of a centralized state. The administration of provinces by intendants made the royal presence felt in the most remote provinces as it had never been before, though one is reminded of the viceroys and corregidors of Philip II. A "land" thus ceased to be merely a part of an estate; it became increasingly part of a centralized state under Colbert's and Louis' direction. Similarly, the taking of a castle had counted for much in war since the year 1000, but now the massive fortifications built by Vauban and his imitators unlocked access to entire regions of Europe, and no longer simply to a "land." Even the feudal aspects of marriages between sovereigns, the rendering of homage, and the presence of kings with their armies on the battlefield concealed more than they characterized in the substance and definition of power. A good example of this is the partition treaties which Louis and William arranged in an attempt to solve the problem of the Spanish succession before the death of Charles II. There is a dynastic basis to these treaties, but in reality both kings sought some sort of partition vaguely involving a balance of power. And yet ancient forms still counted. When Louis refused to recognize William as King of England and kept referring to him personally as "the Prince of Orange," William felt the intended prick of instability and inferiority.

From the beginning, the great Dutch statesman John de Witt had a premonition of the coming battle for Europe and had described it in these terms:

> The two great powers of France and Spain have up to now kept in balance the interests of all the European princes. [But at present with Spain being weak], it is impossible for the equality which divided Europe over such a long period of years to continue after the King of Spain's death. [France] has a twenty-six-year-old king, vigorous of body and mind, who knows himself and acts on his own, who possesses a realm peopled with an extremely bellicose nation with really considerable wealth. [It would be necessary for this king] to show extraordinary and almost miraculous moderation to divest himself of the ambition which is so natural to all princes, for him not to extend his frontiers in the direction where they are the most limited and where France has always been the most disadvantaged by her enemies.[1]

De Witt was in a position to know what was happening. He feared the future, and yet possessed the courage to struggle with the problem. The rise of French power, just as much as the decline of Spanish power, was a fact. As this gradually came to be recognized, the place of England in European affairs became increasingly important. It is for that reason that the assessments of English and French power given by contemporaries are emphasized in these documents.

1. From E. Lavisse, *Histoire de France* (Paris, 1906), VII², 281.

34. *Leibnitz's Advice to Louis XIV*

While in the service of the elector of Mainz, Gottfried Leibnitz (1646–1716) advised diplomats and wrote numerous confidential memoranda designed to help maintain peace in Europe. His *Project for the Conquest of Egypt* (1672) is not only an assessment of the nature of states in Europe, but also an attempt to divert the expansionist energies of France away from Europe itself. If Louis proceeded according to Leibnitz's plan, would not the Rhineland, where Mainz was located, avoid the arrival of French troops? Arnauld de Pomponne, Louis' secretary of state for foreign affairs, invited Leibnitz to Paris; but the *Project* failed to impress the Sun King, who never deigned to receive its author at Versailles. Still, the definitions of power and more particularly Leibnitz's discussion of the relationships between the power of the state, religion, commerce, and so forth make the *Project* extremely interesting as an example of how one of the leading thinkers of the age looked at the problems of international affairs.

V. Until now I have recounted only what I might call the *history of my plan*, going back to the most ancient sources. These are my dreams, if you wish; but I wanted to reproduce the deliberations and the judgments of the wisest men on the subject of an expedition into Egypt. Scarcely noted until now, these things made me reflect all the more and struck me all the more profoundly, when I read them, because this question was then engrossing me more intensely. Now we must return to the very heart of the matter, at which time I believe I can show that an expedition into Egypt is: 1. the most infallible means of assuring one's preponderance; 2. that it is easy, considering the vastness of the undertaking, and especially for the Most Christian King; 3. that it presents no danger; 4. that it is in accordance with the current course of events; 5. that it ought no longer be delayed; lastly, that it should be undertaken in the interest of the human species, of the Christian religion, and, which amounts to the same thing, that it is in con-

SOURCE: Gottfried Wilhelm Leibnitz, *Oeuvres* (Paris: Didot, 1864), V, 42–47, 252–255.

formity with the divine will, that it is just, pious, and hence, that it will be successful.

VI. Preponderance, in other words France's chief concern, is a power such as she might reasonably desire, which she is permitted to hope for, and which is not chimerical.

This will not be, I repeat, a universal monarchy, today less than ever possible among Christians, but a general administration or a sort of arbitration of things. To desire to conquer by military might nations which are civilized, but at the same time bellicose and impassioned for their liberty, as are today almost all of the European nations, would be an undertaking no less ridiculous than sacrilegious. Everyone knows that a good many German emperors ruined themselves in sterile efforts to succeed in dominating in Italy alone, which, however, is not an immense country. Yet how rapidly the fruits of victory evaporated in the hands of Charles VIII and Louis XII! While on the subject of Germany, the great Oxenstierna used to say privately, concerning the liberty of that country [Italy], which Austria then boasted about subjugating, that it was a completely mad claim, when Italy had so many fortified cities, so many mountains, so many rivers, so many illustrious families, and that in the end everything would crumble under the invaders' feet. Indeed, one is forced to have simultaneously several armies in position; when calm seems reestablished in one place, war is rekindled at another; one runs to where the danger is observed, and at the same instant similar agitation occurs elsewhere. Charles Gustavus [Charles X of Sweden], in Poland and in Denmark, was able to test this truth, that in the heart of Christian Europe the conquest of a kingdom is almost impossible, or, if it is possible, is not lasting, everyone finding it to his interest to unite to prevent an event whose consequences are so harmful to the general peace. The treaty, called of the Hague, among France, England, and the Confederate States, concluded at the moment when Denmark was at bay, is an example of this truth for conquerors. Conquests which may result from war between Christian states are of necessity limited to unimportant fractions of territory; those who formulate the most daring plans, and carry out their realization with most perseverance, can scarcely harvest some palpable fruit: for it is a truth of elementary experience that every power which extends its boundaries awakens the suspicions of the others and unites them all against it. Whence it follows that a king aiming at great things, as is the Most Christian King, must—in his wisdom—avoid as much as possible such a manner of increasing his power. To take that road to domination is to assign limits to oneself, to mark for oneself in advance an inflexible *nec plus ultra*, and to gamble the highest and most solidly based hopes for meager results. Those acquisitions which are made with the most ease and gentleness, whose ownership is the most tranquil and the most assured, are those which result from elections, inheritances, and marriages which prepare them. Thus the House of Austria grew, thus the House of Bourbon will increase if it does not stray from the line of conduct it has followed to this day. But since this manner of profiting depends on the fate of other families, to base one's calculations on these eventualities is to desire to attract hatred to oneself and to run risks. Thus, since the diverse means of aggrandisement are: war, inheritance, election, a prudent internal administration of the realm, trade, manufactures, military maneuvers, improvement of the laws and the reign of justice, everything which makes subjects happy, finally authority, that is to say love, then the fear which one inspires in foreigners by the opinion which one creates of one's wisdom and of one's power through alliances, arbitration, protectorates, it is evident that successions and elections depend upon chance; but it is thanks to internal reforms that the security of the monarch and the public good are strengthened. The Christian states will cultivate competitively the arts of peace; trade treaties, industry, maritime commerce are the sole sorts of rivalry appropriate to them. Let France, I agree, rise above the other nations, but let her turn her arms uniquely against barbarians. Finish that war in one fell swoop, as is in the character of the French nation, so that an expedition of this sort seems natural to her; topple and found empires there where failure itself will cause neither fears nor dishonor; there where there is incredible glory to win, and where one can lay the foundations of great power; there where the applause of everyone must follow you, and where the jealous will neither dare nor can oppose you, and the Most Christian King will be proclaimed head or general of the Christians, France will be proclaimed the school of Europe, the academy of illustrious minds, the marketplace of the Ocean and of the Mediterranean. And if we seek honor, indisputable prerogative, the titles and rights of the Emperor of the Orient, usurped by the Turks, will return (they already had them under Baudoin at the time of the Empire of

Constantinople), they will return, we say, to the French, as well as the universal arbitration of affairs more desirable in the eyes of wise men than monarchy. While Europe is at peace, the prosperity of France increases; let her begin a war inopportunely, we shall see her decline at once. As far as trade is concerned, France's very rivals recognize that every year, everything considered, her profits surpass theirs by several million, and she will not lose favor for her manufacture work, if she does not, through unfortunate greed, force the others to conspire against her, not only through alliances but through trade regulations.

On the contrary, an untimely war in Europe, undertaken in particular against the maritime nations, could bring about the ruin of French trade and of the companies founded at such great expense, newborn, not having had time to take root, and thus very easy to topple; such a great misfortune would cast immense discouragement into spirits, and several centuries would scarcely suffice to put them aright. Moreover, a naval war is particularly subject to the caprices of chance, and the most clairvoyant cannot promise any very certain results. But once war is declared upon the barbarians, one must attack Egypt. As for trying something big in America, not only the Spaniards, under whose protection it is placed, but also the Dutch and the English would not allow it, since it is in the interest of them all for things to remain in the state they are now in. One might say almost the same about other undertakings. One could call upon Christians in vain; one would only gain a few allies. On the contrary, none would dare oppose a war against the Turk, as I will show later; even more, many, I shall prove, will concur. If Egypt is invaded, this war, which will have the character, the results, the consequences of a sacred war, which will be applauded as one, will be even more useful than any other, undertaken for a purely human goal: and we shall have conquered not merely Palestine, that desert country which is no longer peopled but by its ruins, but Egypt, the ornament of the earth, the mother of fruits, the center of trade. . . .

XLVI. I have shown clearly enough, I believe, that we can undertake in complete safety an expedition into Egypt; I now pass to the opportune time for it to take place. We should carry out this expedition now, first because circumstances are favorable and because a propitious occasion will perhaps never present itself again. I must thus prove two things: first, that the planned expedition will obtain the approval of all Frenchmen; and second, that if we allow this opportunity to escape, it will perhaps never return. The expedition into Egypt is in accordance with the destinies of the King and of Christendom; the feelings of France and the very actions of the King show it sufficiently. Moreover, this stems, I believe, from the debates and the speeches which have already been made since this question came under discussion. Thus it will suffice if I say a few words on the most salient points and throw them into relief by a parallel.

XLVII. France is called to become the arbiter in the Levantine trade. Egypt is the center of this trade. Once masters of Egypt, we will have gained more in one year than by all our slow undertakings on Madagascar. France desires the ruin of Holland; but Holland will be conquered in Egypt where she cannot defend herself. The fable tells how Meleager's mother, indignant with her son, plunged her unfortunate offspring into the glowing flames and burned out his entrails. A fire as devouring as that one will be lighted in the hearts of the Dutch, and they will go elsewhere to seek food for that flame by opening a more direct route toward India.

France wishes to be the first among nations: well! she will acquire the title Queen of the Orient which she has so much right to seek. France, not content to be called the elder daughter of the Church, would further like a title which is now the appanage of the Emperor. (Those are, moreover, only specious names which push us into many undertakings under religious pretexts.) Here is the opportunity to acquire these two titles and to earn the applause and the approbation of everyone, by waging a war a hundred times more useful than all the wars undertaken for a sacred or profane motive, a war which Machiavelli would approve, Machiavelli who laughed at all sacred things and whose fundamental axiom says that one must hide the profane and the useful under the appearances of the sacred and the honest.

Certainly, religion can indeed play a great role in an undertaking, even when the fruits of that very undertaking would be doubled by the profane advantages resulting from it. In the Church it is indeed permitted to earn one's living from the altar; he who serves at the altar is indeed right in searching for both public interests and his private interests, always combining justice and wisdom. France is thinking of making the authority of the Church in Rome prosper, of reforming abuses and removing taxes. How will she arrive at this result more easily than by sheltering all of Italy from the ruin which threatens it, and above all by becoming absolute mistress of the Mediterranean? I do not know whether France has her eyes on the German Empire; but if such is the case, is there a more efficient means of attracting public affection than by fighting for the Church, for the Empire, and for the Emperor? If the King has the ambition to become the arbiter of the world, a goal toward which a wise monarch ought to strive, is there a surer way than to become more powerful than everyone else, to be the judge who settles all disagreements, to attract the entire world to himself, not only by his reputation for power, but also by his reputation for wisdom, to sacrifice odious details to the public peace, to make France into a sort of military school for Europe from which come forth illustrious warriors, to seduce the great families and the great geniuses by furnishing them with the means to unfurl their talents, finally, to be the avenger of outraged justice, the head of Christendom, the delight of Europe, and of mankind, to be showered with honors and to enjoy in his lifetime the reputation which he will have earned? A vast quarry opens here before the eloquent man, but I detest long, tortuous phrases. I have shown and shed light on what I shall call the nerves of the thing, and I do not wish to go into the consequences; for enlightened men who have talent for writing will easily complete what I have omitted saying. There is not one of the points which I have dealt with in this paragraph which does not merit a chapter, or rather an entire book, if one wishes to treat it as it should be treated. Indeed, one will see a multitude of noteworthy actions present themselves. But I am limited by time; I said, moreover, at the beginning of my discourse, that I would not enter into the minute details for each item, but that I would however furnish enough to persuade and to prove. Certainly, once the thing is done, poets and panegyrists will not be lacking. . . .

35. *The Siege of Vienna and the Struggle for European Dominance*

Whether French armies could have defeated the Turks had Vienna fallen to them in 1683 was the sort of question armchair strategists and generals alike asked once the crisis was over. The following anonymous text reflects a quite dispassionate analysis of international relationships in the late seventeenth century. Neither morals nor religion, but power and "interest," preoccupy the author, which may account for the fact that the work was published anonymously.

Some perhaps will . . . retort that though Vienna had been taken by the Turks, there was no great fear of his further progress into Germany: Because Lewis the King of France surnamed the Great for the things he has done already, would oppose him in such a case with a puissant army, and force him back again to the great loss of the Turks, and his own immortal glory.

This indeed would be great in Lewis the Great; and in truth in such a conjuncture of affairs he would be the only prince of Europe in a capacity to stop the progress of such a potent enemy. But first, we may justly question whether he would in such a case be willing, or not, till such time as he were forced to it, for his own defence. For every one knows that knows anything, that clipping the wings of the Austrian eagle (or House of Austria) will extremely add to the splendour of the French monarchy. Whilst then the Turks were invading Germany on the one side, would not both self-preservation, honour and interest invite the French King to be busy on the other? And divide perhaps Germany with the Turks, since in all likelihood he could do no better. Yea this it seems, might prove his only expedient to put himself in a condition to oppose afterwards the Turkish fury by seizing first upon the neighbouring strong holds and cities of Germany, as not being able to defend themselves. Would not he be then strangely tempted to

SOURCE: *The Present State of the German and Turkish Empires*, by D. A., M.D. (London, 1684), pp. 38–44, 78, 1–5, 7–10, 13–22, 25–51.

attack Philipsburg, Mayence, Spire, Manem [Mannheim], Herminstean, &c. rather than suffer such places to fall into the hands of the Turks; or defend 'em for the Germans, from whom perhaps he would scarce get thanks, and who might prove afterward his mortal enemies. He has been hovering these many years over Millan, Genoa, Flanders, Holland, and threatening England too afar off. The good success of the Turks in Germany would present him with the fittest occasion can be imagined, for such interprises. And if it may be feared, as things now stand, that Flanders will have much ado to escape him; in such a conjuncture, there had been no hopes of saving it from the French yoak. Flanders oweth the remaining part of its liberties to the forces of Germany, who obliged the French to withdraw the best part of their troops from Flanders.

All Europe knows into what extream distress the States of Holland were brought by the French King's first and second campaign against the Hollanders: And had Germany been invaded by the Turks, the lillies [emblem of the French monarchy] perhaps had ere now taken such deep roots in Holland, that it had not been easy (to say no more) to pull them out again. But as Germany was then in peace with the Turks, the Emperour united all the German princes together, for their common interest, and set on foot in the beginning of winter, an army of near 40,000 horse and food, under the command of Muntecuculy [Montecucculi], who at his first arrival besieged, and took in by surrender the city of Bonn, belonging to the Bishop of Cullen [Cologne]. The good success whereof occasioned a great change in the affairs of Holland. For then the French thought it no longer secure for them to remain there, and deserted on a sudden the cities they had taken in it partly by force; partly by a free surrender, so that after having caused the citizens to redeem their liberties with great sums of mony the French retreated from their new conquests, which they have never done, if the forces of Germany had been diverted by a Turkish invasion.

Great Britain I grant if in peace at home may prove always a sufficient protection for Holland, and the Low Countries. Yet in case there had been no hopes of help, or diversion from Germany, by reason of the Turks' invading it, France by the advantage of the neighbourhood, and so many strong cities it possesseth, in the Low Countries, had in all appearance swallowed up that small remainder of the Netherlands, belonging to the Spaniards, before England could be in a readiness to relieve them. Now the Spanish towns being once conquered, by the French, Holland would either submit to the yoak upon fair conditions, or could but make a very feeble resistance. So that their only safety in such a desperate case would be an intire submission to the King of England, and so acknowledge him as their prince and sovereign. Which would engage him to defend 'em with the same zeal he would defend England itself.

Out of all this discourse, we may gather that although the French King were able alone to beat the Turks out of Germany, in case they had succeeded in their designs; it's not certain whether he would have been willing to do it, at least till he had been himself possest of the best part of Germany, of Flanders and Holland likewise; Which some of these people would perhaps have no less willingly bore, than the slaveries under the Turkish yoak: So great is their aversion to the French subjection. But let us invert the medal, and take another view of Germany. I assert that if Vienna had been taken, it had not been easy for the French to hinder the Turks, from overpowering Germany, yea and France too, within a shorter time then we do perhaps imagine. How unhappy then would this dissatisfaction of the Christian princes have proved to all the Christian world, and whitherto would they have tended? If we may guess, or following the opinion of many people, it's more than probable that a peace or a truce had immediately ensued. Which the Turks would no doubt have willingly consented to, in order to the setling their affairs in this Imperial city, and the adjacent countries. But how fatal this peace had proved to all Europe, we may easily guess, if we reflect but a moment on the Turks' true interest, in such a conjuncture. For then all the ambitious and malecontented persons of Germany and France, had flocked to him for support and relief which he would undoubtedly have promised, and in some measure performed, being so necessary in this affair in order to his further progress. Nay rather than fail made his application to the Protestant princes in Germany, as being well perswaded of their aversion against popery, with hopes to draw them to his side by promises of great advantages and a full liberty to serve God after their own manner. . . .

I shall now to give a full satisfaction on to the reader's curiosity, set down a true and most exact account of all the remarkable passages of the late siege of Vienna which gave occasion to the foregoing discourses. I had this journal from an officer of the garrison, of my old acquaintance, a very ingenious man, and a good scholar, I shall but English his words.

An impartial and true account, of all the most considerable passages and actions relating to the siege of the Imperial city of Vienna; being the Memoirs of a considerable officer of that garison, who was actually in service there till the siege was rais'd. Which he thus relates:

Anno 1683

The seventh of July in the forenoon we had a hot alarm, at the arrival here of the Count of Stirum, who desired His Imperial Majesty to send a speedy supply of men to the army, as being much inferior to the enemies in number, and upon that account, unable to stop their progress: But our fears were exceedingly increased by the afternoon, when the Count of Caprara came hither to inform the Emperor of the near approach of the Turks, and to desire him without any further delay, to remove from thence the Archduke, the enemy being not only stronger than was at first reported, but reinforc'd by a considerable number of rebels and Tartars; and accordingly in the evening the Emperor parted from Vienna for Clooster Newburg, intending to go from thence to Lintz. The same day the boors came hither in great numbers, flying from all parts, by reason of the cruelties of the Turkish army, against all such as they met in their passage. . . .

[Two days] after, the whole Turkish army appeared within a German league of Vienna, consisting of one hundred and fifty thousand fighting men, horse and food, commanded by the Grand Vizier in person; with several considerable bassas, and the best officers and soldiers of the Ottoman Empire. The consternation of the citizens at the first sight of this prodigious army cannot be expressed; but Count Staremberg [Rüdiger von Starhemberg, governor of Vienna] showing a chearful countenance, and little fear of this vast multitude, did somewhat incourage the people. . . .

That whole night the enemies undertook nothing; but alighting from their horses remained without any noise. Our men in the mean while lying close in the ravelins, redoubts, and along the *chemincovert* [covered way].

At the break of day we heard the trumpets sound from all parts of their camp, which occasion'd a great concourse of people towards the walls of the city, and was looked upon by some as a forerunner of some interprize: But all this noise was nothing else but an usual ceremony amongst the Turks, when the Grand Vizier is to go first to his quarters before a besieged town; which [quarters] he took the same day at the palace of the Empress Dowager, called La Favorita. His camp then appeared in all its glory, extended as far as Nusdorps, the carriages were without number; the cannon amounted to several hundreds of all sorts: their tents were most magnificent, to the number of thirty thousand and more. . . .

Count Staremberg considering the importance of his trust, and the fatal consequences to the whole Christian world (should Vienna be taken by the Infidels) had a watchful eye on all sides, either to take an advantage of the enemy, or surprise them, which he did often, as well as render unsuccessful their attacks. By this time the citizens had recovered themselves from their first amazement, and beginning now to look the enemies in the face with an undaunted courage, conceived some hopes of a good success: But nothing incouraged them more than the trust they had in their governor the Count of Staremberg who took little rest by day or by night, and gave as little to the enemies.

They first began the siege, without keeping the ordinary forms, as not knowing yet how strong our garison was. And in this method, to the number of thirty thousand horse and foot, they march'd on a suddain from all sides, towards our out-works, causing the neighbouring valleys and hills, to rebound with their shouts. Which mistake of theirs being taken notice of by Staremberg, without further delay, he commanded the whole garison within the walls to be in a readiness, the rest being at their post without to receive the enemy; which they did with great success, by the incouragement and good example of their officers, more especially of their governor. For the Turks were everywhere repulsed with great loss, which made them somewhat more sober, and less daring.

After this great action, which happened the third day after the arrival of the Ottoman forces before Vienna, Staremberg caus'd an exact account to be taken of all the provisions that were in the magazines, and was always present himself at their distribution among the soldiers, as well as scholars and younger brothers that mounted the guard. An oath likewise was by him administred to them, to defend the place to the last, and never to hearken to any proposals from the enemy, how advantagious soever they might be. So that now the siege went on on both sides according to the usual forms, the enemies finding it otherwise impossible to gain the city; after the advices given by their spies of the strength and resolution of the garison and citizens.

To annoy us with their great artillary, which was chiefly managed by renegadoes, they set up several batteries, which gave us little rest either by day or night, though they had little other effect at that time than the dismounting of two or three pieces of cannon, and the killing of some centinels. The Turks made three considerable attacks near the Scotembourg Gate and the Red Tower, but were as often beat off, with the loss of more than six thousand men slain on the place; besides prisoners, among whom some were of considerable quality. . . . Heaps [of dead] together lay about the same place where they fought.

The mortality being taken notice of by the Grand Vizier, and fearing lest the stink of their putrifying bodies should infect the rest of his army, he demanded a cessation of arms, whilst he gave burial to his dead; But the Count Staremberg's return was, that he had no need of a truce, his garison being all very well, and under no obligation to gratify him therein. By which means the dead were unburied; and it was the occasion of the camp's removal from that side a little farther the following day, though they did not for this abandon their attack.

The Count Staremberg lay close for two days after this great action, to give some rest to his men, and take new measures. Neither did the enemy attempt anything more all that time; but yet was not idle, being busy working like moles, both with their hands and feet, under the ground.

The first and only effect of their labour at this time, was the blowing up of a captain and near fifty soldiers, whereof some were only transported from that to another place, without being wounded. About noon the same day we rendred them the like, by springing a mine that ruined one of their batteries which had been the most of all troublesome to us, being so skilfully managed by an English renegado. . . .

The Grand Vizier in the mean time had several ingineers at work under a ravaline not far from the Lebel bastion; they had advanced their trenches towards the ravaline in two days' time in such measure, that they had made themselves a passage into the ditch [dry moat]; which the officer that commanded taking notice of, sends instantly an express to inform the Governor of the imminent danger he was in, without a speedy and strong supply: But before the express came back to give an answer, the enemy had sprung a mine; the effect whereof, was the overthrow of the point of the ravaline, and the loss of about fifteen soldiers and a lieutenant. The Turks making their best advantage of this disorder, without any loss of time, came on furiously with their swords in their hands, they were at first repulsed, and retreated in great confusion. . . . But their design in retreating was only to see what would be the effect of another mine they were to spring near the entrance of the ravaline, with intent, not only to hinder our men from returning into the city, but to put a stop to those that were expected to our assistance: Neither were they deceived in their expectations; for the ravaline was intirely overturn'd into the ditch that surrounded it, where most of those that had escaped the fury of the first attack found their burial places. . . .

They sprang the 18th of August another mine under the same ravaline, and entring the breach, attacked those that defended it . . . and got no other advantage that day, than to lodge themselves at the foot of the ravaline. . . .

This business of the ravaline had so frightened our citizens, that some of them began to murmur, and to say, that Staremberg would sacrifice them all to the fury of the Turks; that it was full time to make some agreement with the enemy; that if he deferred it too long, they should have no quarter given them; that it was the Emperor's interest in this juncture of affairs (since better could not be hoped for) to consider the garison of Vienna as able to do good service to the Empire, and save it from the Turkish fury, provided the composition were in time. These dangerous discourses coming to the knowledge of Staremberg, he was once in a mind to punish exemplaryly such as could be known to have spoken so undescreetly, or rather seditiously: But upon second thoughts he resolved on another expedient, which was to publish an order to this effect, that if any citizen or officer in the garison, of what rank or quality soever he was, should talk of surrendring the city, or making any sort of composition, how seemingly advantagious soever, with the Turks, he should instantly be declared a rebel, and punished accordingly. Which did so influence the citizens, that whatever their thoughts were, they kept their tongues within bounds; and being incouraged by the good hopes Staremberg gave them of relief, they appeared not to be much affraid of being stormed by the Turks, who, the night following after their descent into the ditch, had made a great lodgement there, which they might do with the less difficulty, for that the deepness of the ditch did secure them against the great and small shot of the besieged. Besides that, the works they had raised were of a prodigious height, and like hills round the attack of the counterscarp, which did in a manner cover their passage into the ditch. . . .

Twenty of the best cannoniers were called, and ordered to do their best endeavours to demolish these mounts and hills that did so much prejudice to the city and proved so infinitely advantagious to the enemy. Our cannon began to play at the break of day. . . . The thunder of the cannon was continued with a like success till night, at which time the hills appeared to be near leveled with the ground; yet Staremberg thought it not time to attack the enemy till the next morning.

[Following two inconclusive attacks upon the Turks, Staremberg ordered a third attack.]

They began their march in silence, between eleven and twelve a clock at night; Staremberg remembring them now and then of their duty as they passed, and promising large recompences to such as should distinguish themselves most signally in the performance of their duty. They appeared all to be of a very chearful countenance, and resolved either to dye or vanquish. They took leave of one another as they went by, and bid a last farewell to their friends, embracing and kissing such as came near them; which Staremberg expresly discountenanced, as a thing not before this instant practised in this garison, and seeming an untimely sort of tenderness, which might take off too much of the edge of a marshal courage. There was a great number of torches lighted at several gates, designedly to amuse the enemy, least they should know what way our men intended; but they were of a suddain freed of this doubt, by a showre of small shot, that came frome whence they least expected it. This entertainment in an instant put the whole Turkish army in a motion. . . . The meanwhile pioneers were not idle, they mined all the enemies works, burned their gabions, and the greatest part of their gallery. But all was not as yet done, the retreat was not very easie, a great party of Turkish horse and foot advanced withal diligince to stop our passage into the city; which undoubtedly they had performed, if Staremberg, who had still a watchful eye upon all contingencies, had not prevented their design by charging them unexpectedly with fifteen hundred choice foot, which forced them to retreat, and opened to us a free passage into the city, to the great satisfaction of the Governor, and incouragement of the whole garison.

The enemy resolving on a revenge, gave us a general assault the twenty first of August in the morning, of which take this short and true account: Some janizaries that were taken prisoners, inform'd Count Staremberg, that it was generally reported in the army, that the Grand Vizier had resolved to attack the city in a more furious manner than he had done hitherto; and that for that purpose great preparations were making, so that he hoped either to force us by storm, or compell us to surrend upon thoughts how little we were able to stand out after this general assault. They further added, that the Turks, from the beginning of the siege, had lost more than twenty thousand of their best men; and that it would never have been undertaken, if the Grand Vizier had thought to have met with so vigorous a resistance. They said likewise, that he was informed the city was destitute of all necessary provisions, at least of many things requisite for a considerable or long defence; that the Turks were now beginning to mistrust their good fortune, and somewhat to dispond of a good success in this siege; because that it began to be generally reported that the King of Poland was upon his march at the head of a strong army, accompanied by his son; and that the auxiliary troops were coming a-pace to the King of Lorrain (or so they called him) not knowing what a distinction we put between a king and a soveraign prince. That nevertheless the Grand Vizier was resolv'd to lose his life before Vienna rather than raise the siege; and that trusting to the number and courage of his army, consisting of the best officers, and stoutest soldiers of the Ottoman Empire, he would undoubtedly venture a battel against the whole Christian forces united together. Tho' all this was reflected on by Staremberg, Capeliers, and other officers of the garison, yet their main concern in the present juncture of affairs, was to inquire of the true time and manner of the formentioned assault, save only, that if it succeeded not, the Turks would be extreamly discourag'd, and would perhaps raise the siege by the Grand Siegnior's command, who, they said, had not much approv'd of this enterprize, inclining more to sweep all away before him, than to attack the Imperial seat, and leave the island of Schutz, Raab, Gomorra, and Presburg.

The prisoners dismissed, a counsel of war was held; whereof . . . a short account was sent to the Duke of Lorrain, by a fisherman that swam the river.

The 21st of August, all such as were able to carry arms in the city were commanded to draw to their colours, in the usual places, whence, after they had been provided with match, powder, and other necessaries, they were ordered to retire to their respective stations till further orders.

About midnight a hot alarm was given us by the enemies, who sprang two mines not far from one another under the Lebel bastion. . . . We observed a general motion in every part of the enemies camp, which some looked upon as a disposition to retreat, but in reallity was nothing else but the marching of several detachments . . . in order to give the lately mentioned general assault, which was preceeded both by their great and small shot, whereever they could discover us. We answered them with the same musick, but with a far greater loss on their side than ours. . . . But then on a sudden the enemy marched on all sides towards the ditch, so and in such a crowd, that we had some reason to fear our being overpowered by the number: But we fired our cannon from the wings of the bastions, and other parts so often, that we put them now and then to a stand, till they had either withdrawn; or marched over the huge heaps of the dead. . . . Staremberg's undaunted courage, and chearful countinance, inspir'd the whole garison with a new vigour. He retreated back of a suddain to the city, and although wounded in the shoulder with an arrow, took no rest. . . . [The Turks] were all cut off in less than half an hour. Which action applauded to by the shouts of the garison, beating of drums, timbals, and sounding of trumpets, was followed by a general retreat of the Turkish forces. . . . The loss of the Turks in this attack was little less than six or seven thousand men; on our side we had near fifteen hundred killed or unserviceable; amongst whom were several considerable officers slain on the place.

This action discouraged infinitely the Grand Vizier, who was inraged at the great loss, and did begin to manage his men with more discretion against a better occasion. He was three or four days, though not idle, yet not very busie, his trenches not going on with the wonted diligence. . . .

This city was about this time generally afflicted by an epidemical distemper, a dyssentery, or bloody flux, which carried off sometimes threescore or more in one day. The Governor himself was not free of it, though he never kept within doors: and when he was so weak that he could not walk or ride, he caus'd himself to be carried whither 'twas requisite for him to be. The rumor was a while in the Turkish army, that he was dead; which caused such an universal joy amongst the Turks, that they made upon this account bonfires, hoping that now the city would be soon yielded up. . . .

We were informed [by captive janizaries] . . . that the Turkish army was beginning to suffer much for want of necessary provisions, which were sold at very high rates in their camp; that their greatest want was that of forrage, the adjacent country being quite desolated; that the dead horses did infect their whole army; that the bloody flux had already almost ruin'd or at least much weaken'd some quarters of the army; that the daily loss, what by the sword, and what by various distempers, was esteemed to amount to more than a thousand men; that the Grand Vizier was resolv'd between the 29th of August and the 2d of September, to give so many and so furious assaults to Vienna, that he doubted not but that he should take it by storm before the arrival of the auxiliary-troops, and the junction of all the Christian forces. . . .

The 29th we perceived the Turkish forces drawing up in battalia around the city, and detachments going off towards the ditch. . . . About ten a clock in the morning the Turks came fiercely on with their ordinary shoots and haloo's. . . . Our men according to their orders by little and little giving ground, retreated orderly into the city, where they were instantly divided, and sent to the bastions and rampart; for them onely now we had to defend, the enemy being master of all our out-works. . . .

We were never in a greater distress than in this conjuncture, and began to look upon our selves as lost men; though fully resolved to spend the last drop of our blood, rather than surrender. . . .

Their attacks were not now so open as before, but more dangerous, because under ground, and hidden; they were busie mining everywhere. And on our side likewise, we were not idle, but doing our utmost endeavours, either to find their mines, or give them air by our countermines. Wherein we had often greater success than we expected, or the enemies designed.

They had already undermined not onely the bastion of the court, but were heard working under the Emperour's palace: which so affrighted our enginiers, that surprised to hear the enemies beneath them, they retreated instantly out of the mines, for fear of being blown up. Herein Staremberg was forced to make use partly of his authority, partly fair words and large promises, to ingage them to do what lay in their power to discover the enemies mines. Thus incourag'd, they set to work again, and taking deeper measures than they had done at first, met happily with the Turkish miners, killed some of 'em; and brought the rest up prisoners, taking out of their mines several quintals (or hundreds) of powder. This was a most signal service; and I may confidently say, the happy discovery of this mine, saved this city from being taken by the Turks. . . . Our grenades . . . were all spent; our garison was much diminish'd, consisting now but of six thousand men; the victuals were become scarce, and the bloody flux was become almost universal. But the news of the arrival and junction of the King of Poland, the auxiliary troops, and the Imperial army at Crembs, inspir'd us all with a new life and vigour, and we doubted not now any more of defending our selves at least till such time as the Christians army came to our relief, unless some unexpected accident should happen; which we had always reason to be somewhat affraid of, because of the enemies great skill in mining.

The 3d, 4th, and 8th of September they attack't us again most desperately, but both to their great loss, and ours. They had once arbored the crescent upon the bastions against the Grand Vizier's quarters, and had in all likelihood put us all to the sword, if Staremberg, who was always in action, had not run thither, followed by considerable detachments of all our forces. The enemies were scarce able to abide his first charge, but were at the second intirly routed, and most of 'em put to the sword, or thrown down headlong into the ditch.

This victory weakned very much our garison, so that Staremberg judg'd it now full time to give the signs agreed upon betwixt him and the Duke of Lorrain, of his being reduced to the last extremity. Which accordingly was done after this manner: . . . He went round the city, and gave his orders every where, with a special command to the cannoniers to make all the noise they could with their cannon, trumpets in the mean time sounding, the drums and timbalds beating. . . . He caused all night-fusees, and divers sorts of fireworks, to be cast up into the air, which was the main sign of his utmost distress agreed upon between him and the Duke of Lorrain.

The enemy was somewhat perplex'd at our extraordinary mirth, but could not well judge what could be the real occasion thereof. . . .

The King of Poland, the Duke of Lorrain, and the whole Christian forces, came within sight of the Turks the 12th of September, about nine a clock in the morning. . . .

The Christian army marching close, advanc'd in good order towards the Turkish camp. . . . After a vigorous but short resistance, the Christians enter'd on all sides the Turkish camp, where they found the spahi's and janizaries drawn up in several bodies.

The Grand Vizier in this dangerous position of affairs, took a sudden and generous resolution; which, if successful, had proved fatal to us first, and then to the Christian army. He caused two mines to be sprung under the ramparts of the city, not far from the Scots Gate, which made a breach large enough for thirtie men to march in a front; though not without incumbrance, because the ground was not much levelled, though overturn'd. Staremberg caused without delay ten great guns to be set upon the breach, loaden with musquet-balls, broken horse-shoo's, and such-like things. We wonder'd at first at this attempt of the Turks, in presence of the Christian army; and whilst they were very uncertain of victory. But the Grand Vizier's design was, in case he should take the city by storm, which he doubted not but he could, having the advantage of such a great breach, to draw instantly within the walls of the city, and under the cannon thereof, his baggage, cannon, tents, and the whole train of his army, that so it should be his choice to venture or not venture a battel as he thought fittest.

Our governour was extreamly concern'd at this unexpected accident; for he was preparing for a general sallie out against those that kept the trenches, and had lodg'd themselves every where in the ditch; but was now forc'd to expose his best men against an infinite number of Turks, crowding in at the breach with all imaginable bravery. The ground was disputed on each side for half an hour . . . but at length the Turks were prevail'd upon, and repulsed with a great loss of their best men. . . . In the mean time Staremberg . . . sallied out, as he had first resolved, against those that were left to keep the trenches. . . . After a vigorous resistance, he cut in pieces more than four thousand janizaries, whilst on the other side, the King of Poland, the Duke of Lorrain, the Duke of Bavaria, the Duke of Saxony, Prince Waldeck, and other German princes were putting to flight and to the sword the Turkish horse and infantry; which being taken notice of by our citizens and souldiers, they could scarce be holden within the gates from pursuing the enemy.

The whole Christian army now being near fourty eight hours in action, from the beginning of its march, could not pursue the enemy, but stood in battel-array all that night, and express order being issued out from the generals, that no man under pain of death should quit his rank to plunder, without an express command from the high officers, lest the enemy, as has often happened, should sallie on a sudden, and get an easie victory over an army put into disorder by the libertie of plundering, which was only granted to the Christian troops the next day at twelve a clock. . . .

The Turkish enginiers being under ground, knew nothing as yet of the raising of the siege; and having completed some new mines, came to acquaint, as they were wont, the Grand Vizier with what they had done . . . : they were at first overjoy'd, thinking the Turks, whom they saw no more, had possessed themselves of the city; but being instantly made sensible of their mistake, they beg'd on their knees quarter from the Germans, who told them they must first discover their mines, and carry out the powder they had put in them, and then they should know their doom; which done, [all twenty-three] were put to the sword. . . . 'Tis too well known, that the Turks seldom prove sincere converts to the Christian religion; and such men would undoubtedly leave us, if they were spared, to the great damage of the Christians. . . . Greater severity hapned to the sick the enemy had left in the camp, who were about three thousand, for the most part afflicted with a bloody flux, contracted by their ill dyet, more especially by eating of horse-flesh, which being of a very uncommon digestion, caused an ill habit, which immediately turn'd to a white flux with gripes, and soon after degenerated into a dyssenterie, or bloody flux. Of these miserable wretches the souldiers . . . were resolved to make a sacrifice to the flame, and for the purification of the air (denying them the honour of dying by their swords) which on them all they most cruelly performed; though not without decrying, and for which some of the ringleaders were punished. Also, by an express order of the chief officers, the prisoners were commanded to bury the dead, to cast them into the river, to fill up the trenches, and level the works raised by the Turks, &c.

His Imperial Majesty, the King of Poland, and all the Christian generals entered the city, which they found exceedingly defaced by the enemies bombs and cannon. The Emperour shewed all imaginable kindness to Staremberg, and spoke of him in most honourable terms, acknowledged that the whole Empire, and all Christendom were infinitely oblig'd to his good conduct and valour; that he could expect nothing less in time and place, than an adequate reward. . . .

Thus the second siege of Vienna by the Turks was raised, to the immortal glory of the city, and the eternal renown of those that contributed most to its delivery.

36. The French Policy of Burning and Destruction

Michel Le Tellier (1641–1691), Marquis of Louvois, shared with his father the office of secretary of state for war from about 1662 to 1677, and then held it alone until his death. Both hard and systematic workers, the Le Telliers together built the largest, most obedient, and best-equipped army in Europe. Louvois refined and extended the innovations made by his father to force officers of all ranks, troops, and even munitioners to obey the King. Louvois' powers were so enormous that they became legendary during his lifetime. Yet it is difficult to exaggerate his impact at every level of the government. His manner of ordering about high-ranking princes and nobles, his ability to coerce local officials to supply the troops, and finally his great influence on Louis himself made Louvois the most feared, hated, and respected official in the French government.

In these letters the deliberate confusion of powers exercised by the King and Louvois is very well illustrated. The imperious tone conveys

SOURCE: *Letters of Louvois*, ed. by Jacques Hardré (Chapel Hill: University of North Carolina Press, 1949), pp. 434, 328–330, 340–341, 343.

Louvois' power, though he claims to have none himself. The threat is always to inform Louis, while at the same time the impression is always that Louvois himself has trouble pleasing the King. Louvois is almost humorous about the maps which he requests from Vauban, and he intended this to be funnier than it is. But the power and influence of such a man would make any man, even one of Vauban's influence, have second thoughts before failing to comply with Louvois' requests.

The principal issue dealt with in these letters is French policy on the northern frontier and in the Rhineland in the 1680's. Was Louis himself responsible for the orders to burn villages, fields, and towns? Louvois ordered these reprisals and "contributions" in the King's name, while officers in the field remained reluctant to carry out such brutal orders. The aim, of course, was to force Spain to sue for peace on Louis' terms.

The military strategy of reprisals was anything but new in the 1680's. No major force stood to oppose the French armies; and as had so often been the case, the switch from large-scale military combat to guerrilla warfare and control of the population led to such brutal acts. The French sought to impose their will on a region, to relieve the enormous tax burden on the homeland by having the enemy pay, and to make their troops feared. As recently as the Thirty Years' War such a strategy had been used by virtually every officer in the field. But in the 1680's, with the large-scale actions resulting from the size of the French armies, such a policy seemed more brutal and—more important, in a sense—particularly ineffective.

The increased military power which first the French developed, and then the other European states followed, did not lead to a new assessment of the moral and religious foundations for war which friend and foe alike shared in the seventeenth century. By contrast, the very adverse effect which the French actions had on public opinion did have impact. The policy of "scorched earth" was therefore dropped more because it was ineffective than because it was immoral. In the future Louis XIV and the French would pay for the "policy of terror" in the Rhineland. This same policy of terror also indicated what Louis and Louvois generally believed should be the territorial limits to French expansionism. For Alsace, a conquered people which was to be incorporated into France, a policy of accommodation, not terror and reprisals, was established.

To Monsieur du Montal
Versailles, December 19, 1683

The two letters which you took the trouble to write me on the 15th of this month have reached me. What took place during the time you commanded the troops which were placed under your orders during the months of September, October, and the first days of November both in regard to the Spanish villages spared and to the safeguards which you obliged the region of Liège to take, is so public and has been reported in similar fashion by so many officers that it is impossible to doubt the care you are taking to spare the Spanish villages, into which you have not sent a single detachment since the troops have been in winter quarters, and although it would be true that during the time you were at Thuin you could not have sent large detachments for the reasons which you note, nothing prevented you from sending small ones, and the Spaniards only continued to carry out raids in the region which is under your command because they felt assured that the reprisals which the King has so often ordered you [to carry out] would not be carried out by you. If you will inquire about the state of the receipts for the Contributions from the region which you command, and the small amount of money which has been received in the last two months, you will easily judge that His Majesty would have no reason to be happy with you had I informed him, which you should not doubt that I will do if you do not immediately change your conduct in this regard. Nothing is at the moment more easy than to force the most distant region to pay since His Majesty thinks fit that we should put to the torch all localities which will not pay. The concern that I show in matters touching you, obliges me to give you this last warning after which I would not be able to keep from telling the King of everything that has happened, of the prejudice done to his service, and of the advantage which the enemies gain from your conduct and from your failure to carry out his orders; to which I add that the troops which serve under you are complaining that you make them make substantial marches, with no stops to eat, in order to spare the villages which are found along the road, which still belong to your friends—for whom it will be wise for you to show less concern in the future than for the preservation of His Majesty's troops—and this all the more so since it is his intention that you not only oblige the Spanish subjects to pay the sums demanded of them by Monsieur Fautrier; but that you try to make their region abandoned and absolutely ruined, and that the King's troops may profit from the damage which will be done to the aforesaid region.

You will inform the general officers serving under you of His Majesty's intention in this matter, and you will take measures so that what he orders is punctually carried out.

If you believe you need more troops than you have to cut off the large detachments beyond the Sambre, you will take the trouble to send me a memorandum showing what there is in each of the villages under your command, so that I can make known to you His Majesty's wishes principally on this matter.

To Monsieur de Montbron
Versailles, February 21, 1684

Sir,

There are many villages which have not yet paid the demands which have been made upon them last year and this year; the King's will is that you punish with the utmost severity those who do not finally pay at once; His Majesty expects that after having so precisely directed you [to do so] he will be obeyed to the letter, since his service requires that the Spanish territories be entirely ravaged, or that everything that he has asked of them be paid before the end of the coming month.

Id. to:
Marquis de Boufflers
Monsieur de Lambert
Marshal d'Humières
Marshal de Créquy
Monsieur Dauger
Monsieur du Montal
Monsieur de Langallerie
and Monsieur de Bulondes

To Monsieur du Montal
Versailles, February 18, 1684

Sir,

The King having been informed that the Spaniards put to the torch two barns full of fodder and grain situated at the extremities of the villages of Avenelle and Sepmenier, in the administrative district of Avesnes, His Majesty commanded me to inform you that he wishes you to burn twenty villages as close as possible to Charleroi, and that you distribute handbills saying that it is in retaliation for the burning of these two barns; the King's will is that Gauchelys, Guenets, and Fleuru be among their number, and that you take the necessary steps in carrying this out so that not a single house in these 20 villages remains standing; that in the future at the first notification you receive of a similar thing, you will act in like manner without awaiting further orders from His Majesty; that the above should be carried out by a large detachment, which His Majesty wishes you to command yourself, and which is substantial enough so that there need be no fear of the joining of the garrisons of Namur and of Charleroi.

The same was written to Marquii de Boufflers.

To Monsieur de Vauban
Condé, May 12, 1684

I received your letter of the 11th of this month, which surprised me by not having a map of the trenches; but a lackey whom I had sent had the presence of mind to have one made by an officer. There is laughter over the fact that with fifty engineers under you I cannot get what I want; if that continues I will name some who will do only that and will spare me the shame of appearing before the King without that which he has ordered me to have brought to him daily, when only two scribbles with a pencil would give me the satisfaction I request.

His Majesty noted with pleasure the marked advance of the earthworks and the little they cost. He would have liked you, in making as detailed a report to him as you did, to have indicated for him what you hoped to do in the coming days and approximately what day you believe you will be able to attack the counterscarp, and whether to avoid the effect of the mines you would not try to make yourself master of both at the same time, on which I beg you to explain yourself and, not being content merely to explain to the King what has happened, always to show him what you hope to do in the coming days.

His Majesty noted with pleasure the success registered by the mortars and he hopes that the aforesaid mortars will so ruin the defenses that they will save the lives of many people and will substantially advance the capture of the fortress.

Explain to me a bit how you mean to make progress with half-saps in rock and take care to inform me every day whether you encounter earth and how deep.

I fear that you wrote a little late concerning the abbeys left vacant by the death of Monsieur de Fourbin, but you can be sure that either this vacancy or one of the coming ones will give you the satisfaction you desire and that I would say you deserve it if you had not made me wait so long for the maps I asked of you.

37. A Personal Memoir on the French in the Rhineland

The policy of reprisals and destruction carried out by French troops against Spanish subjects on the northern frontier, 1683–1684, had not aroused animosity in Europe toward Louis XIV in the way the destruction ordered in the Palatinate would after 1689. Though the edition from which this translation was taken was not published until 1789, accounts of this sort circulated at the time aroused immense hostility to Louis XIV in Germany and elsewhere.

As I was returning to Speyer from Kirrweiler on the twenty-third of May of this year [1689] at about five o'clock in the afternoon, I guessed from the conduct and disturbed faces of the citizens that some terrible news had arrived. Two or three of the burgomasters and the townscribe, Wegelaz, came to me to say that about an hour before, the French intendant of war, M. la Fond, had arrived and summoned the chief magistrates and fifteen leading citizens to listen to certain royal commands. To those that assembled he read the following:

"The interests of His Royal Majesty, owing to existing conditions, demand that this town be entirely evacuated within six days. Not only must all wines, provisions, furniture, and other effects be removed, but everybody, whether laymen or clergy, must leave and take refuge somewhere on this side the Rhine or in Philippsburg. These orders are not the result of His Royal Majesty's fear of his enemies, nor has he any grudge against the town, but is well satisfied with its conduct hitherto. Accordingly you need not conclude that the town is to be burned. It is necessary, nevertheless, in order to deprive his enemies of all means of subsistence, to have the town evacuated. You must accordingly transmit this royal com-

SOURCE: J. H. Robinson and C. A. Beard, *Readings in Modern European History* (New York: Ginn & Co., 1908), I, 33–35.

mand to all the citizens and clergy and order its execution, for everything that remains in the town after the expiration of the term set, shall fall to the King and his soldiers."

All remonstrances and pleading were vain, the city scribe translated the order into German, and the citizens could find their only consolation in the promise that the town should not be burned. They pleaded for more time, but were told that it was useless to apply to the King or Marshal Duras, that they must set to work to remove their goods by means of the hundred carts which they had, and that they could store the goods which could not be removed within the time fixed, in the cathedral, where everything would be safe.

When the clergy, the Jesuits and members of the four mendicant orders, appealed to the French officers, they were received with words of sympathy and compassion, but no hope was given. The boys and girls, dressed in white, marched in procession to the intendant and general and besought him vainly for mercy on the town. The officers declared that their orders came from the court at Versailles and that they could not make any concessions.

In the meantime there was much talk of further delay, when on the morning of the twenty-seventh, between ten and eleven o'clock, General Montclair announced that he had received orders to set fire to the town, churches, and cloisters, with the single exception of the cathedral. On May 31, at six in the afternoon, the destruction began as it did at Worms. The fire was started by the Weidenberg and spread gradually—for it was a still evening—through the fish market. There was an old man in the upper story of the bell ringer's house who was miserably burned to death, whether he could not or would not make his escape.

On June 1 the fire caught the houses in the market place and progressed towards the church of St. James and the Horse Market. About ten o'clock a fearful thunderstorm and wind arose which spread the fire with terrible rapidity, so that in an instant it was raging in the Herdgasse, and reached the White Tower. Between eleven and twelve it enveloped the Wolzhausen and the whole neighborhood, for the wind scattered a shower of sparks everywhere, and so it came about that the bell tower of the cathedral was set on fire. This was extinguished no less than three times, but the cloisters were ignited by incendiaries and the near-by buildings caught.

A little flame was then discovered in the tower over the choir. Every effort was made to put it out, but the strong wind, dry wood, and the danger from the stream of molten lead from the burning roof combined to permit the fire to gain the upper hand. When I saw that the cathedral was in the utmost danger, I tried to save the miracle-working figure of the Virgin, but the shower of lead and the thick smoke prevented. Seeing that nothing could be done, I mounted my horse and rode into the suburb of the Carmelites. Here I appealed to the general who had received me with so much sympathy before, to place guards at the doors of the cathedral to prevent plundering.

On June 3 I sent my servants to inspect the cathedral. They found the miracle-working Virgin quite uninjured and brought it thither. We placed it in the church here. It is remarkable that even the artificial flowers which adorned it were not harmed, although one of the doors of the shrine, which I had carefully shut upon my last visit, was burnt for several inches.

On the fifth, I learned that an order had arrived to mine and blow up the towers of the cathedral as well as the buildings attached. I went immediately to Marshal Duras at Odenheim to get the order countermanded, and succeeded finally. I wished then to see with my own eyes the ruin of the noble building, and found it, alas, in a worse state than had been reported to me. The vaulting of the nave had wholly collapsed, the building full of rubbish; and chairs, altars, and everything that had been stored there was reduced to ashes. The sacristy and other portions that had escaped the fire had been plundered. The deacon von Weideberg had gone into the sacristy as soon as he dared, to see if the body of Saint Guido was still there. He found the receptacle broken open and the holy head of the saint stolen on account of its silver crown. The rest of the saint's body he brought to a place of safety. In the choir, moreover, several of the emperors' tombs had been opened; the epitaphs, inscriptions, and everything that looked like metal had been taken and a number of the statues themselves mutilated.

Von Rollingen
Kirrweiler, June 15, 1689

38. A Debate between Sovereigns over the Causes of War in 1688

The French and Latin texts of Louis XIV's memorandum to Emperor Leopold and the latter's reply were translated and published in London in a matter of months after they had become available on the Continent. Both texts had been written to influence public opinion, and the fact that they appeared in London suggests that their authors were successful in reaching a considerable part of the literate public.

Neither Louis nor Leopold, of course, discussed his real intentions or the history of the policies which each had pursued prior to the war. But if these texts do not describe what was going on at the highest levels of government, they nevertheless do something equally important. What Louis and Leopold wanted Europeans to believe was as much a part of their policies as their secret orders were. And beneath these explanations lie assumptions about politics and international affairs which determine policies as much as propaganda. The piety about keeping the peace and preserving Christendom lacks conviction as we read it now, as well it may have in 1688.

More important, in each text the authors and their secretaries attack what they believe to be their opponent's weakest points in the public opinion of the moment. Louis was striving to hold former French satellites and to evoke fears of the Emperor among the lesser German princes. What he omits is as important as what he discusses; the same must be said for Leopold's reply.

Those who shall examin without passion, or any other interest than that of the public good, the conduct which His Majesty has taken from the beginning of the War of Hungary to the present time, will have great reason to wonder that he having always been advertised of the design which the Emperor had formed of a long time, to attack France, as soon as he shall have made peace with the Turks, he should have deferred the preventing thereof even to this hour, and being far from making use of the pretences which the

SOURCES: *The French King's Memorial to the Emperor of Germany* (London, 1688), pp. 5–9, 16–17, 25–26, 29 ff.; *The Emperor's Answer to the French King's Manifesto, Translated from the Latin* (London, 1688), pp. 1–10, 14–18.

rules of good politicks might suggest to him for putting a stop to the greatness of the Prince, he had rather for the sake of peace, even sacrifice the just occasions which have been so often given him to employ the forces which God has put into his hands, as well for taking from the Court of Vienna all means of doing him any hurt, as for putting a stop to the unjust courses and violent usurpations of the Elector Palatin; and to cause a restitution to Madam, the sister-in-law of His Majesty, of what in right belongs to her by succession from her father and brother, and timely to prevent all the leagues and preparations of war that have at length forced him to bring his arms to the banks of the Rhine, and to attack those places by which the Emperor might with most ease renew and maintain a war against France.

All the world is now satisfied that it was the too sincere desire His Majesty had of putting a stop to whatsoever might disturb the repose of Christendom, and the convincing proofs he has given of his good intentions, that have so much contributed to all those occasions of discontents, that have at last tired his patience.

It is very apparent that at the time when His Majesty might have taken advantage of the disturbance which the War of Hungary gave the Emperor, so as to have obliged the Court of Vienna and the Empire to yield to him, by a definitive treaty, all the places which had been reunited to his Crown, in consequence of the Treaties of Munster and Nimweguen: and by this means put a stop to all occasions of misunderstanding between him and the Empire, His Majesty had rather acquiesce to a treaty of truce or suspension, than by his arms be the occasion of diverting the princes and states of the Empire, from affording the Emperor those succors he stood in need of, in order to repel the forces of the Ottoman Empire: and that His Majesty following his pious and generous inclinations had preferred the general interest of Christendom, before the good of his own Crown, contenting himself to obtain that provisionally, which in prudence he ought to have demanded for ever.

It is sufficiently known that this treaty of truce was hardly ratified on both sides, but His Majesty was willing to give fresh proofs of his moderation; and altho he understood the Imperial ministers employed all their diligence and endeavours in most of the courts of Germany, to incline the princes and states of the Empire to enter into new leagues against France. That by the treaty made at Ausbourg [Augsburg], they had engaged a considerable number of the princes and states to subscribe this association. That in the Assembly of Nuremberg all kinds of artifices and suppositions were made use of, to bring all those into this league, who were with held by the consideration of the misfortunes which might be occasioned by a new war, and the advantage which the whole Empire might find in the maintaining a good correspondence with His Majesty. And lastly, that the ministers of the House of Austria have plainly professed on several occasions, that the War of Hungary should no sooner be at an end, than the Emperor would turn his arms toward the Rhine, and that the treaty of truce should not be able to hinder his designs. Nevertheless all these pressing motives, which might immediately have obliged His Majesty rather to carry the war into the countries and estates of this prince, than to expect it in his own kingdom, had yet given place to the earnest desire he has always had of doing what lay in his power for the maintaining of the peace; and he had taken no other precautions for maintaining his dominions from all the mischiefs preparing against them, than to fortifie his frontier places, so as to put a stop to the designs of his enemies. . . .

'Tis true, that the Archbishoprick of Cologne, remaining in the power of a prince, whose intentions were so sincere as those of the late Elector, for the maintaining the publick tranquillity, there needed only to take away so great an obstacle to any new troubles; the only expedient was by fair means, or by foul, to set up a coadjutor entirely devoted to the interest of the House of Austria, and there could not be found anyone that could be so certainly rely'd on for the execution of this design, and the aggrandizing that house, as one of the princes of the same. And it may also be affirm'd, that there is nothing which he has not put in practice for the effecting hereof. But as his offers and promises supported by the presence of the Duke of Juliers, have not had the desired effect, the threatnings which he made use of against the canons, and against the Elector himself, have been so violent and outrageous, that they have drawn upon him the indignation of both one and the other, and of four and twenty votes of which the Chapter is compos'd, they have determin'd nineteen to postulate the Cardinal of Furstemberg to the coadjutorship of the Archbishoprick of Cologne, as judging him with good reason so much the more capable to govern well, that besides the experience he has acquired during the long administration the late Elector entrusted him with, his dignity of Dean, his age, his excellent personal qualities have procured him the esteem and love of all those of the Chapter, who are not obliged to sacrifice their inclinations to other interests than that of their Church. . . .

These were truths well known to His Majesty, and there could not be a man of good understanding, and who was well inform'd of what passed in Europe, who can bring in doubt the least circumstance of what is advanced in this memorial. It would also be to no purpose, to make publick all those other proofs which His Majesty has had of the resolution taken by the House of Austria, to declare war immediately against him. He is throughly perswaded, that after all these instances he has given of the very great desire he has always had to secure the publick tranquillity, all the world will allow that it were to be wish'd, for the common good of Christendom, that those who hope to find advantage by stirring up new troubles had not so good an opinion of the sincerity of His Majesties intentions, and that it is upon them alone that the blame is to be laid, that he is set under a necessity of marching his troops, as well to besiege Philipsbourg (being a place fit to render to his enemies an easie entrance into his estates) as to possess himself of Keisserslouter [Kaiserslautern] till the Elector Palatine has restored to Madam, his sister-in-law, that which belongs to her by succession to the electors, her father and brother.

But whatsoever success it shall please God to give to the arms of His Majesty, he has always the same desire to contribute what on his part he can to the establishment of the publick peace. And to this end he decares, that he will not hold himself bound to make this perpetual, but only the Emperor and his confederates; His Majesty being very willing (that so for the future all occasions of misunderstanding between him and the Empire be taken away, and that no cause may be left for a breach and renewing of the war) that a definitive treaty of peace be made upon the same articles with that of the truce concluded and signed at Ratisbonne, August 15, 1684. It being provided that His Majesty shall not be troubled, nor in any manner disturbed on occasion of the new fortifications he has been obliged to make for the security of his estates, as well at Hunningen [Huningen], as at Fort Lewis upon the Rhine.

And as he has not undertaken the siege of Philipsburg, to open to himself a way to attack the Empire; but only to make secure the entry into his estates, from those who would raise new troubles, so he offers moreover, in order to facilitate a treaty of peace, to demolish the fortifications of the said city of Phelipsburg, as soon as shall have reduced it to his obedience, and that he will cause it to be surrendred to the Bishop of Spire, for him to enjoy it after the same manner as his predecessors have done, before the place was fortified, without authority to rebuild the fortifications. . . .

Furthermore His Majesty is willing to add to these overtures, a more considerable and more convincing proof of the desire which he has to reestablish a good correspondence with the Emperor and the Empire, and to render the same of a long duration; that whereas the extraordinary expence he has been at to make the town of Fribourg a place impregnable, as it is at present, might reasonably oblige him never to part with it from the Crown, nevertheless in order to procure a happy peace to all Christendom, and to make appear that he designs nothing but to secure his kingdom, and not to preserve to himself means of enlarging the same, he is also willing to cause the fortifications of this important place to be demolished, and to surrender it to the Emperor with all its dependences, upon condition that he shall never fortifie it hereafter.

As for the Electorate of Cologne, His Majesty offers to withdraw his troops from thence, as soon as the Pope, either by his own free will, or at the request of the Emperor, shall have confirmed the postulation of the Cardinal of Furstemberg; and he will freely interpose his interest, as soon as the said Cardinal shall be in the peaceable possession and enjoyment of the said Electorate, to cause him to join with the Chapter in such temperaments as may be proposed for the satisfaction of Prince Clement and the Elector of Bavaria, in such sort as that the repose of that arch-bishoprick may not be disturbed, neither at the present, nor in time to come.

His Majesty is also very willing, that nothing may remain of what is past nor any occasion for future troubles, immediately to put an end to those differences which concern the succession in the Palatinate; and he offers on the behalf of Monsieur, his only brother, and of Madam, his sister-in-law, a disclaim of all the places, territories, and countries, as well as the moveables, ordnance and every other thing which ought yet to be restored, satisfaction for the damages being made in mony, according to such estimation as shall be made, at the least within a year's time, by commissioners which shall be named to this purpose; and in case they shall not agree within the aforesaid time, His Majesty gives his consent, that whatsoever shall remain in difference shall be determined by the arbitrage of the King of England and the Republique of Venice, without leaving either one or the other party at liberty any ways to render it ineffectual.

It is upon these conditions which are much more advantageous to the Emperor and the Empire, than to His Majesty and to his Crown, that the public tranquillity may be reestablished and made sure for ever; provided that they are accepted before the end of January next, to which effect His Majesty is ready to send his plenipotentiaries immediately to Ratisbonne. But after that time, His Majesty being obliged to continue at vast expenses, he pretends not to be holden to these his offers; and in case of a too long delay, or of a refusal to accept hereof, he charges from this present, all those mischiefs which the war may bring upon Christendom, upon those who have forced him to resume his arms to prevent their evil designs, and who would not take the advantage of the expedients which he proposes for the immediate assurance of a lasting peace.

Given at Versailles
September 24, 1688

It is known to the whole Christian world that when the Peace of Numigen [Nijmwegen], within a little after its conclusion, was by the French King many wayes violated, and large countrys and provinces, contrary to the express tenour of the said Peace, were, under the new and strange pretences of re-unions and dependencies and the like, torn away from the Roman Empire, (there being a kind of a mock court of justice erected at Metz and Brisac; in which the French ministers acted the parts at once of pleaders, witnesses, and judges) that it was at last agreed in the year 1684 upon the 15th of August, between His Most Sacred Majesty the Emperor on the one part, and the Most Serene King of France on the other, that there should be a mutual cessation from all acts of hostility, to be inviolably observed for twenty years: and that, for the honour of God, and the security of the Christian religion which was in danger, and not without great advantage to the French affairs: it being permitted in the mean time to the French, that they should have quiet and peaceable possession of almost a sixth part of the provinces which after the Peace of Numigen remained of right to the Empire.

It is known also, with what strictness in the mean time, and confidence in the King's word, and favorable interpretation of all suspitious actions, and injuries, which His Majesty the Emperor suffered, and which the princes and states of the Empire often complain'd that they suffered from the Crown of France, the said Peace on the Emperor's side was observed; and how His Majesty the Emperor trusting in the faith of this league, was unmov'd at everything, insomuch that his subjects as well as forreigners did wonder, that he seemed not to be in any fear, though his frontiers lay open every where to the French, if they wou'd break their faith, there being scarce above one or two legions to defend such a large open country, the confederates themselves being call'd away to Hungary, and the frontier garrisons such as Philipsburg, Constance, and the rest, being in a manner neglected and disregarded: and all to the intent that His Imperial Majesty might defend the Christian religion in regions far remote, though he saw in the mean time the French forces unreasonably increas'd, new and unnecessary garrisons made on the bank of the Rhine, which belong'd not to the French King: and that fraud and violence was every where to be fear'd from him.

Certainly to this day there has not been any one action on the account of which the King might justly accuse the Emperor of so much as attempting to break his faith, much less of actually doing it. Nay those little suspicions which France lov'd to make to it self, as if Caeser had in thought, or in his secret wishes inclin'd to any such thing, were by him immediately discuss'd, and the matter fully clear'd, by his great moderation, in that he let alone what he might lawfully have taken, and generously omitted advantagious opportunities lest he might seem by any the least spark, to kindle the flame of the French jealousie.

Yet behold now again that flame breaks out on a sudden which the French Court unwillingly cover'd over for a time. The French seize on the Diocess of Cologne, invade the Palatinate, besiege Philipsburg, and without observing any law or article of the peace, or so much as the ancient manner of kings going to war one with another, the French King falls most unjustly upon the Emperor and the Empire, like one that had been long secretly a contriving it: and at last forsooth in his smooth-tongued fashion, not when he denounced war, but when he had already begun it, he orders his fallacious Memorial to be presented us, in which he does not excuse but openly avow[s] the violence and injustice of his arms, as if he had been provoked to a war, and did not bring it on a sudden, upon those who thought nothing of it.

In those his letters (or that his manifesto) he publishes those which the compiler of 'em calls the causes, whereby the Most Christian King is induced to take arms again against Caesar and the Empire, and by which he says the Christian world ought to be convinced of his sincere desire of the publick tranquillity thereof; that forsooth His Sacred Majesty the Emperor intends to make a peace with the Turk, that he may turn his arms against France.

This he will have to appear, first, in that presently after the Peace concluded, the Emperor sought new alliances, which by divers artifices, and craft were transacted at Ausburg [Augsburg] and Norimburg [Nuremberg], contrary to the French interest.

Secondly, for that, although the Emperor were perswaded even by the Pope's ministers, to turn the twenty years' truce into a perpetual peace, yielding only thus much to France, that what the French now enjoy'd for so long, by vertue of the truce, they should enjoy for ever, by this peace, yet Caesar would by no means yield to it.

Thirdly, for that the Most Serene Elector Palatine, has violently invaded and taken possession of divers goods, moveable and immoveable, which belongs to the Dutchess of Orleans, by inheritance, from the deceased lords, her father and brother; and hitherto detains 'em, finding means to elude by divers arts the patience both of the King and his brother, but depending all the while upon the protection of the Emperor, whom he therefore has perswaded to make peace with the Turk, and to bring back his arms to the Rhine, having enter'd into divers leagues for that purpose.

For that in the fourth and last place, the Cardinal of Furstemburg contrary to the Holy Canons, the freedom of the Chapter, and the instrument of peace, his former faults which by the Emperor had been pardon'd, being brought into remembrance, and allegd'd against him by the Emperor's ambassador before a session of the Chapter, is openly and expresly excluded from the electoral dignity, and the Most Serene Prince Joseph Clement of Bavaria by base arts, the Pope himself being seduced, and a brief of eligibility, as they call it, obtain'd from him, to the scandal of all people, and the forces of the Protestants being brought into the Electorate of Cologne, is violently thrust in, in his stead; with this malicious intention, that he the said Clement of Bavaria, being by entring into orders, hindered from marrying, if the Most Supreme Elector of Bavaria should happen to dye, as he is at present, without issue (which may easily be, he exposing himself continually to so many dangers in the war) then a family suspected alwayes by the House of Austria should be taken out of the way.

By all which ('tis said) it may appear clearer than the sun at noon-day, that the Emperour not regarding the desolation of the Arch-bishoprick of Cologne, and the oppression of the Catholick religion, does endeavor to have war made upon France at the charge and hazard of the electors, princes and states of the Empire, that so the Roman diadem may at least settle on the head of the King of Hungary (now a child) and all Germany, large as it is, being torn away from the King's friendship, may fall under the most miserable tyranny and servitude of the House of Austria: even as these things are more largely and invidiously set forth in the foresaid writing.

When His Sacred Majesty, the Emperor, read this infamous libel, (infamous not to him, but to the author or authors of it) and saw in it not so much as a shadow of reason, but the most impudent slanders wickedly forg'd, both against His Sacred Person and the Pope's, as also against the Most Serene Elector Palatine, he easily perswaded himself, that it was quite contrary to the sence of the Most Christian King, and therefore far from having been read or approv'd by him, but that rather it was compil'd by some malicious French minister of state; for that he believ'd the French King would not suffer willingly, that His Imperial Majesty, in a way so unusual betwixt crown'd heads, should be so unworthily reproach'd, which matters he certainly knew in his conscience to be false, or that the reasons of his own actings, such as they are, should be written in such an impudent stile, and with such venomous reflections and interpretations of things; and therefore His Imperial Majesty doubted a great while whether he should think it worthy of an answer, and not rather pass it over in silence: but forasmuch as the French Court is not asham'd, irreverently to publish it, by its ministers as well in the Emperor's own Court, as at Ratisbone in the Dyet, and endeavours by such false and contumelious reasons to justifie their bringing on us a cruel war, in a way little better than downright treachery and perfidiousness, without so much as denouncing it before hand, as the law of nations does require, and has been often agreed; and without letting us know what injury they had to complain of, but even deceiving us all by their fresh assurances of constant friendship and pretended kindness: therefore His Imperial Majesty thought it necessary to demonstrate to the world the vanity and insignificancy of all those undeserved imputations.

To begin therefore with that which is the foundation, on which all the French reasoning stands, viz. that the Emperor had resolv'd to make a peace with the Turk, that he might fall upon France, that can with no more truth be charged upon him now, than it was the last year at Rome in a proposition made by Cardinal d'Estrée. And as impartial judges will hardly believe, that so religious a prince, supported by God's help in the present war, and having all the success he desired, forc'd by no necessity, would so much as think of making a peace with the Turks, without the privity of his allies, thereby to defile his conscience with the rash breach of a league made against the Ottoman Empire, and at the same time to incur the just censures and complaints of the Pope, the King and Senate of Poland, and the Commonwealth of Venice; so how vain a suggestion the other is, that His Imperial Majesty should have an intent to make war with France (when he has neither an army nor provisions at hand, nay when all his strong places, cities and provinces, as the event shews, by too much trusting the King's word, are left in a manner destitute of souldiers, and of all kind of necessaries for defence, and his whole strength gone against the enemy of Christianity) every one will easily see who will but take the pains even slightly to consider, upon how weak and frivolous arguments that surmise is grounded.

Those arguments certainly amongst those that know nothing of the matter will scarce seem to bear the weight of a thin and brittle conjecture; but to those who do understand it they will appear to be mere fictions, which yet if they were true, would prove nothing to this purpose. For who is there that can draw so much as a probable consequence from hence, that because the Emperor favors the innocent in defence of himself, and of the alliances which his friends have made, because he refuses to turn a twenty years' truce into a perpetual peace, without first hearing those that are concerned in it, and without any discussions of the matter, because by his counsel and help he sustains his father-in-law, the Elector, that France may not have the deciding of his cause. Because lastly, he removes Furstemburg, the man that has been so fatal to his country, and promotes to the Bishoprick of Cologne a prince of great expectation, of the family of the dukes of Bavaria, which has deserv'd very well both of their country, and of that archepiscopal see: who I say can hence draw but a probable consequence, that therefore the Emperor intends to take the first opportunity to make war with France.

Nay France it self, if it would but remember what was remonstrated in letters to the Pope, and to His Most Christian Majesty both by words and writing, the last year, by the Count Lobcowitz, the Emperor's embassador, would doubtless acknowledge, that all the other superadded arguments, and especially that drawn from the league established at Ausburg, were vain and frivolous. For this league brought on nothing that was new, but only established some ancient agreements betwixt the Emperor and some of the circles of the Empire: it renew'd what was necessary betwixt the princes and states of the Empire for the circumstances of the present time: it tended to the hurt of none, but only to that which is most innocent, and allowed by all law, their mutual defence: and besides it took in but a moderate number of heads, and a small strength into it: and therefore the mighty Crown of France did not need to be afraid of it.

Truly the forgetfulness of the compiler of this libel is very wonderful, that he will not so much as remember that his own King, to prevent all just occasion of quarrelling with the Emperor and Empire upon that account, before the signing of the truce, did promise, that after it was sign'd he would not be against the Empire's consulting the best ways for its own safety. Nay, and it was expresly declared in the very league of truce, that such agreements of the Empire might be strengthened by any kind of guaranty of forreign princes. But the same author's ignorance is yet much more to be admir'd, that he shou'd not know that there is nothing more antiently receiv'd in the German Empire, nor nothing more agreeable to its laws, than that the members should always most closely adhere to the head for the preservation of the whole body. And lastly, his arrogance or his folly is greatly to be admired, that whilst he presumes it lawful for his own King to make vast preparations of war in his kingdom, nay and under pretence of a league unjustly made with some of the Chapter of Cologne, to send his forces into that Arch-bishoprick, he supposes the Emperor in the mean while to have so little to do in the Empire, that he may not so much as meet with the princes and states thereof to consult about the peace of their country, without doing such an injury to France as must be revenged by force of arms.

His second argument has much the same degree of force and validity in it, viz. that the Emperor refused to turn the truce into a peace: if he had wholly refused it, and that upon other conditions, that were not so unworthy of the Emperor, and noxious to the whole Empire, as those which at that time happened to be prescribed rather than propounded by the Court of France, had that been any crime? The twenty years' truce ought certainly to have been stood to, and during the continuance of that a peace should have been treated of, which His Most August Majesty never refused, provided the King would agree to a peace that was honourable, maturely considered and just: there ought therefore to have been a meeting appointed, and both sides heard, and all the chief controversies concerning matters of right, in those things which were attempted by France as well before as after the truce, should have been examined; and then might have ensued a peace, everyone having their own restored to 'em, by common consent, and such as might have been likely happily to continue.

The Most Christian King might remember, that at his desire the truce was lengthened out to twenty years, both that there might be time enough to discuss and determine all controversies, as it was fit, and that the electors, princes and states of the Empire, might with the greater security take arms against the common enemy of the Christian name: and therefore that it cannot be without the French King's breaking his agreement, and violating his word; that when scarce two years of the twenty are gone about, and while the Turkish War yet lasts, he should so change his mind, that nothing now forsooth should remain to be discussed or determined, but a sixth part of the provinces of the Empire must at once by a full and irrevocable right be made over to him. Now this is what the Emperor could not lawfully have done, if he would: it would have been contrary to right, and to the tenour of the truce, and they who had thought themselves injured would doubtless have withstood it. . . .

He endeavours to amuse their minds with such stuff lest they shou'd agree and join together for their true honour and common security, thinking that the French King will easily rout 'em all severally, though if all shou'd joyn together, they wou'd quickly drive him away. And therefore he strives all he can by fraud and craft, to cause Germany to forsake the patronage and auspicious conduct of the House of Austria. But the House of Bavaria is not so weak, nor the German nation so silly, as not to understand these artifices which cannot easily be hid. And as the Most Serene Elector of Bavaria do's gratefully acknowledge the kind offices which the Emperor at his bequest did for his house in the election at Cologne, so according to its usual wisdom, it will but laugh at such little sparks of suspition, as it has done already having had experience of these prating sowers of dissension; and will easily see, that there is nothing to be hop'd for from the French who seek but what they can get. But the German whoever he is, that is free from the iron yoke of the French, may easily see by the oppression of the people even in Germany it self where they come, and from the condition even of their own nobility and gentry in France, whether comes nearer to tyranny the governour of the House of Austria, or the French manner of ruling; and will rejoyce truly that the Roman Crown do's not fall that way, whither the French Court has often shewn that they have designed it, and then especially, when after their ancient fashion without any regard to honesty, to their faith, their good name, or to conscience, they have not only cherish'd the rebels in Hungary, followers of the Turk, by sending 'em captains, messengers, arms, money and large promises, but also, as it is done even at this day, have stirred up and encourag'd the very enemies of the Christian name against His Imperial Majesty. As it may be manifestly prov'd by the authentick letters of the French emissaries and of the rebels and others, which are ready to be produced.

And this is that which His Imperial Majesty has order'd to be answer'd with as much brevity as possible, to that contumelious libel or French manifesto, not to injure the reputation of the Most Christian King, whom he believes to be induc'd to this unjust breach of the peace by the malitious and false suggestions of those who seek gain by these troubles, and who he believes wou'd not approve of such ill language and unjust railing against His Sacred Person, but to wipe off all the scandal which this impudent writer has endeavoured to fix upon the House of Austria, and which the ministers of France do every where scatter about, and to defend his own innocence.

And moreover that this his cause may be more and more publickly known and testified to all the Christian world he does publickly declare and call the Omniscient God to witness, that he never thought any thing of breaking the truce, but that he was alwayes firmly resolv'd, and it is still his true and serious purpose to keep it inviolably, if it will at last please His Most Christian Majesty to stand to the covenant of truce, and the declarations which he made and reitereated but the last year from Paris, and not to endeavour to make any alterations. But as for passing this truce into a firm and perpetual peace, he persists in that, that he will most candidly and willingly shew forth all readiness in endeavouring it, provided that a commission being appointed for the dividing of the borders, and discussing the controverted rights, may proceed in that manner and order as is agreeable to the laws made betwixt France and the Empire. Wherefore if there be any regard to justice in the Most Serene K[ing] of France (as it is hop'd) His Imperial Majesty has good reason to believe and trust, that he will of himself chastise and correct the calumnies and slanders of this scandalous French print, will withdraw his unjust arms, restore dammages, bring back all into its primitive state, permit the Most Serene Prince Clement, long since legally confirm'd by His Holiness, to enjoy quietly the Electorate and Arch-bishoprick of Cologne, and will remit the cause of the Prince Palatine to a competent court of judicature, in which His Imperial Majesty does promise that justice shall be faithfully and impartially done: and lastly, that he will suffer the peace which he sayes he wishes for, to be procured in the time, manner and order as is set down in the truce.

But if he be not willing to do these things, none can then suppose there is any other cause for the French King thus to revive the war, than that the singular favor of the Divine Providence, and the wonderful defence it has afforded to the House of Austria, are things displeasing to him, or that he fears the great encrease and enlargement of that august family, by their late victories which have carried the Empire beyond Belgrade; or that he has a desire to raise up agains the beaten and depressed Turks by diverting our arms, as 'tis said he has promised them. Or lastly, that through too greedy a desire, not only of assuring to himself for perpetuity, what he has got for a time by the articles of the truce, but also of conquering the whole Roman Empire, he thinks himself not oblig'd by any pacts or covenants, but that he may break them at any time at his pleasure. Whatever it is, the Most Glorious King of France shall not escape the infamous mark of a perfidious prince that violates his faith. And therefore His Most Sacred Imperial Majesty does protest before God and the whole Christian world, that the said King is free to stretch forth his hands either to the fire or the water, and either to abuse the felicity of his present power, or in time to fear those adversities which he provokes the Omnipotent God in anger to send upon him. But as for himself, being driven to the necessary defence as well of his provinces, as of the Sacred Roman Empire, the electors, princes and states thereof, he shall be blameless and free from all the guilt as well of the calamities like to follow from the war, and the effusion of Christian blood, as of the Mahometan superstition continuing still in Europe, and of the destruction of so many Christian souls, miserably groaning under the yoke of the Turk.

The author indeed of this print boasts and glories that His Most Christian Majesties arms are proved just from Heaven by their success wheresoever he moves 'em; but with what truth let him shew if he can. His Imperial Majesty being fully satisfied of the goodness of his cause, is resolved if it shall please God in this occasion to give prosperous success to the French arms, he will never the less adore and magnifie the secret counsels of God, who has sometimes chastized and corrected even those whom He loved, by such as Attilas: but he is glad that he has cause to hope better in this world. The Most High has thrown down and humbled the Turk that broke his league but a little before it was ready to expire: and He will also throw down and humble the French violater of a league which should have held sixteen years longer.

Vienna, Octob. 18th, 1688

39. The Glorious Revolution

William of Orange (1650–1702) profited from war and instability for himself and his dynasty more than any other prince in Europe. Without the French invasion of the Netherlands in 1672, William might not

SOURCE: J. H. Robinson and C. A. Beard, *Readings in Modern European History* (New York: Ginn & Co., 1908), I, 28–31.

have succeeded in wresting power from the strong republicans in the Netherlands; and in 1688, the pro-Catholic and absolutistic policies of James II of England provided still another opportunity for William to increase his power.

By proclaiming that he had come not to violate English laws and customs but to preserve them as a Protestant defender, William appealed directly and forcefully to those Englishmen disaffected from James II. The climate of fear and near-hysteria about "Popery" and "enslavement" which had developed in England under James could be exploited by a clever statesman. In this William succeeded, not only for his wife Mary, daughter of James II, but also for himself. William carefully avoided a direct attack on, or even criticism of, James himself in order not to arouse sentiments of loyalty to the Stuarts or fears of violence and revolution. Moreover, as a prince all too familiar with the power of the mob and the yoke of representative institutions, William moved quietly and slowly in his attempt to gain the English throne without the loss of regalian rights. Here he was somewhat less successful.

The impact upon European politics of William's successful invasion of England was immediate and enormous. Suddenly a great power appeared to the north of France able to sustain long and costly wars in a way neither the Dutch nor the English could have done alone.

The Declaration of His Highness, William Henry, by the Grace of God, Prince of Orange, etc, of the reasons inducing him to appear in arms in the Kingdom of England, for preserving of the Protestant Religion, and for restoring of the laws and liberties of England, Scotland, and Ireland

I. It is both certain and evident to all men, that the publick peace and happiness of any state or kingdom cannot be preserved where the laws, liberties, and customs established by the lawful authority in it are openly transgressed and annulled: More especially where the alteration of religion is endeavoured, and that a religion, which is contrary to law, is endeavoured to be introduced: Upon which those who are most immediately concerned in it are indispensably bound to endeavour to maintain and preserve the established laws, liberties, and customs, and above all the religion and worship of God, that is established among them; and to take such an effectual care that the inhabitants of the said state or kingdom may neither be deprived of their religion nor of their civil rights; which is so much the more necessary, because the greatness and security both of kings, royal families, and of all such as are in authority, as well as the happiness of their subjects and people, depend, in a most especial manner, upon the exact observation and maintenance of these their laws, liberties, and customs.

II. Upon these grounds it is that we can't any longer forbear to declare, that, to our great regret, we see that those counsellors, who have now the chief credit with the King, have overturned the religion, laws, and liberties of these realms, and subjected them, in all things relating to their consciences, liberties, and properties, to arbitrary government, and that not only by secret and indirect ways, but in an open and undisguised manner. . . .

XII. They have also, by putting the administration of civil justice in the hands of Papists, brought all the matters of civil justice into great uncertainties; with how much exactness and justice soever these sentences may have been given. For since the laws of the land do not only exclude Papists from all places of judicature, but have put them under an incapacity, none are bound to acknowledge or to obey their judgments; and all sentences given by them are null and void of themselves: So that all persons who have been cast in trials before such Popish judges, may justly look on their pretended sentences as having no more force than the sentences of any private and unauthorized person whatsoever. . . .

[The King's evil counsellors] have not only armed the Papists, but have likewise raised them up to the greatest military trust, both by the sea and land, and that strangers as well as natives, and Irish as well as English, that so by those means, having rendered themselves masters both of the affairs of the church, of the government of the nation, and of the courts of justice, and subjected them all to a despotick and arbitrary power, they might be in a capacity to maintain and execute their wicked designs, by the assistance of the army, and thereby to enslave the nation.

XIII. The dismal effects of this subversion of the established religion, laws, and liberties in England appear more evidently to us, by what we see done in Ireland; where the whole government is put in the hands of Papists, and where all the Protestant inhabitants are under the daily fears of what may be justly apprehended from the arbitrary power which is set up there; which has made great numbers of them leave that kingdom, and abandon their estates in it, remembering well that cruel and bloody massacre which fell out in that island in the year 1641.

XIV. Those evil counsellors have also prevailed with the King to declare in Scotland, that he is cloathed with absolute power, and that all the subjects are bound to obey him without reserve: Upon which he assumed an arbitrary power both over the religion and laws of the kingdom; from all of which it's apparent what is to be looked for in England as soon as matters are duly prepared for it.

XV. Those great and insufferable oppressions, and the open contempt of all law, together with the apprehensions of the sad consequences that must certainly follow upon it, have put the subjects under great and just fears; and have made them look after such lawful remedies as are allow'd of in all nations; yet all has been without effect. . . .

XX. And since our dearest and most entirely beloved consort the Princess, and likewise we ourselves, have so great an interest in this matter, and such a right as all the world knows to the succession of the Crown: Since all the English did, in the year 1672, when the States General of the United Provinces were invaded with a most unjust war, use their utmost endeavours to put an end to that war, and that in opposition to those who were then in the government; and by their so doing, they run the hazard of losing both the favour of the court and their employments: And since the English nation has ever testified a most particular affection and esteem both to our dearest consort the Princess, and to ourselves, we cannot excuse ourselves from espousing their interest in a matter of such high consequence: And for contributing all that lies in us for the maintaining both of the Protestant religion, and of the laws and liberties of those kingdoms, and for the securing to them the continual enjoyment of all their just rights. To the doings of which, we are most earnestly solicited by a great many lords, both spiritual and temporal, and by many gentlemen, and other subjects of all ranks.

XXI. Therefore it is, that we have thought fit to go over to England, and to carry over with us a force sufficient by the blessing of God, to defend us from the violence of those evil counsellors. And we, being desirous that our intention in this might be rightly understood, have for this end prepared this declaration, in which, as we have hitherto given a true account of the reasons inducing us to it, so we now think fit to declare, that this our expedition is intended for no other design, but to have a free and lawful Parliament assembled, as soon as possible, and that the members shall meet and sit in full freedom. . . .

XXV. We do in the last place invite and require all persons

whatsoever, all the peers of the realm, both spiritual and temporal, all lords-lieutenants, deputy-lieutenants, and all gentlemen, citizens, and other commons of all ranks, to come and assist us, in order to the executing of this our design against all such as shall endeavour to oppose us; that so we may prevent all those miseries, which must needs follow upon the nations being kept under arbitrary government and slavery: And that all the violence and disorders which have overturned the whole constitution of the English government may be fully redressed in a free and legal Parliament. . . .

XXVI. And we will endeavour, by all possible means, to procure such an establishment in all the three kingdoms that they may all live in a happy union and correspondence together; and that the Protestant religion, and the peace, honour, and happiness of those nations may be established upon lasting foundations.

Given under our hand and seal at our court in the Hague, the 10th day of October, in the year of our Lord 1688

William Henry, Prince of Orange
By His Highness's special command

40. *English in Favor of Continuing the War*

General weariness with war, high taxes, and economic dislocation raised doubts in the minds of some Englishmen about the wisdom of continuing the war against Louis XIV. This pamphlet, published anonymously in 1692, attempts to rally support for the war and indirectly to aid William III at a time when the King faced considerable opposition to his policies in Parliament. Military operations in 1692, after tremendous efforts on the part of both the Allies and the French to defeat each other, ended that year in something like a stalemate, with little hope of peace in sight.

It is not difficult to discern which public the anonymous author was most concerned about in his efforts to sustain opinion in favor of the war. His arguments and appeals are directed mainly toward English merchants. But in addition to his assessments of trade, his mercantilistic, nationalistic, and historical conceptions of the nature of war make the

SOURCE: *The Present War no Burthen to England* (London, 1692), pp. 1–6, 7–9.

text particularly interesting. Similar texts, and refutations of them, may be found in the Dutch, French, Spanish, and German pamphlet literature of the time. There are differences in each tradition which deserve to be systematically explored. A comparison of this text with that of Sir Peter Pett found in document 32 reveals that a more complex analysis of their economic situation was available to literate Englishmen.

Some sort of people having wearied out themselves in finding fault with the government, and reviling sometimes the Dutch, as ready to strike up a private peace; sometimes the whole body of the Allies, as none of them having done their duty: the general cry of that party now is, that money being carryed abroad for the payment of our forces, it will in time exhaust the treasure of the nation, and impovrish it: which seems so palpable a thing, and begins to gain so much ground upon the belief of many (otherwise well-affected) people, that a longer delay in shewing the falsity of that notion, might seem of a dangerous consequence: therefore I think it will not be improper, to prove, that the war increasing our trade, and occasioning a greater vent and exportation of our manufactures, and of the product of our ground, inriches the nation, and augments its stock.

In the first place, the vent [sale] of our woollen manufactures is greater than heretofore, which appears not only by that it is generally advanced in price, but in that there is a greater quantity now exported than in times of peace, as may be seen by the entries in the custom-houses.

Secondly, the manufactures of silk, linnen, paper and others, have since the war been considerably forwarded; there is no longer need of importing flowr'd and mixt silks, good quantity of plain silk is made here, as likewise of linnen and paper, which saves and keeps so much money in the nation, as formerly was sent out to purchase those commodities.

Thirdly, corn (which by the blessing of God hath been hitherto plentiful amongst us, although very scarce amongst our neighbors) tobacco, sugar, and many others the products of our ground, bear a better price than they should in a peaceable time, by the greater exportation abroad; the Netherlands alone taking more of these commodities and of our manufactures, than what is remitted thither for the maintaining of our forces, comes to; I say, taking more, over and above what they did in time of peace. For how can it be imagined that so small a tract of ground, as the Spaniards have left in the Low Countries, which doth not extend to above thirty miles in breadth, and an hundred miles in length, and which by the great and numerous armies that continually harass it, yields little or nothing; should suffice to maintain two hundred thousand men and horses of the Allies, besides the inhabitants of eleven great towns, and of an innumerable quantity of villages, castles, and strongholds: certainly that prodigious number of people must be supported and maintained from the neighboring countries. The Dutch, indeed, supply them a good measure, (for otherwise being obliged to send money thither for the payment of their forces, their treasure also would in time be exhausted, and they impoverish't) but they draw the greatest part of their maintenance from us; our wheat, our malt, our oats, our tabacco, our sugar, go thither for their food; our cloth, our serges, our bayes [baize], our stockings, our hats, are sent them for their cloathing; our coals for their fuel; our lead, our powder, our arms, for their warlike service; our tallow, our pewter, our leather, and thousands of other things, for their other necessary uses: nay, our wine, our brandy, our salt (that we take from our enemies as prize, and which otherwise would be destroyed) are sent and vended amongst them, and the money it produces turned to the nation's advantage; so that the fifty or sixty thousand pounds a month we remit thither for the payment of our forces, comes monthly to us again for the payment of all those necessaries; from whence perhaps this inference might be drawn, that the more forces we send into Flanders, provided the Allies do send an answerable number, the better England will fare, and the richer grow.

Fourthly, trade in general is much increased.

1. The plantations and West-Indies trade is no less, but rather better; that of Jamaica especially, which is now treble of what it was before the war, by the great transportation of linnen, and other things from that island, to the coast of terra ferma of America.

2. That of Turkey is as considerable, there going now as much cloth for Turkey in one fleet, as formerly did in two or three years.

3. That of Spain as good, we now sending thither some of the commodities the French used to carry into Spain, and drawing

from thence, wines and other commodities in a greater quantity than heretofore.

4. The trade to Italy is considerably increased, not only by our getting from thence more paper and silk; (this last for the carrying on our manufactures here at home) but likewise by our sending thither abundance of cloth, and other woollen manufactures; lead, tin, leather, and other things for the service and cloathing of the forces in Piedmont, the Milanez, and other parts of Italy. The islands of Sicily and Sardinia; the Kingdom of Naples, and the State of Milan, by the prohibition of French commodities, drawing now from us several sorts of goods which they usually got out of France.

5. That of Portugal hath received a considerable improvement; we fetching from thence more wines than we did formerly, and sending thither in return, a much greater quantity of lead, tin, coperas [copperas], serges, bayes, sayes [say, a type of serge], &c. than in time of peace.

6. The trade to all northern parts, as Russia, Sueden, Denmark, Norway, is more considerable, by our greater importation of hemp, pitch, tar, and other products of those cold clymates.

7. The Germany trade, as that of Dantsick [Danzig], Lubeck, Hambourg, Bremen, is three times what it was heretofore, by the great quantities of linnen we import from thence, not only for our own use, but likewise for transportation to Jamaica and Spain; and also because we send them more cloth, and all other woollen manufactures, more tin, lead, coals, wines, brandy, and salt, than we used to do.

8. That of Holland and Flanders, what a vast addition hath it not received? By the prodigious quantities of corn of all sorts, sugar, tobacco, tin, lead, coals, cloth, bayes, sayes, serges, stuffs, stockings, &c. of our own manufacture and product, we send thither; in such a degree, that where there was formerly one vessel trading between the Netherlands and the island of Great Britain, there is now scores of ships imployed in the mutual service of both countries.

9. The trade of France indeed is lessen'd, but is much more advantagious: our money (and in a considerable quantity too) was yearly sent to that kingdom for its products, whereas now whatever we get of French commodities costs us nothing, but is sold by our privateers, and merchants concern'd with them, in Flanders and Germany, for good money, which is so much profit, that accrues to the nation. . . .

If from trade, we turn our thoughts to other parts of the nation; is there any sort, or rank of people that can complain they suffer: the wages and salaries of labouring-men are rather higher than in time of peace: the handycraft-men want no work, and vend it easily, and at good rates: nay, several handycrafts are set up by the war, which are needless in time of peace: the farmer sells his corn, his timber, his hops, his cattel, better than at any other time, and thereby is enabled to pay better his rent: the shop-keeper hath as good and as great a retail: the rich-mony'd-man an opportunity of lending his money to a better advantage: the land-man indeed must pay taxes, and if the tax were equally laid, a small share of his revenue, (which is the only visible hardship); but in lieu thereof, how many gentlemen are there, that have imployments, and by those imploys, get more than they give towards the war? What family is there, that hath not either a brother, a son, or some other near relation in the fleet, or in the army? And thereby is put in a capacity not only of maintaining, but of raising it self: many a younger brother, that in time of peace had been ready to starve, hath now by the war, hundreds to spend a year; nay, many vagabonds, and other idle people of the nation, have by the war an opportunity of honestly and lawfully getting a lively-hood in the service of their country.

War is said to be a curse to a nation, 'tis true, but 'tis only so, where the seat of war is, where all is committed to plunder, rapine, fire, flames and utter destruction. But how many nations have raised their name, and rendred themselves famous and rich by war? The Persians, Macedonians, Romans, Suedes, are memorable instances of it, who all grew great, potent and rich by their wars.

The Dutch, when they form'd themselves into a commonwealth, were a handful of people, and had neither ships, money, or strong towns to boast of; but under the ever auspicious conduct of the princes of Orange, and by a fourscore years' Spanish war; they grew to that vast wealth and immense grandeur, we have seen them arrived at.

And what have not advantagious wars brought into this nation? Our conquests in the West-Indies have for certain advanced our riches: the fifty years' war of Edward the Third against France, cost England an immense treasure, and yet all our chronicles say, England was never so rich as in his time: our great Queen Elizabeth had not always a peaceable, though a happy and golden reign; Oliver [Cromwell] was not in peace, whilst he govern'd; but no body then complained the nation grew poor, every body was sensible it grew rich: and had not the Richards, the Henries, and others our heroick princes, render'd by their wars abroad the English name formidable throughout the world? I don't know, what our last thirty-years' peace would have brought us to, and whether we had been not the prey of a neighbouring prince, otherwise greedy and powerful enough, but who perhaps was daunted by the remembrance of our ancient valour; and the glorious atchievements of our ancestors.

41. An Assessment of French Strengths and Weaknesses

After some preliminary political and moral arguments regarding France's weaknesses, the anonymous author turns to an analysis of Louis XIV's revenues. Note his reluctance to see the French as any more brutal than the Confederates (Allies) as a consequence of the burning and destruction of the Palatinate. Not even the revocation of the Edict of Nantes stirs him much emotionally; the author is chiefly interested in the effect of this decision upon the French economy.

Though the description and analysis of French taxation may not be entirely accurate, it is a very worthwhile introduction to this complex subject. A comparison with the figures which Colbert provides in document 17 may reveal that the English author conscientiously sought to estimate France's ability to continue at war, rather than to supply false figures which would have propagandistically suggested to a war-weary public that Louis was in a weaker position that he actually was.

There are few persons that suffer not their eyes to be daz'led at the first sight with the great power of France, and the appearing riches of that kingdom. The repose which one would think she enjoys within her self, her progress abroad, her naval strength, her prodigious armies, and the great number of towns and fortresses which she has won within her enemies' countries and upon their frontiers, which render her own provinces as it were inaccessible; all these

SOURCE: *The Present Condition of France, in Reference to her Revenues, comparing them with the Infinite Expences she is forc'd to be at, Demonstrating thereby that it is impossible for her to support her self if the War with the Confederates continues*, Done out of French (London, 1692), pp. 1–12, 23.

things joyn'd together, are enough to deceive the eye. But pry into her more narrowly, and you will find that if on the one side this great power appears invincible, and these immense riches inexhaustible, the first cannot support it self, but must inevitably sink under the burthen of its own weight, if the second, which is the revenue, the principal sinews of the other, and the main spring that moves that mighty fabrick, comes once to fail, or but to abate considerably, which has already come to pass. The people who supply'd these revenues, but are now tumbl'd into utmost misery, are an evident proof of what we assert, altho' we wanted others much certain. But the display which we are about to make is without any reply. Tis true; that a crew of anonymous scriblers and others, by setting forth a prodigious number of pamphlets, have us'd their utmost endeavours to make it out that if the grandeur of France draws to a period, she her self has procur'd her own misfortune. They have set forth, with great care, the violences which she has perpetrated both abroad and at home, within her own provinces, her ravishings, her falshood, her breach of all her promises, contracts, and treaties; her usurpations, burnings, sacriledges, her persecutions and extortions.

They have prognosticated that all these proceedings were as so many avant curriers and occasions of her approaching downfall. I must confess at the same time that all this is not without good grounds. For if we look upon the thing, in respect of Providence, it is impossible that Divine Vengeance should suffer a domination so long to prosper that has no regard to any laws, either divine or humane, when the contest was for grandeur and dominion, and many times committed many mischiefs meerly to pleasure a haughty fancy, when there was no advantage to be reap'd by the crime. If we consider her conduct, in respect of the princes that are become her enemies, it is impossible but all these lawless actions must have provok'd 'em to that degree, as never to hope for any reconciliation. Her allies may also judge by that, what they do expect from her, if once they should happen to kindle her anger, or if it should only come into her head that their ruine might be serviceable to exalt her grandeur. And lastly, it cannot be but that even her own subjects must be highly disgusted at her government, in regard that though these rigorous tyrannies did not directly concern themselves, as it has many times happn'd upon several occasions, yet it is always an unhappy thing to serve such violent masters; as well for that the hatred which forreigners conceive against a sovraign rebounds upon the subjects, as for that they ought to expect the same usage, should it happen by misfortune that the war should come home to their own doors; and that he to whom they yield obedience should be constrain'd to abandon their defence. In a word, I am perswaded that if the Confederates, for example, should come to penetrate into the Dauphinate, the French would deal by that province as they did by the Palatinate. So that those writers that have made the violences of France an argument of her approaching ruine, have not been altogether in the wrong. But however it be, all these reasons cannot pass for any other than reasons of plausibility, not sufficient to satisfie and convince certain people who, being accustomed to more solid arguments, submit to nothing but demonstration.

I shall therefore quit these sort of reasons in this little treatise, or if I make use of 'em, it shall only be as accessories, upon which I shall not put any great stress. My principal aim is to shew that by comparing the revenues of France with her expences, and examining the nature of these revenues, we shall find that the expences vastly exceed the income; I shall also shew by undeniable proofs that the revenues of France are very much abated, and that it is impossible but they must fall every day more and more. So that if the war continues, she must of necessity sink under the weight, without any possibility of being able to support her self. But it is time to conclude this long proem, least the impatient reader cry out with Horace, "*Quid dignum tanto feret hic promissor hiatu?*"

Let us come then to matter of fact. 'Tis certainly true that before the war which blazes now all over Europe, the Crown of France might reckon upon rents and revenues which were appropriated and annexed to it, to the value of about a hundred threescore and two millions; besides casualties, which formerly, and before the war in 1672, the French had mounted up to threescore millions. 'Tis also true that since the year 1685 that open hostility was absolutely proclaim'd against all the Reformed in the kingdom, the rents have fallen near ten millions, by reason of the interruption and disorder which it caus'd in trade. Which was the reason that they began to grant considerable indemnities to the [tax] farmers, though they had taken the farms at a fix'd and certain rent; and of this the contradictory decrees and declarations that ensu'd are testimonies so notoriously publick that they are no way to be call'd in question. 'Tis also certain that the Reformed were they who had the principal and the greatest interest in these farms, considering their trade both within and without the kingdom. The duties for entrance, passage, and carrying out of merchandize which they pay'd, amounted to a vast summ in the receipts of the farms, customs, *foraines*, *traittes estrangeres*, and *tariffes*.* There are also some French merchants in Holland, and in other places, of which the meanest dealer pay'd before the persecution above 25,000 livers [livres] (or 3125 £ sterling) every year in duties to the king, and who the next three years after that of 1685 never pay'd above 177 £ odd money. And therefore it was that the deceas'd Monsieur Colbert, who foresaw the damage that would accrue to the Crown by the edict prohibiting the Reformed to be admitted to publick offices and management of the king's affairs, and lamented their being persecuted as they were every day, could not forbear to oppose it with all his might. But all his remonstrances could not prevail against the Jesuitical counsels and resolutions which were then taken utterly to extirpate the Reformed out of the kingdom, whatever it cost.

It is therefore evident that before the revocation of the Edict of Nantes, the persecution had caus'd a considerable abatement in the king's farms.

Now if we compare this time with that which follow'd after, when several rich merchants who still drove a considerable trade, though much abated, were forc'd to fly the kingdom, and carry'd along with 'em almost all their effects, which was for the most part in ready money, and settled their manufactures and traffick abroad; when several families also, that rais'd the king's duties by the consumption of several commodities, were likewise withdrawn, and that the manufactures were almost utterly laid aside in all the cities of the kingdom, as well as because they had not vent [sales], as for that the workmen were hal'd away to the wars; there is no doubt but all this caus'd a far more considerable abatement in the king's duties.

Nevertheless, the French make it their business to spread it

* *Foraines* is an imposition of trelupence tournois, on the fourth part of an English shilling upon all goods imported. *Traittes estrangeres* is an imposition of the twentieth part of the value of all goods imported and exported. *Tariffes* are the books of rates upon all spiceries and custom-house goods. [Author's note]

abroad that the farms of all the grand demesnes that were lett in the years 1689 and 1690 receiv'd no diminution by this present conjuncture, and yet that the price of 'em was rais'd too. But this is such a wonderful thing that it may well be question'd whether they who presum'd to divulge so idle a story, had not a purpose to make themselves merry, by ridiculing the prince, in whose favour they forg'd a fable so incredible. For from whence should such an enhancement proceed? Could it be from the increase of trade? With whom should this mighty traffick be? Certainly it must be with the people of the Antartick regions, which the ships of the French had lately discover'd. For as for any trade which they pretend to with the known parts of the world, we see but little they have. But quite the contrary, excepting Switzerland, a country very improper to augment the king's farms, and some parts of Italy, all other commerce is forbidden 'em. But perhaps the preceding farmers got too much, and the new ones are contented with a meaner profit. But had it been so, we should infallibly have seen some tax impos'd upon 'em. Besides, that though there is something to be gain'd, they are too sharp sighted in France to let the farmers gain so considerably by the bargains which they make.

Then again, all France is sensible that the new farmers are so far from acting independent in the management of the farms, that they only act as overseers, for the better ordering and receiving of the king's duties and demesnes. The labour which they take, and the conduct which they observe in all the places where the king's duties are demanded, evidently prove this to be a truth. 'Tis well known that these overseers had for their expences, as also for their advancing-money beforehand, and for their good management, two sous in a livre, and were oblig'd to give an account for no more than they receiv'd. Nor is this the first time that the farmers have been at this lock. Le Gendre, Fauconet, Saunier, du Frenti, Bout, and some other general farmers, before the year 1689 though they had taken the farms at a set rate, were admitted, at least they who desir'd it, to account for no more then they receiv'd, because it was clearly seen they had been losers by the abatements that had happen'd in their farms, by reason of those accidents and casualties already mention'd. Others there are who have only obtain'd considerable abatements; which is so well known over all the kingdom that there are few people who know anything of business that can be ignorant of it. The declarations and decrees that have been publish'd upon these occasions, and the great failings of the principal farmers, have been too publick for any body to deny what a ticklish undertaking it is to meddle with those great farms.

Now if in time of peace, and in the flourishing state of France, they were constrain'd to allow the general farmers considerable abatements and indemnities, what may be thought of it now that the best cities of the kingdom are ruin'd, that the nation is depriv'd of all forraign trade, and that the King is forc'd to hurry his militias, his bans, and arrier-bans, from province to province, and frontier to frontier, equally tiring out both gentry and peasant, and exhausting all his subjects with marches and counter-marches, and lying up and down the country remote from their homes and habitations. All this shews that whatever care is taken to publish the contrary, the revenues of France amount not to above the half of what the adorers of the Gallick Monarch would make the world believe. The particular examination will make this out more clearly to be true.

I shall begin with the taxes real and personal, which the Crown levies over all the extent of the kingdom, excepting in some provinces which are govern'd by States [*pays d'État*]. These taxes were enhaunc'd before the war, 1672, and three years after, to fifty-one millions a year. But then the poverty of the people and the interruption of trade was such that in the year 1676 they were reduc'd to forty millions, and in the year 1678 to thirty-six millions, and so they continued sometimes more, sometimes less, till the year 1690.

But in that year it was that the receivers of the taxes, having made it out that it was impossible to collect 'em any longer according to that rate, by reason of the poverty of the people, and the decay of trade, the desertions of the Protestants, and the waste of the younger sort in the wars, the taxes were reduc'd to thirty millions. Maugre this abatement, in regard the same inability still continu'd, there was a decree of the General Council by which all cities, with their dependencies, should in the body of their corporation be answerable for themselves, the solvent for the insolvent, to make good the summ that was impos'd upon the corporation, which put those that were taxable to unimaginable confusions and disorders, and contributes not a little to augment the miseries of the people.

The *taillon*, subvention, and subsistance,* which is receiv'd as a tax by the extraordinary treasurers at war, before the war 1672 was enhaunc'd to three millions and five hundred thousand livres, since which time it has vary'd in rising and falling, till it fell to thirteen hundred thousand livres, that is to say till it fell to two millions, two hundred thousand livres.

Before the war in 1672 there were great variations in the price of the general farm of the *gabells*[*gabelles*], or imposts upon salt; but it never exceeded nine millions, one hundred and thirty thousand livres. During the first war, it fell above six millions; and at length the farmers who desir'd greater abatements were admitted to account for what they receiv'd. After the Peace in 1678, this farm could not be enhaunc'd again any higher then twenty seven millions, two hundred thousand livres, though the *gabells* of the conquer'd countries were compriz'd therein; and at another time it was let at twenty six millions, with conditions of abatement in case of war; which shews, that though the general *gabells* had been considerably augmented by the addition of those of the conquer'd countries, by the duties impos'd upon tabacco, tin, and by a sous in a livre impos'd upon dry'd, fresh, and salt fish, in the provinces of Normandy and Picardy, nevertheless there was an abatement of above three millions; now if this happen'd during the preceding war, and in a time of peace at home, may we not believe what persons of credit and fidelity write from all parts, that in the present condition of France, the *gabells* for the year 1690 did not amount to above sixteen millions. This truth will be easily believ'd, if we do but never so little consider what has been said of the heart of France; and when we call to mind that the product of this farm chiefly proceeds from the abundance of trade. But in regard there are few people that understand what is meant by *gabells*, and what duties they include, I thought it necessary to give a short explication of the word. Under the name of general *gabells* are comprehended the three bishopricks of Metz, Toul, and Verdun, the

* The *taillon* is a tax that was rais'd by Henry II, An. 1549, toward the increase of the pay of the gens d'armes that were billetted in towns and villages, to enable 'em to pay for what they call'd for, and prevent disorders. Subvention, is a duty of the 20th penny, or one sous in a livre, laid upon all merchandizes, to supply the necessities of the State. Subsistance, an impost lay'd upon the people for the maintenance of the soldiers in their quarters. [Author's note]

demesnes and salt-pits of Lorrain, the salt-pits and demesnes of Francht Conte [Franche Comté]. They are the principal product that swell the Five Great Farms [*cinq grosses fermes*], which consist in the duties that are lay'd upon merchandize, provisions, druggs, and spices, imported and exported out of the kingdom. They are call'd the Five Great Farms, by reason of their being joyn'd to those of the same nature in the frontier provinces, as Normandy, Picardy, Champaigne, Burgundy, and Lionnois, comprehending also the provostship of Nantes, convoy and comptably of Bourdeaux, exportations from Charente, customs of Lyon and Valence, patent of Languedoc, Provence, and Arzat, the transportations from Rousillon, duties of fifty sous per tun upon fraights of foraign vessels, duties upon tabacco and tin, and the sous in every livre upon fish in the provinces of Normandy and Picardy.

If there were any part of this grand demesne of which the price ought to be fix'd, that would be seignioral demesne, and in funds of land, as rents, fines for alienation under the name of lods and ventes, of which the first are more chargeable than the second. Reliefs,* fifth penny, and fifth part of the fifth penny, quit-rents, escheats, bastardies, together with other duty and redevances, or duties annually payable to the lord of the fee, in money, corn, or day-labour, and annexed to seignioral and demesne duties; besides all this, houses, castles, cultivated lands, mills, meadows, ponds, woods, and other estates, in the nature of funds; nevertheless it has been known that these demesnes before the wars in 1672 have been taken by the farmers at 43 millions: but during the first war, they suffered two abatements, and were reduced to 36 millions, 300 thousand livres; but after the war, these abatements fell so considerably that no body would take the farm at a set rent, without great abatements, so that at present it is manag'd by persons under the name of commissioners, who for their advances, their pains and expences, which are very great, have two sous in a livre; which is notoriously known in France: and what is more to be admir'd in this, that all these demesnes have never been let higher, before the year 1663, than at three millions, which makes many believe that the excessive rates to which they were afterwards rais'd was the

* The whole year's profit of land, due to the lord upon every redemption, collateral descent, or change of the tennant. [Author's note]

occasion of those acquittances, by vertue of which the farmers sav'd themselves harmless.

There are another kind of duties which are call'd *aydes* [*aides*], which seem to be fief-rights, and almost of the same nature with those before-going; which nevertheless have suffer'd a very considerable diminution. But to make a better judgment of this, it will be requisite to enumerate the parts that compose the body of these rights: these duties therefore call'd *aydes* comprehend several impositions upon wine, sold over the whole kingdom, either by whole-sale, or re-tail, brandies, strong-waters, cider, beer, and other drinks, vinegar, the entries of Paris and Rouen; upon wood to burn, and timber, wrought and unwrought; duties of *pie*[*d*] *fourche*,* the fief-duty for the mark of iron, the duties of nine livres, ten sous per tun, and a sous, for every pot of Picardy, and passage over the Somme, the imposts and billio's† of the province of Bretagne; duties upon weights to the duke of the said province; the demesne toll for the stalls and curateries of Rennes; the one half of the tolls and assessments granted for corporations of towns and cities to lay upon themselves; a third part of the alienated duties allow'd to certain officers, except those of the civil government of Paris. The duties of subvention and subsistance in the cities of Orleance [Orléans], Rennes, Troyes, Diep [Dieppe], Caen, Chalons, Bourges, Havre de Grace [Le Havre], Amiens, and other cities, as they are settl'd in the book of rates of the city of Alanson [Alençon]; the duties of the ancient *pied fourche* of Rouen; five sous upon every bale of wood, thirty sous upon every pack of madder, four new deneers upon every bale of merchandize carried into the country; ten sous and six deneers for every hundred of white linnen cloth, as much for a hundred of canvas; by the duties that arise from the privileg'd assessments of the city of Rouen, by the doubling the mark in gold; and lastly, by the duty upon mark'd paper and parchment.

All these duties were let to farm before the year 1672 at 17

* A duty collected at the gates of some cities, upon all cattel that are driven in to be spent. [Author's note]

† An impost upon wine, of the twentieth, fourteenth and fifteenth deneere [denier], at the pleasure of the king. [Author's note] These percentages, expressed in the seventeenth century by the number of deniers, can be obtained by dividing 100 by the denier; thus the twentieth denier equals 5 per cent. [Ed.]

millions 150 thousand livres; during this war they suffer'd two diminutions, as appears by the leases, of which the most considerable amounted but to 4 millions. After the Peace in 1678, they were let at 18 millions, and 18 hundred thousand livres, comprehending the *aydes* of the new conquests. 'Tis true, that in the year 1689 the lease was made for no more than 14 millions, but to be rais'd in case that things remain'd in the same posture, and that peace continu'd; but in case of war and loss, to give an account only for what was receiv'd. Now if we reflect upon the nature of these imposts that make up the *aydes*, upon the present state of affairs, and the diminutions which these duties have suffered at several times, we must conclude that they are now more considerably abated.

'Tis true that the Crown has received every year since the Peace in 1678 ten millions and something more for the farms let out at a certain rate of the demesne of the new conquests of the Low Countries, besides what is contain'd in the general farms already mentioned: these demesnes lye in the cities and castellanies of Tournay, Douay, L'Ile [Lille], Cassel, Ypre, Balieul, Verni, Verneton, Paperingue [Poperinghe], Loo, and their dependencies: the city and verge of Menin, St. Omer and Aire, Valenciennes, Condé, Bouchain, Mauberge [Maubeuge], and Bavet [Bavai], Cambray, Cambresis, and all their dependencies.

After the truce in 1684 all the demesnes of the country of Luxemburg were augmented by the uniting of Strasburgh and a great number of other places and countries, which the Royal [Court] Chambers of Metz, by an unjust decree, without example, adjudg'd to the Crown, under the name of dependencies, encourag'd and supported by the violences of France, and by that means extended her limits and usurpations, I will not say beyond what the treaties prescribe, but contrary to all manner of treaties and agreements. All which countries joyn'd together, yielded a revenue of about six millions, and two hundred thousand livres; but since the war there have been considerable falls and abatements, being manag'd only by intendants that give an account for no more than they receive.

It must be acknowledg'd that neither the desertion of a great number of Protestants, nor the present war, which has exhausted all the provinces of the young and able people, and particularly those of Languedoc, Lyonnois, Provence, and the Dauphinate, nor the misery with which the people are overwhelm'd, could hinder the general farm of the *gabells* of salt from being still fix'd at 9 millions and 100 thousand livres, as well for that it is a commodity which no body, tho' never so poor, can any more be without than without bread, as for that they have rais'd the price to supply the abatement which the depopulation of the kingdom has occasioned.

Before the present war, it was look'd upon as good as certain that the sales of offices amounted to five millions ever year, together with the taxes upon officers and the annual duty, call'd Paulete [*la paulette*],* but within these two years that revenue is become casual and was rais'd one time to 18 millions, by the great number of new taxes that were laid upon all sorts of officers, and by the creation of new offices and masterships of corporations, for which they were to supply the king with large summs, by way of loan. But besides that, these are funds which are not altogether inexhaustible, or rather are such as will suddenly be drain'd dry, since it is impossible to create new officers ad infinitum, and for that they who are created have not presently so much knowledge of their great business, which is to fill the king's coffers; and this also shews the poverty of the kingdom: for though these officers have the most ready money in the kingdom, next to those that are interress'd in the revenues, yet there are many of them that the King has been forc'd to acquit either in part or altogether of their new taxes, as being convinc'd of their inability. 'Tis true that to conceal their weakness in this particular, the King has pretended to discharge 'em for some good services done him; but these are State devices, which only delude those who know not such pretences have been made use of more than once, to hide the infirmities of the pocket. It is also true that part of these new offices which have been erected have been fill'd up; but 'tis as well known by what means it has been done: they apply'd themselves to those who are known to have money by 'em; and they were told by the by, that it was better to lay out their money in the purchase of an employment, which would bring in something every day, than constrain the King to lay a tax upon their heads; and the financiers, who hate nothing so much as the word taxing, had rather lay out their

* A duty which the officers of judicature and the revenue pay to the king at the beginning of the year, to preserve their offices to their widows and heirs in case of death, settl'd at the rate of the fiftieth penny of the value of the office, in the year 1605. [Author's note]

money upon that bad merchandize, than having nothing at all; and yet notwithstanding all these tricks, all the offices are not fill'd up neither; another argument of the poverty of the kingdom.

The tenths upon the clergy of the kingdom amount every year to two millions; and the benevolences of the States [Estates] of the provinces of Languedoc, Provence, Burgundy, and Bretagne are well worth six millions, and five hundred thousand livres. 'Tis true they are given out to be much more worth in the public declarations; but every body knows that the King makes 'em abatements afterwards, as it were out of favor. All these gifts have suffer'd no diminution during this war; and one would think they should have rather encreased, in regard the clergy of the provinces afore-mentioned have given more freely than in the preceding years; and yet it is very certain that all these revenues have not mounted higher than what we have already declared.

'Tis also true that they whose business it is to invent new ways to get money have procur'd the King of France above fifteen millions, by fifth pennies, and fifths of fifth pennies, collation of benefices, mortmains, estates and possessions of all the clergy; eighth and tenth pennies, by countenancing and tolleration of the goods of the Church alienated, which has caus'd a strange confusion among the clergy, as also among all private persons; in regard that to raise money to preserve or regain 'em, both the one and the other find themselves almost ruin'd; besides that, 'tis a question whether the law suit, the indemnities, and protections will not exceed the principal; so odious, troublesom and doubtful, is the verification of these rights, there being very few families in the kingdom that are not entangl'd in these affairs, and forc'd to pay these duties; neither is any ecclesiastical person that has not a temporal estate exempted. . . .

'Tis a truth acknowledged by all those that understand the fertility of France, that in regard this fertility is not very great in corn, it is impossible there should be enough for the subsistence of the people; and if corn were not frequently imported from forraign countries, the dearness of provision would produce considerable calamities. In a word, those persons that have been employed in the seaport towns, to collect the duties of importation and exportation, have observed that for one load of corn carried out of the kingdom, there is imported four. . . . But then again, here is another thing that has extreamly augmented the misery of the people, which is that the vines in most part of the provinces were killed by the rigour of the fore-going winter. . . . That the fertility of the soil of France is hardly sufficient to support the people; and if it come to fail never so little, they are exposed to great hardships. . . .

Machiavel set up a maxim that was carry'd into France by Cardinal Mazarine, and practised there by him and his successors in the ministry, *that the people ought to be kept low*, and that 'tis sufficient that they can only live, because the soveraign thereby has 'em better at command. . . . I know not whether this maxim be true, but this I know, that 'tis not to be practised in France, and that 'tis absolutely impossible but that the whole monarchy must sink at last, if that maxim be much longer made use of; that is a maxim only for princes to follow who have prodigious riches of their own, vast settled demesnes, and not for a French monarch, whose riches and demesnes only consist in the sweat, labour, trade, and commerce of his subjects. . . .

V

The State and French Society

The two principal ways in which Louis XIV's subjects came into contact with "his" state were through justice and taxation. Whether on a remote Provençal field, in a Norman abbey, or in a Parisian *hôtel*, the royal judges and tax collectors enforced the King's will and made his presence felt to all Frenchmen in varying ways according to their social status. Ever since the first Capetians had acted as little more than lords and tenants-in-chief in the eleventh century, their justice and dues had constituted the main secular link binding governed and governor in the society.

Over the centuries layers upon layers of royal officials would gradually be established, and royal justice, taxes, and laws regulating virtually every aspect of life would be extended to newly acquired territories and downward toward the peasantry and the artisans. Nonroyal justice never entirely disappeared in the *ancien régime*, nor did local autonomy; but the state increasingly permeated and regularized everything from the economy to morals. In the reign of Louis XIV this extension of the state into French society occurred at a greater and more significant rate than at any time since the fifteenth century.

Historians generally agree that the weight of royal government on French society, not only as a financial burden but as a pressure for change, increased after 1660, but they have as yet been unable to formulate a general analysis of why and how this was accomplished. Colbertian economic policies have so far received the most attention, but the impressive codification of French law, new taxes such as the *capitation*, royal control of the Church, and the impact of huge standing armies have yet to be assessed. These are only a few of the classic topics which deserve intensive study. Still more innovative would be research on the charitable, educational, and military institutions supported by the Crown, for these expressed in concrete terms the aims and motives of Louis XIV and his ministers in fundamental and as yet unexplored ways. This interaction between the state and society should be neither political history nor social history, but both combined. The third element, which is the history of values in the society and the aims or motives of statesmen, must never be treated simply as the history of ideas. Values and aims are always expressed in a specific social context, and often in response to specific political issues. Hence the value of studying the interaction of the state and society.

The extension of royal government after 1655 occurred during a profound crisis brought on by both civil and foreign wars. The disturbances, violence, high taxes, and ideological outbursts of the Fronde ended only very slowly and left individuals at virtually every level in the society feeling the need for order and administrative coherence. This dialectic between revolt and order—or, in other words, the relationship between the Fronde and Louis XIV's absolutism—is clearly discernible after 1655. Indeed, it was not a coincidence that the building of the first modern army, totally obedient to the state and able to repress rebellion anywhere, occurred concurrently with the regularization of the intendancies, the founding of general hospitals, and the beginning of legal reform. The price of revolt had been high, psychologically as well as materially; and it is only in this context that the urgency for fiscal reform and extended royal power can be understood.

But in building an increasingly absolutist state—one in which the state would recognize no limits on its power—did the motive and moral aims which lay beneath royal policies change in response to the Fronde? This question is impossible to answer on the basis of our current knowledge of seventeenth-century France. It would seem, however, that new organizational and bureaucratic patterns for enforcing traditional values and legislation characterize most of the government of Louis XIV. Bigness and centralization, unity and conformity—rather than innovation, pluralism, openness, and toleration—developed in the years of major reform, 1661–1685. The response of Louis' subjects suggests that the Crown provided what the vast majority of Frenchmen wanted. This is indicated by the general decline in the level of violence during the last decades of the seventeenth century. Urban and rural revolts never disappeared, princely and parlementary opposition remained as a potential brake on royal power, while theologians and men of letters, whether Protestant, Jansenist, Quietist, or something else, would persistently challenge not only the moral underpinnings of the state, but the beliefs of typical individuals as well. Louis' efforts to repress dissent and heterodox thinking never were very successful, but they nevertheless earned him the confidence and support of the majority of his subjects. Even in the grave test provided by the revocation of the Edict of Nantes, internal opposition never became as important to the state as the anti-French storm of protest which it aroused in much of Northern Europe. Even the meaning of the peasant revolts is very ambiguous in the general context of political and administrative development, since they seem to have been caused as much by policies designed to regularize taxation and relieve the peasantry as by the traditionally enforced fiscal legislation. Colbert may well have exceeded the limits of innovation acceptable to the French public; his "revolution from above" threatened public tranquillity in a way not fundamentally different from the "revolts which spread from below."

42. *Military Reform under Le Tellier and Louvois*

Born out of decades of war with the best armies of Europe, the French troops under Turenne and Condé had gradually learned to stand their ground against the Spanish and finally to become the most powerful fighting force in Europe by 1660. But while the Franco-Spanish war continued, and for that matter while Turenne and Condé still lived, fundamental reforms would scarcely be possible. The armies had traditionally been controlled by princes and great nobles with the result that the king's orders were often ignored by the officers of his army. Still worse, the troops lived off the king's subjects, with the distinctions between quartering and pillaging often completely ignored. The lessons of the Fronde, with the endless rebellions led by treasonous generals commanding pillaging troops, could scarcely be ignored.

After the Peace of the Pyrenees in 1659, the secretary of state for war, Michel Le Tellier (1603–1685), had the opportunity to enforce the first major reforms which his son, the Marquis of Louvois (1641–1691), would eventually complete once the last great heroic commander, Condé, had disappeared from the head of "his" troops. Abso-

SOURCE: Philippe Sagnac, *La Formation de la Société française moderne* (Paris, 1945), I, 66–70.

lute obedience to the King and his ministers by officers, promotions on the basis of merit, and an adequate supply system which would ensure the possibility of enforcement of rules against pillaging all seem quite obvious to persons in the twentieth century, but armies as late as the Thirty Years' War had lacked these characteristics.

No brief collection of Le Tellier's letters or Louvois' regulations would convey this profound transformation which made France the strongest single military power in Europe for the better part of a century. For this reason a text by a modern historian which includes numerous quotations from the original documents has been published here. A final word to the specialists of the seventeenth century, who might wonder why P. Sagnac's work has been selected over that of L. André: as a matter of fact, it has not. Sagnac's brief synthesis relies so heavily on André's work that it is nearly what the latter himself wrote, except of course that André takes several hundred pages to provide the rich detail expected in a French doctoral thesis in history.

The consequences of these reforms for French society remain one of the best subjects as yet unstudied by historians. Here the activities of the state as represented by Le Tellier and Louvois resulted in the loss of political independence for the nobles. And for the population as a whole, did the decline of urban and rural revolts result as much from the decrease in pillaging as from the fact that the newly obedient army was a much more effective agent for repression?

The Military Administration

Through its wars and its conquests, through the enormous and continuous effort which they required, the French monarchy became a great military monarchy, the strongest in Europe. The administration of the army thus occupied a conspicuous place in this transformation. And since it used a very great number of nobles, its duty was to reduce all of this nobility of the sword to the strictest obedience, from the simple lieutenant up to the marshal of France. But, after so much indiscipline, so many shocking betrayals, how difficult it was to control this turbulent group! A painful task—and one which constantly had to be begun again—for Michel Le Tellier, secretary of state for war, who had already worked at it indefatigably, with a remarkable consistency in outlook and with remarkable perseverence and diplomacy. Yet how much remained to be done by him, and later by his son Louvois, his associate after 1666—Louvois, whose personal influence began to be felt during the Dutch war and who, after Nimwegen [1678] would be the true master of the government, recognized as such by the Venetian ambassadors, who called him "principal minister and accepted as such."

The task began with the signing of the peace treaty [between Spain and France], with the "reform" of 1659 to 1661, over which Le Tellier presided; but it was applied only to a peacetime army, which totaled merely thirty thousand men, and which was to be transformed, after 1665, into a more numerous army, ready for the offensive.

However, the system of venality in military offices continued, despite efforts which had already been made to suppress it among the elite troops: in 1664 in the "body guards," and in 1672 in the companies of *gendarmes*. For lack of funds, the monarchy was incapable of abolishing the abuses which this regime brought with it. Colonels and captains continued to make money on their regiments and companies.

At least the great offices which came between the king and his army were gradually abolished, as circumstances permitted: that of colonel general of the infantry, upon the death of the Duke of Épernon—henceforth the King would name officers in the infantry; that of grand master of the artillery, when the Count du Lude, the King's aide-de-camp, purchased this position from the Duke of Mazarin—resulting in the incorporation of the artillery into the royal army; finally—though the position of colonel general of the cavalry continued to exist, being held by Turenne, a great commander and the conqueror at the battle of the Dunes [1658]—the power to name cavalry officers was in fact reduced after 1667. As for the governors of provinces or strongholds, who, having troops paid by them and loyal to them, had in the past laid down conditions to the king or had even gone into open revolt, they were now named for a period of only three years, subject to renewal, it is true (1660); but, in fact, these great nobles—still dreaded for their power in the provinces, where they possessed a considerable amount of landed wealth, and for their enormous influence over the entire nobility and the cities—were gradually invited to no longer put in their appearance, except in exceptional cases, and to leave the exercise of their functions to lieutenant generals named by the king.

Henceforth the sole master of the army would be the king. His secretary of state for war was a civilian, a man of the robe, who commanded in his name. This civilian minister would regulate the hierarchy of regiments and officers, would institute the *ordre du tableau*, promotions according to seniority; it was he who would fight against all the abuses in an army in which irregularity, absence, and indiscipline had reigned before 1660. To make the officers obey, to supervise their conduct, Le Tellier and Louvois—it would be difficult to separate the two—organized an entire civil administration, entrusted with inspection and control, which informed the ministers. At the summit were the general inspectors, then the "intendants for the army," next the "war commissioners," and finally the "extraordinary treasurers," all naturally odious to the officer caste, which saw itself being strictly watched by them and denounced to the king.

Officers would agree, at the beginning of a war, to enlist so many recruits for a fee; but sometimes, having taken the fee, they did not raise the troops. One war commissioner, in 1672, warned the secretary of state of this "negligence which is so great that for the three months that the captains have been recruiting they have not sent in a single man." Louvois became irritated and wrote in 1671 to Marshal Humières, "If between now and Christmas, when I go to Lille, the companies are not in the state the King wishes, I will bring with me orders to cashier them, which will be carried out while I am present." And when war broke out, he wrote to Captain Marcé (March 4, 1674): "If after the two months since His Majesty has had you paid in full, your company is not complete, you may expect not only to be cashiered, but also to be arrested and made to repay the money which you received for the men you do not have."

But enlistments were often made by force; hence loud protests by several provincial intendants. The intendant of Montauban wrote: "They take, without enlisting them, and without paying a thing, passersby, travelers, shepherds, peasants, carters, even children and old men," in the countryside the flocks are "without shepherds, who flee as soon as they see a horseman or a person who is walking and has a sword at his side." "Formerly they were satisfied," wrote Caumartin, intendant of Champagne, "to enlist drunkards and those who had half consented. But now captains take whom they want, shepherds in the countryside, guides, the leading men of the parish, merchants in the towns; no one can escape, and if you do not take the word of a sergeant or an officer's valet when he tells you a man has enlisted, although all appearances are to the contrary, the captain cries for mercy and is ready to abandon his work of enlisting. . . . I admit that when I saw a wretch with a sword wound through his body because he did not want to enlist, I did not think I should allow that deed to go unpunished." Indeed, Lieutenant Colombet had wanted to take by force a blacksmith's young assistant and had wounded him. The subdelegate had arrested the officer; but the war commissioner refused to intervene. Louvois was very unhappy with this intrusion into the authority of his department and wrote to the intendant that "in the future he should abstain from having officers arrested." But the facts remained, and forced enlistments continued, for at all costs the minister needed soldiers. This explains the many desertions, which were likewise seen in all the armies of Europe.

After the very serious abuses over enlistments come those of the *passe-volants* who were seen only at reviews, and those concerning pay, which often came belatedly or was even totally forgotten by the officer. The war commissioners were ordered to end this. "The war commissioner," Louvois ordered the commanders of a stronghold in 1671, "being obliged to take precautions to prevent the abuses which the captains intend to commit, you must open the gate of the fort to him as soon as he appears and you will facilitate everything he may require of you as regards his work."

Another abuse, and not one of the least, was the frequent absences of the officers. Le Tellier wrote to Marshal Bellefonds in 1668, "The absence of officers is almost universal. It stems in many places from the ease with which those in command can grant leaves and the liberty which several officers have taken to leave without permission. It is not an easy thing to make them return promptly to their posts, since they are spread throughout the provinces and it takes time for them to learn that His Majesty wants them to return to their garrisons." Again, in 1674, in the midst of the Dutch war, in the corps commanded by Marshal Bellefonds, there were, observed a commissioner, "very few officers"; and he added, "I believe there is one regiment where there is no officer at all." However, the ordinance of 1661 had stated: "Henceforth a third of the officers of a garrison will always be present"; then the system of 1665 had established the semester. But officers did only what they wished. However, their obstinancy ran headlong into that of Louvois; they had to obey. Abuses thus were reduced.

Finally, in the countryside, if soldiers pillaged, the officers also sometimes took their share of booty. One of Louvois' main agents, Robert, pointed out a pillaging officer to the minister: "Monsieur de La Marck makes me despair. We are at sword's point with one another. He takes everything, pays for nothing, and has already sent back to France, from what I have learned, in a boat which he is sending to Rouen, Dieppe, or Le Havre, a quantity of tapestries, paintings, and other things. . . ." Turenne paid no attention to maintaining discipline and let his soldiers pillage; thus he drew stern reprimands from Louvois and even from Louis XIV. All the armies, however, did not behave that way; there were no abuses at Bergues or at Tournai in 1667; in Lorraine in 1670 the troops "did not take a pin."

It must be said also, and above all, on behalf of a mass of officers, that very often they did not receive their pay—as a result of the considerable increase in the number of troops—that they were sometimes poor, as Intendant Robert indicated in Holland. And yet officers, even those lacking money, were devoted to their soldiers. "It is true," wrote Commissioner Benoît to Louvois on July 12, 1672, "that there are officers who have been obliged to pawn their finery to make loans to their companies." Louvois tried to remedy this sad situation; but he could not do everything: "I shall see," he answered Créqui on January 30, 1671, "whether the treasurer has the funds so they can get their money." Though officers committed abuses; though marshals in wartime refused to obey a commander-in-chief named by the king; and though ferments of independence still agitated the noble class in the service—chivalric, disinterested, and generous sentiments also animated a number of them. However, in spite of everything, by the glorious time of Nimwegen, the nobility of the sword was no longer the same as in 1660; it obeyed the king, forced to by the war and the harsh severity of the ministers—especially Louvois, who did not have the conciliatory manner of his father and who often gave his orders with a hitherto unknown sort of brutality. This was the price that the army paid to become a royal army, obedient in the king's hands, and no longer a feudal one. Louis XIV was very careful to let Louvois have complete liberty, did not spare his praises, and assured him "of his friendship and his confidence." Upheld in this way, the great minister was able to carry out his work, as an absolute master.

43. *Colbert's Instructions for a General Survey of France*

During the Fronde the intendants and commissioners had proved themselves to be the Crown's most loyal officials in the provinces. Despite political attacks and threats to their lives, the intendants carried out Mazarin's and Anne's orders with dogged determination. Once the crisis had passed, of course, rewards in money and offices were expected by the intendants, and Mazarin never forgot a loyal servant of the state.

The regularization of the intendancies in the provinces was one of the major consequences of the social and political upheaval which had occurred, 1648–1651. Under Le Tellier's—and later Colbert's—direction a new layer of officials, the intendants, was established in order to wrest power from tainted local officials. Moreover, after Mazarin's death, Colbert undertook an immense program of fiscal, legal, and social reform which required, if it were to have a chance of success, a much more centralized and responsive public administration. As local matters were increasingly referred to Paris for decisions, and as more ambitious programs were implemented to harness the wealth and economic power of twenty million Frenchmen to serve the necessities of the state, the need for more information about provincial conditions became apparent in the capital. The plan to conduct a complete survey of the realm was not original with Colbert, but it was he who actually ordered it in September 1663. The results—mountains of reports which still survive and which have almost completely defied systematic exploration by historians—gave Colbert and his successors a new power to govern. He realized more than anyone in the Council of State, including Louis XIV himself, how knowledge of provincial conditions would enable the centralization of political power. The claim of absolute power was given more substance by the survey of 1663.

SOURCE: "Instruction pour les Maîtres des Requêtes, commissaires départis dans les provinces," September 1663, *Lettres, Instructions, et Mémoires de Colbert*, ed. by Pierre Clément (Paris, 1877), IV, 27–43.

Instructions for the Maîtres des Requêtes, *Commissioners Who Have Been Sent into the Provinces*

The King wishing to be clearly informed concerning the state of the provinces within his realm, His Majesty has ordered that this memorandum be sent to the *maîtres des requêtes* so that each may work within the confines of his office and study carefully and exactly all the articles contained below.

MAPS—It is necessary for the said sieurs to look up the maps which have been made of each province or *généralité*, carefully checking to see whether they are good; and, in the event they are not accurate or even are not complete enough, they are to find some capable and intelligent person to redraw them, in the same province or in the surrounding ones. His Majesty wants them to employ [these persons] to work continuously and without interruption; and in the event they find no person capable of this work, they are to have very precise memoranda drawn up for the old ones, both to correct them and to make them more detailed, which His Majesty will place in the hands of the Sieur [Nicolas] Sanson, his official mapmaker; and on the basis of these memoranda, the said sieurs will see to it that the divisions among the four administrations—ecclesiastical, military, judicial, and financial—are clearly drawn, not only in general, but even in the details and the subdivisions of each, namely:

FOR ECCLESIASTICAL ADMINISTRATION—The bishoprics distinguished from one another; in each bishopric, the archdeaconries and the arch-presbyteries; the names of all the parishes in each division, so as to show the total number in the bishopric; the abbeys and other benefices, with a distinction between those which are subject to the authority of the bishops and those which are exempt; and, in the event that the latter have exempted jurisdiction over an expanse of land or parishes, that this also be mentioned.

FOR MILITARY ADMINISTRATION—The distinction between the different general [military] governments; all the parishes dependent upon each government should be clearly marked [on the maps]; and, in the event the governments overlap, this should be mentioned. . . .

FOR JUSTICE—It is necessary to show the divisions between the extent of each parlement, and in the event there are several of them, which rarely happens, it is necessary to make the distinction; likewise with the *bailliages*, and the *présidiaux* and royal justices [old judicial divisions].

FOR FINANCES—To show the limits of the *généralités*, the *élections*, and the *greniers à sel* [which administer the *gabelles*];

and to be certain everywhere, in all the four types of government, that we know the correct number of cities, towns, and parishes of which each of these general and particular divisions is composed.

While the said commissioners are working to become acquainted with all these divisions, His Majesty wants them to draw up accurate reports about everything concerning which he wants to be informed, namely:

ECCLESIASTICAL—In regard to the Church, the names and number of bishoprics; the cities, towns, villages, and parishes subject to their ecclesiastical jurisdiction, their temporal seigniorial holdings and the cities and parishes of which they are composed; especially if the bishop is temporal lord of the cathedral city; the name, age, estate, and inclinations of the bishop, if he is from the region or not; if his permanent residence is there; how he performs his episcopal visitations; what influence he has in his bishopric and what effect he might have in time of trouble; his reputation among his people; if he confers any benefices on his chapter; if he is engaged in any lawsuits against [the chapter]; the amount of his revenues; the names and the values of the benefices which he bestows.

In addition to the bishoprics and all related matters, it is necessary to report the names and the number of all the ecclesiastical houses, secular and regular, in the province; the names and the number of abbeys founded; their order; by which monks they are occupied; if they are reformed or not; the number of monks in each of them at the time when the reform was introduced, and thirty or forty years earlier; how many there are at present; what is their reputation for their way of living and their morals; for how many monks the abbeys were founded.

If, before the reform, there were gentlemen and were they of good family or not; if this is likewise the case with the reformed monks; if in the past one had to be a gentleman in order to enter one of the said abbeys, if one had to provide proofs of nobility or not; the origin of this requirement.

If the abbey is exempt from the bishop's jurisdiction, if it has exempt spiritual jurisdiction over several parishes; its temporal seigniorial holdings; the cities, towns, hamlets, and parishes dependent upon it; the name of the commendatory or regular abbot, his ancestry, his age, his state of health, his influence in the region and the effect he might have in time of trouble; whether or not he resides in the abbey; the names, number, and value of the benefices he confers; the total revenues of the abbey, namely: the abbatial house, the conventual [house], the small convent, and all the cloistered houses.

After having mentioned all the endowed abbeys for men, divided by the different orders to which they belong, beginning with the Benedictines, the same must be done for the endowed abbeys for women, and then for the nonendowed mendicant orders for men and women, so that, by this complete explanation which His Majesty desires, he can know truly and in general the revenues of the Church from each province; how much from its temporal possession; the number of its vassals and its subjects, the conduct of the leaders who are in charge of caring for the salvation of the others, and generally everything concerning the ecclesiastics, who form the first order of his realm.

MILITARY—As for the military government, which concerns the nobility, which is the second order of his kingdom, although His Majesty knows all the talents of the governors and lieutenant generals of his provinces, he nevertheless wishes, in order to make these reports thorough, that the *maîtres des requêtes* begin their inquiry on the nobility by naming the said governor generals, their ancestry and family ties in the province, whether they currently reside there; their good and bad conduct; if they are accused of taking money or of vexing the people in any other way, whether these accusations are plausible; if the people are complaining about them; what influence they have among the nobility and the people. And since the principal and most important concern that His Majesty wishes the governors of the provinces to have is to support justice firmly and to prevent the suppression of the weak by the violence of the strong, His Majesty wishes to be particularly informed of the past conduct of the said governors, in order to judge what he should and may expect from them in the future. In case some violent outbreak occurred, in each province, His Majesty wishes to be informed in detail along with how the governor conducted himself.

It is necessary to be informed of the same things concerning the lieutenant generals.

After having examined everything concerning the governors and lieutenant generals, His Majesty desires to be especially informed about everything relating to the nobility, namely: the principal families of each province; their family ties, their possessions, and the extent of their lands and seigniories; their morals and good behavior, whether they do violence to the inhabitants of their lands, and in the event some notable act of violence has been committed which went unpunished, he will be very glad to know the details; whether they favor or prevent the proceedings of royal justice in the *bailliages* and *présidiaux;* their influence in the region both on other gentlemen and on the people.

For the lesser nobility, it is good to know the number and the names of the most respected. If, in general, many have gone to war, or not; whether they cultivate their land themselves or whether they rent it out to tenant farmers, this being one of the most essential signs of their inclination toward war or toward remaining at home.

For the nobility in general, His Majesty would be very happy to know the correct number, divided by *bailliages* and *sénéchaussées;* the number of the chief nobles, not only taking into account their ancestry, but also their merit and their service; the number, and the income from the lands and goods they possess.

JUSTICE—As far as justice is concerned, in the event that there is a parlement or another sovereign company in the province, it will be necessary for the *maîtres des requêtes* to carefully examine in general and in particular those who make up [the parlement]. For the general, its entire conduct during His Majesty's minority must be examined, by what motives it was guided, and the means used by the principal members, who guided it for better or for worse. If its [conduct] was bad, to learn whether the reasons which might have made it change since then are strong enough to lead one to believe that in a similar situation they would hold firm, or whether it is to be feared that they would once again lapse into the same errors.

And since it is assuredly the most important matter which is to be examined in the province, it would be good and even very necessary to know in detail the concerns and the talents of the principal officers of these companies, and particularly whether those who led them into this behavior are still alive. . . .

First they must find out in detail in what fashion the company renders justice to the king's subjects; whether or not there is corruption; the causes and the persons who are suspect. If some manifest injustice has taken place, which has stirred up talk in the province and which has resulted in the oppression of the weak in favor of some friend, relation, or for some other equally vicious motive, His Majesty desires to be informed of it, and also about the length of lawsuits and excessive legal fees, in both the sovereign and the subordinate companies, it being important to know in great detail about these two matters, which are a great burden upon His Majesty's subjects.

Since these great companies were established by the kings to administer their justice, and since their principal object must also be to employ the authority entrusted to them to protect the weak from the powerful, it must be learned whether, in all acts of violence, such as murders, assassinations, or ill usage, committed by gentlemen or by the principal [persons] of the provinces, they firmly upheld the same authority, and whether they fearlessly carried out the proceedings and meted out stern justice to the guilty persons, as they were obliged to do.

His Majesty having also often received complaints that the officials in the sovereign companies in various localities force owners to sell them land they desire, he would be happy to be specially informed concerning the places where this occurs. It will likewise be necessary to present in the memorandum all the landed possessions which are owned by each of the officials of the said companies. . . .

After having examined the sovereign companies, the same thing must be done for the *bailliages*, *sénéchaussées*, and *présidiaux*. . . .

FINANCES—As for finances, in the provinces where there is a *Cour des aides*, it will be good to know the names of the officials, their attainments, and their family ties in the province, especially those of the first president, then of the other presidents, and the principal members of the companies; what is their reputation in the province concerning their manner of rendering justice; if there is manifest corruption among them; if someone has caused a stir, learn about it in detail; if the tax farmers and receivers are pleased with their firmness in supporting them; if the people complain of any vexation on their part; and of unraveling the concerns of these two different parties in order not to take false cognizance.

In addition a study must be made of the vexations which the people experience, either through the length of the trials or by excessive legal fees; and appropriate remedies must be sought for all these evils, and the easiest ones possible. Also since the greatest surcharges which taxpayers suffer come from the quantity of false nobles to be found in the provinces, who were created in part by letters of the king and in part by simple edicts of the *Cour des aides*, it is very important and necessary to seek out appropriate remedies for both these evils.

In regard to the nobles created by letters of the king, His Majesty will consider the remedies which he can bring forward on the basis of the report which will be made to him concerning the number in each province and the injury which his subjects suffer. But in respect to the nobles created by decrees of the *Cour des aides*, not only must they be suppressed but also a means must be found to cut away the root of this disorder so that it will be permanently suppressed in the future. . . .

THE KING'S REVENUES—It remains to examine the king's revenues and matters concerning them. They consist of the Crown lands which are all alienated and which in consequence produce no revenue; and of the tax farms for import and export duties, *aides*, *gabelles;* and diverse other duties and tax farms; and the *tailles*. Concerning these five kinds of revenue, it is necessary carefully to discover how much His Majesty collects annually from each province. . . .

After having learned the value of all these different types of revenue and by this means everything which the king collects annually in the province, it will be necessary to examine in detail all the difficulties encountered in levying and collecting them, either because they cause a decrease in the said revenues or because they are prejudicial to the people. . . .

Concerning the *aides*, there is a general rule to follow for all kinds of taxes levied on the people, which results assuredly either in their overburdening or in their relief, which consists in knowing well all those who are subject to [taxes], and whether each pays his part according to his resources; it being certain that by the inequality of burdens, that is to say when the most powerful or the richest (because of the privileges of the estate to which they belong) have their burden removed or lightened, the poor or the weak are overburdened; and this inequality causes in the provinces poverty, misery, and difficulty in recovering what is due the king, which occasions the irritation of the tax receivers and collectors, the sergeants, and generally all sorts of evils. So that the commissioners in the provinces must always keep this fundamental maxim and this certain rule in their minds, and should never stray from it, in order to know the true strength of all those who are subject to paying the said taxes . . . and to prevent all the powerful persons of all the orders of the province from . . . granting relief to certain communities or individuals. . . .

Concerning the provinces [subject to the *gabelles*], it is necessary to see whether the schedule of the said tax was established long ago and whether it has since remained almost unchanged; and since the original schedule was established with reference to the number of inhabitants in each province or community, and that number has changed, either through war or through changes in the fairs and markets, or through any of a number of other reasons which cause increases or decreases in the population of various localities, it happens that this schedule is currently no longer proportionate to the number of inhabitants. Since it is absolutely necessary to reestablish this proportion, this first schedule must be produced in each *grenier* [*à sel*], to see the difference when compared with the most recent one, to compare the tax list with that of the *taille*, and even to make a summary statement—while the said commissioners are in each *élection* and *grenier à sel*—of the number of inhabitants in each parish or community, in order to make a new apportioning of the taxes, more just and in proportion to the number of inhabitants.

Concerning the *taille*, it is necessary to find out by means of [the reports of] the royal commissions sent each year to the financial offices and *élections*, which the said commissioners shall request to see, how much the *taille* has amounted to in the past six years, in order to know exactly the increases and reductions granted by the king. Next, through the annual reports of the *élus* for those years, it is possible to determine whether these increases and reductions have been followed; and if they have not been followed they should be asked to explain why. Finally, [the commissioners are] to justify and become accurately informed, by diverse means, of the state of each parish in the *élection*, during the period the commissioner stays there. It will be good to do the same thing, as much as possible, in regard to the lists of each parish. . . .

THE SITUATION IN THE PROVINCES—After having commented upon all the things which must be known about the four sorts of government in the provinces of the realm, it remains only to examine the advantage which His Majesty can obtain from each. To this end, the commissioners must carefully examine the mood and the spirit of the people of each province, of each region, and of each town; whether they are inclined to war, to agriculture, or to commerce and manufacturing; whether the provinces are maritime or not; and, in case they are maritime, the number of able seamen and their reputation as sailors; the condition of the soil; if it is completely under cultivation or if there are some uncultivated regions; if fertile or not, and what sort of crops it produces; if the inhabitants are industrious, and if they not only strive to cultivate their land well, but even to learn the best use of their lands, and whether they are good managers; if there are forests in the province, and what condition they are in; on this point, it is well to point out that the King has had drawn up a memorandum dealing with everything which must be done in reforming [the laws concerning] the forests of the realm; what sort of trade and commerce, and what sort of manufactures, are carried out in each province.

COMMERCE—And, on these two points, which are assuredly the principal ones, because they concern the industry of the inhabitants, His Majesty likewise wants to be informed of the changes which have occurred in the past forty or fifty years in the trade and manufactures in each province of his realm; and, among other things, whether during all this time, and even before, some commerce was established in foreign countries which has since stopped; the reasons for this suspension and the means of reestablishing it; if manufactures have been abolished; the reasons, and the means of reestablishing them.

His Majesty wants the commissioners to pay particular attention to these two points, commerce and manufactures, which he considers as the two sole means of attracting wealth into the realm and of making an infinite number of his subjects live comfortably, who will even increase considerably every year, if it please God to maintain the peace which Europe has enjoyed to the present.

NAVY—To this end, they must learn the number of vessels belonging to His Majesty's subjects; they must strongly urge the chief merchants and traders of the cities to buy them and to increase their number, to form companies for foreign trade, even to undertake long sea journeys; they must promise them all the protection and help they will need, and even must discuss with them all the things they might desire, there being nothing His Majesty will not do to give them his complete protection, provided that, on their side, they strive to augment their trade and the number of their vessels.

MANUFACTURES–The same must be done in regard to manufactures, not only to reestablish all those which have been lost, but to establish new ones; and since His Majesty is very attached to this question, in the event the commissioners find cities which are truly eager to carry out these reestablishments and if they lack the means, not only will His Majesty give them his protection, but even, as appropriate to the proposed plan, will willingly assist them with certain sums for the reestablishment, and even with an annual revenue for the maintenance and enlarging of the manufactures; this is to depend upon the prudence of the commissioners, who, nevertheless, will make no final arrangements without having received orders from His Majesty.

In the event that the commissioners deem it necessary to grant privileges, even honors and precedence in the towns, either to merchants who are making efforts to build vessels and who are maintaining a number of them at sea or to the founders of sizable manufactures, His Majesty will readily give them, by these favors, proofs of his goodness.

In all things, [the commissioners] must recognize and ask the advice of the most intelligent persons in the province, so that they can form their opinions, and the King will make a decision which will render the success commensurate with his good intentions.

CANALS–Moreover, His Majesty will be very glad to be informed about all the navigable rivers. Although he has already ordered the suppression of all tolls, which considerably decreased the advantages which river navigation ought normally to provide, he wants the commissioners to strive carefully to discover all the obstacles which the navigation of the said rivers might encounter, and the means which may be used to eliminate them and to facilitate trade and the transportation of merchandise, both within and without the realm.

In regard to nonnavigable rivers, His Majesty wants his commissioners to inspect them personally, assisted by experts and persons familiar with them, and to make a summary of all the methods which could be used to make them navigable, of the necessary expenditures and the compensations which would have to be paid; which regions would benefit, and whether all or part of the expense could not be levied upon the region which would benefit.

BRIDGES AND ROADS—Moreover, His Majesty wants the commissioners to visit in each parish the paths, bridges, and construction which have been completely abandoned; they are to have summaries made by intelligent and economic persons, so that next repairs can be ordered and the necessary funds provided for this purpose, according to public need and necessity; even, should the commissioners deem that, to facilitate commerce and the transportation of merchandise, it is necessary to undertake new work, [the king] agrees that they should have reports and estimates made.

STUD FARMS—Finally, His Majesty desiring to have stud farms reestablished in the realm, as being very necessary not only for public utility during peace and war but even to prevent very sizable sums from being used for the purchase of foreign horses and by this means taken out of the realm, he wants to be informed of the reasons why all those who formerly were raising mares—be they peasants, for daily work, or gentlemen or persons of quality, for their utility, service, and pleasure—stopped; which gave rise to the importation of foreign horses into the realm.

His Majesty desires that not only should the commissioners examine the means by which we could succeed in obliging the peasants to resume the custom of using mares, but even that, in his name, they should urge gentlemen and persons of quality to reestablish stud farms and to create new ones . . . , that they should assure the gentlemen who are lords of [suitable] localities that they can render no more agreeable service to His Majesty than by reestablishing stud farms.

In order to facilitate this, His Majesty has ordered a number of horses from Spain and from North Africa to be used as stallions and which shall be given to those striving to satisfy his wishes.

The said *maîtres des requêtes* must be informed that the King intends them to make their visits and carry out all the points included in these instructions within the period of four or five months' time, at the end of which His Majesty will send them orders to go to another province, leaving memoranda and instructions of all work undertaken which they have not been able to finish, to be followed up by the one who will succeed them; His Majesty wishing that, by assiduous work and extraordinary diligence, the said *maîtres des requêtes* will visit the entire kingdom in a period of seven or eight years' time and will as a result become capable of the highest employment; His Majesty reserving for himself the right to judge which have done the best, by the reports which they will give him in his council, in order to reward them with tokens of his satisfaction.

44. *An Intendant Reviews Tax Assessments*

Jean-Jacques Charon de Ménars (d. 1718) served as intendant in the *généralité* of Paris, directly under Jean-Baptiste Colbert, who was controller general of finances. Ménars was Colbert's brother-in-law and no doubt owed his intendancy to Colbert's favor at Versailles. Hard-working and loyal, Ménars sought to please those in power at court and to fulfill the obligations of his office. Ménars' activities are therefore very instructive for understanding the functions of the intendants, since he may have functioned closer to the ideals which Colbert and Louis XIV had in mind than those intendants less indebted to Colbert and in remoter provinces.

In this document Ménars describes to Colbert his review of the *taille* assessments made on a crucially important group in rural society, the *laboureurs.* Though living on the land, the *laboureurs* generally were wealthier than the average peasants, field hands, and other still poorer rural residents. The *laboureurs* not only tilled their own soil, but with hired workers rented their plows and ox teams to those who had none; they often kept inns and sometimes bought small contracts for raising revenues on seigniorial domains as well. In the general assessments by the leading parish members, the *laboureur* often escaped having to pay a *taille* commensurate with his income. In some instances, the *laboureurs* were among those making the assessments, and they took advantage of this situation to assess themselves lightly.

Assessments upon Offices, Made by the Intendant for the Généralité *of Paris, for the* Taille *of the Year 1683*

Paris, this last of November, 1682

I am sending you, in accordance with your orders, the statement of the assessments on offices which I have made. I examined, during my last visit, all the rolls for the *taille.* Those who did not pay what

SOURCE: A. M. de Boislisle (ed.), *Mémoires des Intendants sur l'État des Généralités dressés pour l'Instruction du Duc de Bourgogne* (Paris, 1881), I, 506–508.

they ought according to their means and their trade, the collectors of the *taille* who had decreased their own assessments, and the officials who owned two offices, one of which exempts them from the *taille*, were taxed, which I did under the terms of the King's declaration of November 13, 1680. Those who earn money in several parishes have been taxed in the one in which they reside, and I lightened proportionally the assessment on the parishes in which they earn money. You will see, Sir, that—my only concern being to relieve the poorest—all the judicial officers and the tenant farmers of the nobles who paid nothing are now taxed. I hope that the work I have done will facilitate the collection and will decrease its costs; they have decreased by a third in the last two years. I shall try to do even better this year, and to prove to you, by my assiduous attention to the [King's] service, my perfect gratitude and deep respect, etc.

MÉNARS

THE *Élection* OF PARIS

Ivry-sur-Seine

Jean Cressy, tenant farmer on a farm of the archbishopric of Paris and *laboureur* with two plows belonging to others, will pay .... 400 livres

Palaiseau

Jean Liévain, lieutenant of justice, *laboureur*, and innkeeper, for what he earns in Palaiseau as well as what he earns in the parish of Igny, will pay 500

Michel Richard, *procureur fiscal*, for his property and for what he earns 350

Vitry

Gilles Chalouvrier, tenant farmer of the domain [of Vitry], because of his large business and his possessions 700

Orly

Philippe Carron, tenant farmer of the domain of the Chapter of Notre-Dame [of Paris] 700

Athis

Germain Bogne, *laboureur* with two plows, who was tax collector last year, who assessed himself only for 20 l., although the preceding year he paid 150 l., will pay 150

Fresnes-lès-Rungis

Louis Parent, tenant farmer for the domain [of Fresnes-lès-Rungis], will pay 700

La Chapelle-Saint-Denis

Simon Le Faucheux, tavernkeeper, who paid only 100 l. on the list of 1682, will pay, because of his large business 400

Braquet, lieutenant and surgeon, who, through his plotting, is not on the list, will pay 60

Villiers-le-Bel

Jacques Tavernier, lace seller, for his large business 400

Sarcelles

Louis Ferret, lace seller, clerk for permits [to transport merchandise], for his business 350

Antoine Bursier, *laboureur*, routinely assessed for 400 l. in 1682, will pay 440

Nicolas Bethemont, receiver, who paid only 70 l., will pay 100

Le Bourget

Jacques Cotelle, tax collector, who in 1681 paid 60 l., and who assessed himself in 1682 at 20 s[ous], will pay 100

Saint-Cloud

Jean Déon, officer of Monsieur's kitchen, assessed because of his *dérogeance*, at 100

Chevreuse

Louis Gourlier, merchant, who was on the tax roll for only 75 l., will pay 100

Cernay

The monks of Vaux-de-Cernay, because they earn money on two plows in the parish of Cernay-la-Ville, and on two others in the parish of Saint-Benoît, in the *élection* of Mantes, will pay 100

Pontault

The mayor, earning money on three plows 200

Chelles

Claude Bonnescuelle, *laboureur* with three plows, who was assessed at only 260 l. for 5,500 l. worth of tenant land which he cultivated, in addition to costs, will pay 500

François Regnard, *procureur fiscal,* and *laboureur* with two and a half plows, who paid only 330 l. on the list for 1682, will pay 450
Jacques Billard, *laboureur* with one and a half plows, who only paid 4 l. on the list of 1682, will pay 100
Antoine Billard, [legal] practitioner, who only paid 10 l., will pay 50

Essonnes

Eustache Picard, *laboureur* with two carts, innkeeper at the sign of the Swan, who is assessed for only 70 l., will pay 200

Périgny

François Moustier, receiver for the domain [of Périgny], who paid only 60 l., will pay 120

Crosnes

Nicolas Morin, receiver and *laboureur* with two carts, assessed for 90 l. in 1682, will pay 140

Brie-Comte-Robert

Nicolas Bourdin the father, merchant grocer, with a large business, will pay 600
Antoine Robelin, merchant for wood and wheat, and *échevin* 350
Jean Cousin, merchant for wheat, wood, and linens, with a large business, and *échevin* 600
Jean Château, merchant for wheat, wood, tiles, and lime, and *laboureur* with one cart, will pay 500
Pierre Roblain, wheat merchant and process server, who on the list is assessed for 40 l., will pay 100
Étienne Bertot, *procureur,* who pays only 22 l., will pay 70
François Bonleu, town clerk, process server, and wheat merchant, will pay 100
Master Charles Lainé, *bailli,* who is not on the lists, will pay 100
Master Tessier, *procureur du roi* and doctor, who is not on the lists, will pay 10

Sevran

The priests of the Mission, because they earn from their land at Saclay and Sevran, which are in two different parishes 500

Épiais

Jean Guiard, for two plows with which he earns money in the parish of Épiais, although he is domiciled in the *élection* of Meaux 200

Bessancourt

Nicolas Verrier, for two plows with which he earns money by his own labor at Frépillon, for which the tenant farmers paid 150 l., and for collecting the tithes, will pay 300

Piscop

The Sieur de Braque, gentleman, for what he earns at Saint-Brice and at Piscop, which are in two different parishes 150

Saint-Gratien

Master Jean Garrault, town clerk for the *prévôté*, receiver for the land, notary and scribe, clerk in the office of the *aides*, who paid only 56 l., will pay 100

Gennevilliers

Denis Bulot, who rents a farm worth 1,800 l. and paid only 144 l. in 1682, will pay 200

Andrésy

The tax farmers and guarantors for the general lease of the tithes and other possessions and rights previously leased to Jean Desforges 500

The tax farmers and guarantors for the seigniorial rights and other possessions acquired by the Chapter of Notre-Dame of Paris 300

Châtenay

Antoine d'Auxerre, tax collector, who assessed himself in 1682 for 20 s., and who was assessed in 1681 for 44 l., will pay 50

René d'Orléans, vine grower, tax collector, who assessed himself in 1682 for 20 s., and was assessed in 1681 for 70 l., will pay 80

Jacques Ferrault, vine grower, also tax collector, who assessed himself in 1682 at 20 s., and who was assessed in 1681 at 65 l., will pay 70

Argenteuil

Claude Grimon the younger, merchant, tax collector, assessed in 1681 at 108 l., which he himself reassessed in 1682 at 13 l., will pay 150

Pierre Bré, cooper, tax collector, assessed in 1681 at 86 l., and who reassessed himself in 1682 at 11 l., will pay 120

Jacques Pionnier, vine grower, also tax collector, assessed in 1681 at 63 l., and who reassessed himself in 1682 at 10 l., will pay 80

Pierre Drouet, quarrier, tax collector, assessed in 1681 at 60 l., and who reassessed himself in 1682 at 10 l., will pay 60

Thillay

Jean Bernier, innkeeper and cartwright, tax collector in 1682, who in 1681 paid 105 l., and who assessed himself, on the list for 1682, at only 20 l., will pay 150

Passy

Jérôme Hautan, *laboureur* and butcher, who is on the list at only 60 l., will pay 150

Le Bourget

Eustache Pierre, *laboureur*, taxed routinely in 1682 at 240 l., will pay 260

Tremblay

Claude de la Mare, *laboureur*, will pay 2,100

Louvres

Claude Le Rouge, *laboureur*, will pay 900

Jacques Bimont, *procureur fiscal* 230

Marly-la-Ville

Nicolas Malice 550

Montmorency

François Genuit, *procureur* 100

Franconville

Guillaume Cailleux, innkeeper and *laboureur* 330

Ermont and Cernay

Louis Larcher, *laboureur* 300

Argenteuil

François Brûlé, merchant 550

Louis Thuillier, *bailli* 200

Colombes

L'Éguillier, tavernkeeper 260

Dampmart

Louis Labour 160

Marcoussis

Léon Pouillier 660

Longjumeau

Marin Le Bigot 260

Marolles-en-Hurepoix

Louis Guillemain 350

Montainville

François Maugeant 330

45. Louis XIV's Income in 1692

Though the figures are rounded off, this document describes the basic types of French taxation and the amount of revenue each brought to the Crown. With this information, some rough estimates might be made about the proportion of excise, *taille*, and other taxes falling on about twenty million Frenchmen. These income figures might also be compared with what English observers were publishing about the condition of France during the war (cf. document 41).

In the list of *aides* (excise taxes) from the plain country of Paris (*plat pays*), note the prevalence of agricultural products being taxed.

Summary of the King's Revenues for the Year 1692

The general tax farms of the *gabelles* of France, the *cinq grosses fermes* and related fees, tobacco, the *gabelles* of the region of Lyons, the *gabelles* of Provence and of the Dauphiné, the *gabelles* of Languedoc and Roussillon, of the western domain, of all the French islands of Canada and America: two millions' increase in the *gabelles* for each year, in 1689; the general tax farms of the *aides*, the domains of France and related fees; the old and new paper and parchment taxes; the fees for measures and brokerage

SOURCE: A. M. de Boislisle (ed.), *Mémoires des Intendants sur l'État des Généralités dressés pour l'Instruction du Duc de Bourgogne* (Paris, 1881), I, 484–486.

reestablished on October 4, 1689; the new *pied-fourché* established in 1690; the new taxes on hats, [established] in 1690: the whole, in conformity with the union of the general tax farms on September 11, 1691, in order to pay during the war . . . 61,000,000 l[ivres]

And in time of peace 63,000,000 l.

The new taxes established on tea, coffee, chocolate, cocoa, sherbets, and vanilla, on January 22, 1692, for the first year	100,000
And for each of the 2nd and 3rd years, 220,000 l.	
And for each of the 4th, 5th, and 6th years, 420,000 l.	
The French and foreign postal systems	2,900,000
Equipment for soldiers	9,000,000
Waters and forests	2,600,000
Duties paid by each hearth in the province of Brittany	528,000
Parties casuelles, average year	3,200,000
General financial receipts from the Franche-Comté	800,000
General financial receipts for Flanders	1,600,000
General financial receipts for Lorraine and regions connected with it	1,423,990
Powder and saltpeter of France	200,000
Free gift from the French clergy	2,400,000
Free gift from Provence	800,000
Free gift from Burgundy	300,000
Free gift from Brittany	1,500,000
Free gift from Languedoc	3,000,000
For the canal [of Languedoc], they gave	82,000
Free gift from Bigorre	10,000
Free gift from Navarre	7,000
Free gift from the County of Foix	7,000
Free gift from Béarn	17,000
Free gift from Artois	400,000
Free gift from Mons	162,500
Taillon and soldiers' pay from the *pays d'états*	373,764
Paris	3,789,194
Soissons	889,240
Amiens	919,544

General receipts from the *tailles* for	Châlons	1,541,689
	Orléans	1,939,868
	Tours	3,042,439
	Bourges	634,684
	Moulins	1,335,595
	Lyons	1,295,086
	Riom	2,574,013
	Poitiers	2,177,735
	Limoges	2,008,087
	Bordeaux	3,276,291
	Montauban	3,372,669
	Rouen	2,259,800
	Caen	1,581,627
	Alençon	1,440,439
	Grenoble	1,362,147
Grand total for the contents of this summary		127,851,401

Summary of the Income from Entries into Paris and Rouen, and the Tax Farms Which the Gentlemen Concerned Administer Under a Lease with Pierre Pointeau

Aides and related fees from the plain country about Paris are worth	700,000 l.
Fees for measures and brokerage	1,800,000
Aides and related fees from the *élection* of Chartres	230,000
Stamped paper for Paris and the *généralité* of Paris	528,000
A sou per livre on the sale of calves in Paris	120,000
The great duty of Picardy, which consists of 9 l. 18 s. per *muid* of wine passing through Flanders and elsewhere	51,000
Duties on all merchandise passing over and under the bridge of Joigny	200,000
French wines in transit through Paris, and which are not inspected	5,996
Entries into the city of Rouen	433,700
French wines entering Paris in bottles	7,337

Brandies entering Paris, including taxes upon consumption	200,000
Liqueurs entering and sold at retail in Paris	100,000
Wholesale and entry taxes on all French wines arriving in Paris, by water or by land	5,600,000
River duties upon wines and other merchandise	481,881
Apple and pear ciders entering and sold at retail in Paris	4,578
Retail and corking fees upon all winesellers in the city and faubourgs of Paris	1,200,000
The old *pied-fourché*	700,000
The new *pied-fourché* established in the year 1690	500,000
The doubling of the *marc d'or*	160,000
The first half of the tolls which has been set aside	40,000
Total of the said entries into Paris, Rouen, and the tax farms which the gentlemen concerned are administering during the lease with Pointeau	13,062,492

46. Definitions of Nobility by the State

For centuries French kings had claimed the power to regularize the status of nobles in their realm, but in fact the enforcement of royal social legislation had been ineffectual or nonexistent before the reign of Louis XIV. As a consequence of nonenforcement of the law, persons bore titles and coats of arms to which they were not entitled, they claimed exemptions from the *taille* on the grounds of nobility when in fact they were commoners, or still more frequently they violated with impunity laws which all Frenchmen were expected to obey. Specific laws promulgated for the second estate, regulating the dress of nobles or establishing their hunting rights or military service, filled the law books but were largely ignored.

The monarchy's efforts to legislate the status of nobles and to force them to obey royal laws began in earnest once again under Richelieu, for the civil wars of the sixteenth century had undermined the previous structure of definitions and patterns of enforcement. The Cardinal forced obedience to the Crown by punishing all nobles regardless of their status when they violated the law against dueling. Similarly, Richelieu and Louis XIII actively promoted officials in Paris and the

SOURCE: Isambert, *Recueil Général des Anciennes Lois Françaises* (Paris, 1830), XX, 261–262, 400–402.

provinces to all kinds of offices on the basis of the legal distinctions between gentility and nobility which had developed in the sixteenth century as a result of the massive sale of royal offices conferring nobility upon their purchasers. "A nobleman is made, a gentleman is born," became the legal principle as well as the conventional one depicted in literature; and eventually the nobility as a social group accepted the definitions of status being enforced by the royal courts. This was a major victory for absolute monarchy in the reign of Louis XIV. The Fronde had been partly a reaction against the regularization of the conduct of the princes and the great nobles who claimed a special place in society by virtue of their blood and courage; but they too submitted to royal law, in a way, when they accepted the rigid etiquette governing their conduct at Versailles.

Directly inspired by Colbert—a bourgeois according to the Duke of Saint-Simon, but legally a nobleman though not a gentleman—Louis XIV instituted a major effort in the 1660's to discover false nobles and to punish them. Extensive genealogical research had to be conducted even by the true nobles and gentlemen in order to prove their status. Thus the second estate as a whole slowly came to accept the definitions of itself formulated by the state. But the enforcement of laws governing nobility was never simply a matter of social status. Colbert had sought to force false nobles to pay the *taille*. Indeed, social legislation in the *ancien régime* always had a fiscal aspect to it and reflected the Crown's insatiable need for money.

The edict of March 1696 reflects this need for money. Service, honor, and the other characteristics of nobility are given lip service only; the legislation amounts to the blatant sale of nobility. One generation later the sons of the purchasers would legally "pass" as gentlemen, though a stigma would still remain. By contrast, the edict of 1701 reflects a long-range policy of the Crown to remove the social stigma from nobles engaging in wholesale trade. On this point, despite the Crown's efforts, in most of France engaging in trade continued to be considered degrading for nobles long after Louis XIV's death.

Edict Conferring Ennoblement in Return for Financial Contributions upon Five Hundred Persons Chosen from among the Most Distinguished of the Realm

Versailles, March 1696

LOUIS, [King of France], etc. If noble origins and the antiquity of the bloodline which confers so much distinction among men is merely the gift of blind fortune, the title and the source of nobility is a gift of the prince who knows how to reward with discernment the important services which subjects render to their country. These services, so worthy of the gratitude of sovereigns, are not always rendered with weapons in the hand; zeal is shown in more than one way, and there are occasions on which, in sacrificing one's own possessions to maintain the troops which defend the state, one earns as it were the same reward as those who pour forth their blood to defend it. It is this which has made us resolve to grant five hundred letters of nobility in our kingdom, to serve as a reward for those of our subjects who, in acquiring them for a modest sum, will contribute to furnishing us the aid which we need to repel the obstinate efforts of our enemies.

For these reasons, etc., we ennoble in our realm, country, lands, and seigniories obedient to us the number of five hundred persons who will be selected from among those who are the most distinguished through their merit, virtues, and good qualities. Given preference will be those who, by the posts and offices which they have held or hold, have made themselves praiseworthy and worthy of being elevated to this degree of honor and distinction; even businessmen and merchants carrying on wholesale trade, which they will be able to continue without forfeiting the said quality of nobility, to each of whom we shall send our individual letters of ennoblement, which will be registered in our parlementary courts, *Chambres des comptes*, *Cour des aides*, and financial offices, as well as in the registries of our *bailliages*, *sénéchaussées*, and *élections* where the grantees are domiciled, the costs of all of which registrations will be moderately taxed by decree of our council, by virtue of which letters we desire that they be held, considered, and reputed as nobles, together with their children and their posterity, born and to be born of loyal marriage, just as if they had been born of noble and ancient families, and as such, that they be honored and respected in all acts, assemblies, and occasions, and that they may assume the title of squire and attain the degree of chivalry and other [privileges] reserved for our nobility, to enjoy and use all the honors, prerogatives, privileges, preeminences, freedoms, liberties, exemptions, and immunities which the other nobles of our realm enjoy without distinction. And also that they can acquire, hold, and possess all fiefs, lands, and noble seigniories, whatever their title and rank may be. We permit them to bear crested coats of arms, regulated by our judge of the arms of France, which will be imprinted and emblazoned on our letters of ennoblement; on condition that they live nobly, without *dérogeance* from the said rank, and that they pay us the sums for which they will be moderately taxed in our council by the lists which will be established there, upon the receipts of the guard of our royal treasury now in office, which will be delivered to them, without the said ennoblements being liable to suppression or revocation by us and by our successors, nor subject to any tax, for confirmation, in view of the sum which they are paying us in the urgent needs for which we are granting them. So we grant . . . etc.

Edict Granting Permission to Noblemen, if They Are Not Magistrates, to Conduct Commerce without Dérogeance

Versailles, December 1701

LOUIS, [King of France], etc. The concern which we have always shown to make trade flourish in our realm, having made us realize the advantage which the state gains from the industry of those of our subjects who have honorably attached themselves to business, we have always looked upon wholesale trade as an honorable profession, and one which involves no obligations not reasonably consistent with nobility; which has even led us on several occasions to grant letters of ennoblement in favor of several of the leading businessmen, to show them our esteem for those who distinguish themselves in that profession. We have moreover been informed that a great number of those of our subjects who are of noble origin or who have become so by the positions and offices which they have acquired, as well as those whom we have ennobled by our favor, encounter difficulties in undertaking to carry out or continue any trade, even wholesale, other than that at sea, which we have already declared will not cause them to forfeit their nobility, through the fear of being prejudicial to that [nobility] they possess; and wishing to encourage all those of our subjects noble and otherwise who may have an inclination or talent for trade to devote themselves to it, and to induce those who have embraced this profession to remain in it, and to raise their children in it, we believe we can do nothing more appropriate than to show to the public the value we have always placed on good businessmen, who by their cares and their labor attract wealth from all sides and maintain abundance in our states.

For these reasons . . . by confirming and renewing to the extent necessary the edict of the month of August 1669, concerning trade at sea, which we understand shall still be carried out according to its form and tenor, . . . we desire and it pleases us:

1. That all our subjects, noble by birth, by office, or otherwise, except those who are currently holding judicial offices, may freely carry on any sort of wholesale trade, both within and without the realm, for their own account or on commission, without *dérogeance* from their nobility.

2. We desire and understand that the nobles who conduct wholesale trade will continue to have precedence over other businessmen in all general and private assemblies, and will enjoy the same exemptions and privileges granted their nobility, which they enjoyed before entering trade.

3. We permit those who carry on only wholesale trade to possess offices as our councillors, secretaries, to the house and Crown of France, and in our finances, to continue at the same time their wholesale trade, without needing to this end decrees or letters of compatibility.

4. Shall be deemed and considered merchants and wholesale businessmen, all those who carry out their trade in a warehouse, selling their merchandise by bales, cases, or entire lots, and who do not have open shops or any display counter and sign at their doors and houses.

5. We desire that in the cities of the realm where until the present it has not been permitted to carry on a business or make money without having been received into some merchant guild, nobles will be free to carry on a wholesale business, without being obliged to seek admission to a merchant guild or to prove any apprenticeship.

6. And so that the families of wholesale merchants or businessmen, both on land or on sea, will be known to enjoy the prerogatives which are granted them by these documents, and to receive the marks of distinction which we judge appropriate to grant them, we desire that those of our subjects who devote themselves to wholesale trade will in the future be obliged to inscribe their names on a list, which will to this end be placed in the commercial juris-

diction of the city in which they live, and in the individual chambers of commerce, which henceforth shall be established in several cities of our realm.

7. We desire and understand likewise that in the provinces, cities, and localities where lawyers, doctors, and other principal bourgeois are admitted to the offices of mayors, *échevins*, *capitouls*, *jurats*, and first consuls, those merchants carrying on wholesale trade may be elected concurrently to the said offices, notwithstanding all statutes, regulations, and customs to the contrary, which we have expressly annulled and annul to this end by these documents.

8. We likewise understand that the wholesale merchants can be elected consuls, judges, priors, and presidents of the commercial jurisdiction, as well as the merchants received into the merchant guilds and brotherhoods, which have been established in several cities and localities of the realm.

9. We also desire that the head of each commercial jurisdiction, whatever title he may bear, shall be exempt from lodging soldiers, and from watch and guard duty, during the time of his office.

10. And to preserve as much as we can probity and good faith in a profession so useful to the state, we declare stripped of the honors and prerogatives granted above those wholesale merchants and businessmen, as well as other merchants, who have gone bankrupt, asked for letters to extend debts, or made contracts for deferred payment with their creditors. So we issue, etc. . . .

47. *The Problem of Religious Uniformity*

Fervent supporter of Cardinal Richelieu, man of letters, and member of the French Academy, Paul Hay du Châtelet (1592–1636) summarizes some of the principal arguments and strategies which were already being used in the 1660's to restore religious uniformity to France. More a work of synthetic propaganda than of original thought, Châtelet's writing enables us to see the origins of what would become an almost national movement for the "conversion" of the Huguenots.

SOURCE: Paul Hay du Châtelet, *Traitté de la politique de France* (1666), Chap. V. This text and translation have been supplied by Professor Alfred Soman of Carleton College, Northfield, Minnesota.

A king can have no object more worthy of his care and attention than to maintain in his realm the religion which he received from his ancestors. For diversity of belief, cult, and ceremony divides his subjects and causes them reciprocally to hate and despise one another, which in turn gives rise to conflicts, war, and general catastrophe. On the other hand, unity of belief binds men together. Fellow subjects who pray to God in the same church and worship at the same altar will rarely be seen to fight except in the same armies and under the same flags. Since this maxim is universally true in the politics of Christian nations, and since our religion is the only one which offers salvation, princes are obliged to maintain it with all their might and to employ for its glory the sovereign power which they derive from its beneficence.

The pagans, who conducted themselves so prudently and equitably, and who have bequeathed to us so many examples of wisdom and probity, held so firmly to the principle of not allowing any novel opinion which might offend common beliefs that they forbade anyone to disabuse the populace of its errors. The books which were found by the tomb of Numa Pompilius were ordered by the Senate to be burned, even though they contained the ancient religion of Rome; for the praetor, Rutilius, who had been commissioned to read them, affirmed by oath that they contained things capable of overthrowing the religion observed by the people at that time. Furthermore, they refused to open their eyes to the light of truth, even though they knew it to be true, when it seemed that the people would find it [too] new; they preferred to maintain the fables hallowed by time and the traditional devotion of the multitude. Similarly, the Athenians believed they were performing a necessary act of justice when they condemned Socrates to death for having taken it upon himself to persuade the people that there is only one God. They knew, however, that the true [teaching] of this philosopher was the wonder of their age, the glory of the city and of all Greece. The wisest among them were convinced of the soundness of this doctrine, and the Stoics made it an article of belief. Thus one should recognize that the ruin of the Gentiles and the destruction of the idols was accomplished by the Hand of God, who alone can perform prodigies of grace and omnipotence.

The royal ancestors of His Majesty exercised constant diligence inviolably to preserve the Catholic religion. They were always the unfailing protectors of the Church and of the Holy Apostolic See.

They expelled the Arians; they bore arms and risked their lives against the Albigensians, whom they defeated and destroyed; they chastized the Waldensians [*Pauvres*] of Lyons; in sum, they prevented any attack on Christianity in all places to which their authority extended.

In the last century a new monster rose up against the Church. France witnessed its birth and watched it mature, abetted by impiety and revolt. History will show posterity how much blood was shed during the course of nearly eighty years in order to repress this dangerous sect and how the reigns of six of our kings were occupied by the zeal to reduce the heretics to their duty. The glory of cutting off the last head of this Hydra was reserved for His Majesty; but it would be well to inquire into the proper weapons for performing this long-awaited execution.

There can be no doubt that, by the principles of Christianity and by the maxims of politics, it is necessary to reduce the King's subjects to a single faith. Although those who profess the so-called Reformed Religion are today without weapons, without fortified positions, without money, and without a leader or allies, they are nevertheless to be feared. They retain the memory of their audacity and of their past rebellions. They look upon those cities which they had overrun, and from which it was necessary to evict them by armed force, as their proper heritage stolen from them by injustice. In their hearts they nurse the same old hatred of order and discipline, and they are still inclined toward revolt, confusion, and anarchy. While they do not bother to appoint leaders, they could [easily] do so by delegating authority to those of their number who are soldiers. They are convinced that if they should arm they would lack neither money nor friends. They believe that the greatness of the King arouses as much jealousy as admiration, and that his power inspires as much anger as terror among his neighbors. In sum, there is reason to consider that he has more than 100,000 potential enemies in the bosom of his realm as long as France harbors Huguenots who, perhaps, are only waiting for a chance to rebel. Thus they are perpetual obstacles to any projects which may be undertaken; and although they are weak, they are to be feared because of their well-known animosity. It is true that sensible men [*honnêtes gens*] of their sect are well aware that they could never have greater peace and security than they now enjoy by the King's favor and under the protection of his edicts; but in such matters mass opinion prevails. It is like a torrent which, by its very swiftness, overturns rocks which seemed immovable.

It might be argued that the lenient treatment accorded the Huguenots sustains the friendship of the German princes for France, and if they were dealt with more harshly the King would lose his most eminent and powerful allies. This is mere idle talk and has no foundation. Not only are the German princes of a different religion from our heretics [i.e., they are Lutherans, not Calvinists] and have no direct interest in whether the King guarantees the Huguenots their so-called liberty of conscience; but [more importantly], since the military strength of France protects [the German princes] from the power of Austria and especially the Emperor (who has various designs on them), they cannot withdraw from the alliance they have contracted with His Majesty and would not do so even if all the Huguenots were to be put to death. Inasmuch as the might of the King is so vital to all Protestants, it would be to their interest to drive the Huguenots out of France rather than to take up arms to maintain them. And this is so, because if these Huguenots were to create a disturbance, the King would be preoccupied in quelling the revolt; and, the King being thus distracted, the Emperor could seize the occasion to extend his dominion—which is what Charles V did while Francis I was powerless to aid [the German princes]. Since it is certain, therefore, that German freedom is dependent upon the King's armies, they would not trouble themselves about the affairs of the Huguenots in France. While the Protestants are attached to the King by considerations other than those of religion, they will continue to act as before, and His Majesty, for his part, will still have the same reasons for coming to their aid—even if there were not a single Huguenot in France.

Neither should one expect England to assist them. It is too small a state to attempt anything against France. If every last Englishman crossed the Channel and the Island were emptied of soldiers and munitions, it would still not be enough. Moreover, their affairs remain exposed to the violence and fickleness of the populace. Holland and Sweden are in a similar situation and have other matters than the problems of the Huguenots to settle with the King. Denmark is not strong enough. The policy of the Calvinists is truly wonderful, for they wish us to believe that whatever is not Roman

Catholic is French Huguenot; whereas in fact the German Lutherans have less in common with them than with us.

Thus the King has nothing to fear on the part of the so-called allies of the Huguenots. However they are dangerous, as I have said. If there were some extraordinary upheaval in France, such as civil war, or some great invasion by foreign enemies, we would see them act as they did during the Fronde, when they took up arms and protested respectfully that they were devoted to the King. But if peace had not come when it did, they would not have failed to join in the fray [*de se croire necessaires*] and to demand anything they might have believed advantageous to their party. They would have asked that their strongholds be returned to them; they would have insisted on the restitution of their temples, on an increase in their so-called privileges, and on the free practice of their religion; and, in their admirable manner, they would have complained and threatened [at the same time]. And if, by some misfortune, a victorious foreign army, either Catholic or Protestant, invaded the kingdom, the King would have to resign himself to the prospect of a revolt of the heretics or else satisfy all their claims—which would mean plunging the realm into the calamities with which our ancestors were [only too] familiar.

These Huguenots are ill advised to make so much noise and such a parade about the Edict of Nantes; they obtained it by violent extortion, sword in hand. Moreover, it was [intended] only as an interim settlement, until such time as they should have seen the light of truth—for which they have had sufficient time. Did not they themselves violate it by the war of Languedoc, Cévennes, and La Rochelle? They summoned the enemies of the state to their aid and put the whole kingdom to fire and sword. Finally, in matters of government, what is good at one time is often not at another. One must always adapt things to the general rule of politics, which is to strive incessantly for the good of the state. When the Edict of Nantes was granted it was intended for the well-being of France; and if that same well-being today requires that the Edict be revoked, the choice is clear: either it must be revoked, or all that I have said must be disregarded. It follows that the King is completely justified in protecting himself against those of the so-called Reformed Religion and in reducing them to a condition in which they cease to be a threat.

Perhaps it will be said that the Huguenots serve a useful purpose in France because they oblige the Catholic clergy to strive to live more modestly and observe more strictly the regulations of their vocation; but this is a frivolous point. The Church of God is not sustained by human means. Christ dwells within it and governs it by his Holy Spirit which pervades and animates it. If France were rid of the Huguenots, there would be fewer wicked persons and more men of good will—which ought to gratify the King, since it is a rule that states are maintained by men who love virtue, etc. It can thus be taken as proved that the King should prevent the Huguenots from causing harm and creating suspicion.

It remains for us to inquire into the fastest and most efficient means to achieve this purpose. I am not of the opinion that we should compel the Huguenots to leave France, as the Moors were driven out of Spain, to the great detriment of that country. It would be inhumane to do so; they are Christians even though they have withdrawn from the Church. And furthermore, it would deprive the state of many good families and would deny these wretches any hope of conversion and salvation. It seems to me that in this case the King should imitate the Church (Mother of all Christians), whose justice always mingles gentleness with severity and whose punishments are always indulgent.

The first method the King should employ is to encourage Huguenots to associate with Catholics more freely than they do at present. For by such association they will gradually correct their misconception that we hate them. They will lose their aversion for us; they will come to know our ways and learn the true mysteries of those doctrines which now offend them. This will cause them to confess, as did St. Augustine, that they have not correctly understood the teachings of the Church. In the long run, I do not believe there is a more efficacious way to convert the heretics than by this kind of intercourse. With the passing of time, their hearts must be touched, just as sunlight dissipates shadows . . . and truth triumphs over falsehood.

The second [method] would be to reward honorably those who might convert and to create an inexhaustible fund for that purpose. I do not think it a good idea to exclude Huguenots from every kind of employment; they should be allowed to hold lesser offices though not the more important ones. The rationale behind this is that if they were totally excluded, they would grow accustomed to idleness, lose their ambition, and perhaps ultimately make it a point of religious doctrine not to work. If, on the other hand, they are employed in minor positions, they will become accustomed to living among Catholics, and their ambition will be aroused when they compare themselves with their superiors.

The third means is legally to harass private individuals on religious [technicalities], thus forcing them to live near court. Lawsuits of this kind might be instituted against gentlemen on the grounds of the religious services they conduct in their homes. There is no one who would not be liable to that charge, and the bishops would gladly lend their support. Moreover, the King's attorney general is justified in investigating whether marriages, baptisms, and burials are properly conducted in private homes and whether accurate and faithful records of these matters are being kept. Inasmuch as many such records may have been lost, this will provide a [suitable pretext] against those nobles who abuse the concession they were granted to hold religious services in their châteaux . . . on the condition that they do not violate the terms of the Edict of Nantes by regularly admitting persons other than their domestic servants.

The fourth means is to oblige the Huguenots to reestablish in their houses the ancient chapels which they have profaned or demolished; and this ought to be enforced by each bishop in his own diocese. It would not be necessary to make this a general law applicable to all Huguenots; rather [it would be sufficient to restrict it] to certain individuals. Nothing could be more reasonable. For they had no right to destroy temples consecrated in perpetuity for divine services according to the religion practiced by the King and throughout the whole realm—the religion of our ancestors.

[As for] the fifth method, when there is a lawsuit of the sort I have just described, the deputies who are spokesmen for the Huguenot community should not be permitted to intervene. There are three reasons for refusing their intervention. The first is that the Huguenots may not incorporate in France or hold an assembly without the explicit permission of the King. In the second place, lawsuits of private individuals must not be made public affairs. Third, the King will dispense justice without their intervention. We must not abolish these deputies of the Huguenots by a single stroke of the pen, but neither must we heed everything they say.

The sixth method would be for the King to forbid Huguenots to dwell or practice their religion in any fortified towns other than those belonging to the King. They should especially be excluded from fortresses whose lords are followers of the so-called Reformed Religion. For example, Vitré in Brittany belongs to the prince of Tarante, a Calvinist, since M. de La Trémouille resigned in his favor. The Huguenots have a temple there and practice their religion publicly. We should make them exchange this town for another, and we shall not lack reasons to justify this substitution. Nothing could contribute more toward converting them; for it will cause them incredible distress to live among strangers with whom they have no ties of interest or of blood.

The seventh method is to allow Huguenot judgeships to expire upon the death of the incumbents. The *Chambres mi-partis* established by the Edict of Nantes are henceforth unnecessary.

The eighth method is to appoint Catholic commissioners to attend all Huguenot synods. (Formerly these commissioners were always Catholics.) They should be competent in matters of religious controversy and adroit enough to foment the quarrels which always arise. We must not refuse when they ask permission to hold regional synods, but we must never permit them to hold national assemblies. At the end of each synod we should demand that the pastors furnish money for the King—either in the form of loans, taxes, or upon some other pretext.

The ninth is to have them prosecuted for their communal debts and to order the sale of some of their temples, which are nontaxable property.

The tenth is to forbid all subjects to leave the country without the King's permission. For the Huguenots must not be allowed to leave France, and they will be included in the general prohibition.

The eleventh is to have confessors make poor Catholics realize that their souls are in peril when they work for Huguenots.

The twelfth is to have the police force Huguenots to observe the same fasts as the Catholics, on the same grounds that we oblige them to observe holidays out of respect for public religion. Those who violate either of these two rules should be severely punished.

The thirteenth method is to try to marry Huguenots to Catholics and to have all the children of these marriages raised in the Roman faith.

The fourteenth is to prevent Huguenots from selling any real estate they may own, because this form of property attaches them to the interests of the state.

The fifteenth and last is to transfer their Academy of Saumur to some other town, such as Vangé or Beaufort. We have a precedent in the case of the Academy of Montauban, which was moved to Puylaurens. The pretext for making them leave Saumur is that the town lies at the crossing of the Loire, which affords the [main] communication for several large provinces; and therefore the King cannot be too cautious. Moreover, this Academy of Saumur is illegal; the Huguenots never received letters patent to establish it. It will be pointless for them to claim that Saumur is one of their strongholds; for other subjects of the King do not demand strongholds, and henceforth the Huguenots are to be treated no differently from the rest. Think of the situation if every group demanded fortified towns. What madness!

In addition to the above, we could also require that divinity students who aspire to the ministry be obliged to teach one course in philosophy or two years of theology. The result would be fewer ministers, and as their number decreased, infallibly the number of Huguenots would diminish. The King could even order that divinity students appear before royal commissioners and be forced to undergo a rigorous examination. For His Majesty has an interest in seeing that these ministers are properly prepared, lest they be not pastors but seditious rebels. In such an examination, the said students could be obliged to reply to Catholic theologians on whatever disputed questions of doctrine [the Catholics] might see fit to ask. The Huguenots could hardly refuse this suggestion since the students are supposed to be prepared on all subjects. Furthermore, since the Huguenots say that their pastors are their bishops, no one must be allowed to become a pastor before the age of twenty-seven.

These, in brief, are what I believe to be the most useful of human means to convert those of the so-called Reformed Religion.

48. The Revocation of the Edict of Nantes

Opposition to the program of "converting" the Huguenots never really materialized, especially after the princes and great nobles who had led the Protestant cause died, were exiled, or converted to Catholi-

SOURCE: D. D. Scott, *The Suppression of the Reformation in France* (London, 1890), pp. 341–344.

cism. The conversion of Marshal Turenne to Catholicism in 1668 and the zeal of ex-Protestants such as Paul Pellisson for their new faith seemed to confirm Le Tellier's and Louvois' assertions to Louis XIV that there were practically no Huguenots left in France by 1685. Jean Racine, poet and Jansenist, had had the courage, through an address he wrote to be given by a provincial abbot, to condemn use of "fire and sword" to convert souls; but coming to the defense of the Protestant cause apparently was out of the question for non-Protestants at court.

As is the case with all royal edicts in seventeenth-century France, a historical accounting or evocation of old precedents for the legislation is given. In this instance, Louis XIV's primary claim is that he was accomplishing what Henry IV would have done had he lived long enough.

In Europe, Catholic countries greeted Louis' decision to revoke the Edict of Nantes as a great victory for monarchy and the Roman Church, while for Protestants in England, the Netherlands, and Germany, the suspicion that the Sun King was the devil incarnate seemed confirmed. In the context of Louis' foreign aims, as he struggled to assert French dominance over Europe, the revocation was a political blunder of immense proportions. It helped Protestant sovereigns to rally their subjects in a great coalition war against France, while Louis gained little from papal or other Catholic supporters.

Edict of the King

Prohibiting any farther public exercise of the Pretended Reformed Religion [P. R. R.] in his kingdom. Registered in the Chamber of the *Vacations*, Oct. 22, 1685.

Louis, by the Grace of God, King of France and Navarre; to all present and to come, greeting. King Henry the Great, our grandfather of glorious memory, being desirous that the peace which he had procured for his subjects after the grievous losses they had sustained in the course of domestic and foreign wars, should not be troubled on account of the P.R.R. as had happened in the reigns of the kings his predecessors, by his edict granted at Nantes in the month of April 1598, regulated the procedure to be adopted with regard to those of the said religion and the places in which they might meet for public worship, established extraordinary judges to administer justice to them, and, in fine, even provided by particular articles, for whatever could be thought necessary for maintaining the tranquility of his kingdom and for diminishing mutual aversion between the members of the two religions, so as to put himself in a better condition to labour, as he had resolved to do, for the reunion to the Church of those who had so lightly withdrawn from it. And as the intention of the king, our grandfather, was frustrated by his sudden death, and as even the execution of the said edict was interrupted during the minority of the late king, our most honoured lord and father of glorious memory, by new enterprises on the part of the said persons of the P.R.R. who gave occasion to their being deprived of divers advantages accorded to them by the said edict: Nevertheless the king, our said late lord and father, in the exercise of his usual clemency, granted them yet another edict at Nîmes in July 1629, by means of which tranquility being established anew, the said late king, animated with the same spirit and the same zeal for religion as the king our said grandfather, had resolved to take advantage of this repose for attempting to put his said pious design into execution, but foreign wars having supervened soon after, so that the kingdom being seldom tranquil, from 1635 to the truce concluded in 1684, with the powers of Europe, nothing more could be done for the advantage of religion beyond diminishing the number of places for the public exercise of the P.R.R. by interdicting such as were found established to the prejudice of the dispositions made by the edicts, and by the suppression of the *Chambres mi-partie*, these having been appointed provisionally only. God having at last permitted that our people should enjoy perfect repose, and that we, no longer occupied in protecting them from our enemies, should be able to profit by this truce, which we have ourselves facilitated, by applying our whole endeavours to the discovery of the means of accomplishing the designs of our said grandfather and father, adopted as these have been by ourselves since our succession to the crown. And now we see with the thankful acknowledgement we justly owe to God, that our endeavours have reached their proposed end, inasmuch as the better and the greater part of our subjects of the said P.R.R. have embraced the Catholic. And inasmuch as by this the execution of the Edict of Nantes and of all that has ever been ordained in favour of the said P.R.R. remains useless, we have determined that we can do nothing better in order wholly to obliterate the memory of the troubles, the confusion, and the evils which the progress of this false religion has caused in this kingdom, and which furnished occasion for the said edict and to so many previous and subsequent edicts and declarations, than entirely to revoke the said Edict of Nantes, with the particular articles accorded as a sequel to it, and all that has since been done in favour of the said religion.

I. We give you to wit that for these causes and others us thereto moving, and of our certain knowledge, full power, and royal authority, we have by this present perpetual and irrevocable edict, suppressed and revoked, suppress and revoke, the edict of our said grandfather, given at Nantes in April 1598, in its whole extent, together with the particular articles agreed upon in the month of May following, and the letters patent expedited upon the same; and the edict given at Nîmes in July 1629; we declare them null and void, together with all concessions made by them as well as by other edicts, declarations, and *arrêts*, in favour of the said persons of the P.R.R. of whatever nature they may be, the which shall remain in like manner as if they had never been granted, and in consequence we desire and it is our pleasure that all the temples of those of the said P.R.R. situate in our kingdom, countries, territories and lordships under our crown, shall be demolished without delay.

II. We forbid our subjects of the P.R.R. to meet any more for the exercise of the said religion in any place or private house under any pretext whatever, even of *exercices réels*, or of *bailliages*, although the said exercises may have been maintained hitherto in virtue of orders of our council.

III. We likewise forbid all noblemen of what condition soever, to have the religious exercises in their houses and feudalities, the whole under penalty, to be exacted of all our said subjects who shall engage in the said exercise, of confiscation of body and goods.

IV. We enjoin all ministers of the said P.R.R. who do not choose to become converts and to embrace the Catholic, Apostolic, and Roman religion, to leave our kingdom and the territories subject to us within fifteen days from the publication of our present edict, without leave to reside therein beyond that period, or during the said fifteen days, to engage in any preaching, exhortation, or any other function, on pain of being sent to the galleys.

V. We desire that such of the said ministers as shall convert themselves, continue to enjoy during their lives, and their widows after their decease, during their viduity, the same exemptions from taxes, and from giving quarters to soldiers, which they enjoyed during the exercise of their functions as ministers; and, moreover, we shall cause to be paid to the said ministers a life annuity of one-third greater amount than they had as ministers, half of which annuity shall be continued to their wives after their death, as long as they shall remain in viduity.

VI. That if any of the said ministers wish to become advocates, or to take the degree of Doctor of Laws, it is our will and pleasure that they enjoy dispensation from three years of the studies prescribed by our declarations, and that after having undergone the ordinary examinations, and been found to have the requisite capacity, they be admitted as doctors, on payment of the half only of the usual dues received on that occasion at each of the universities.

VII. We forbid private schools for the instruction of the children of the said P.R.R. and in general all things whatever which can be regarded as a concession of whatever kind in favour of the said religion.

VIII. As for children who may be born of persons of the said P.R.R. we desire that from henceforth they be baptised by the parish priests. We enjoin parents to send them to the churches for that purpose, under penalty of five hundred livres of fine, to be increased as the case shall happen; and thereafter the children shall be brought up in the Catholic, Apostolic, and Roman religion, which we expressly enjoin the local magistrates to see being done.

IX. And in the exercise of our clemency towards our subjects of the said P.R.R. who have emigrated from our kingdom, lands, and territories subject to us, previous to the publication of our present edict, it is our will and pleasure that in case of their returning within the period of four months from the day of the said publication, they may, and it shall be lawful for them to reenter into possession of their property, and to enjoy the same, as if they had all along remained there; on the contrary, that the property of those who during that space of four months shall not have returned into our kingdom, lands, and territories subject to us, and which property they shall have abandoned, shall remain and be confiscated in consequence of our declaration of the 20th of August last.

X. We repeat our most express prohibitions to all our subjects of the said P.R.R. against them, their wives and children, leaving our said kingdom, lands, and territories subject to us, or transporting their goods and effects, therefrom under penalty, as respects the men, of being sent to the galleys, and as respects the women, of confiscation of body and goods.

XI. It is our will and intention that the declarations rendered against the relapsed, shall be executed according to their form and tenor.

XII. As for the rest, liberty is granted to the said persons of the P.R.R. while waiting until it shall please God to enlighten them as well as others, to remain in the cities and places of our kingdom, lands, and territories subject to us, and there to continue their commerce, and to enjoy their possessions, without being subjected to molestation or hindrance, under pretext of the said P.R.R. on condition, as said is, of not engaging in the exercise, or of meeting under pretext of prayers, or of the religious services of the said religion, of whatever nature these may be, under the penalties above mentioned of confiscation of body and goods: Thus do we give in charge to our trusty and well-beloved counsellors, &c. Given at Fontainebleau in the month of October, the year of grace one thousand six hundred and eighty-five and of our reign the forty-third.

Signed "LOUIS *visa* LE TELLIER," and further down, "By the King, COLBERT." And sealed with the great seal, on green wax, with red and green strings.

Registered, heard, &c. at Paris, in the Chamber of Vacations, the 22d of October, 1685

Signed DE LA BAUNE

49. The Camisard Revolts

In the rugged hills of what is now the department of the Lozère in southern France, the Protestants refused to submit to the Catholic religion. Even before the revocation of the Edict of Nantes, violence had developed between royal officials, guards, Catholic priests, and the Protestant inhabitants of the region. Violence would flare up again and again for decades.

The Crown's answer to the defiant Protestants of the Cévennes Mountains was military repression. Troops, the famous dragoons who had been the terror of many battlefields, arrived to defeat the small forces of untrained Camisards. But familiarity with the terrain and guerrilla tactics on the part of the Protestants gave them a fighting chance against crack royal regiments. Attacks by night, ambushes in the mountain passes, and terrorism against Catholics by Protestants, and vice versa, soon turned what was originally considered a minor military operation into a war.

SOURCE: *Journaux Camisards* (1700–1715), ed. by Philippe Joutard (Paris, 1965), pp. 30–31, 41–42, 64–66.

The son of a peasant, Abraham Mazel (1677–1710) was one of the first Camisards to prophesy and take up arms. One of the principal leaders during the zenith of the Camisard rebellion, he saw his companions executed or forced to surrender as the balance turned against the Protestants in 1704. Arrested and imprisoned, Mazel escaped and fled to London. While there, he dictated this account of the uprisings in an attempt to counter English skepticism about the divine inspiration of the rebellion. In 1709 Mazel returned to France, attempted to raise the region east of the Cévennes, but was betrayed and killed.

Although God abundantly poured forth his Spirit over the people of our Cévennes, so much that these preachers of repentance were counted by thousands, people of all ages and sex, we nevertheless had such great respect for the [Huguenot] ministers and such a high idea of their ministry that although the majority of us were too young to have known them before the persecutions which obliged them to leave the kingdom, we ardently wished that some of them would come among us to console, to fortify, and to lead this remnant of a flock with—having been unable to flee when the wolf had come to wreak havoc, and having been abandoned by the shepherds—had been scattered throughout the mountains, afflicted, beaten, wounded, left in a state of devastation, be it in the towns or in the countryside. No one is unaware of the history of the persecutions which we have undergone for more than twenty-five years.

Finally, Jean Rampon and Pierre Esprit . . . received by divine inspiration this extraordinary order which greatly surprised them. They were forbidden to comb their hair for several weeks, and they were told that this sign would be explained to them. They faithfully carried out this order, and when the time had expired, and they were commanded to comb their hair, they were told by inspiration that as many lice as fell from their heads, that many ministers would they see return to the region to preach the gospel to them and to administer the sacraments as before the persecution. These two inspired men were sure they would see an abundance of lice fall from their heads, since in the wretchedness in which they lived, being vagabonds and fugitives, sleeping completely clothed in caves, unable to change their linens to keep clean, this vermin had so invaded them that all their efforts could not keep them free from them. Consider their circumstances and their prejudices in favor of the ministers: how astonished they were to see that not one louse fell from their heads, which they combed to the point of scalping themselves. They were very saddened at being able to find none for the sake of the ministers for whom they had as much love as they had hatred for that vermin which was eating them alive.

A few months before taking up arms [in 1702] and before the least thought of doing so had come to my mind, I dreamed that I saw in a garden some big and very fat black oxen which were eating the cabbages in the garden. A person whom I did not know having ordered me to chase the black oxen from the garden, I refused to do so; but having redoubled his entreaties and his orders, I obeyed and chased the oxen away from the garden. The Spirit of the Lord having subsequently come upon me, it seized me as usual in the form of a powerful and strong man who cannot be resisted, and having opened my mouth, it made me declare among other things that the garden which I had seen represented the Church, that the big black oxen were the priests who were devouring it, and that I was called to carry out this vision.

I had several inspirations by which I was told to prepare to take up arms to fight with my brothers against our persecutors, that I would bring iron and fire against the priests of the Roman Church, and that I would burn their altars. . . .

At dusk . . . we set out for Saint-André de Lancize to carry out another order uttered by my mouth, which was to put to death the priest of the locality, to burn his house, to topple the altar, and to set fire to the church. The next morning we entered the priest's house, where we found no one, for as the priest was a persecutor, fear had seized him since the death of the Abbot of Chayla [whose murder by the Camisards in July 1702 had opened the war in the Cévennes], and he was at the top of the bell tower, with provisions and weapons. After having burned his house, we broke down the door of the church and toppled the altar, destroying the images and the grotesque figurines, according to our orders. We collected everything we found in the middle of the church, the altar, its trappings, the benches, and faggots which we brought from outdoors, and set fire to it. Although our inspirations told us that the priest was there, we withdrew after having sought him in vain, for we did not then know that he was in the bell tower; but he revealed himself by throwing stones at us. Immediately some of our men pulled down the ladder leading to the tower and carried it outside, by means of which four of them climbed to the roof of the church armed with pistols and halberds. The priest wanted to fire at them with his weapons, but not one would fire. The priest received a pistol wound, and the schoolmaster of the parish who was with him also was wounded and died two weeks later. The priest, seeing that we were climbing into the bell tower and that he was irretrievably lost, being unable to use his weapons, jumped from the tower and killed himself. Someone shot him with a pistol to take from him a remnant of his miserable life which he still seemed to have. I said that the priest's weapons had refused to fire upon us in his hands; I can also say that in ours, never were there better weapons than those of this priest, for they never misfired. . . .

Before continuing, I must point out that the war in our Cévennes whose beginning I have just described appeared so inconsequential at its birth that Intendant Bâville and the others in charge of the province thought they could easily stifle it by means of the regular troops used to patrol the country, by the bourgeoisie [*sic*] in case we resisted, and by a few free companies which had been recruited recently in the province, in order to disperse and prevent the assemblies of inspired persons, without tiring the court [at Versailles] with such a contemptible matter, which the wheel and the stake could doubtlessly end. Seeing, however, that this was not enough, they increased these free companies to forty-two. And finally seeing that the situation was worsening, and that the court would of necessity have to be informed, shortly afterward armies commanded by marshals of France were sent against us. Monsieur Bâville had imagined that wretched peasants, beaten, ruined, unarmed, restrained on all sides, and in the heart of the kingdom, would never be able to undertake anything of that nature which would not immediately be suppressed by the careful precautions which had been taken against any uprising. First they had sent Captain Poul, who had been a famous guerrilla in the Vaudoise valleys against the troops of the Duke of Savoy. This wretch did a great deal of harm at the beginning. He was bold and brash, and had boasted that he and his single company of dragoons would exterminate us if ever he could attack us in open country. The occasion presented itself, apparently as favorable as he could wish, toward the Christmas holidays of last year [1702], when troops of Cavalier [a Camisard] were near Nîmes, who himself had secretly entered there to take out some munitions.

The Count de Broglie and Poul went out on the notification

they had been given and met the said troops of Cavalier commanded by Ravanel in the plain of Val de Bane near the Gaffarel farm two leagues from Nîmes. These gentlemen, seeing that our men were awaiting them without wavering, were a bit astonished. Brave Poul's courage seemed to deflate, but the Count de Broglie bolstered it by recalling to him what he had said, that the opportunity could not be better. Poul, stimulated by these words, advanced. Our men received him, singing Psalm 68: "Let God arise, let his enemies be scattered."

His fire had no effect; he was wounded in the throat and fell from his horse. The Count de Broglie fled at once. However, Poul arose in order to remount his horse, crying, "Help me, dragoons! Help me, dragoons!" But several of our most puny men, falling upon him with hatchets, pitchforks, and clubs, showed him, by taking his life from him in that manner, that God, when he wishes, overthrows the strongest and the most haughty by the weakest and the most scorned. It must be noted that those who had firearms pursued the fugitives. Four of his dragoons remained [dead] on the spot; the others and the soldiers fled to Nîmes; several of those who had presented themselves for the battle withdrew seriously wounded.

I do not know whether it was this event which caused the disgrace of the Count de Broglie, who was the king's lieutenant in the province, but he was recalled. Monsieur Julien was sent with his troops, and shortly afterward Marshal Montrevel, with a greater number. So much that they calculated that there were in the province twenty-five thousand men as regular troops, including the free companies and the Miquelets [Catalonian mercenaries], in addition to the bourgeoisie.

It was after Poul's death that they began to call us the Camisards. I do not know whether it is because we often made *camisades* [night attacks] that we were given that epithet, or because we usually fought in our shirts or camisoles. We also were called "fanatics" because of our inspirations.

50. *An Intendant's View of the Camisard War*

The role of the intendants in the Camisard war became something of a cause célèbre even during the lifetime of Louis XIV. Had an ordinary intendant, or one who was inefficient or corrupt, been in charge of Languedoc, the Camisard war might not have become a kind of test case for the centralized ministerial government which developed in the Sun King's reign. Nicolas Lamoignon de Bâville (d. 1724) was neither inefficient nor corrupt; hence his reactions to the Protestant insurrection were those of the royal government at its best, if one approved of bureaucratic centralization, or at its worst, if one did not.

Lamoignon de Bâville was *the* intendant par excellence. His social origins and career corresponded almost exactly to the ideal of this official. Born in 1648 into one of the most distinguished Parisian judicial families, Bâville quickly moved up from being a lawyer as early as 1666 to a councillorship in the Parlement in 1670, when he was twenty-two. The critical moment in his career occurred in 1673, while Colbert's power was at its height, when he became a *maître des requêtes*. His loyalty and efficiency in that post earned him a promotion to the intendancy at Poitiers in 1682. His fame rests, however, on his thirty-three-year record as intendant for Languedoc, a post he held throughout the Camisard war.

Bâville had recommended the repressive responses of the Crown, and in court circles his name became associated with the violence which occurred as troops tried year after year to repress the Huguenots. Thus when the small circle of opponents to Louis XIV's ministers developed, first in the court of the young Duke of Burgundy (see document 58) and later among aristocrats and merchants, the intendant's role was criticized. One of the leaders in this public opposition was Count Henri de Boulainvilliers (1658–1722), who prepared and published this quite distorted summary of Bâville's report on the Huguenots in Languedoc. This document therefore is doubly valuable in that it describes Bâville's views, as well as those of one of the major critics of the intendants. It is not at all difficult to discern the parts where Boulainvilliers makes his critique.

English efforts to support the Camisards with money and arms were largely unsuccessful; but their role in supporting the "rebels," as well as the hopes for a general defeat of France by the Protestants which

SOURCE: Monsieur le Comte de Boulainvilliers, *État de la France* (London, 1727), II, 526–527.

Bâville attributed to the Huguenots, illustrate the relationships between internal and international developments late in Louis XIV's reign.

The author [Bâville] ends this article on the state of the Church in the province, by considering the new converts, who really form a separate people in Languedoc. There is no province where they are so numerous; the count of them was made several times, and it totals 198,483 souls, spread over seven dioceses, Nîmes, Alais [Alès], Viviers, Montpellier, Usez [Uzès], Castres, and Lavaur; but in the two other [dioceses of Languedoc] they are incomparably weaker. Among the new converts are 440 families of gentlemen, of which 109 have no children, or have only daughters; so that they can be considered extinct, and among them are none deserving of special attention, except the Marquis de Malauze in the diocese of Castres, who is moreover believed to be a good Catholic. Their possessions for the most part are not very substantial. There are fifteen who have between 5,000 and 12,000 livres' income; the others are below, and few exceed 3,000 livres. Which shows that there is no one in a position to become party leader; for in the case of merchants, although rich and numerous, the author does not believe they would ever dare risk their fortune. He adds that in general they are all more hard-working and industrious than the old Catholics. But their principal strength stems from their spending almost all their life in a region to which access is difficult and of which they know all the strategic advantages. We know how in the same localities the Albigenses resisted the strength of a formidable league and also that people there have for a long time been hatching in their minds feelings of independence and revolt which should bring them to the full attention of a prudent government.

Therefore, to relate their history in few words, the author says that after the revocation of the Edict of Nantes, which he calls the "General Covenant," the Huguenots of Languedoc balanced for some time between love for their religion and [love] for their possessions, but that the latter won out and that they remained in the region. To be honest, it seems that he should have added that they were forbidden to leave. However, about 4,000 crossed into foreign countries, and 600 returned. He admits that of those who remained few are Catholics, and the reason he gives for their failure to be persuaded is that during the entire war of the Prince of

Orange [the War of the League of Augsburg] they were deluded into thinking that events favorable to their religion would occur and that they would shortly see their churches and their worship services reestablished. Preachers returning from Holland reeled off these prophecies as certain truths; they kept on among themselves saying their prayers together secretly; and animated by resentment born of constraint, they rejected everything proposed to them which was contrary to the prejudices of their birth. It happened that several priests were assassinated at the beginning of the war [of the Camisards]. Fanatical preachers descended upon the area about Viviers, and they would have stirred up unfortunate outbursts if the author's attentiveness in watching over, punishing, and repressing everything contrary to the estabished order had not contained them.

He used two principal means to cut short all their hopes. The first was to lay paths over the entire expanse of the Cévennes wide enough to allow cannon to pass and mortars to be carried should the need arise. That taught them that there were no inaccessible places, and they themselves were forced to work upon these fateful roads which extinguished the last spark of their liberty. The second was to make use of the strength of the old Catholics. First eight regiments of militia paid by the province were recruited, and when the King deemed it proper to use them elsewhere, they were replaced by fifty-two [or twelve]* other regiments which, though unpaid, are always ready to march on short notice, having handpicked officers, arms and munitions, and strict discipline. Troop reviews are conducted annually in view of the new converts, and the author claims that by dint of seeing these, they have finally understood that, being unable to employ, in order to sustain themselves, the same methods, they must either remain quiet or be resolved to perish wretchedly, being leaderless, weaponless, and without troops. In addition the King had three forts constructed at the entrance to the [Cévennes] mountains: Nîmes, Alais, and Saint-Hippolyte [-du-Fort]. They even selected castles and defensive positions in the region, where they established posts for controlling the interior. Who would not have thought that with these masterly precautions these people would bend to necessity? But experience has shown that [these precautions] served only to

* Brackets are Boulainvilliers'.

inflame their despair, overwhelmed in regard to religion, which gave birth to a guilty conscience, stripped in this regard of any sort of liberty, reduced moreover to a deplorable state of poverty, which was said to predispose them to obedience and which was considered a result of the author's harshness. These wretched people took the last decision which seemed left for them to try, if rebellion or death did not put an end to their suffering. The consequences of this decision were only too disastrous. A hundred thousand men perished, immolated to justify the author's conduct; and of this number a tenth died at the stake, by the rope, or on the wheel. The Albigensian war was no more tragic: but what is indeed deplorable is that these upheavals are not yet ended* and that the least incident is capable of resuscitating the rage of both.

What the author adds concerning the methods appropriate to use in winning over these people seems to be more correct than the rest, except that he relies chiefly on the quick death of those living. He therefore wants great stress laid upon educating their children and that schools be established to this end in all sizable localities; that boys be placed in *collèges* and girls in convents, when the fathers have the wherewithal to pay their board. Second, he wants the utmost done to train good priests to fill the positions of parish priests and vicars in the parishes; he even asks for one qualification beyond high morals, which is talent in speaking, because the entire religion of the new converts amounts to, according to him, listening to the gospel. In vain have we tried to compensate for their usual pastors with missions: it is a question of winning hearts, and that is not the work of a day. A parish priest works his entire life, talks with his flock, wins it over imperceptibly; this the missionaries are unable to do, in addition to the fact that their vulgar manner of preaching is the complete opposite of that of the ministers to whom these people are accustomed. We must therefore reach their minds and their hearts simultaneously: which is not so difficult, since the ministers have always manipulated them as they pleased. But above all we must, according to him, avoid the sacrileges in which we usually involve them. It is an established principle that the new converts take communion as often as they wish and confession likewise. It is therefore appropriate to adopt in this respect a means of conciliation which only the pastors are in a position to understand.

* Boulainvilliers' note: The author was apparently writing this in 1705.

51. *Absolutism, Bourgeois Values, and Charity in Paris*

The conception of monarchy which the seventeenth century had inherited from the Middle Ages included the notion that the king was responsible for both the spiritual and the physical welfare of his subjects. Henry IV had founded two large hospitals in Paris, had forced the Hôtel Dieu and other charitable institutions to reform, and had granted special taxes for the support of the poorest of his subjects. In the provinces the royal will could often take only the form of strong exhortations to city fathers to found new hospitals and to increase the money available for those already established. But the high costs involved, despite the emphasis laid on charity by such saints as St. Vincent de Paul, often meant that the Crown's orders and suggestions went unheeded.

The Parisians, and the poor in the countryside around the capital, experienced a decade of terrible physical suffering beginning in about 1645. Rising food prices, exceedingly heavy taxes, high land prices and rents, and interruption of food supplies as well as pillaging by armies combined to reduce thousands to roaming the streets of the capital as beggars, prostitutes, and *gens sans aveu*, or "do-nothings." Historians have yet to determine whether the number of needy actually did increase, or whether a new sensibility about begging and poverty developed, inspiring clergy, laymen, and royal officials alike to increase their efforts to help the poor. Another explanation for the increased need for charitable institutions is that the improved care for the poor in the cities actually attracted increasing numbers of poor from the countryside.

In any case, the sufferings and constant begging of the poor, a new spiritual impetus to help the needy, and the conduct of these hungry crowds during the Fronde all led the property owners in the capital to found a secret society for religious and charitable regeneration. The Company of the Holy Sacrament thus had a lofty program from the beginning and included many prominent and rich Parisians among its members. But in undertaking to aid the sick and to reform the beggars, members soon found that they had tackled a much bigger task than they could finance or manage.

SOURCES: "Institution des Enfans de l'Hospital de la Trinité avec la forme du gouvernement et ordonnance de leur vivre," July 1, 1645, Bibliothèque Nationale, manuscrits français 18606, fol. 233 ff.; *L'Hospital Général de Paris* (Paris, 1676), pp. 17–41.

The first of these two documents dates from this period and deals with the founding of a home for children. Historians have not yet investigated the question of whether any of this legislation is innovative. The attention to moral and spiritual rectitude, as well as training for work, pervades the legislation for the poor in the seventeenth century. Attention to minute detail characterizes all this legislation and enables us to perceive the values of a society very different from our own. And yet there are continuities, not the least of which is the problem of knowing whether or not the legislation for charitable institutions was in fact enforced.

The founding of the General Hospital resulted from these efforts of the Company of the Holy Sacrament to help needy Parisians. But this hospital was not charity alone. Beggars and prostitutes were virtually taken into custody and were sent to the particular part of the General Hospital reserved for them. Once behind the bars of the various houses, sermons, food, uniforms, and work were mandatory for those well enough to recover without major medical attention. Others—children, pregnant women, the insane, and the aged—received help for as many years as necessary. When the numbers interned soon rose into the thousands, the Crown had to interfere not only to supply funds, but to regularize the admission and care of indigents. These selections from the founding charter give an overview of social legislation in the capital, as well as of the centralization and financing of charity by the government. The General Hospital was in reality a merger of several older charitable institutions—La Pitié, Savonnerie, and Bicêtre. Details concerning the general conduct of the hospital have been deleted, for it was to be very similar to that of the Trinity. The government provided certain tax exemptions and sources of revenue, only a few of which can be included here. But were the strict codes about begging, prostitution, and work also the product of the royal government? The moral heritage of the property-owning bourgeois remained very marked in the activities of the General Hospital until the French Revolution.

The Founding of the Children of the Hospital of the Trinity with the Form of Government and Organization of Their Care, July 1, 1645

I. Be it understood that in the said hospital, which is located in Paris, rue Saint-Denis, before the Church of the Holy Savior, there be two locations separated one from the other; in each of which are a dormitory, a refectory, and a school, which are arranged one for boys and the other for girls. These children are taken and admitted from the poorhouses of the city and faubourgs of Paris, born of legal marriage, and [these children] are to be separated from one another.

II. Nevertheless, both are directed by the same governors, the same dole from the alms which are collected for the said hospital, and the revenues which since its founding have been turned over to the said hospital.

III. For directing [these children] six governors have been appointed by the Court [of the Parlement], to watch over the said hospital.

IV. Also, appointed by the said governors are three churchmen of good morals and capable of instructing the boys without in any way communicating with the girls, other than by an iron grille placed on the said girls' side so they may hear Mass and the services conducted in the church.

V. Also appointed by the said governors are worthy women and schoolmistresses for guidance and management, and two nurses, one to care for the boys who are sick, the other for the girls similarly sick, whose infirmaries shall be separate.

VI. In the morning at five o'clock in summertime, and in wintertime at six, at the sound of the bell, the oldest boys shall rise, and immediately upon having risen shall prostrate themselves on the floor and recite the antiphon of the Trinity, with other prayers and intercessory prayers.

VII. Having done this, they shall go down into the chapel, in which they shall hear Mass, recite the seven Psalms and the service; to each of them, after the Mass, shall be given five ounces of bread for their breakfast and at once they shall withdraw into the schoolroom, there to be instructed in the Catholic faith; so that each of them will know the Ten Commandments of God, of our Mother the Holy Church, and will be so educated that none of them will lack justification for their belief; also they shall be taught the Psalms, and shall be instructed in singing, psalmodizing, and the art of writing.

VIII. At eleven o'clock, at the sound of the bell, all shall go to the chapel, where an antiphon shall be recited and afterward the blessing shall be said in the room in which all dine in common, and they shall eat, during which the child appointed for that week shall recite the commandments of God.

IX. The meal over, offering thanks to God they shall return to the school, where they shall be regularly taught to read, sing, write, and psalmodize.

X. At the hour for vespers, the said children shall go to the church to sing vespers each day, and shall recite immediately after them the usual hymns according to the day.

XI. Having done this, they shall all assemble in the refectory, in order, before partaking of the meal, to say the blessing as at dinner; and during this meal, one of them shall recite the commandments of God and of the Church, and other things which will instruct them about the love and fear of God and of one's neighbor, in the presence of the said churchmen who, similarly, shall take their meals in the said refectory with the said children.

XII. The meal over, giving thanks to God they shall afterward return to the school until eight in the evening.

XIII. At the said hour of eight o'clock, they shall all assemble in the dormitory to take their rest; before going to bed they shall recite several intercessory prayers and other prayers.

XIV. This done, they shall go to bed in the said dormitory, each one sleeping separately, unless they are occasionally forced to put the little ones two by two because of the crowd.

XV. On holy days all the said children shall confess before churchmen, and those who are old enough shall receive the body of Our Lord Jesus Christ.

XVI. The same and likewise is to be done for the girls, in regard to managing, instructing them, and organizing their subsistance.

XVII. Their garment is a garb of blue cloth,* a bonnet, a little trunk hose, and knit stockings in white serge with shoes.

XVIII. And each child for food is issued daily a loaf of bread weighing one pound, for his breakfast, dinner, and supper, six ounces of raw meat which comes to four ounces cooked with soup; and their drink is water from the fountain in the said hospital donated by the *prévôts des marchands* and the *échevins* of the city of Paris.

XIX. It must also not be omitted that in each of the localities, for the boys and for the girls, there is to be an infirmary in which are nourished, fed, and doctored the children who fall sick, visited by the doctors and surgeons appointed and delegated for this purpose, the whole at the expense of the revenues of the said hospital.

XX. And since the said hospital has only about three hundred livres' income, each of the said children has been allotted six deniers tournois per day, to be taken from the alms for the poor of the said

* Hence their sobriquet, *les Enfants bleus.*

city, which shall be paid by the general treasurer of the poor, by order of the governors of the said hospital.

XXI. And in addition a decree of the court has permitted alms to be solicited for the said children in the said city and in its churches; which shall be done on feast days.

XXII. Now after such a time as the said children have been instructed in the Christian faith at the said hospital, some of them shall be placed in a trade for a given period, and according to the ordinances issued concerning the trades in the city of Paris.

XXIII. Nevertheless, two-thirds of the three to four hundred of the said children who have been placed as apprentices and placed in a trade have left their master's service, and also some through malice who rob their masters; some because of bad treatment by their masters, and others by instigation of their father and mother and other relatives, despite the prohibitions heretofore made to the said fathers, mothers, and all others, in accordance with and pursuant to the decrees of the said court, posted at the crossroads of the said city, that the said children in a trade be neither dissuaded nor taken away, as has been said; to the point that the said governors have been and are constrained to change the said children in three or four trades and each time to garb them anew to the great detriment of the said hospital because it is impossible to bear and continue the said expenses. Other children return to begging and stealing as they did in the past, so that the trouble which the governors and administrators of the said hospital take is wasted and comes to no profit. . . .

XXV. As a means by which to counter the above, and to be sure that the said children not be lazy and that the older ones have some means of earning their livelihood and that of the small children who are placed there, who are not yet able to work, owing to their young age, and who are being instructed in the Christian faith and are being shown the first elements of reading and writing, it seems useful and expedient to teach trades to the said children in the said hospital in accordance with their mental capacities; and to this end several trades and diverse manufactures have been established at the said hospital, and it happens that some of them have of themselves begun to learn the trades which have been proposed for them; which trades they do not wish to continue when they are in the city, and they escape, as has been said; and being in the said hospital to learn a trade, they shall be unable to avoid it.

XXVI. Thus, from the age of seven, the said children shall learn trades and will have learned them in three years, after which they shall earn their living; others from eight to twelve, and the rest in like manner, according to the quality of the trades and the amount of time deemed fitting for teaching them the said trades.

XXVII. After they have learned the trades which are shown to them, they will earn money to live and more, and will show the other children who will subsequently be admitted to the said hospital.

XXVIII. By doing this, the said hospital can admit all children from the age of seven, of which there are a great number begging in the said city of Paris, who are children of the poor, on the alms lists of the said locality.

XXIX. In addition this will prevent the excessive prices at which the masters of products made in the city are forced to sell their said products, because their apprentices and those who know something about the said trades, being badly instructed and of bad character, they debauch themselves and frequent taverns and public places, on feast and on working days, so that the said masters of trades cannot get them away, and must increase their salaries, because they do not care for drudgery; this is one of the principal causes which forces the said masters to increase the prices of the said products.

XXX. And when the said children have learned and taught the said trades at the said hospital, the products will be cheaper and less costly to produce, since a quantity will be made in the said hospital, under [supervision of] the artisans of the city of Paris for such a fee per day as will be established. And also the said children, having been some time in the said hospital, will be able to establish a work-room in the said city, where they can be given out to the masters of trades. The said children having been nurtured in sobriety and work will retain something of that nurturing, so that the said masters of the said trades will not be obliged to use apprentices and workers who frequently debauch themselves and demand higher salaries; and by doing this, there will be more workers in this city of Paris than there presently are.

XXXI. It must also be recognized that the majority of young boys finishing their apprenticeship, although they have no possessions, immediately marry before they have attained the age of twenty years, with girls as poor as they who have nothing: so that a short time later, they have a great number of children whom they cannot nourish in the great poverty to which they have been accustomed since their youth and are obliged to beg or have the children beg; this will not happen when the said children are instructed and taught in the said hospital, because they shall not be released from the same, nor freed, until they are experts in their trades, which have been shown to them, and also the children will be given (after they have learned the said trades) some money of the profits which they have earned by their industriousness in the said hospital, and they will be able to marry girls who have been instructed and taught a trade in the said hospital; by this means both will have a way of earning their livelihood, and the survivor of them will be able to nourish the said children if they had any and not send them begging as one usually sees them do.

XXXII. And inasmuch as there is no income for the said hospital to supply the money required for the salary and wages of the said artisans, who will show and teach the said trades to the said children, some artisans and other persons of the city of Paris can be found to show them, receiving the profit which the said children would earn from the manufactures made by them over a period of six years, or such other time as is deemed advisable by the said governors of the said hospital; and by this means there will be no great expenses for the hospital.

XXXIII. Or a stipend could be paid (alms which might in the future be made to the said hospital) to some master craftmen to be workers, to make mail shirts and brigandines, which are imported from foreign countries; trimming makers, some of whom shall make metal and silken braids, the others gold and silk cloths; and after having taught some of the said children the said trade, [the teachers] shall earn five sols a day. And a quantity of children can be employed in the workshops of the said artisans, some on looms from the ages of thirteen, fourteen, fifteen, and sixteen years; others at winding off silk and in making spools, and this from the ages of nine, ten, eleven, and twelve years; the others fustian, serge, and other things made in foreign countries.

XXXIV. Some [would be] embroiderers, others painters, others tapestry weavers, who might also be in great number; and children from the ages of seven to eight years would draw wool; the girls would be able to spin it, others would card it; those nine years of age would comb it, and those above the said age would put it to use. And the above would cause no harm, would have no effect upon the trades conducted in France, because the majority of the said manufactures which it has been deemed useful to set up at the said hospital, some of which have already been begun in order not to keep the children in idleness, are manufactures and crafts which we are forced to seek out and have brought in from foreign countries at great expense. The other children will be pin makers, needle makers, purse makers, makers of carding combs and other tools used in France, and this would result in a reasonable price for supplies and products of the said trades, which today are very costly.

XXXV. And expenditures for the support of the said master craftsmen will come to only about five hundred livres a year, during and for the period of six years, and within which time there will be a number of the said young children who would become workers and would be able to show the others; and thus France would have workers for manufactures which it is constrained to bring in from foreign countries. Thus there would no longer be young children begging in the city, and thus the children of the said hospital could live and be supported by the money obtained from the profits on these manufactures, and without its being henceforth necessary to ask for alms or to burden the people. . . .

Royal Edict Establishing the General Hospital for the Confining of the Poor Beggars of the City and Faubourgs of Paris

Issued at Paris in the month of April 1656. Verified in the Parlement the first of September following, and in all the other Sovereign Companies.

LOUIS, by the grace of God, King of France and of Navarre, to all present and to come, hail. The kings our predecessors during the last century issued several ordinances for the maintenance of order, and strove by their zeal as much as by their authority to prevent begging and idleness, the sources of all disorders. And although our Sovereign Companies have supported by their efforts the execution of these ordinances, they nevertheless became with the passage of time fruitless and ineffectual, either through the lack of the funds necessary to support such a great plan, or through the lack of a well-established board of directors suitable to the nature of the work. So that recently and during the reign of the late King our very honored lord and father of blessed memory, the evil having grown even greater as a result of public licentiousness and the dissoluteness of morals, it was recognized that the chief fault in the execution of this program to maintain order lay in the fact that beggars were free to wander everywhere, and that the relief obtained did not prevent secret mendicity and did not make them cease their idleness. On this basis was planned and carried out the praiseworthy plan to confine them in the House of Pity and its dependencies. And *letters patentes* were granted to this end in the year one thousand six hundred and twelve, registered in our Court of the Parlement of Paris, according to which the poor were confined; and the adminstration was entrusted to good and renowned bourgeois who, successively, one after the other, contributed their industry and their good conduct to make this plan succeed. And nonetheless no matter what efforts they made, it was effective for only five or six years, and then very imperfectly, as much from a failure to employ the poor in public works and manufactures as because the directors were not supported by the powers and authority necessary for the great size of the undertaking, and because as a result of the disorders and the misfortunes of the wars, the number of poor increased beyond common and ordinary credence, and the illness became more powerful than the remedy. So that the libertinage of beggars went to excess, by their unfortunate abandoning of themselves to all sorts of crimes, which bring down God's curse upon states when they remain unpunished. Experience having shown the persons involved in these charitable undertakings that several of [the beggars] of one or the other sex are living together without being married, many of their children are unbaptised, and they are almost all living in ignorance of religion, in scorn of the sacraments, and in the continual practice of all sorts of vices. That is why, since we are indebted to Divine Grace for so many favors and for a visible protection which it has made apparent in our actions at our accession, and in the happy course of our reign, by the success of our arms and the happiness of our victories, we believe we are more obliged to show [Divine Grace] our gratitude by a royal and Christian attention to the things involving its honor and its service, by considering these poor beggars as living members of Jesus Christ, and not as useless members of the state, and by acting in carrying out such a great work not in the name of the maintenance of public order, but with the sole aim of charity.

Firstly,

For these reasons . . . we desire and order that poor beggars both healthy and invalid, of both sexes, be confined in a hospital to be employed there at works, manufactures, and other tasks according to their capacities. . . .

V

We desire that the localities serving to confine the poor be called the General Hospital for the Poor; that the inscription be placed with our coat of arms over the portal of the House of Pity and its dependencies.

VI

We intend to be the preserver and protector of the said General Hospital and of its dependencies, since it is a royal foundation. . . .

IX

We very strictly prohibit and forbid all persons of all sexes, and places, and ages, whatever their social standing or birth, and in whatever state they may be, healthy or invalid, sick or convalescent, curable or incurable, to beg in the city and faubourgs of Paris, or in the churches, or at their doors, or at the doors of houses, or in the streets, or anywhere else publicly or secretly, by day or by night, no exception being made for solemn feast days, pardons, or jubilees, or assemblies, fairs, or markets, or for any other reason or pretext whatsoever, under penalty of being whipped for the first offense; and for the second offense the galleys for men or boys, and banishment for women and girls.

X

If anyone begs in houses, we permit and specifically command owners and tenants and their domestic servants and others to keep the said beggars until the directors or the officials named below can be notified to impose upon them the above penalties, as the case demands.

XI

We do not intend the above prohibitions to include the alms collections for the Hôtel Dieu [hospital] and its dependencies; those for the Grand Bureau of the Poor [maintained for the non-begging poor] and its dependencies, the blind of the Hospital of the Quinze-vingts, the children of the Hospital of the Trinity, of the Holy Spirit, and of the Red Children,* begging monks, the Sisters of the Ave Maria, and others entitled to poor boxes or alms collections, all of whom we exempt, such privileges being generally forbidden to all others; and on condition that the blind, the children, and others entitled to seek alms remain at the doors of the churches, or near their boxes; and that they are forbidden to solicit elsewhere in the churches, under penalty of being stripped of their rights.

XII

We give and confer upon the directors . . . all power and authority for the direction, administration, legal authority, jurisdiction, policing, correction, and chastisement of all the poor beggars in our city and faubourgs of Paris, both within and without the said General Hospital. . . .

XIII

To this end the directors shall have posts, iron collars, prisons, and dungeons in the said General Hospital and its dependencies. . . .

XIV

The directors shall have a hospital bailiff, sergeants of the poor, [and] guards at the gates and entrances, with halberds and other suitable weapons, and all other necessary officials, both to carry out their ordinances, and to capture the beggars and escort to the hospital or its dependencies those who are to be admitted, to send away, eject, or arrest those who are to be excluded from it, and to accompany passersby. . . .

XV

We enjoin the bailiff, and the other officials who shall be appointed by the directors, to make a careful search each day with the sergeants of the said hospital, to remove all sorts of beggars from the streets, . . . under penalty of being sent away and punished; [and they shall carry out this search] without taking anything from the poor, or others, or granting them favors or

* The children in the Hôpital des Enfants Rouges wore red uniforms.

tolerating them, or mistreating them, the whole under penalty of corporal punishment. . . .

XVII

We prohibit and forbid all persons, whatever their social standing and position, to put alms into the hands of beggars in the streets and above-mentioned locations, no matter how moved by compassion, urgent necessity, or other pretexts whatsoever, under penalty of a fine of four livres parisis, which shall be given to the hospital. . . .

XVIII

We likewise forbid owners and tenants of houses and all other persons to lodge, shelter, or keep with them . . . the poor who are or would be beggars, under penalty of a hundred livres' fine for the first offense, of three hundred livres for the second, and higher, in case of repetition, the whole to be given to the poor of the General Hospital; to which end the owners, tenants, and others can be compelled by seizure of their belongings and imprisonment of their persons. . . .

XX

We forbid the soldiers of our guards, even the bourgeois of our said city and faubourgs, and all other persons, whatever their social position, to molest, insult, or mistreat the bailiff, officials, or any of those employed in capturing or escorting, expelling, ejecting, or accompanying the poor . . . under penalty of being imprisoned at once and criminal proceedings being lodged against them. . . .

XXI

We order the commissioners of the quarters . . . and others not to allow anyone to reside in their quarter without first verifying at the police office that he has the possessions, industriousness, or vocation sufficient to nourish himself and to support his family: with the exception of the humble poor who are being helped by parishes or elsewhere, and the married poor now begging, who will receive alms from the General Hospital according to the certificate which they will bring back from [the hospital] . . . ; and that every month [the commissioners] will bring in the list to the office of the said hospital, under penalty of a fine of forty-eight livres parisis for each person not appearing on the list. . . .

XXXV

Inasmuch as the care of the poor concerns all sorts of persons, and since by our ordinances, police regulations, and old edicts, each one is obliged to contribute to the feeding of the poor, according to his means, we desire and order that . . . all secular and regular religious communities [with the exception of those serving the poor], of both sexes, in our city and faubourgs, *prévôté*, and viscounty of Paris, and all lay groups, the vestrymen of the churches, the guild chapels and confraternities, and others of that nature, even the trade guilds and all other persons shall contribute to the establishing and maintenance of the said work, each in proportion to his wealth. They are invited to do this, and if they fail to do so willingly, they will be assessed in accordance with the former edicts, by our Court of the Parlement. . . .

XXXVI

We permit the directors [to use] all alms collections, poor boxes, collection plates, and large and small boxes in all the churches, crossroads, and public places of our said city, faubourgs, and *prévoté* and viscounty of Paris; and that the said boxes may be placed in the merchants' warehouses, offices, and shops, in inns and coach halts, in public markets, covered markets, and fairs, at bridges, city gates, and passageways, and in all localities where one might be urged to give alms, even on such occasions as baptisms, marriages, funerals, burials, and memorial services, and others of that sort. . . .

XXXVIII

[We grant the said hospital] a quarter of the fines or sentences stipulating that the guilty party give alms, ordered for misdemeanors, malversations, and usurpations of the Waters and Forests of France, both in the past and in the future, for which the directors, as litigants, can carry out the prosecutions in our Council or elsewhere.

XXXIX

A quarter of the police fines, and of all merchandise or other things declared acquired and confiscated.

XL

And also a third of all the [fees paid for] letters of [guild] mastership, which have been and shall be by us in the future and by the kings our successors issued and registered in our Parlement, either owing to the marriage or birth of [royal] children of

France, an accession to the throne, or other special cause, intending by this to include those previously issued by us, and not yet registered.

XLI

All officials who are received into our Sovereign Companies established in our city of Paris, others besides those of the said companies, and also those who will be received into subordinate seats and jurisdictions, both ordinary and extraordinary, similarly established outside our said city, will upon their reception be obliged to contribute some modest sum to the said General Hospital, and they shall be obliged to bring back the receipt before the edict or judgment of their reception shall be delivered to them. This sum or tax shall be determined by our said Sovereign Companies, each one individually, and a list of them [shall be] drawn up, taking into account the rank of the said officers.

XLII

We also desire all journeymen in trades, when they receive their certificates of apprenticeship, and masters, when they complete their masterpiece or test, or are elected as guild officials, also be obliged to give some modest sum to the said General Hospital, and likewise to bring back the receipt before the said certificates of apprenticeship or letters of mastership shall be delivered to them. . . .

LV

In order to favor and patronize further the establishment and subsistence of the said General Hospital, we desire each trade guild of our said city and faubourgs of Paris to be obliged to provide, when they are asked, two journeymen, and the mistress seamstresses two girls, to teach their trade to the children of the said General Hospital, as they shall see fit; and in doing this the said two journeymen and girls will acquire a mastership in their guilds and trades, after having served for the period of six years in the said General Hospital, and certificates shall be delivered and signed by the directors, to the number of at least six, with the right to keep a shop, as do other masters and mistresses, and with no distinctions between them. . . .

LVII

We also want the apothecaries' and surgeons' guilds to each give two members of their said group, capable of serving free in the said hospital, and of helping the poor there and its officials and domestic servants; and after a similar six-year period, the said apothecary and surgeon members shall likewise earn their mastership, with certificates from the directors in like number, and shall have the same rights and privileges as all other masters.

LVIII

And those who have served as schoolmasters and mistresses for ten years in the General Hospital, with the approval of the directors, can be masters and mistresses in the city and faubourgs, with no examination, letters, and permits beyond the directors' certificate confirming their service. . . .

LXIV

We also forbid all inhabitants, assessors, and collectors for the parishes, and all others, to tax or to assess, or to cause to be taxed or assessed, upon the lists of the *tailles*, *taillons*, subsistences, utensils, or other ordinary or extraordinary duties, either for us or for individuals, levied or to be levied, of any nature whatsoever, the tax farmers, sub-tax farmers, receivers, or clerks of the said General Hospital, or its farms, houses, and their dependencies; but in the event that they are eligible to pay, they will be taxed for a modest amount by the *élus* according to the regulations and considering their possessions, without including in them the possessions and the income of all or part of the said General Hospital, which we intend to be entirely exempt, under penalty of the said assessors, collectors, and others, and even the chief inhabitants of the parishes being held answerable for it jointly, in their own and private names, and being compelled by seizures, distraint, and sale of their possessions, of furniture, and buildings, and imprisonment of their persons, to repay the money which had been paid, and all expenses, damages, and interest. Even in the cases of surtaxes on surtaxes which were routinely issued; for which reason we permit the directors to intervene or to take the affair in hand, and to settle it directly in our *Cour des aides*, without the need to make any previous appeals. . . .

Issued in Paris, in the month of April in the year of grace one thousand six hundred and fifty-six, and the thirteenth of our reign.

LOUIS

52. *Accounts and Statistics of Royal Charity in Paris*

The General Hospital, charitable monastic institutions, and the reform and expansion of the Hôtel Dieu did not eliminate the need for alms on the parish level. Indeed, each curé continued to have as part of his duties the care of the needy in his parish, and he cajoled wealthy church members to supply funds and to administer alms to their poorer neighbors. Regular lists of poor and sick residents in the parish were established, making distribution on the basis of need the fundamental principle of charity on the local level.

Partly to relieve the burden on the wealthier Parisians and to gain their support for the Crown, Colbert instituted a regular monthly subsidy for some parishes in the capital during the season when the poor suffered the most. The first document briefly summarizes this activity and gives a breakdown of expenditures by parishes.

The second document, a list of the status and number of the poor in the General Hospital, provides a very interesting list of categories for those on welfare in the *ancien régime.*

Report on the Distribution of Royal Charity in Paris *February 29, 1708*

Among the several fine establishments which Paris owes to Monseigneur Colbert, that of poor relief is not the least important. Each year he carefully would order distributed to the curés of that city who have faubourgs in their parishes the sum of 80,000 l[ivres], at the rate of 20,000 l. for each month of December, January, February, and March, to help the poor get through the hard winter weather. And in the spring, he had silk, wool, and other merchandise for their trades distributed to them, to put them back on their feet and put them in a position so they can subsist by their own labor during the rest of the year. I do not know whether this latter help was continued after his death. Monsieur Le Fouyn was in charge of the funds for the poor; Monsieur Le Peletier replaced him by Monsieur de Rosset, and Monseigneur the Chancellor

SOURCE: A. M. de Boislisle (ed.), *Mémoires des Intendants sur l'État des Généralités dressés pour l'Instruction du Duc de Bourgogne* (Paris, 1881), I, 418–420.

[Louis Phélypeaux, Count of Pontchartrain], while controller general, ordered me to succeed the Sieur de Rosset in 1695. The 80,000 l. were paid regularly until the year 1702; but the war interrupted this relief several times in the last six years. The last order for 20,000 l., issued for this expenditure on December 3, 1707, is that in complete payment of the 80,000 l. for the winter of 1706.

Of this 20,000 l., Monsieur de Nointel paid:

December 30, 1707	3,000 l.
January 21, 1708	5,000
And the 28th of the said month	1,500
Total	9,500
He still owes	10,500
Grand total	20,000

No order was issued for the winters of 1707 and 1708.

The distribution of the 80,000 l. was done according to a statement of which the said Sieur de Rosset gave me a copy, and it has not been changed in the thirteen years since it was entrusted to me:

The parish of	Saint-Sulpice receives	13,200 l.
	Saint-Laurent	12,000
	Saint-Eustache	6,160
	La Villeneuve	7,200
	Saint-Paul	6,600
	Saint-Nicolas-des-Champs	5,000
	La Ville-l'Évèque	4,600
	Saint-Hippolyte	4,000
	Saint-Martin	3,000
	Saint-Médard	7,200
	Saint-Jacques-du-Haut-Pas	2,600
	Saint-Étienne	4,400
	Saint-Benoît	400
	Saint-Nicolas-du-Chardonnet	450
	Saint-Roch	300
	Saint-Sauveur	2,630
To several individuals		260
	Total	80,000

These funds are used according to the orders of the said curés, for the distribution of bread, soups, shirts, clothes and other garb, food for the sick and for women in childbed, milk and flour for children, etc.

When the 80,000 l. are paid, I present the journal-register of payments and the receipts of the said curés to Monseigneur the controller general, and he puts his sign of approval on the register.

CLAIRAMBAULT

List of the Status and Number of the Poor in the General Hospital May 11, 1713

House of Pity [*La Pitié*]	
Little boys from five to eight years, in the care of governesses	152
Little boys in school, from six to ten years, who are employed at knitting	210
Carders and spinners for the royal manufacture, from ten to fourteen years of age	242
Boys for deliveries, from twelve to fifteen	220
Scrofulous, misshapen, of various ages, ten years and over, employed at knitting	57
Male officials, schoolmasters, and others	38
Girls serving in the supply room, kitchen, and as alms collectors	61
Female officials and bursars	6
Ecclesiastics	8
Total	994

House of Saint-Louis of the Salpêtrière		
Children from	six months to two years	122
	two to five years	153
	five to eight years	340
	eight to twelve years	362
	twelve to fifteen years	189
Pregnant women		55
Nursing mothers and their children		94
Children with scurvy, measles, of various ages, under seven years of age		125

Girls who are burned, misshapen, crippled, and deformed, from two to sixteen years	129
Girls with scalp diseases or scurvy, of the above ages	150
Violent and harmless madwomen	300
Epileptics of various ages	92
Paralytics of various ages	268
Senile women of great age	294
Blind old women, from seventy to seventy-six years	176
Married men and women, living as couples, from seventy to seventy-five years	260
Girls working at making linen, canvas, and woolen cloths [*tiretaines*] for hospital use	100
Laundresses for the smaller linens of the various houses [of the General Hospital] and all the sacristies	28
River [washer] women, for all the linens of the various homes	47
Women [interned] by *lettre de cachet*, order of the court and usual judicial practice and sentence	295
Libertine girls being corrected, working at carding and spinning wool	250
Ill and convalescent women who have returned from the Hôtel Dieu	70
Common female beggars and vagrants	355
Apprentices, workers in the poultry yard	60
Governesses and servant girls	238
Bursars, male officials, shopkeepers	40
Female superiors and officials	31
Ecclesiastics, including the rector	11
Total	4,634

House of Saint-Jean of Bicêtre

Paralyzed old men, from sixty-five to ninety years	486
Scrofulous, deformed, misshapen, and with scalp diseases, taken while begging	120
Violent, imbecile, and harmless madmen	182
Epileptics of various ages	40
Blind men captured while begging	70
Syphilitic men and women	70
Common beggars and tramps kept in the houses by force	195

Persons [interned] by order of the king and for purpose of correction	150
Bursars and male officials	64
Female officials	4
Ecclesiastics	4
Total	1,385

HOUSE OF THE HOLY SPIRIT

Orphan boys and girls from Paris	81
Officials entrusted with the building, and servants	14
Ecclesiastics	5
Total	100

HOUSE OF SAINTE-MARTHE, CALLED SCIPION

Bursars, officials, and servants for the bakery and butchery	90
Lying-in hospital	130
House of Saint-Antoine	180
The Red Children [a name derived from the uniform worn by the children residing there]	90
Foundling hospital, which is entrusted with their nourishment and clothing, and leaving them in the country with their wet nurses, over three years of age	1,460
Total	1,950

The total of all the houses of the General Hospital is 9,083 persons.

There are 250 persons fewer than in the previous list, presented during the month of February, because the number of poor people is greater during the winter.

53. *Selections from a Treatise on Torture*

After a long career as a soldier in Italy, secretary in Spain, and magistrate at Dôle in the still-Spanish Free County of Burgundy, Augustin Nicolas (1622–1695) later rallied to the French Crown. Something of a man of letters and legal philosopher, Nicolas' work on torture belongs to a group of works which delineated the "evil" of accusing and torturing persons to find out if they were witches, yet did not deny the existence of witchcraft itself. His work was dedicated to Louis XIV, to whom he looked because of "his absolute power . . . to correct so many unjust means of arriving at the knowledge and punishment of crimes."

While discussing torture, Nicolas presents what were views generally accepted by French judges on the relationships between Christians and supernatural beings. Nicolas' sense of Christian charity may have led him to question the value of torture, but according to R. Mandrou, *Magistrats et Sorciers en France au XVII*[e] *Siècle* (Paris, 1968), his conclusions were shaped in part by the arguments of another non-French legist, F. Spee (p. 484).

For a long time I wavered between the desire to sustain the innocence of those who might suffer unjust torture in legal proceedings, where it is a question of their life and their honor, and the fear of giving the public something which might seem contrary to customary opinions; but finally I became convinced that there is more merit in saving one innocent person than in causing criminals to perish; and knowing that the [ancient] Romans themselves, whose laws I have undertaken to study, did not hesitate to pay greater honor to the person among them who saved the life of one of their citizens than to another who might have killed a thousand of their enemies, I thought I could render more service to human society by saving innocent people than by condoning through my silence procedures which can cause them to perish as if they were criminals. . . .

SOURCE: Augustin Nicolas, *Si la Torture est un moyen seur à verifier les crimes secrets; Dissertation morale et juridique* (Amsterdam, 1681), pp. 7–8, 49–55, 77–78, 152–154, 157, 162–163, 169–170, 188–189.

One of the Demon's most clever stratagems is to insinuate himself into the minds of men in the guise of the most august things. We could not deny that he has introduced, under pretext of religion, some of the greatest cruelties among men. In order to remain in disagreement with these truths, one would have to be unaware of the fact that idolatry produced sacrifices of human blood, sacrileges, blasphemies, and all sorts of impieties. Our profession of Christianity has not been free from these baneful excesses, when misguided zeal made us arm ourselves against our rebel brothers, to take vengeance upon them in the name of the Divinity, for their debasement of the worship service and of the faith which we owe Him. Could justice, in such a feeble subject as man, be free from this corruption among so many abuses which can corrupt it, as much through excesses as through shortcomings? We must not first become infatuated by a blind prejudice about the status and the normal aim of that virtue, nor believe that everything done in the name of justice cannot, in its execution, be a mixture of injustice and tyranny through our misuse of it. [Justice] is necessary for order among men, and it is with the aim of being profitable that laws and administration introduced it to us; but it is no less true, for all that, that we must not deceive ourselves by labeling as "justice" everything which religious or judicial zeal undertakes and carries out. . . .

I therefore beg every man, whatever his nature or condition, to put off all heated zeal and prejudice about my views until he can acknowledge dispassionately, and by long and serious thought, what I am presenting to him as the proof and foundation of this discourse. Those who use insults as their whole argument, and who think they can weaken an argument by attacking its author with the crass reproaches of "lawyer for sorcerers," and "protector of impunity," doubtlessly have a presumptuous and vain mind, since they condemn before they have heard, and they confuse things and prefer their authority or their personal interest to that [interest] which all of human society has a right to take in the clarification of a matter concerning it. Their entire study consists of proving to us that these matters of sorcery are possible, as if we were casting doubts upon the existence of sorcerers and the justice of punishing them. They hasten to prove to us that these sorts of criminals exist and that they must be chastised; and the whole result of this great zeal is that they want to kill all those who are accused of sorcery, because they might all be sorcerers. And if someone replied to them that torture and the infamy of atrocious crimes do not depend solely upon the possibility, but upon the obvious reality of these crimes committed in deed by the accused, they maintain that in order to certify this evidence, or at least moral soundness, one must refer to the depositions of witches, recognized enemies of mankind, slaves of Satan who are infatuated with his illusions or are incited into [making] these false declarations by the pact which they have made with him. And if you beg them to consider that it can virtually be assumed that in the case of Satan's fiends [such declarations] are to be considered suspect, then they refer you to torture, recognized and admitted to be an invention of tyrants and an almost obvious mouthpiece for lies. Judge whether the peace of mankind and the life of innocent people are securely founded upon such fine maxims?

It is not the pain of the human body which impels a criminal to confess his crime, but the contrition and the pain in his soul. It is this affliction of the spirit which produces in us the repentance which proceeds from the true confession of our crimes, because it is made to God, who cannot be fooled; but torments inflicted upon our body only draw injured cries from us. Everything is forced; everything is subject to the plea of force or of fear, sworn enemies of liberty, of artlessness, of truth. . . .

As for me, I confess naïvely that I do not understand how a judge can be at rest after he has condemned a man on a confession which he knows and admits is uncertain and subject to so many assumptions that it may be false.

All the reasons which are usually used to uphold such a strange practice are reduced to saying that in moral matters there is no infallible truth, and consequently a judge must be content with a probable truth and must base his conscience on what laws and legal practice tell him should be a rule for his actions; but if his conscience clearly bothers him that the proof upon which he based his judgment concerning the life of a man is uncertain, I do not see how, in such a serious matter, he can be confident enough to calm himself, nor how the public authority which he exercises can justify itself before God or before men. I do not understand how the chastisement of a few guilty persons can be so important to the public welfare that in order to show severe justice in punishing the wicked or in preventing the effects of a number of possible crimes, one must risk causing the innocent person to perish as a criminal. . . .

I am not afraid to say that it is credible that hell and all its fiends have no finer hold on man and against the calm of states than [the hold] they gain from the use of torture in seeking our crimes of sorcery. They have only to incite the stupid populace to whisper about some poor woman, old and ugly, as they naturally are. Behold, there is a witch to question and, according to several [learned] doctors, to torture, on the basis of a general rumor. The devil has only to take the shape of a man, or of a respectable woman, either in real witches' Sabbaths or in the fancy seen by the fascinated eyes of a witch who is sleeping or watching, as he can in a thousand ways. This witch, infatuated by these illusions, or urged by the force of the torture, will say and will swear that she saw everyone they wish in all the witches' Sabbaths of the world. But one does not have to be a witch to do that. The most respectable man will say the same thing about himself, when moved by the duress of anguish; that is why almost all modern theologians have been induced to state by their tenderness that a sufferer who feels pushed beyond endurance by these horrible pangs can without mortal sin make a false confession in order to obtain for himself, by a quick death, the cessation of those hellish torments. . . .

We must chastise public crimes which can harm human activities and [which can] bring down divine vengeance upon those states which neglect to punish them when they are legitimately proved and recognized; but we must not hope that torture will help us learn about secret crimes. It will make us martyrise four times more innocent people than the number we will prove to be criminals; it is the real means not only of establishing tyranny, but of assuring the triumph of Satan, whose sole aim is the doom of mankind, and who will gain more through the unjust torture of one innocent person than he will lose through the deaths of a thousand guilty ones. In the city [Besançon] where God saw fit that I be born—the Inquisition having become involved in that infinite progression whose inevitable consequence is that violent injustice which ends in the accusations of accomplices and in confessions obtained under torture—two persons accused of witchcraft had already claimed they had seen the Inquisitor at a witches' Sabbath; and if the Holy

Office in Rome had not taken care to stop these proceedings, the Inquisitor, and all his convent, and all the respectable persons of the city and of the province, would have been embarrassed by these special trials.

It is a very certain sign of ignorance to deny that there are sorcerers. If I had undertaken to prove their perpetual existence from the very beginning of the world, I would not have had a very hard time succeeding. . . . Torture and its deplorable effects are not necessary in order to prove to us that the devil knows how to get even with innocent persons for what he lost by the demise of paganism, since torments gain for him more injustices than he lost in ten centuries thanks to all the inquisitors. . . .

It is for you, Sire, and for all the wise princes to weigh the degree of discretion one can be assured of through the use of a method which can only earn [discretion] by being abolished. If it is pernicious to so many innocent persons, as ten thousand examples attest, its use cannot be continued without indescretion, and it is vain for someone to promise discernment in handling a thing which at its best is recognized and admitted to be uncertain, misleading, cruel, and dangerous in oppressing innocent persons, [and is admitted to be so] by those very persons who introduced it to work in the interest [of the innocent], and who have admitted it to be so in practice. . . .

As for the accusations of accomplices, there is no solution to this argument. The person who accuses someone during torture is either guilty or innocent; if he is a criminal and is really a sorcerer, what faith can one place in the testimony of a person shown by a thousand proofs to be the sworn enemy of mankind, and who has sworn to the Demon that he will work toward its doom by all possible means? . . . But if this accused person is innocent, and is forced to admit his guilt by the duress of torture, he does not know what goes on at a witches' Sabbath, since he has never been there; however, if you demand that he name accomplices, can you hope that he will show more concern for the honor and life of another while undergoing this torture than he has been able to show for his own? No one's conscience can stand the strain. He will accuse, if you wish, all the saints in Paradise, and all the Blessed Spirits, in order to buy his way out of that hell, in the hope of being able to retract his statements about them later. But either he will not remember this owing to his extremely disordered state of mind, or, if he remembers, the fear of undergoing unbearable torture up to three times more or the announcement that these retractions will be useless to him makes him decide to die without retracting. I let the wisest persons judge what certainty there can be in seeking out crimes by torture. . . .

That modern author who accused the Parlement of France of incredulity because it does not subscribe like him to all these strange procedures should remember on this subject the poor wretch who was burned as a sorcerer in the county of Burgundy and whose story was told by the confessor who was attending him at his death, a story which [the confessor] himself tells us in turn in his ignorant incredulity. This poor man had been accused as a sorcerer in these famed accusations by accomplices, and impelled to make false confessions by that infallible constraint which is called torture, "he confessed that he was a sorcerer, as they had said. He was accepting death willingly as a chastisement for such a great crime, since they wanted him to be guilty of it; but he begged this good priest, who at these words shivered with horror and burst into tears, to tell him whether one could be a sorcerer without knowing it?" If this priest, who knows the inevitable effects of these injustices and of torture, had been able to collect his wits, instead of excusing the judges who were exposing themselves to such horrible injustices through the prejudices of these [contemporary] Roman laws, ought he not to have stated, unequivocally, that these judges fairly deserve the punishment which they make so many innocent persons suffer unjustly? . . .

Since I believe that this discourse is doing the Christian Republic the greatest service which can be rendered to it, I do not fear to direct it to all the Christian princes, nor to beg them very respectfully to have it read to them and to study it seriously. It is they that the matter primarily concerns, since these laws and injustices have neither strength nor authority over the people except by the tacit approval which they give by permitting them without being aware of them; and since it is almost impossible that any of the persons preoccupied by these strange maxims will become the instrument of their discrediting, and will plead against their own profession by revealing to the princes the true reasons which damn its use, [I] must by this volume expose myself to public indignation and attract to myself alone all the envious darts of those among them who remain obstinate about fomenting and supporting the continuation of these abuses.

If we expect the princes to decide by themselves, we do so in vain. While scholars and wise men do not dare to speak their thoughts to them, the princes, who rely upon their officials, will never completely know the precise situation. We are not freed before God of so much innocent blood which torture has unjustly spilled while seeking out secret crimes, crimes which are prosecuted in a special manner, by saying as our only excuse: "It is up to the sovereign princes to abolish by their authority both torture and those injustices [which their authority] has sustained until now in their courts." It is up to those who know its sad consequences to present them to [the sovereign] clearly, since in addition to relieving their consciences, they will do them the greatest service which a subject and an official can render to his sovereign. . . .

54. The Merchants and the State

The economic crisis which set in and caused great hardship after 1680 prompted leading merchants to criticize Louis XIV's ministers and their policies. The dislocation of international trade caused by war, high taxes, high protective tariffs, and other rigid economic controls fed this opposition until the ministers decided that something would have to be done.

After consulting among themselves and with leading merchants and financiers, the ministers recommended to the King that a council of commerce be established to hear grievances and collect information about economic conditions. The decree of June 29, 1700, which established the council clearly states its purpose. Note how the merchant councillors were to be chosen on the local level.

Now royal officials at least heard what influential men in French commerce thought of the international market, France's place in it, and the Crown's policies. The conflicting interests of southern and western merchants rendered joint recommendations to the Crown impossible. The "memorials" presented by the two groups reflect a continuity of different interests, as well as little opposition to the Colbertian conceptions of a state economy.

SOURCE: *Memorials presented by the deputies of the Council of Trade in France* (London, 1736), pp. ii–iv, 31–34, 36–46.

An Arrêt *of the King's Council of State for Establishing a Council of Commerce, June 29, 1700*

The King having at all times been sensible of what importance it was to the welfare of the State, to favour and protect the commerce of his people, as well within the kingdom as out of it; His Majesty has, on divers occasions, issued several edicts, ordinances, declarations, and *arrêts* [decrees], and made many useful regulations upon that subject: But the wars which have intervened, and the multitude of indispensable cares which took up His Majesty's thoughts, 'till the conclusion of the last peace, not allowing him to continue the same application thereto, and His Majesty being more disposed than ever, to grant a particular protection to commerce, to shew his esteem of the good merchants and traders of his kingdom; and to facilitate to them the means of making commerce flourish, and extending it, His Majesty judges that nothing can be more capable of producing this effect than the forming a Council of Commerce, which shall be wholly attentive to the examining and promoting whatever may be most advantageous to commerce, and to the manufactures of the kingdom . . . the King being in his council, has ordained, and ordains, that for the future a Council of Commerce shall be held, at least once, every week, which shall be composed of Monsieur Daguesseau, Counsellor in Ordinary of State, and of the Royal Council of the Finances; of Monsieur Chamillart, Counsellor of the said Royal Council, and Comptroller-General of the Finances . . . and of twelve of the principal trading merchants of the kingdom, or such who shall have been a long time engaged in commerce. That of this number of trading merchants, two shall always be of the town of Paris; and that each of the other ten shall be taken from the towns of Rouen, Bourdeaux, Lyons, Marseilles, La Rochelle, Nantes, St. Malo, Lille, Bayonne, and Dunkerque.

That in the said Council of Commerce shall be discussed, and examined, all the propositions and memorials which shall be sent to it, together with the affairs and difficulties which may arise concerning commerce, as well by land as by sea, within the kingdom and out of it, and concerning works and manufactures, to the end that upon the report which shall be made to His Majesty, of the resolutions which shall be taken thereupon, in the said Council of Commerce, His Majesty may order what shall be most adviseable. . . . That those [merchants] who shall be chosen to be of the said Council of Commerce, be men of known probity, and of capacity and experience in matters of commerce, and that for this purpose the towns above mentioned shall assemble in the month of July next, in each respective Townhouse, to proceed to the said election, so that the trading merchants thus elected, and named, may be able to arrive at Paris or where the Court shall reside, by the end of September. . . . That the said elections shall be for one year only, and shall be renewed yearly, in the manner above mentioned, with a proviso that the time of service in the said Council may be prolonged, if it shall be judged proper to do so. His Majesty ordains that the fore-named Comptroller-General of the finances shall nominate two persons interested in His Majesty's [tax] farms, to be called to the said Council when the nature of affairs shall require. . . . Done in the King's Council of State, His Majesty present, at Versailles, the 29th day of June, 1700, signed Phelypeaux, and sealed.

A Memorial of the Deputies of the Trading Towns in the West of France, Concerning the Commerce with the Levant, the Goods Used in That Trade; and Why Marseilles Alone Has the Privilege of Trading Thither

Experience teaches us that the English carry on the trade of the Levant with much greater advantage than our nation; their woollen clothes are better made, are better and cheaper than ours, and therefore are more in request, and have a greater vent [sale]: they carry thither lead, pewter, copperass, logwood, which are goods that they are masters of, together with a great deal of pepper: And that they may not drain their country of its gold and silver, the ships which are freighted with those goods are laden likewise with dry fish of their own catching, sugars from their colonies, and other goods of their own product which they sell on the coasts of Portugal, Spain, and Italy, and receive the produce in pieces of eight, which they carry to the Levant, to add to the stock necessary for purchasing the merchandizes which they take in there and carry to England.

This way of trading is very beneficial to England, since by supplying themselves with coyn from foreigners, they draw so much less from home; and besides, they make a profit by the goods they sell in their passage upon the coasts of Portugal, Spain, and Italy. . . . Upon the like plan, it would be more advantageous to France to permit the towns of the West to carry on this trade in the same manner directly. We have, as well as the English, woollen cloths, stuffs, paper, silks, tobacco, fish of our own catching, and linen cloths which they have not . . . thus, the towns of the West might carry on this trade without sending our money abroad, our manufactures would be consumed in greater quantities as far as the competition with those of the English would permit, and we might bring back in our ships all the merchandizes of the Levant. . . .

Since the towns of the [Atlantic] Ocean have been obliged to go and unlade their goods at Marseilles, instead of endeavouring to continue and increase that trade, they have been forced to relinquish it absolutely, and indeed, how can it be expected they should come from the extremity of the Levant to pay their respect to Marseilles? Subject themselves to consume a fourth or a third more of victuals than usual? Pay greater wages to seamen, and higher rates for insurance? . . . By the *arrests* [decrees], none but the towns of Dunkirk and Rouen can receive goods from the Levant directly without touching at Marseilles; nor they without paying 20 per cent for entry; the other ports complain of being excluded: This extraordinary duty has been laid on since the year 1685, whereby the throwing up of that trade has not only been continued, but it has likewise given occasion to the [tax] farmers to be very vexatious in extending that duty to merchandizes which are not subject to it. . . .

Consequently our manufactures have laboured under this dearness; which is contrary to the views we ought to have of increasing the export and vent of them to foreign parts. . . . The town of Marseilles, which is solely empowered to manage the Levant trade, thrives by the exclusion of the other maritime towns, to the prejudice of the publick. . . . Marseilles, by being a free port, by its near situation to the Levant, and the settled correspondence of its merchants there, will always have sufficient advantage over the ports and towns of the West. Marseilles is not excluded from any commerce permitted to the towns of the West (or ports of the Ocean), therefore what justice is there in appropriating the trade of the Levant to that city alone. Besides, the manner in which Marseilles carries on this commerce cannot be approved, since it is manifest that the goods which it sends thither, of the growth or make of the kingdom, being in moderate quantities and of little consideration, the merchants of that town make the greatest part of their remittances in pieces of eight and in other sorts of coyn. . . . The merchants of Marseilles lay out a great part of such remittances in linen-cloth and stuffs of the Levant, which whatever precaution be taken, do not fail of being dispersed about the kingdom to the prejudice of our own manufactures. . . .

A Memorial of the Deputy of Marseilles

It is a very difficult task, when a single man is obliged to answer such knowing and acute persons as the deputies of the ports of the Western-Sea; and if I had not a just cause to defend . . . I should distrust my ability through want of practice in drawing up memorials so well put together and so politely turned as those given in by those gentlemen: But as the present dispute is about facts, and that the trade of the Levant has been ever allowed to be the most beneficial to the State, the council will please to permit me to lay before them my reason in the best manner I can. . . .

The pretention of these gentlemen is not new; they have often endeavored at the same thing. . . . It is certain that the permission which they require of driving a trade to the Levant is not proper to be granted them because neither in their own towns nor among their neighbors can they find a consumption of divers gross commodities which they would be forced to take in to make up the trading of their ships, as does Marseilles which enjoys this advantage. . . .

One sure proof that this trade is not proper for them is that it does not appear they ever set about it, notwithstanding the permission which all the ports of the West had to drive this trade before and after the establishment of the free port of Marseilles which was in 1669 until 1685. For the ports of Rouen and Dunkirk had this permission because of the convenience of having their Levantine merchandise by way of Holland and England, more easily than by fetching them from thence directly, which they find very difficult, always put them upon that prejudicial practice of giving their profits to those foreigners and enemies to the damage of the King's subjects, and if His Majesty had not put a stop to it by his decree of Aug. 15, 1685, which lays a duty of 20 per cent on Levantine which should come from England or Holland into France . . . it is certain that by this time [*c.* 1702] those nations would have supplied France with all the Levant goods, and the King's subjects would have utterly lost that trade, so important to the State. . . . It is well known what Cardinal Richelieu said to the advantage of this trade, and what was done by Monsieur Colbert after mature consideration. . . . How can men, after this, think of procuring any change in this establishment? . . .

Marseilles has a very particular and advantageous situation and proximity to the Levant; she has in her town, her province, and in those of Languedoc and Dauphiné her neighbors, all sorts of manufactures proper for the Levant, and has had settled correspondence, and been used for some ages to this trade which by experience she manages with perfect economy; and it looks as if God had endowed her with these advantages for the good of the State. . . .

The deputies of commerce represent, that seeing His Majesty has declared he will be pleased to protect and favour trade, they presume that what might contribute to promote His Majesty's designs would be the granting to the merchants some marks of honour and distinction which might make them value themselves on their condition, and for that purpose it might be necessary that His Majesty would be pleased to grant what follows.

That all the King's subjects, who are noble by extraction, by office, or otherwise, may be permitted to traffick and deal in all commerce by wholesale, as well by sea as by land, either for their own account or by commission, without derogation from their nobility, in consequence of the edict of the month of August, 1669, by which the King has declared that commerce by sea does not derogate from nobility, provided gentlemen do not sell by retail. . . .

That the children of* nobles may, for their instruction in business, put themselves to merchants within the kingdom or out of it, for such a time as they think convenient, and this without derogation of their noblesse. . . .

All retailers shall be forbidden to take upon them in publick acts

* The eighteenth-century English translator noted: "of nobility or gentry, the French having but one word for what we distinguish by two."

or otherwise the title of negociant, on the penalty of 100 livres for the first time, 200 for the second, and 300 for other times; one third to go to the informer, another to the hospitals of the area, and the other third towards the maintenance of consular houses.

That all mechanics ["artisans and ouvriers"] shall be enjoyned to confine themselves to the title of their trade, and forbidden to style themselves merchants, on the penalty of 10 livres for the first time, 30 for the second, and 50 for other times, applicable as above.

55. *Boulainvilliers' Critique of the Intendants*

While linked to Fénelon in the little Duke of Burgundy's entourage, the Duke of Beauvillier had requested the provincial intendants in the late 1690's to prepare detailed and lengthy descriptions of the geography, economy, and spiritual and moral life of the peoples in each *généralité* of France. These reports were prepared, but nothing much was done with them until Henri, Count of Boulainvilliers (1658–1722), edited them and had them prepared in manuscript as an *État de la France* about the time of Louis XIV's death.

First published in London in 1727, these edited reports of the intendants became an important source of opinions and facts about the reign of Louis XIV. Boulainvilliers' own aristocratic contempt for Louis' "bourgeois" ministers, whom he saw as power-hungry, influenced Montesquieu greatly and fed the propaganda machines of the aristocratic party during the eighteenth century. Opposition to bureaucratic absolutism and the centralization of political power in Paris focused on the ministers of Louis XIV and their cohorts, the intendants. Note Boulainvilliers' portrait of Bâville, because it is representative of what aristocrats stripped of political influence by the Sun King wanted to believe about those they felt had displaced them.

But shortly afterward how surprised and indignant I was when the report of the *généralité* of Paris and subsequently those of the other provinces revealed to me the incapacity or the negligence of those who had been entrusted with the execution of such a fine project. Who would not have believed that—[being] personally concerned in serving the prince from whom they received their orders, obliged by the intimate obligations which bind us to king

SOURCE: Monsieur le Comte de Boulainvilliers, *État de la France* (London, 1727), I, Pt. II of Preface, ii–xii.

and country, and honored by the master's confidence—they would at least have made the usual efforts to carry out the just desires of his son. . . . If ever the intendants' consciences were closely involved in the functions of their ministry, they were in this instance; the poverty of the people, which they saw but did not heed, found a favorable opportunity to be portrayed to the mind of a naturally just and compassionate prince, who would never have forgotten it. . . .

If men are classed according to their different characters, the greatest number is certainly those lacking in application, the second, those who are incompetent, and the third are persons predisposed by certain passions. The reading of the reports which the intendants supplied our prince shows that, unfortunately for France, none of them in the years 1697–1698, and 1699 . . . were really excluded from one of these three character types: incompetence, inapplication, and prejudice; so that one can truly say that in one way or another it is almost impossible for the truth to ever reach kings. . . .

States form large families; the same economy which sustains our [families] makes the other [families] prosper; but can there be any conception of economic virtue without a knowledge of revenues and expenditures? The desire for arbitrary power, which I call the stumbling block of the virtue and fortune of kings, often makes them imagine that they are the masters of all their subjects' possessions. . . .

Among the miseries of our century, there is none which merits [the name] more than the administration of the intendancies. I do not doubt that the kings who created this arbitrary jurisdiction thought they had reasons for establishing it, when their only reason was multiplying the means of making themselves obeyed, since Italian maxims had convinced them that love did not suffice; but at the same time one must admit that the opposition which almost all the people in the monarchy are showing to this innovation was the last effort of French liberty, and that after the weak and useless resistance which they showed, the plagues with which we have been smitten followed one upon another almost year after year, and finally reduced us to our present prostration.

Our fathers did not foresee all the consequences of this innovation; the parlements thought it would deal a mortal blow to regular justice, and that did not happen; the flow of lawsuits was not diverted, this allurement remained for the higher and lower judges; governors of provinces and forts thought that their authority, their functions, their profits were going to be taken away, and they were not mistaken; the nobility saw in general that attention was going to be focused too closely on them; those of this group whose conscience bothered them over injustice or violence feared for their lives; but this same nobility did not see that it was going to be degraded to the point of being reduced to proving its social station before these new judges; that it was going to lose its natural authority over its own subjects to the point of being not confused with them (for indeed the distinction was supposed to remain), but so debased that the peasants, who originally were only free and owners of their possessions through the grace of their lords, would in the future have the right to impose the *taille* upon the nobles and their possessions, and that they would remain forever excluded from their natural right to direct and lead this blind populace.

The *peuple*, on their side, did not know what an intendant would be; but since they always like novelties, and since without foreseeing the evil to come, they thought only of freeing themselves from an existing yoke, they imagined that [an intendant] would be a protector for them against the authority of the nobility, which, although so old and so legitimate, even though stripped of its original strength, still continued to annoy them, less through [this authority's] being exercised than through its constant presence; experience having subsequently shown [the *peuple*] that the intendant was a sovereign judge, who would have the power to change, to overthrow arbitrarily the provincial institutions, they easily transferred to him their adoration and the gift of their possessions; but they learned only long afterward, through more painful experience, that the new magistrates were to be the immediate instruments of their misery, that their lives, their possessions, their families, everything would be at their disposal, masters of their children to the point that they could enlist them by force, masters of their possessions to the point of taking away their subsistence, masters of their lives to the point of prison, the gallows, and the wheel. . . .

Two passions currently govern men: fear and pride; our ancestors put piety in the place of pride, but the times having changed; one scarcely encounters [piety] these days. As for fear, its imprint is to be found in all the intendants' reports. One appears to tremble in speaking of the "king's rights," for this is the generic term for everything called taxes; another shows the weight of the yoke but searches for excuses and insinuates that the evil lies in the manner in which it is imposed. . . .

But what terms should I use to depict the disorders and misfortunes resulting from pride, when it is combined with one of the preceding character types, and when it has corrupted the heart sometimes without harming the enlightenment of the mind? The report for Languedoc, and the conduct of its author [Bâville], will show [these disorders] better than anything I could say; it is nevertheless necessary to comment upon it briefly.

It is certain that this report is the best written of all; the intelligence, the organization, the talents of the author are noticeably superior to the others; but I dare say that this does not make [the report] any less pernicious to the prince and to his subjects; here one can see the character of a man drunk with the authority which he has acquired from both sides, who senses the power he has over the monarch's trust, earned by having kept such an important province under control, and that he nevertheless fears blame for being the cause of the rebellion which has been going on there for so long: on the one hand, he shows ostentatiously that he alone supplied more than a hundred and sixty million to the King during the nine years of the war of the Prince of Orange [the War of the League of Augsburg]; but without saying that the excessive surcharge on these taxes threatened an imminent revolution, he strives only to show his foresight in preparing the means of averting the storm which, in spite of the terror over punishments, was developing before his eyes; moreover, insensible to the poverty he has created, and to the deaths of several thousand men sacrificed in order to maintain his authority, he speaks only of the need for obedience, in order to be entitled to have it applied in his case; if he criticizes taxes, if he investigates their origins carefully, if he even refers to some secret of the previous reign on this subject, one can see that it is only in order to attract more approbation for his book and more commendation for the new taxes he has invented; thus the creator of the *capitation* clears himself of all the evils which he has caused, and also has succeeded in having his book read with pleasure by the prince. Can one nevertheless keep from viewing him as one of the cruel instruments of public poverty and as the most dangerous seducer of our prince's piety?

It is intendants of this sort whom I call professional intendants, of whom one can truly say that never did the earth bear more dangerous citizens; these men, possessed of an ambitious fury, remorselessly sacrifice their country to their desire to command, as they sacrifice their consciences to favor at court; their aim is gaining authority for themselves; favoritism is the means of establishing it; thus as slaves of the ministry, they become by this very slavery tyrants over the people; they never conceive of plans which are beneficial to liberty, to calm, and to abundance; lovers of the public good are always criminals in their judgment; one is only permitted, according to their maxims, to be well off by means of work, action, and intrigue; they are so far from thinking that natural blessings belong to the people that they scarcely leave them [the blessing] of being industrious; never has helplessness excused anyone before them: it is a vain allegation which they usually class as disobedience and laziness; they are harsh, inflexible, and scornful. Sworn enemies of the nobility, whom indeed they crush while flattering it, or rather whom they insult by the sumptuousness of their repasts. But I have not mistakenly assumed that pride and ambition possess these intendants without bringing prejudice to their insights; for one must confess that, despite the harshness of their prejudices, they saw and sensed the current calamity. . . .

56. La Bruyère on War and Human Nature

Born in Paris, the son of a bourgeois *contrôleur des rentes*, Jean de La Bruyère (1645–1696) became one of the most brilliant satirists in France during the reign of Louis XIV. While a preceptor in the household of the Grand Condé, as a result of Bossuet's patronage, La Bruyère had the opportunity to observe courtly society during the 1680's not only from a bourgeois perspective but also from that of this staunchly proud, independent prince of the blood who kept his distance from Versailles. La Bruyère's description of the pretentious, modish, corrupt, and hypocritical aspects of courtly society in his anonymously published *Les Caractères* made him instantly famous once the identity of the author was discovered.

Relying on brilliant writing rather than on originality of thought,

SOURCE: *Oeuvres de La Bruyère*, ed. by M. G. Servois (Paris, 1865), II, 128–131.

and not caring particularly whether the portraits he made of individuals under quite obvious pseudonymous names were accurate or not, La Bruyère demonstrated by his success the moral and religious uneasiness in the French governing elites. In an age when Louis' military victories were officially recognized as bounty from God, and the King himself was endlessly compared to Alexander and Caesar, La Bruyère used the age-old literary device of comparing human and animal behavior to make his criticisms of war. With the entire literary focus trained on Versailles, La Bruyère could write:

> Caesar wasn't at all too old to think of conquering the universe; no other beatitude was available to him than that of a good life, and a great name [for himself] after his death; born proud, ambitious, and carrying himself well as he did so, he had no better way to employ his time than to conquer the world. Alexander was certainly too young for such a grave project; it is astonishing that at his early age, women or wine did not break up his enterprise sooner.[1]

And the French public would immediately think of Louis XIV.

Little men, six feet tall, at the most seven, whom you confine at fairs as giants and as rare items which one must pay to see, as soon as you reach eight feet; upon whom you shamelessly bestow *highness* and *eminence*, which is the most one could grant those mountains [which are] neighbors to the sky and which witness the clouds forming beneath them; species of glorious and superb animals, which scorns every other species, which cannot even be compared with the elephant and the whale; approach, men, give a little reply to Democritus. Do you not say in popular idiom: *ravenous wolves, furious lions, malicious as a monkey?* And you others, who are you? I hear constantly blaring in my ears: *Man is a rational animal.* Who gave you that definition? Is it the wolves, the monkeys, and the lions, or did you confer it upon yourselves? It is already a ludicrous thing that you gave the worst there is to the animals, your confreres, in order to take for yourselves the best there is. Let them describe themselves a bit, and you will see how they will forget their own interests and how they will behave toward you. I am not talking, O men, of your flightinesses, of your follies, and of your caprices, which place you beneath the mole and the tortoise, who go soberly on their way, and who follow undeviatingly their natural instinct; but listen to me a moment. You

1. ¶ 105, "Des Jugements," Les Caractères. . . .

say of a male falcon who is very fleet and who swoops down nicely onto a partridge: "There is a beautiful bird"; and of a greyhound who captures a hare at close quarters: "That is a good greyhound." I also accept your saying of a man who chases the wild boar, who puts it at bay, who strikes it and stabs it: "There is a brave man." But if you see two dogs barking at one another, who meet face to face, who bite and tear one another, you say: "Those are stupid animals"; and you take a stick to separate them. If someone told you that all the cats in a great nation met by the thousands on a plain, and that after having meowed their fill, they threw themselves furiously upon one another and played tooth and claw together; that of the melee there remained [dead] on the field between nine and ten thousand cats from both sides, who infected the air for ten leagues around by their odor, would you not say: "That is the most abominable witches' Sabbath ever heard of"? And if the wolves did likewise: "Such howls! Such butchery!" And if one or the other told you that they love glory, would you conclude from this discourse that they earn it through being at that fine meeting place, to thus destroy and annihilate their own species? Or after having concluded this, would you not laugh with all your heart at the ingeniousness of those poor beasts? You have already, as reasoning animals, and in order to set yourself apart from those who use only their teeth and their nails, invented lances, pikes, darts, sabres, and scimitars, and to my mind very judiciously; for with your mere hands what could you do to one another besides tear out your hair, scratch your faces, or at the most gouge your eyes from your heads? Instead here you are, armed with convenient instruments, which serve to make reciprocal large wounds from which your blood can pour to the last drop, without your risking a chance of being saved. But since you become more reasonable year by year, you have nicely improved upon this old manner of exterminating yourselves: you have little globes which kill you at once, if only they manage to hit you in the head or in the chest; you have others, heavier and more massive, which cut you in two or disembowel you, without counting those which fall upon your roofs, crush the floors, go from attic to cellar, collapse its vaults, and toss into the air, with your houses, your wives in childbed, the child, and the nursemaid: and there again is where *lies* glory; it loves hullabaloos, and it is fracas personified. Moreover, you have defensive weapons, and according to the proper rules in war you should be clad in iron, which truly is a pretty ornament, and which brings to my mind those four famous fleas which in days of old used to be exhibited by a charlatan, a clever artisan who had found the secret of keeping them alive in a vial: he had given each of them a helmet for its head, had put a breastplate on each, armlets, knee pieces, a lance at the thigh; they lacked for nothing, and in that attire they went jumping and bounding about in their bottle. Imagine a man the size of Mount Athos,* why not? Would a soul be disconcerted at animating such a body? It would have more room. If that man had eyes keen enough to discover you somewhere on earth with your offensive and defensive weapons, what do you think he would think of little urchins equipped like that, and of what you call war, cavalry, infantry, a memorable siege, a famous battle day? Will I never hear you buzzing about anything else? Is the world now divided solely into regiments and companies? Has everything become battalion or squadron?

57. *Bâville on Fiscal Policies after Louis XIV's Death*

One of the characteristics of bureaucratic government is established routines and procedures. This often results in hostility to innovation in procedures and reforms on the part of bureaucrats. On September 1, 1715, Louis XIV had died, leaving immense royal debts and a society tired of both old and new taxes. Pressure to eliminate the *capitation*, a head tax based on income, and to reduce all other taxes fell on the ministers whom Louis left behind. After some scurrying, which resulted in an increase in power for the Parlement and the princes—the latter increasing their power in the polysynodal councils established to curb the powers of the ministers during the Regency of Louis XV—a general debate about taxes and the royal debt quickly developed.

Intendant Nicolas Lamoignon de Bâville's position on tax reform was not long in reaching the capital. It is a classic statement of fiscal problems as seen by an official in the provinces. The refrains about hostility to fiscal innovations on the part of the king's subjects, the

SOURCE: A. M. de Boislisle (ed.) *Mémoires des Intendants sur l'État des Généralités dressés pour l'Instruction du Duc de Bourgogne* (Paris, 1881), I, 486.

* The Greek architect Dinocrates wanted to transform Mount Athos into a sculpture of Alexander the Great.

high cost paid for the collection of taxes, and the promise of a reform proposal were already traditional and obvious by 1715, but they would continue to be recited right down to 1789.

Letter from Monsieur de Bâville,
Intendant in Languedoc, to Noailles,
President of the Council of Finance

Montpellier, December 26, 1715

I have made, Sir, no plans about the new manner of assessing taxes; it is a matter which has always appeared to me too difficult and of dangerous consequences; in the past I have closely examined only the plan of Monsieur the Marshal de Vauban, and after having thought about it a bit, I confess that I was convinced that it would be a very rash act to put it into practice. I concluded that the people pay through habit, that they feel almost no repugnance at the old taxes, and that whatever is collected, for example, under the name of the *taille* appears much less onerous to them. Though that *taille* be increased considerably, they bear it patiently; but if it is a new tax, even though much lighter, they cannot endure it. We instituted a tax, the individual tithe on their land, which they could not tolerate in this province; having found the way to make an assessment through the estates, and this assessment having thus been blended in with the old taxes, there was no more difficulty [in collecting it]. For this reason, if a new plan were followed, such as the one of Monsieur de Vauban, or of someone like him, it is greatly to be feared that the people would accept only half of it, that is to say, they would no longer pay according to the old manner of assessing taxes, and that in regard to the new, they would create a lot of difficulties, which would throw things into great confusion. Moreover, the sums to be collected would have to be much less substantial than they are, in order to make such an attempt, and a trial run would have to be made in some *canton* before applying it in general. But it would never succeed, in my opinion, as long as taxes are as exorbitant as they now are. I therefore believe that what could be done now is to give a great deal of attention to preventing excessive costs in tax collection, in which there is certainly a great deal of abuse. The main rule should be to cost the people money only when they are in a position to pay, at certain times of the year, after their various harvests, after the fairs which are held in all the provinces, where they sell wool, cattle, grain, and other produce. At that time the *receveur* cannot act too promptly, because indeed the persons owing money have the wherewithal to pay; but all the rest of the year, during which we know there are no sales or any money in the hands of individuals, all the money we cost them is pointless, and only overwhelms them, without producing anything for the king. In Poitou, I have seen through experience what I have the honor to tell you [in this letter]: the *receveur général* at that time had an excellent and very well-meaning clerk; he acted on this principle, collected his tax money very well, and with little cost, because he did it only when it should be done. That the people pay without constraint, this is an ideal which we will never attain; it is a question of moderating this constraint, and of exercising it only at an appropriate time. There still may be a great deal of abuse concerning excessive costs, which should be settled, once and for all, without our allowing them to exceed the prescribed amount. I have not been in the territory of the *taille personnelle* for such a long time that I cannot tell you now what abuses may be occurring there. I see that in Languedoc, which is a territory of *taille réelle*, there are very many abuses in the collection of the *taille*, that collection costs reach excessive totals; the rules which have been established for these collections are very faulty and need to be corrected. I am going to work on a plan which will concern this province, and which will serve in the others of the *taille réelle*. I will have the honor of sending it to you upon completion; it is a matter indeed worthy of your attention and of the great care which you take to relieve the people. It is the reply which I owe to the letter which you have done me the honor of writing me on the 18th of this month.

I am with respect, Monsieur, your very humble and very obedient servant,

BÂVILLE

58. Fénelon's Critique of Louis XIV's Policies

Disappointed courtiers and idealistic reformers often constitute a single group in a monarchy when the inevitable attempt to control the education and patronage of the heir apparent develops into a party.

SOURCE: *Oeuvres Complètes de Fénelon* (Paris, 1850), VII, 182–188.

Louis XIV's reign was no exception to this rule, for as both he and his oldest legitimate son aged, the entourage of his little grandson, the Duke of Burgundy (1682–1712), became a hotbed of ambitious critics of the Sun King and his policies. This opposition had to be covert, of course, because Louis could disgrace these critics and force them to leave Versailles (as he in fact did later on); thus, while in the coterie around Burgundy, their criticism was limited to Louis' ministers and did not include the King himself.

The Duke of Burgundy's preceptor, François de Salignac de La Mothe-Fénelon (1651–1715), became the leader of this party of courtiers and critics. Highly intelligent, witty, ambitious, and charming, Fénelon covertly accused Louis of ruining France through his military and social policies. Not opposed to war on principle, but critical of it because of the high costs in blood and treasure for the French people, Fénelon feared rebellion and a general political and moral collapse for the kingdom. His opposition to the rise of commoners and even of nobles (as opposed to gentlemen) to high places of influence around the King echoed the nostalgic refrain of princes and peers who had once held greater political power than Louis would ever allow them after their conduct during the Fronde. Repugnance for new men of wealth and contempt for any who served the Church or the state except out of devotion and loyalty are basic premises in Fénelon's critique of Louis XIV's state.

More important for the developments at Versailles over the next seventy-five years, Fénelon and his circle formed a body of ideas which the aristocratic opposition would develop against the Crown right down to the Revolution, which the nobles themselves would unleash.

Governnment Projects Worked out with the Duke of Chevreuse to be Proposed to the Duke of Burgundy, November 1711

Article I
Project for the Present [Situation]

1. To make peace—must be bought at any cost. Arras and Cambrai very expensive for France.

If, through extreme misfortune, peace was unattainable at any other price, we would have to sacrifice these strongholds.

If [peace] cannot be achieved, diligence to be ready by the end of March. Forage, grain, carts; no rivers against the enemies. – Castile.

2. To wage war.

Choice of a general who has respect and confidence, who knows how to make an excellent defensive.

No new marshals in France. They would neither be more able nor have more authority, humiliation for the good lieutenant generals.

Choice of a moderate number of good lieutenant generals working with the general.

The presence of Monsieur the Dauphin in the army, pernicious without an able and zealous general, a second general working closely with him, well-chosen lieutenant generals, the authority to decide first, and the firmness of a fifty-year-old man.

To avoid battle while protecting our strongholds, even allowing the small ones to be lost.

In direst extremity, battle, at the risk of being defeated, captured, killed with *gloire*.

Generals: Villeroi, painstaking with order and dignity. –Villars, quick and not very well liked, because he is scornful, etc. –Harcourt, ill; little experience, good sense. –Berwick, organized, vigilant, timid in council meetings, curt, stiff and a man of parts. –Bezons, irresolute and narrow-minded, but level-headed and an honest man. –Montesquiou. . . .

General officers–Do not urge all courtiers to continue their service; disgust, inapplication, bad example. –Good treatment for old officers of repute. –Regular council of war. General officers good to listen to, not always to believe; many are very mediocre.

Council of war at court, composed of marshals of France and other experienced persons, who know what a secretary of state cannot know, who speak freely on troubles and abuses, who devise plans for campaigns together with the general in charge of carrying them out, who give their opinion during the campaign, who, however, do not prevent the general from deciding without awaiting their opinion, because it is of capital importance to profit from the moment.

Article II
Plan for Reform After the Peace

§I–*Military Situation*

Military force, reduced to a hundred and fifty thousand men.

Never a general war against Europe. No sticky points with the English. Readiness for peace with the Dutch. We will easily pit the one against the other. Ready alliance with half the Empire.

Few strongholds. Works and garrisons ruin [us]. Multitude of strongholds fall as soon as we lack money, as soon as a civil war comes. Superiority of the army, which is easy, does everything.

Moderate number of regiments, but large and well disciplined, without any venality under any pretext; never given to young men without experience; with many old officers. –Good treatment for soldiers for pay, victuals, hospitals: elite group of men. –Good emoluments for colonels and captains. –Seniority of officer counted as nothing, if it is the sole consideration. –Care not to let those seen lacking in talent grow old in the service. Promote men of marked talent.

Plan for reform. Listen to Messieurs the Marshals of Puységur, Harcourt, and Tallard.

Fortifications by the soldiers, by neighboring peasants, limited to medium-sized garrisons.

Militias throughout the realm. Very free enlistments, with punctuality in mustering-out after five years. Never any amnesties. Instead of the Hôtel des Invalides, small pensions for each invalid in his own village.

§II–*Order for Expenditures at Court*

Reduction in all the unnecessary pensions at court. Moderation in furnishings, retinue, clothing, food. Exclusion of all useless women. Sumptuary laws like the Romans. Sacrificing of buildings and gardens. Cessation of all double employment: make each one stay within his function. Exact calculation of the funds for the royal household: no increase under any pretext.

Reduction in all work for the King: let the arts flourish through rich individuals and foreigners.

Exact calculation of all the emoluments of governors, lieutenant generals, etc., of military staff, etc., of unavoidable pensions, of wages for offices in the parlements and other courts.

Exact calculation of all the King's debts; distinguishing those which carry interest from those which should not; an accounting with each *rentier*, with reduction for enormous and obvious usury, with postponement of many others, with general reductions to 3⅓ per cent, with the exception of certain privileged cases; cleaning up each account, if possible, finishing by a rough estimate, if one cannot get to the bottom of it.

Calculation of the total funds necessary for the royal household and the court, of all the necessary emoluments, wages, and pensions, of the interest on all debts, of the subsistence of the entire military force.

Exact comparison of these total expenditures with the total revenues which can be collected by restoring agriculture, the useful arts, and trade.

§III—*Internal Administration of the Realm*

1. Establishment of the Board, a little assembly from each diocese, as in Languedoc, composed of the bishop with the lords of the region and the Third Estate, which fixes the raising of taxes on the basis of the land registry, which is subordinate to the Estates of the province;

2. Establishment of individual Estates for all the provinces, as in Languedoc; they are no less submissive there than elsewhere, they are less [financially] exhausted. Composed of deputies of the three Estates from each diocese, with power to administer, correct, allocate funds, etc. To listen to the reports of the deputies of the Boards; to calculate the taxes on the natural wealth of the region, of the commerce which flourishes there;

3. Cessation of the *gabelle*, the Five Great Farms, the head tax, and the royal tithe. Adequacy of the sums which the Estates would raise to pay their part in the total sum of the expenses of the State. —An order from the Estates always more comforting than one from the King's tax farmers or from *traitants*, without the drawback of perpetuating ruinous taxes and of making them arbitrary. For example, taxes by the Estates of the region on salt, without *gabelles*. No more speculators.

4. To increase the number of provincial governments, limiting them to a smaller area, over which a man can watch carefully with the lieutenant general and the King's lieutenant. At least twenty in France would be the rule for the number of individual Estates. —Resident governors and officers. —No intendants; only *missi dominici* from time to time.

5. Establishment of the Estates General.

Usefulness: Estates of the entire realm will be peaceful and friendly like those of Languedoc, Brittany, Burgundy, Provence, Artois, etc. —Regulated and uniform conduct, provided that the King does not alter it. —Deputies interested in contenting the King because of their goods and their hopes. —Deputies interested in taking care of their own region, where their goods are, while the speculators desire to destroy in order to enrich themselves. — Deputies see at first hand the nature of the land and commerce of their province.

Composition: of the bishop of each diocese; of a lord of old and high nobility, elected by the nobles; of an influential man in the Third Estate, elected by the Third Estate.

Free election: No recommendations by the King, which would become an order; no permanent deputies, though they would be eligible for reelection. No deputy will receive a preferment from the King until three years after the end of his term as deputy.

Superiority of the Estates General over those of the provinces. Correction of things done by the provincial Estates, on the basis of grievances and evidence. General inspection of the accounts of the individual Estates for funds and ordinary expenditures. Discussion about funds to be raised for extraordinary expenses. Undertaking of war against neighbors, of navigation for commerce, of correction of potential abuses.

Authority of the Estates, through representation, to assemble every three years in a fixed city, unless the King proposes another one. —To continue the deliberations, as long as they judge necessary. —To include in their deliberations all questions of justice, administration, finance, war, foreign alliances and peace negotiations, agriculture, commerce. —To examine the census made in each Board, checked by the individual Estates, and reported to the Estates General with the description of each family which is being financially ruined through its own fault, which is becoming richer through its toils, which has so much and owes so much. —To punish violent lords. —To leave no land unused, large new game parks, to fix the number of *arpents*, if untilled; abuses of captaincies in large hunting areas, because of too much wild game, hares, etc., who spoil the grain, vines, meadows, etc. —To abolish all privileges, all abusive *lettres d'état*, all those noncommercial moneychangers, except the necessary bankers.

§IV—*Church*

1. Temporal power: compulsory authority to make men live in society, in subordination, and with justice, and moral honesty. —Examples: so lived the Greeks and the Romans. Temporal authority complete in these examples, with no authority for religion.

2. Spiritual power: Definition: noncompulsory authority to teach the faith, administer the sacraments, see that the evangelical virtues are practiced, by persuasion, for eternal salvation. –Example of the early Church until Constantine, it created pastors, assembled the faithful, administered, preached, acted, corrected, excommunicated; it did all this without temporal authority. –Example of the Protestant Church in France. Example of the Catholic Church in Holland, in Turkey. –Church permitted and authorized in a country should function all the more freely there. Our kings left the Protestants in France free to elect, to depose pastors; delegates to the synods. The Grand Turk [Sultan] leaves Christians free to elect, to depose their pastors. Putting the Church in France in the same position, we would have a liberty which we do not now have to elect, depose, assemble. –The prince's protection ought to support, facilitate, not hinder and subjugate.

3. Reciprocal independence of the two powers. The temporal comes from the community of men, which is called the nation. The spiritual comes from God, through the mission of his Son and of the apostles. –The temporal is, in a sense, older: it freely received the spiritual. The spiritual, in a sense, is also older: the worship of the Creator before the institutions of human laws. –Princes cannot fulfill the pastoral functions of acting, teaching, administering the sacraments, creating pastors, excommunicating. Pastors cannot control the temporal administration. –Mutual aid: prince can punish an innovator against the Church; pastors can strengthen the prince, by exhorting subjects and excommunicating rebels. –The two powers, separated during three hundred years of persecution, united and in agreement, not fused, since peace. They should remain distinct, and mutually free in this agreement. –Prince is lay, and obedient to pastors for the spiritual, as the lowest layman, if he wishes to be Christian. Pastors are obedient to the prince for the temporal, as the lowest subjects: they must set an example. –Thus the Church can excommunicate a prince, and the prince can have the pastor executed. Each must use this right only in the direst need; but it is a true right.

4. The Church is the mother of kings. It strengthened their authority, through binding men by their conscience. It directs the people to elect kings according to God. It works to unite the kings among themselves; but it has no right to set up or to depose kings;

the Scripture does not say so; it simply notes the voluntary submission for the spiritual.

Kings protectors of canon law. Protection means neither decision nor authority over the Church. It means supporting it against its enemies and against its rebellious children. Protection is ready help to follow these decisions, never to forestall them: no judgment, no authority. –As the prince is master of the temporal, as if there were no Church, the Church is mistress of the spiritual, as if there were no prince. –The prince is only obeying in protecting decisions. Prince is only external bishop, in that he sees that the administration set up by the Church is enforced exteriorly. Whoever says simple protector of canon law says a man who never makes any canon or rules, but who has them carried out when the Church has made them. –From that it follows that the prince ought never to say in this manner: We wish, we enjoin, we order. This is only since Francis I.

5. Mixture of the two powers–mixed assemblies: councils where the princes and ambassadors were with the bishops. Special councils of Charlemagne: capitularies, rules of ecclesiastical discipline and of the secular administration. –Christianity became like a Christian republic, of which the pope was the head. Examples: the Amphictyons, the United Provinces. –Pope became sovereign, crowns [became] fiefs of the Holy See. –Bishops became the first lords, heads of the body of each nation, to elect and depose sovereigns. Examples: Pepin, [Pope] Zacharius. Example of Louis the Pious. Example of Carloman; Charlemagne. –Two different functions in these first bishop-lords, which must not be confused.

6. Royal line.

Christian and Catholic religion–less ancient than the State, freely received into the State, but older than the royal line–which received and authorized the royal line. Example: Pepin, Hugh Capet.

Remains or signs of election: kings receive the *sacre* [anointing] during their father's lifetime, until St. Louis.

The *sacre* consummated everything, because the people wanted only a Christian and Catholic king. –Contract and oath of which the formula still remains. Examples of Peter the Cruel, of John Lackland, of Emperor Henry IV, of Frederick II, of the Count of Albigensian Toulouse, of Henry IV King of France, of the Greeks in Italy in the time of Gregory II. Examples of heretics: King of Sweden; James, King of England; his grandfather, James I.

7. Rome. Center of unity, head of the divine institution for confirming brother-bishops, daily until the consummation. Must be every day in the communion of this see, principally for the faith. —Person of the Pope, by the confession of the Ultramontanes, can become heretic: then he is no longer Pope. —Osius, Bishop of Cordova, presided over Nicene Council in the Pope's name. Legates to the other councils. —Necessity of an independent center of unity for the individual princes, for the churches of the nations.

Power of Rome over the temporal—absurd and pernicious—obvious, although fallible, when it is reduced to deciding on the oath, by consultation; but deposition by no means follows. —In the interests of the individual churches to have head independent of their temporal prince. Greater independence of the spiritual, if there were no temporal to watch over. —The ecclesiastics ought to contribute to the burdens of the state out of their revenues.

8. Gallican liberties concerning the spiritual.

Rome employed an arbitrary power which troubled the order in the individual churches: expectancies, frivolous appellations, odious taxes, abusive dispensations.

We must confess that these ventures have greatly diminished. Now these ventures come from the secular power, not from Rome. King, in practice, more head than the Pope, in France: liberties as regards the Pope, servitude toward the King. —Authority of the King over the Church falling to lay judges; laymen dominate the bishops, the Third Estate dominates the chief lords. Example: *arrêt* of Agen; primateship of Lyons. —Enormous abuses of the appeal by writ of error, of royal cases, to reform. —Abuse of not putting up with the provincial councils; national [councils] dangerous. —Abuse of not letting bishops discuss everything with their head. —Abuse of wanting laymen to ask for and examine bulls concerning matters of the faith.

Schismatic maxims of the Parlement: kings and judges can be excommunicated; King names man who confers, etc. Collation is *in fructu*. —Real right of possession; chimerical claim of ownership.

Formerly the Church, under pretext of an oath between contracting parties, judged everything. Today laymen, under pretext of right of possession, judge everything.

The rule would be that the bishops of France should be sustained in their canonical functions; that the King should protect them in order to sustain himself canonically, according to their desire; that Rome should sustain them [the bishops] against the usurpations of lay power; that they should remain subordinate to their head in order to consult him unceasingly, for appeals, in order to correct them, to depose them, etc.

Abuse of the assemblies of the clergy, which [assemblies] would be useless, if the clergy were not obliged to contribute to the State. They are recent. —Impending danger of schism by the archbishops of Paris.

9. Gallican liberties concerning the temporal.

Full liberty for the purely temporal as regards the Pope, for the King and the people, even for the clergy. —Utility of the Church's being unable to alienate property without him [the Pope?].

Right of the King to reject bulls which would usurp the temporal. No right to examine those which are limited to the spiritual: to send them back to the bishops, who will perform their duties in this regard.

10. Means of achieving reform.

Reestablish free interchange between bishops and their head to consult and be authorized.

Agree with Rome over the procedure for deposing bishops. Example: former bishop of Gap.

Do nothing in general without conferring with the papal nuncio, and without having it discussed in Rome by a French cardinal.

Have elected as pope the most enlightened and most pious persons.

Distrust the overstated maxims of the Parlementarians.

Put some pious, knowing, moderate bishops into the Council, not as a formality, but for all matters.

Remember that they are all naturally the first lords and councillors of State.

Accept the Council of Trent, whose principal points have been accepted in the ordinances, with modifications for the purely temporal points.

Create an office of lay and pious magistrates, [and] good bishops with the nuncio, to settle upon the appeal by writ of error.

Bring to an end all the exemptions of chapters and monasteries which do not live by a rule.

Continue the reform or suppression of the less edifying orders. Example: Cluny, Cordeliers.

Leave to the bishops, with the exception of the simple appeal, the liberty over their procedure, to visit, correct, interdict, dismiss curés and all ecclesiastics.

Leave to the bishops the liberty to judge themselves in their courts.

Only name to the papacy, and to the cardinalate, those learned, pious men who often reside in Rome. –In the conclaves leave them entire liberty to follow their oath in the most dignified way.

Request erudite and zealous nuncios, not political and worldly ones.

Have a Council of Conscience, to choose pious and capable bishops; select them not by position but by merit. Not do it at the present time.

Plan to uproot Jansenism. Ask Rome for a decision on the relative and alternative necessity. Have the bull accepted by all the bishops. Have those who refuse deposed.

Remove the abbot doctors, private teachers, vicar generals, professors, seminary superiors. Give doctrinal rule to Oratory, Benedictines, and regular canons.

§V–*Nobility*

1. Register of the nobility made for each province after detailed research.

The state of the honors and certain proofs [of nobility] of each family, the state of all the branches of which the lineage is clear, of which it appears doubtful, which appear bastard.

Each child registered–general register in Paris–no branch recognized without registration.

Inventory by alphabetical order of the *Chambre des comptes* of Paris, of the Royal Archives, of the provincial *Chambres des comptes*, with the listing for each family of what belongs to it.

2. Education.

One hundred children of the upper nobility, pages of the King, chosen for fine bearing: studies, exercises.

Lesser nobles, or of poor branches, younger sons in the regiments. Relatives, friends of colonels, of captains.

Royal household filled with only chosen nobles, guards, light horses.

No venal military position. Nobles preferred.

Maîtres d'hôtel, ordinary gentlemen [of the King], etc., all verified nobles. –Chamberlains or gentlemen of the bedchamber, instead of valets or chamber boys for common service. All other more important positions to verified nobles.

3. Support for nobility.

Each family will have a permanently entailed estate; *majorasgo* of Spain. For families of the upper nobility, not small [entails]; less for middle nobility.

Freedom to carry on wholesale trade, without derogation.

Freedom to enter the magistracy.

Mismatching forbidden to both sexes.

Those acquiring land with noble names, with the name of still-existing noble families, forbidden to assume these names.

Ennoblement forbidden, except in the case of conspicuous services rendered to the State.

Order of the Holy Spirit only for families distinguished by their splendor, and by their origins in the forgotten past.

Order of St. Michel to honor the services of the good minor nobility.

Neither one nor the other for military men without appropriate birth.

No duchy beyond a certain number. Dukes, of high birth: favor insufficient. No duke [who] is not a peer. Fixed ceremonial. One would have to await a vacant place to obtain one. One would only be admitted in the Estates General.

Letters for marquises, counts, viscounts, barons, as for dukes.

Separate honors for military men. Various chivalric orders, with tokens of esteem for lieutenant generals, brigadier generals, colonels, etc. –Purely honorary privileges.

4. Bastardy. Dishonor it to repress vice and scandal. Take from bastard children of kings the rank of prince: they did not used to have it. Take from all the others the rank of gentleman, the name, and the coat of arms, etc.

5. Foreign princes.

Leave the long-established ranks.

Cut out everything which seems doubtful and contested.

Rule that each younger son will have honors only when the King judges him worthy.

Not easily give these families offices, governments, benefices.

They will never believe there is any sovereign other than the eldest of their family.

Bouillon, Rohan, elders [are] dukes, younger brothers, cousins, etc.

No other family, with no rank other than that of dukes.

§VI—*Justice*

1. The chancellor should watch over all tribunals and establish the jurisdictions between them.

Must know the talents and reputation of each principal magistrate of the provinces; procure advancement for each one, according to his talents, his virtues, his services; force those who do not do their work well to leave their purchased offices.

The chancellor, head of the Third Estate, ought to have a lower rank as in the past.

2. Council composed not of *maîtres des requêtes* introduced without merit for the money but of people chosen in all the tribunals of the realm; established to reform with the chancellor all inferior judges.

Councillors of State sent from time to time into the provinces to correct abuses.

3. Parlements. Gradually eliminate the *paulette*, etc. Purchased offices greatly decreased; such offices to decrease further through reform; leave for life all the upright and sufficiently instructed judges; have their worthy children succeed them gratis; allocation of honest wages from public funds; examples of advancement for those who do the best.

Few judges. —Few laws. —Laws which avoid difficulties over wills, marriage contracts, sales and exchanges, imprisonings and warrants. Few free arrangements.

Great choice of first presidents, *procureurs généraux*. Preference for nobles over commoners of equal merit, for positions of president, councillor. Magistrates [from the nobility] of the sword, and with the sword instead of the robe, when possible.

4. *Bailliages*. No presidial courts: their jurisdiction transferred to the *bailliages*. Reestablish the right of the *bailli* from [the nobility of] the sword to carry out his functions there. —Lieutenant general and criminal lieutenant, nobles if possible. —Fixed number of councillors, not based on the money one wishes to make, but

according to the real needs of the public: forty years [of age] and beyond.

No [seigniorial] justice for individual lords, nor for the King in the villages on his lands. Let them keep justice concerning property, honors of the parish, hunting rights, etc. All the rest immediately to the nearest *bailliage*.

Maintenance by lords of certain rights or their vassals for their fiefs, of guard duty and military service over their peasants.

Regulate the hunting rights between lords and vassals.

5. Office for jurisprudence.

Assemble selected jurisconsults, to correct and collect all customs, in order to shorten the procedure, to eliminate the *procureurs*, etc.

An account rendered to the chancellor by this office in the Council of State. Thorough examination to make a good Code.

6. Suppression of tribunals. No more Grand Council. No more *Cour des aides*. No more treasurers of France. No more *élus* [local tax officials].

Additions to §VI

Council of State where the King is always present. —Six other councils for all the affairs of the realm. No inheritance of purchased offices, governorships, etc.

Permit any foreigner to come to live in France, and to enjoy there all the privileges of natural and naturalized citizens, by declaring his intention before the clerk of court of the royal *bailliage*, on the basis of the certificate of life and morals which he would bring and the oath which he would take, etc. All free of charge.

§VII—*Commerce*

Freedom. Great trade in good and abundant commodities in France, or of work done by good workmen.

Commerce of silver through usury, outside the necessary banks, severely criticized. —Sort of censure to authorize gain by real trading, not gain by usury; know the means by which each becomes rich.

Deliberate in the Estates General and the individual Estates whether import and export tariffs for the realm should be abandoned.

France rather rich if she sells a lot of wheat, oil, wine, linens, etc.

What she will buy from the English and the Dutch are spices and incomparable curiosities: allow liberty.

Routine and uniform rule in order never to vex or wrangle with foreigners, in order to make it easier for them to buy at a moderate price.

Leave to the Dutch the profits from their austere frugality and work, from the danger of having few sailors on their ships, from their good public administration for joining together in commerce, from the abundance of their commercial ships.

Merchants' office, which the Estates General and the regional Estates, as well as the King's Council, consult on all general arrangements.

Sort of Mont-de-Piété [pawnshop] for those who want to trade and have no money for down payments.

Manufactures to establish, in order to do better than foreigners, without excluding their products.

Arts to make flourish, in order to sell, not to the King until he has paid his debts, but to foreigners and rich Frenchmen.

Sumptuary laws for each class. Through luxury, nobles are ruined in order to enrich merchants. Through luxury the morals of the entire nation are corrupted. This luxury is more pernicious than the profit on fashions is useful.

Pursuit of the financiers. They would no longer be needed. Some sort of censors would examine in detail their profits. Financiers would turn their efforts toward commerce.

Additions to §VII

All this controlled by the Council of Commerce and the administration of the realm, and the report of the results always taken to the Council of State where the King is present.

Moderate-sized navy, without pushing it to excess, proportionate to the needs of the State, for whom it is not proper to undertake war at sea alone against the powers which put all their strength into their navies.

Regulate captures [at sea]. —Commerce from port to port, etc.

59. *Death and the Common Virtues*

The funeral sermon in seventeenth-century France was always an occasion to edify those who came to pay their respects to the deceased; it was not a time for talking about his sins, which would be disquieting to his family. These sermons recounted his noble deeds, pious works, love, friendship, and loyalty toward others.

But what if the deceased had not been particularly pious or had never done anything noteworthy? Clergymen may have strained on many occasions to edify their parishioners about the life of the deceased, while both he and they knew that his virtues were being exaggerated. In this popular burlesque of a country sermon about a deceased bell ringer, Michel Morin is not an individual but a type. His virtues sometimes are identical with those of the village idiot. Were not the bell ringers those too old or too limited in intelligence to do anything else?

As a literary work this "eulogy" has none of the rhetorical elegance of a Bossuet sermon. Note the preacher's use—or misuse—of Latin and his contemptuous attitude toward the parishioners. The play on words is raucous and obvious enough for the barely literate to enjoy. Note the reference to the deeds of Alexander the Great. That such a subject could be found in a burlesque suggests that the subjects fashionable at court trickled down to quite low levels in the society. And what of Morin's soul? The subject may have been beyond the burlesque.

Funeral Elegy for Michel Morin: Omnis homo mortalis

We are all mortal: I made that important observation long ago, my dear brethren. We are mortal and subject to death, because we are men: *Omnis homo mortalis*. The past centuries provide us with books informing us that the Alexanders, the Caesars, these awesome men, these terrible warriors, and so many other men of distinguished rank have died: *Omnis homo mortalis*. However, all the

SOURCE: "Éloge funèbre de Michel Morin," from Robert Mandrou, *De la Culture populaire aux 17e et 18e siècles* (Paris: Stock, 1964), pp. 201–205.

reading which I have done has not touched me as much as the death of poor Michel Morin afflicts me today, as you well know.

It was yesterday that he died, yesterday Death sealed his fate; and he died in the flower of his age, and we will see him no more. Last Thursday he was in his garden, and he said to me: "Hem, hem! What do you say, isn't my appetite good?" While biting into a thick crust of bread rubbed with garlic and eating it heartily with both hands. Alas, my dear brethren, who would have believed it? Here he is dead, and we will see him no more; we have all suffered a great loss, for he alone rang the church bell, cut up the blessed bread, went to take up the offering, and sang at the music lectern; he alone chased dogs out of the church, in a word he was the *Omnis homo* of our village. Ha! Ha! Yes, laugh, poor idiots that you are, you who know no Latin; for if you had studied in school, you would know that *Omnis homo* means a jack-of-all-trades [*homme à tout faire*]; but because you are ignorant, you believe that Michel Morin was a fool, since he wore a reddish shirt and white stockings; see the consequences of what you say! If you were to see me when I get up in a nightcap and drawers, you would therefore say that I have no wit: clothes do not make the man. . . . If Michel Morin had been a gentleman of the sword, they would have written of his actions in big letters in the gazettes, but because he was a villager, dressed as a peasant, nothing that he did was noticed; however, no one has ever seen anything more admirable in history books. Pay attention to this.

One day the son and the son-in-law of big Colas were fighting in the garden over some plums, and these two boys were pulling out their hair and socking each other; Michel Morin noticed; at once, with a determined air he jumped over the hedge, zip, he took both of them by the pigtail, socked one, kicked the other, piff, paff, separated them, threw their hats into the street, and no one spoke of the matter again. That shows how charitable Michel Morin was toward his neighbor; for without him they would still be fighting, and you would not stop them, poor folk that you are! If I were telling you here fables or stories of the past, you would say: he is pulling our leg, these are tall tales; but I am speaking to you of our own time. For example, what stronger thing could one see but to watch Michel Morin mow a meadow? As soon as he took off his doublet, he took his scythe in both hands and mowed all about him, and frist and frest, in one breath all the way to the end of the meadow; and without wasting time he took his whetstone hung at his side in a case, and zist and zest; then he spit into his hands and, head down, he began again; you would have said that he was going to cut down everything; that is why they called him the great oak cutter. He was the terror of the forests; with a pruning knife, frist, frest, he cut off entire branches; no one has ever seen such a worker; crick, crack, in two twinklings, there is a faggot of sticks tied up, and what faggots! Conscientious faggots! The faggots of Michel Morin were good faggots; they were not those faggots stuffed with leaves which the merchants sell; his faggots were well-faggoted faggots, the best faggoted of all the faggoters of faggots. What more marvelous thing can be seen! Is there a man on the earth who resembles Michel Morin? No, there is not his equal in the air; this is what I will show you, for I shall never tire of saying that he is a veritable *Omnis homo*.

Michel Morin was admirable in the air: I remember on this point (some of you were there), it will be two years on Sunday, while the preaching was going on, ha! Do you remember, when the birds were making their nests in the vault of the church? They were making such a great racket that you couldn't hear the sermon; you all stood there watching these animals, your arms crossed and like statues, and you did not dare to chase them away. There was only Michel Morin, the *Omnis homo*, who, by his cunning and courage, found the means to make them leave; and here is how he went about it: he went out of the choir, opened the church door, took the pole used for removing spiders, climbed up on a bench, and ho and hum, and gee and haw, and you'll get it, and you'll go, and so you'll not go: he did like that from one end of the church to the other, and chased away all the birds and fledglings, tipped over their nests, so that not a frick nor a frack remained. Well, now! Without Michel Morin where would we be? By Our Lady, he did not go about it roughly, he was a noble champion; that is why you should profit from his good deeds.

But let us speak more seriously. Michel Morin, with his handsome looks and his commanding appearance, dressed in his Sunday clothes, resembled the *procureur fiscal* of the parish. That is not all, he was also a great carillonneur. Everyone, on feast days, came to hear him ring the bells; you have heard him yourselves: he made our bells say anything he wanted, you would have said they were speaking; however, he had not studied music, and his poor mother used to say: "It's a shame that he hadn't gone to school, for he would have passed in the sciences, if he had had the chance." But now, to return to our bells, he rang very nicely; he held the bells with his feet, with his hands, and he threw himself about like a madman: ding, dong, ding, dong, tra-la, tra-la, a drink for Michel Morin. How marvelous you are! the great *Omnis homo*, the great jack-of-all-trades!

He had a steadfastness which was completely heroic; it is this which made a learned man, who was passing through here, say that in extreme necessity he would have spoken to the king; and indeed he was not a fool, like you; he sold his merchandise like a marvel; he knew the plainsong like an oracle, he deciphered an antiphon better than anyone, and wore the cope like a bishop, for he had good bearing and looked grand when marching, plick, plack; he had only wooden shoes; this was not through vanity, since his father-in-law was a shoemaker. He had a voice so terrible and beautiful that when he began to sing all the dogs fled from the church. If I did not fear slander, I would believe that he was the son of some gentleman; but I suspect that at least he had been exchanged by the wet nurse, since he was born for such noble actions, as you will see.

One day he took a gun on his shoulder to go hunting: when he was at the end of Jean Michaud's hedge, he aimed at a hare: puff, he killed it, he jumped the jump and took it, carried it off, larded it, put it on a spit, cooked it, put it on a platter, served it at table, and ate it! Oh, the excellent man! Oh, the good eater! The admirable *Omnis homo!* Would one find his equal? No, for he was fur and feather. You have seen him without equal on the earth and in the air: he was even worse in the water; he was intrepid everywhere, as you will see.

Michel Morin, my faithful friend, had long zealously done me service to the supreme degree. Seeing one day four of my friends who were coming to eat my soup, I think that it was the evening before or two evenings before a feast day or a Sunday; but no matter, it is enough that it was a fasting day and that I had nothing to treat them to; as soon as he learned of my trouble, he stripped himself naked and threw himself headlong into the river; we thought he had been drowned; not at all, in a moment he returned to the bank swimming, with some big fish as long as from here to tomorrow. "Well," he said in his laughing manner, "what do you say about that?" By Our Lady! The fact is that the king's men are not fools: and without wasting time he rolled his sleeves up to the elbow, and his coattails up to his jerkin, then he pulled his knife from his pocket, spit upon it, sharpened it on a cobblestone, and frist, frest, he gutted a fat pike, made us a fish stew with such a good sauce that they licked their four fingers and their thumbs. Oh, what an excellent cook was Michel Morin! I shall never tire of telling you that he was an excellent *Omnis homo*.

I finish with the last and beautiful action of his life, which surely proves his big heart, his cleverness, and his selflessness: the poor man wagered that he could unnest the magpies in the big elm; he climbed up to his misfortune without a ladder; when he was at the top of the tree, he cried out: "I've won," and turned his head, showing the nest; but the branch broke, crick, crack, arms and legs lost hold, and his heart was smashed into his belly. Ha! for a pint, Michel Morin, how cheaply you died! It is true that he was selfless, for he would have run a league for a gallon of wine; besides, not vainglorious, he would drink with the first comer to pay for his pint.

Let us weep, let us thus weep over the death of Michel Morin, because of the loss we have suffered: let us not forget the fine deeds which he did in his life; for example, his great zeal for the public good, in chasing the cows from the cemetery, in separating the people who were fighting over plums; his good faith in making up faggots, his skill in mowing meadows, his industry in chasing birds from the church, his supernatural talent for hunting; his dauntlessness in fishing; his skill in making sauces: what am I saying? I am forgetting his natural instinct for bell ringing! for in two strides he would quickly climb to the bell tower. That is why I exhort you to instruct your children in the marvels of Michel Morin; lullaby them with the fine things you have just heard, put them to sleep with the songs he used to make our bells sing, for he was a great man in his poverty.

60. Education and the State

Jean Racine's brilliant account of the rise and travails of the Jansenist monastery of Port Royal explains the origin of the crucial Jesuit opposition to the Jansenists as resulting from the "little schools" which the latter founded in 1638. At first glance Racine's contention would seem absurd. How could such a seemingly minor matter as founding a school become the basis for the famous and intense quarrel between the Jansenists and the Jesuits?

Two religious movements both fanatically elitist and zealous for God, the Jesuits and the Jansenists placed great emphasis on the education of children. Control of the education of robe and genteel sons, the future members of the Parlement and the royal household, was considered one of the principal methods of combating heresy and of carrying out long-range reform in the Church. The commitment of the Society of Jesus to teaching had been one of the most important reasons for its rapid growth throughout Europe. Indeed, by 1638 the Jesuits already had schools in most of the cultural and political centers of France. Though never total, Jesuit control and influence over French education remained enormous from the later sixteenth century until the Order's expulsion from France in the mid-eighteenth century.

The "little schools" had boasted some of the most erudite men in France as teachers; and some of the graduates, including Racine himself, would be even more illustrious. Once the pedagogical principles had been established, Walon de Beaupuis (1621–1709) was selected as first headmaster for the school, while Pascal's sister Jacqueline became headmistress for the girls' school.

Walon's brother, a former pupil in a "little school," left this account of daily life before the dispersal of all Jansenist schools was ordered by the Crown in 1660. Within Walon's text are hints about the principles and conduct of the Jansenist schools which he thought made them different from the other schools of his day. A number of leading thinkers wrote texts for the boys, and some dukes and high robe officials enrolled their sons. Hence the "little schools" did represent a challenge to the Jesuits in a highly elitist society in which the social status of a pupil rather than his intelligence added prestige to the general cause of either side. The Crown's decision to favor the Jesuits may well have

SOURCE: Charles Wallon de Beaupuis, quoted in Nicolas Fontaine, *Mémoires pour servir à l'Histoire de Port Royal* (Cologne, 1738), I, cxix–cxxiii.

come for more important reasons than the threat posed by the "little schools," but the history of seventeenth-century education suggests that their role was of great significance not only to intellectual and cultural life but also to political and bureaucratic developments.

These schools [le Chesnay, les Trous, and the *granges* of Port Royal] were organized in the same manner. There was a master in each bedchamber with five or six children. The beds were arranged in such a manner that the master saw them all from his own. Each had his separate table, and they were arranged so that the master could seen them all, but [the children] could not talk to one another. Each had his own drawer, his desk, and the necessary books, so that they were not obliged to borrow anything from their companions. The number of boarders was not very great, because a master was assigned only as many as there were beds in his room.

They rose at half past five and dressed themselves. Those who were too small were helped by a valet. Common prayers were said in the room, and then each one studied his lesson for the morning, which was prose. At seven o'clock each recited it to the master one after the other. Next they breakfasted, and in winter warmed themselves. After breakfast, they went back to their worktables. Each child did his translation [into French], which they were advised to write out carefully. Translations completed, they read them to the master one after the other. If time remained, they were made to comment upon [*expliquer*] the next portion of their author which they had not prepared. At eleven o'clock they went to the refectory, and one of those who had been confirmed recited a versicle of the New Testament in Latin. The children from each individual room ate at the same table with their master, who was careful to serve them their food and even their drink. During the meal someone read aloud. Upon leaving the refectory, they went out to play in the garden in all weather, except when it was stormy or after dark. Since the garden was very spacious and full of woods and meadows, it was forbidden to leave a marked area without permission. The masters strolled in the same place without ever losing sight of their children.

At one o'clock they went into a common room until two. There the children learned geography one day and history another. At two o'clock they went back up to their rooms to study poetry, which they recited to the master at four o'clock, after which they snacked. Then they studied Greek in the same fashion as the other lessons, and they recited.

Toward six o'clock they supped. Everything went as at dinner. The recreation period which followed this meal lasted until eight o'clock, when the children went up to their rooms to study their lesson for the following day. At half past they said prayers together. All the children of the different rooms, the *Messieurs*,* and the servants attended. After [prayers] were finished, each returned to his room to go to bed. The master of each room was present; thus he went to bed last and rose first.

Sundays at eight o'clock, the superior conducted the catechism combined with a lesson. Then they went to the parish Mass. Upon their return, if time remained it was spent in pious readings. After dinner, which was conducted as usual, they had recreation which lasted until two o'clock, when they went back into their rooms to do some reading, either in common or alone. They went to vespers in the parish church.

They were free only in the afternoon. They spent this time playing in the garden or sometimes walking to neighboring houses.

Since these schools were more for piety than for knowledge, they did not pressure the children so much in their studies, in which they were, however, given solid principles. This is what produced the fine Greek and Latin manuals and some other works which might have been followed by others. In the manner of instructing them in their subjects, reason rather than custom was followed. Thus they were made to translate [into French] several fine Latin authors, before being made to write in that language and translate [into Latin]. For how does one expect a child to write in a language which he does not know, and for which he has only learned the rules? Instead the reading of good authors enables them to write a composition next, and to use the expressions of the authors they have studied.

Such was the plan followed at the schools of Port Royal. There they showed more concern for the soul than for the body. Chastisements were very rare there. A single look from the master made a greater impression than severe treatment would have done, which would have turned the children against the masters rather than

* The *Messieurs* of Port Royal were resident laymen who frequently served as masters.

have really corrected [their behavior]. If someone was observed to be a truly bad example for the others, he was sent away, with no reason being strong enough to let him remain. They were all dressed alike, so that there would be no jealousy among them, if some had been better dressed than others. They were taught to write letters well, according to the various occasions which presented themselves. They were made to exercise their bodies during recreation periods, either by running or by games of skill; but at the same time care was taken to keep them within bounds so that they would not become upset. When they could not go out to play in the garden, there were in one room billiards, chess, and checkers. There were also games to teach them history, either ecclesiastic or profane.

Through such an education, excellent persons could have been molded, either for the Church or for the State. . . . These schools did not last long, as we have already noted.

VI

The Last Agony of Making Peace

Ever since the 1660's Louis XIV and his ministers, generals, and diplomats had been preoccupied one way or another by the problem of the Spanish succession. For Louis, lack of heirs was something that God alone could do something about, and failing that divine decision, his pride as a Bourbon, son of a Spanish Hapsburg and husband of another, would lead him to fight for everything he considered to be his inheritance. Alliances, wars, and treaties had been made decade after decade, always with the problem of the Spanish succession in mind.

When Charles II of Spain finally died in 1700, Louis faced the impossible choice between accepting the dead Spanish King's will, granting his grandson the Spanish empire, or respecting a partition treaty which had been worked out with William III of England and the Netherlands. A European—indeed, a world—war was probably inevitable one way or the other, since the German Hapsburgs would accept neither the terms of Charles' will nor those of the partition treaty. But war against only the subjects of Leopold I (1658–1705), "Holy Roman Emperor, King of Bohemia, Hungary, etc.," would not have involved a major struggle. Only the renewal of the coalition of England, the Netherlands, and the German Hapsburg state would bring about a general conflict.

Louis helped provoke the renewal of the coalition by again recognizing a Stuart pretender after James II's death; and the haughtiness of the French King toward the Dutch also contributed to a growing war fever among William III's subjects. The war which followed became the bloodiest and costliest that Louis and Europe would fight. The staggering defeats inflicted on the French at Blenheim, Ramillies, and Oudenarde left the Allied armies under Marlborough and Eugene of Savory masters of all non-French and non-Spanish territory. The French no longer were capable of delivering a blow in the home territories of their enemies.

The result was a brief flurry of peace negotiations. The Dutch were feeling especially cocky and made extremely steep demands for a settlement, which the French rejected. Louis considered the defeat of his armies a punishment from God, but this in no way meant that he would give up. The French monarchy had undergone terrible tests before, including an extensive civil war, when peace terms favorable to France could not be had. Another round of terrible fighting had to occur before the belligerents would make peace.

The collapse of France's ability to fight beyond her borders in no way meant that she was defeated, as Marlborough and Eugene discovered to their surprise and chagrin. Under Vauban's direction the French had built a line of immense fortresses on the northern border; these would have to be taken before a march to Paris would have any hope of success. Then, too, up to this point in his long career in warmaking, Louis had largely been able to conduct an offensive war. He had never encountered the level of opposition which had developed in the 1640's against Mazarin; and this time, in 1709–1710, he once again made a very successful appeal for his subjects' support. It is doubtful if Louis himself, or his foreign minister Colbert de Torcy, realized how much support would be forthcoming when the kingdom was faced with invasion. Poor harvests, high taxes, and high casualties notwithstanding, the French sent out a ragged but disciplined and loyal army under Villars in 1709.

The Battle of Malplaquet was neither a victory nor a defeat for either side, but it did end all English and Dutch hopes for an invasion of France. News of the thousands of casualties from Malplaquet reached London and Amsterdam to strengthen the peace parties in both cities. In London, the peace party finally gained the upper hand as Godolphin and Marlborough himself lost favor with Queen Anne.

Every European capital had a bevy of minor and would-be diplomats, each with his special contacts. These men had talked and talked for years, but until there was some basis for peace their role remained insignificant. The Dutch proved intractable, but Queen Anne's new ministers, Harley and St. John, slowly and carefully sounded out the intentions of Versailles. Louis had been anxious for peace for years, but he could not concede to the demands made by the Dutch and the English before Harley and St. John had made concessions. The negotiations of the general peace of Utrecht, signed on March 31, 1713, lasted about two years after Matthew Prior's crucial visit to Versailles. Only one small aspect of these negotiations can be presented by documents here.

61. Matthew Prior's Negotiations in France

By the time the English ministers had decided to send the poet Matthew Prior (1664–1721) to Versailles with the feeblest possible instructions, weeks and months of secret conversations had already transpired. When Prior arrived, Torcy hoped that he would at last be able to deal in specific terms with the English and work out a settlement. But all Prior was supposed to do was "communicate our preliminary demands, according to Queen Anne, and to bring us back an answer." Despite Torcy's disappointment, serious talk got under way, as Prior's account of his trip proves.

The audience with the King is remarkable because, like a good ambassador, Prior put down exactly what the King said to him. Note Louis' cutting phrase, "*ceux qui gouvernent l'Angleterre*" (those who govern England), and Prior's quick retort by referring to "*Sa Majesté la Reine de la Grande Bretagne*" in the first line of his reply. French recognition of Anne as Queen would come later, especially in a touching, ceremonial way. When Anne died, the old King was seen wearing mourning bands, a sign that he recognized her at last as a sovereign.

1711, July 12–23, N.S.—M. Torci had upon his table three letters which he had received from Petkum, these he read to me, two of them were in cipher, the third a very long one in plain characters, received that very night; the substance of them was to desire that the King of France would be pleased to renew the negotiation with Holland, that he was sure the [Dutch] States were in great want of a peace, and were ready to send half way to Paris if they could hope France would treat with them, that he was sure His Christian Majesty [Louis] might have better terms from them than from

SOURCE: Great Britain, Historical Manuscripts Commission, *Report on the Mss of His Grace the Duke of Portland* (London, 1899), V, 34–41. This text was supplied by Professor Joseph Klaits of Oakland University.

England. M. Torci likewise showed me the answer he had given to the second of these letters, which was really very great, not to say a little fierce; expressing his master's resentment of the usage he had received from Holland, and his resolution of not entering again into any particular manner of treating with the States. Petkum's third letter which as I said was received but that afternoon was more pressing than either of the two former, and its being writ at length without cipher showed plain enough that the writer did not fear that it should be opened; from whence it is evident that it was writ by the knowledge and order of the government in Holland. It began with his great sorrow that there was still so unhappy an aversion on this side to the treating with Holland; that he hoped it diminished, and would be overcome; that the Dutch desired more than ever to renew the conferences, and were ready to give the French whatever terms of peace they could ask. He begged M. Torci to believe that he acted for his service, and was sure it was for the interest of France to close with the Dutch proposal, that this was the time in which they might have what peace they pleased, and repeated again that the States were ready to come half way to Paris in case he might have the happiness to tell them that France would treat with them; that we, the English, would deceive them; that the Whigs indeed would act in concert with the Dutch, but that the Tories were privately concerting measures with the Imperialists, and were resolved to continue the war. At this passage I could not forbear laughing, and said that if M. Petkum was no better apprized of the inclinations of the States towards a peace than he was of desires of the English towards the prolonging the war, I thought his advice would not weigh much with M. Torci. I said this would make a good pasquinade in England, as we had already two or three in the name of M. Petkum. "I show you these letters," said M. Torci, "that you may see the plainness and openness with which His Majesty will treat with England, if the propositions you bring leave any possibility for it;" I said I was very sensible of the manner and kindness with which he treated me, and was sure I might thank him in Her Majesty's name upon that account. After this M. Torci began, by asking me seriously if I had not another memoir to give him, for that he would be desirous to see something that could possibly be complied with. I answered that I hoped he, with a serious air, rallied me, and I laughing was serious when I said I had no other memoir, nor the power to recede one iota from any point in this. "*La paix ne se fera pas donc, Monsier; tenez, dit-il, lisez vous-même vos demandes préliminaires.*" I did so, and returning him the paper, I said I had obeyed his orders, and hoped he was going to fill the other side of the paper with such answers as I could carry back. "*Monsieur Prior, dit-il, vous avez été dans le commerce, réfléchessez* [réfléchissez] *un peu sur ce memoire;*" so beginning at "*Pour la* Great Britain *plus particulièrement*," he said that we asked no less than to be master of the Mediterranean and Spain, to possess ourselves of all the Indies, and to take away from France all that appertains to that crown in America. I answered that as I had all the reason in the world to think that France designed to act as his (Torci's) own letters had expressed *sincèrement et de bonne foi*, it was in the same intention that the four persons most concerned in the Ministry whom I named, my Lord Treasurer, the Duke of Shrewsbury, the Secretary, and the Earl of —— [sic], whom I said I hoped was by this time likewise in the Ministry, all of them and Her Majesty herself desirous of a peace had agreed upon these propositions, founded upon his letter, which was the ground of our present negotiation; that our trade in the Mediterranean was not sufficiently assured without Gibraltar and Port Mahon, which, to make use of his own argument, we ought to have, being already possessed of them, as much as K[ing] P[hilip] should have Spain; and upon the same foot that the like might be said as to what we possess or have taken in North America from France, except we should hereafter come to some equivalent; and that, as to our being possessed of some places in the Spanish West Indies, France might make such exception as to those places that Spain would have little reason to fear from our settlements, which were to secure us from pirates and robbers, particularly in the South sea, who I said, for the honour of my own nation, were most Englishmen, and some French, particularly Dunkirkers, which by the way was a new argument for our insisting upon the demolition of that nest of pirates, whom France, as it was always a generous nation, hated as much as we, and from whom they sometimes suffered as much as we in those remote parts of the world; and that the Spaniards themselves would thank us for protecting them from the violence of these buccaneers, which would be an advantage to them, though to be sure we meant it for the security of our own factories. "You will never make Spain believe," said he, "that it is for their advantage to take away their country;" that we should soon fortify any place that should be given us even those which we desired to have assigned to us for our Assiento trade, in case that demand could be complied with, that it was a constant rule of Spain, not to let in any other nation amongst them in America; so that he was assured, and told me plainly that this article was impossible to be granted. Here my heart ached extremely and I was ready to sink, but recollecting myself, I thought it time to say that if this was to continue a maxim, I was very sorry that my coming hither was of no effect, and that I looked upon myself as very unhappy, while I told him with the same plainness, *ouverture de cœur*, that he used to me, that it was impossible the peace should be made upon any other condition.

"*Voici encore une autre impossibilité*," says he, and reading the next article "*la terre neuve*," &c., he observed that we intended to be masters of all that belonged to France, and would keep it, and desired them to give us whatever they were masters of; he asked the equity and reason of this. "Now," says he, "say whatever you please for Newfoundland, we can say the same and more; it is the nursery of our seamen, our fishers are obliged, as yours are, to take young men to perform that voyage, who at their return are en-registered at St. Malo, Brest, and other ports on the west side of France, and for the fish we have more need of it than you, for we are indispensably obliged to consume it ourselves, while you for the greatest part propose to yourselves only the profit of selling it to others." As I saw him very intent upon this, and knew that some temperament might be found in the negotiation upon this head from our being already possessed of Port Royal, and consequently of Acadie, and possibly of some part of Canada, and knowing likewise that it is not of so great consequence to us, provided we remain possessed of their part of Newfoundland, I did not say any more to this article than that all Hudson's Bay was originally ours, that the name spoke it, that Hudson, in the year 1610, sailed through and possessed himself of that bay, that the names of all the banks and towns even in the French maps have always been and are now English, and as to Newfoundland, the words *terre neuve* is but the interpretation of the English name, and even before that name was given to the place it was found by Sebastian Cabot, possessed by the English in the time of our Henry the Eighth, and known by the name of Avelon.

As we went thus through the articles, M. Torci still took some little notes upon each, and returning again to the barrier for Holland, he said, "At least I have endeavoured to please you in this," and took up the paper and read it. I told him I thought it very ample and well, and such as I believed we were very well satisfied with, as I hoped the Dutch would be in the execution of it. "I wish," said he, "I could satisfy you as well upon all your demands." I said I did not doubt but that he would, and in that hope would attend his further orders. "*Agitez* [agissez] *à cette heure, dit il, avec moi en ami, et dites ce qui vous contentera.*" I told him I had really done so, and showed him again the letter with which the Queen had honoured me, assuring him I had no further power, but to report the answer which His Most Christian Majesty should be pleased to make, which, to be sure, I had all the reason in the world to wish would be favourable, and such as I might carry back with satisfaction, the peace of my country, the desire of my queen, and possibly my own fortune by it. He said he could answer me as I answered him, that he was only the "*rapporteur de ces propositions,*" that he had laid them before His Majesty, who, he could already say, could not agree to them, and was commanded to lay them before him again in a more particular manner, which he would do the next day. I took this occasion to tell him that at the same time I had a particular favour to beg of him, which was that he would let His Majesty know that, as far as a private person might with manners express himself to so great a prince, I had an entire pleasure in finding His Majesty in so good health. I always retained the greatest veneration for his person, and remembrance of his favours whilst I was in France, and I hoped His Majesty would contribute whatever he could towards the perfecting that peace which would make him a friend to my queen and to my country.

July 14–25, nine at night. Monsieur Torci desired to speak with me in his lodgings. I was there about a quarter of an hour before he came. He asked my excuse for having made me stay so long, for that the King had kept him; and after a little discourse of the palace, gardens, &c., he began in a serious manner, and a discourse which I thought particular and premeditated. That as he had promised he would do, he had laid the proposals before His Majesty, and that His Majesty's sentiments of them were that they were such as could not possibly be complied with, though the King had the greatest mind to make a peace, for, said he, you ask no less than to be masters of Europe and America; Gibraltar and Port Mahon give you the domination of Spain and of France in the Mediterranean. Your maritime force is such as renders all the commerce to the two crowns, even the possession of Spain, precarious, but your demands in the Indies are such as the Crown of Spain, by all the laws, maxims, and interests of that kingdom, can never consent to, and which the Dutch themselves were as averse to as France or Spain could be; and for the rest, said he, you ask in America all that which [with] our sweat and our blood we have been endeavouring for a hundred years past to acquire. Notwithstanding all this, said he, the King will not send you back with an absolute refusal, but has ordered his council, and to that council has added those persons who are most versed in the mercantile affairs to consider of and report their opinion upon the proposals which you bring: These persons will as soon as it is possible come hither, the council will be ready to confer with them, and I shall be able in six or eight days to give you His Majesty's answer. In the meantime since it is a thing of so great consequence, I hope your stay will not be thought long, nor the delay I ask, affected, for the King desires a peace, but to obtain it he cannot give up France and Spain.

I said that I thought it very reasonable that the proposals should be justly weighed and examined; that we should be better satisfied with an answer to them taken up [with] mature deliberation than if it had been given immediately and in haste, that I was very far from being weary of staying here, since Her Majesty's order had not confined me in point of time, and I met with all the civility here which I could expect. As for that, said he, you know very well it is the circumstance of the time in which you come and the manner of your coming that hinders us from showing you how welcome you are. I said first that I presumed he always kept to what he had been pleased to declare to me at first, that His Majesty had full and complete power to treat for Spain, so that I was not to attend any other answer than such as should be made by France, and immediately from His Majesty's council here. He answered they were those who understood the marine and mercantile affairs, they were now at Paris, and he had already writ for them to come hither, that they would here confer with Mr. Desmaretz, and from their report His Majesty would form in relation to Spain an answer to the proposals, or rather return such a plan as a just and reasonable peace might be founded on.

I said that, with all due deference to what he had said *en ministre et pour la France*, I could not but hope that His Majesty and his council were too *éclaircis* to think that what we demanded from them took anything in reality from France or Spain; that as to the assurance of our commerce in the Mediterranean we asked no more than what was already assigned us by Monsieur de T[orci's] letter, for that gave us Gibraltar, and we were now actually possessed of Port Mahon, that as his letter, by "*sureté réelle pour notre commerce,*" understood the actual possession of some places, so the "*sureté réelle pour notre commerce aux Indes*" must have the same interpretation, and that we must, consequently, have the actual possession of some places in those parts; and, said he, do not we know what you are doing? Have you not put all the money in England upon that chance, and do you not intend to do in the West Indies as you have done in the East, to possess yourselves of the places to fortify them, and to make yourselves masters of the whole trade of the world. I said that, as I had told him before, we most certainly propose to ourselves some advantage in making the peace, in order to recompense us for the prodigious expense we had been at in continuing the war, and that though the present course of trade made us direct our view to the West Indies, yet our designs in that behalf were such as could not give the French, much less the Spanish, occasion to suspect that we should any way become masters in those parts; that four places in so great a tract of land were so few that the number itself was an answer to the objection, and that, as I had before said, the desire of our possessing these places was rather to defend ourselves in those remote parts of the world against robbers and pirates, than to annoy the Spanish, to whom, in matters of trade, we should rather be a help and assistance. Sir, I added, I see nothing in this demand that concerns France, nor that forbids France obtaining some collateral advantage of the same kind from Spain, but that is no way my affair. France may have other politics and other views. We are a trading nation, and as such must secure our traffic; Her Majesty and her ministry judge it absolutely necessary that this branch of our trade be secured.

1711, Sunday, July 16–27, nine at night, in the gardens of Fontainebleau—M. Torci desired to meet me. Gautier was with us. It was dark enough to conceal who we were. He had sent me the printed news which came in the day before from Holland and

Flanders, and after some common discourse, he asked me if I had read the Dutch gazettes; and, said he, your South Sea Company makes a great deal of work. The Dutch are extremely surprised at it. I said it was time we should look a little to our own interest, who ever were surprised at it, and I hoped we should have a peace, and see the good effcts which that company would have, which, if it were advantageous to us, would not be disadvantageous to France, and to Europe in general it would cause a more equal distribution of traffic. You will never convince us of that, said he. I said I hoped that in the answer I should receive upon that article, as upon all the rest which I had the honour to give him, I should find that France thought our proposal reasonable, and I did not question but that he gave his assistance to render those answers as favourable as he could. We are all at work for you, he said, the answers will be ready before the end of the week, but I doubt if they can possibly come up to your demands, if you do not ask to ruin Spain, "*abîmer l'Espagne*," and to engross all the traffic of the world to yourselves. We are dressing such a plan as cannot but be thought reasonable and equitable, "*mais pour les places, Monsieur, vous croyez qu'il ne s'accordera jamais.*" I said I looked upon that as the only base and foundation of a negotiation upon which a peace could be had, that in a tract of land of above seven hundred leagues it was impossible that four places should annoy the Spanish, as it was impossible we could have any advantage in matter of trade without having some communication and places proper to receive and disperse our goods; and that I had already explained myself very fully upon that head; that for what the Dutch gazettes said, France was too wise to mind it. Everybody printed what had been heard in the next coffee house, and the paragraphs from England were generally supplied by the French refugees at London, so I passed off that discourse as well as I could. Our negotiants here, said he, are terribly alarmed at your company. I answered that I neither saw any reason why they should be alarmed, since it would make the whole commerce of Europe circulate, nor did I see what we asked hindered France any way from making what bargain they could with Spain. Upon this he said, people thought Philip's being King of Spain was of great advantage to France, but he could assure "*foi d'honnête homme*" that France was no way upon a better foot with that kingdom than it was in the time of King Charles the Second; but, on the contrary, the Spaniards were most jealous of the French since a prince of the house of Bourbon [was placed] upon the throne.

1711, July 19–30, Wednesday, nine at night, at Monsieur de Torci's lodging—We sat, and he began in the same grave and concerted manner as he had done the Friday before, that the King's Council had been revolving and considering our proposals, but that the more they laboured the more difficulties they still found; that the King was so desirous of a peace and so resolved to show that he acted seriously and honourably with us; that though he could not submit, as he expressed it, to some terrible articles in the memorial I had given him, he was resolved to send us a plan as reasonable and as extensive as he could, and till he had our answer he would no way hearken to the offers which were every day made him from the other side, though they were certainly more easy and advantageous to him. I did not offer to put in the least word till he at last desired me to answer. I said I asked his pardon if I did not well understand what he meant by a plan; that the ministry in England looked upon that memorial which I had the honour to give him as a plan, and that my orders were to receive the answer which he should think good to make to those heads. He said that should be done, but it was impossible any accommodation could be made, since I had no power to recede from those articles, except somebody that had a full power from France of explaining the King's intentions and of agreeing with us in England upon them, or of breaking off the negotiation in case he did not agree, should go over to England with me and the answer they should make to our memorial; and he said that the King and he himself asked my advice in this matter, for if you are for a peace we must not lose time in this matter, it will be too long till you or somebody else returns with your answer, a want of power on each side will still be alleged, the campaign will draw to an end, we shall be providing subsidies for another year, the present disposition we are in may be changed, and we shall be obliged to endeavour at a peace where we can get it cheapest, or to continue a war which, God be thanked, we can yet do.

I said we knew the state of the French nation very well, and we had a great deal of reason to be acquainted with that of our neighbour the Dutch, that I would not question but that the answer I should in a day or two receive from him would be such as a peace might be built upon, and that whoever went to England with me would have little left to explain there, that I could only answer that the person should be received with the same kindness and hospitality which I had found in France, and the only thing that would make that person truly welcome to our ministers at London would be, their seeing that my voyage hither had not been useless. He said again the person whom the King would send should be fully instructed and empowered, and that I should have an answer in a day or two. He showed me in this conference another letter written from Petkum to the President de Rouille, in which Petkum again says that this is the time for France to have what conditions they can desire from Holland towards making a peace glorious for this nation, that Count Galas had assured the Pensionary that all sort of negotiation between France and England was broken off. Petkum desires again to be believed in this point, and asks a passport for his own coming to Paris, where he does not doubt but that he may bring about a peace between France and Holland.

1711, July 21–August 1. Friday, nine at night—Monsieur de Torci gave me the answer to the memorial I brought hither, I read it over with him, and upon it I observed, that it was only an answer to the former part of my memorial, as to what related to the allies in general, but that there was not a word in answer to what concerned Great Britain in particular. He answered that all that matter must be settled and agreed in England, that as he had said before the gentleman whom the King had named to go back with me, was fully instructed and apprized of His Majesty's mind upon those heads, that he wished it could be adjusted here, but since I had no power to recede from those positive demands which the King could not agree to, there were but two things remaining; one to break off the negotiation, which he said His Majesty and he hoped we were unwilling to do, the other to try, if there were a possibility of accommodating in what we desired as to our trade; that this gentleman, whom he named Monsieur de Mesnager, would be at Fontainebleau on Monday, to receive those orders which His Majesty had resolved on. I read the answer again to him, and "have you not heard," said Monsieur de Torci, "how the Duke of Marlborough asked *Le Terre Neuve au nom de Dieu, faites la grace à la reine ma maîtresse de lui rendre la terre neuve, il me semble que vous la demandiez d'une toute autre manière.*" I said that this way of speaking was according to the Duke's way, easy and familiar, that it was true I did not ask it *au nom de Dieu pour la reine ma maîtresse, mais au nom de la reine ma maîtresse pour la grande Bretagne;* that the Duke was a great general and unacquainted with the particular ways of treaty, provided the thing had its desired effect, the manner was some times neglected; that there was some time a small omission in some former treaties, particularly in that we call the Barrier treaty, where care was taken for the Dutch in matter of commerce upon the tariff 1664, while it was only specified for England "*on tâchera de faire un traité de commerce pour l'Angleterre,*" and this I hope will be redressed as it is mentioned in the memoir I had the honour to bring him; that in what I asked I should always endeavour to preserve the dignity of the crown of Great Britain and preserve the respect due to the minister of France with whom I then spoke.

Audience.

1711, July 24–August 3, N.S.–Monsieur Torci having the day before delivered to me the answer to the memoir, and M. Mesnager being now appointed, and empowered to go with me into England, M. Pecquet came to me in the morning and told me, the King would see me at six in the evening in his closet. Accordingly at that time M. Pecquet went privately with me through the lodgings, and Monsieur Torci came out from the King's cabinet, and introduced me to His Majesty. The King was walking, he stood still when I came in, and as I made my obeisance to him he nodded a little, bowed to me at my third bow, and sitting or leaning his back rather upon a table behind him, as I came up to him, he began, "*A ça, Monsieur, Je suis bien aise de vous voir, vous parlez Français je sçay.*" [Well, now, Sir, I am very glad to see you. You speak French, I know.]

I: "*Sire, pour pouvoir exprimer la joie que je sens de revoir votre Majesté dans une santé si parfaite, je devais mieux parler Français qu'aucun de vos sujets.*" [Sire, in order to express the joy I feel on seeing Your Majesty again and in such perfect health, I would have to be able to speak French better than any of your subjects.]

He: "*Eh bien, Monsieur, c'est bien honnête, vous savez la réponse que j'ai donné[e] à votre mémoire, et vous savez la volonté où je suis de convenir et de traiter avec l'Angleterre. J'y envoye un ministre avec vous, qui s'expliquera en mon nom sur l'affaire; vous pouvez assurer ceux qui gouvernent l'Angleterre et qui vous en-*

voyent que nous ferons tout ce que nous pouvons, moi et le Roi d'Espagne, pour les contenter. Nous voulons la paix l'un et l'autre, j'y contribuera[*i*] *de ma part tout ce qui me sera possible*." [Well, Sir, that is very polite. You know the reply I gave to your memorandum, and you know my willingness to please and to negotiate with England. I am sending a minister with you who will speak in my name concerning the matter; you can assure those who govern England and who are sending you that we will do everything we can, I and the King of Spain, to please them. We both desire peace. On my side I shall contribute everything possible to it.]

He having named the Roi d'Espagne, I said.

"*Sire, la commission dont S.M. la Reine de la Grande Bretagne m'a honoré, le mémoire que ai donné à Monsieur de Torci et les discours qui* [*que*] *je lui ai tenus là-dessus sont des preuves convainquantes que l'Angleterre souhaite la paix. J'espère, Sire, que votre ministre est muni d'un pouvoir ample et plein*." [Sire, the mission with which Her Majesty the Queen of Great Britain honored me, the memorandum which I gave to Monsieur de Torcy, and the talks which I have held with him on that subject are convincing proofs that England desires peace. I hope, Sire, that your minister has been granted ample and full powers.]

He: "*Il est, Monsieur*." [He has, Sir.]

I: "*Sire, il trouvera l'Angleterre prête à faire tout pour la paix, qui puisse consister avec l'honneur de* [*la*] *nation et la sûreté de leur commerce*." [Sire, he will find England ready to do everything for peace, which is consistent with the honor of the nation and the safety of their commerce.]

He: "*J'en ferai de même, sur ce fondement la paix se fera, entre deux nations descendues du même sang, et qui ne sont ennemis que par nécessité; il ne faut pas perdre du temps*." [I shall do the same. On this basis peace shall be achieved between two nations descending from the same blood and which are only enemies out of necessity; no time must be wasted.]

He recommended me again to Monsieur Torci who stood at a distance while I spoke to the King, and coming up presented M. Gaultier to His Majesty, upon which I took the liberty to say in that gentleman's behalf what really his behavior merited.

"*Sire, voilà un de vos sujets à qui nous devons que la négotiation est prevenue [parvenue] jusques ici; il a pris beaucoup de peine et surmonté beaucoup de difficultés.*"

[Sire, here is one of your subjects who is responsible for negotiations having proceeded this far; he has taken great pains and has overcome many difficulties.]

62. The Correspondence of Henry St. John

The letters of Henry St. John (1678–1751), created Viscount Bolingbroke in 1712, brilliantly describe further serious negotiations which led to the Peace of Utrecht. At the center of everything as a secretary of state, Bolingbroke moved carefully and surely as a member of the Tory party in order to end the war.

The negotiations between England and France necessarily involved deception on the part of the English toward their Dutch allies. James Butler, Second Duke of Ormonde (1665–1745), had the difficult task as captain general of the English forces in the Netherlands of dealing with the Dutch as if England were continuing the war. Like all the Tories instrumental in making the peace, Ormonde was severely punished by the Whigs when they regained power upon Queen Anne's death.

Not only does Colbert de Torcy (1665–1746) include interesting points about the peace negotiations in his letter, but he also presents a high royal official's view of the place of the Estates General in the French constitution.*

In the eighteenth century there was a difference of eleven days between the New Style (N.S.) Gregorian calendar adopted in most Continental countries and the Old Style (O.S.) Julian calendar retained in England.

To the Duke of Ormond[e]:

Whitehall, June the 7th, 1712

My Lord,

All Your Grace's letters are come safe to my hands and have been laid before Her Majesty. I am now to answer such parts of them as I have received the Queen's orders upon.

SOURCE: Lord Visc. Bolingbroke, *Letters & Correspondence* (London, 1798), II, 369–377, 380–390.

* We owe this reference to Professor Sheila Biddle of Columbia University. The editors have translated the Torcy letter from French.

The first point I am to mention is the satisfaction with which Her Majesty hears the account of that exact obedience which Your Grace has paid to her orders.

The Queen commanded me particularly to take this notice to you, and to express her confidence that you will proceed in the same manner.

Inclosed, Your Grace will receive copies of two letters, and a memorial, which will be dispatched this day to the Marquis de Torcy. They have been prepared by the Queen's order, in answer to the last express which came from France, and you will perceive by them, My Lord, that Her Majesty insists on the execution of the article relating to Spain, and on the delivery of Dunkirk, as points without which she will not declare for a cessation of arms in the Netherlands. At the same time Your Grace will find that Her Majesty is positively resolved to continue no longer on the present foot. This matter, therefore, is now brought to a very short issue. If these conditions are accepted, and sent signed by Monsieur de Torcy, and Dunkirk put into your possession, you are publicly to own that you can no longer act against the French. If they are not consented to, you are entirely free from restraint and at liberty to take all reasonable measures that are in your power for annoying the enemy.

My Lord Strafford will be going hence in the beginning of next week, and we hope he will find the Dutch become more tractable than hitherto they have been; in which case the Queen will do her utmost to settle the terms of a cessation, and a peace too, in the best manner for them. It is with the greatest regret that Her Majesty finds herself constrained to come to such extremities with her allies. But what remedy has she left, when either she must follow this course, or submit to be used worse than any petty prince, and have the negociations wrested out of her hands, for no other reason but because some benefit is likely to accrue to her subjects by the peace?

I observe by Your Grace's letter that you have been pressed, I may say indecently, to give an account of what orders you had received. The Dutch Minister questioned me in much the same manner, but I answered him by demanding what the private instructions are which the [Dutch] States have given to their deputies and generals.

It is probable that Mareschal de Villars may receive the orders which will be sent him from Versailles within a day after this letter may come to your hands. Your Grace will therefore lose no time in acquainting him that you are in expectation of receiving from his court that which must determine your proceedings; and that, according to the King's resolution, you are either to look upon yourselves on both sides as freed from any restrictive orders and in full liberty of acting against each other, or that you are openly to declare for a cessation, whilst the best means possible are used to prevail on the rest of the allies to do the same; but the Queen's declaration, however, is to be positive.

Your Grace is, to be sure, informed of the endeavours used by the States to debauch the troops in Her Majesty's pay from her, and to borrow money for carrying on their subsistence. She makes no doubt but Your Grace is on your guard and that you will take the best precaution to make them steady to Her Majesty's interest, and to prevent any surprize. I shall not fail to let the several ministers know in what manner the Queen will resent any step of this kind; and I believe Your Grace will do well to speak the same language to the generals of the foreign corps paid by the Queen. Among other things they will, I believe, reflect twice on the arrears which are due to most of them.

These, My Lord, are all the instructions which I am at present directed to transmit to Your Grace, and these are of such a nature that I lose no time in sending the courier away, though he for France is not yet gone. I am ever, My Lord, &c.

P.S. I forgot to say in my letter, and therefore I say it here, that in case France agrees with the Queen, and Your Grace, by consequence, refuses publicly to act against them, I think the allies will have little reason to complain, since Dunkirk is something more valuable than Quesnoy, and since a town delivered up is more cheaply acquired than a town taken by siege.

To Mr. Harley (Edward, 1664–1735?)

Whitehall, June 7th, 1712

Sir,

I received this morning, with My Lord Privy Seal's, the favour of the 14th instant, N.S. from Utrecht.

Time has lain heavy no doubt on your hands; Holland is never, I believe, a very agreeable place to one of your temper, but in this ferment it must be particularly disagreeable to you on many accounts.

Our whole attention has been given for several days to the securing of the negociation in the Queen's hands, which the grateful Dutch and the honest Whigs (for the Imperialists are not worth naming) make so many efforts to wrest from her. At the same time, we have been working with France to secure a public suspension of arms, a private one being neither safe nor honourable to continue any longer. My dispatches to My Lord Privy Seal, and the papers from the office, will sufficiently apprize you how these matters at present stand. I am sanguine enough to believe that all will go well, but surely never negociation laboured under so many unnatural, as well as unnecessary difficulties.

I thank you for your intelligence from Amsterdam, and am glad to hear that Hop succeeded no better in his embassy [to Prince Eugene of Savoy on how to best win over the English troops in Flanders]; this seems to be the utmost pitch that passion and rage can carry those people to, unless they should go, as some have been saucy enough to insinuate, as far as to attempt seizing the British troops in Flanders. The provocation indeed is great, the Queen treats for herself and them, when they refuse to concert with her; and this peace, if it takes effect, will contain some articles beneficial to Britain. I should have been glad you had specified who the ministers are that consented to take their masters [*sic*] troops from the Queen; one of them I can easily guess at. All I know is that in this case the Queen may very justly think herself freed from all obligations of treaty or of any other kind; and I think she will gain more by the breach than she could be the union with such allies. I have informed My Lord Treasurer* that you are alive; he received the news with much satisfaction. The House of Lords is this moment in debate on the Queen's speech, and His Lordship, while I am writing to you, may very probably be employed in wiping off some of the dirt which that scavenger Wharton throws at him. I go to him from hence, and perhaps he may write to you by this messenger.

By Tuesday's post you will receive your orders to proceed to

* Robert Harley (1661–1724) Earl of Oxford.

Hanover, and you will have another letter for the Elector; what instructions Her Majesty may think fit to send you shall be sent at the same time.

I have ordered my brother to stay and wait on you to Hanover; I hope you will forgive the liberty I take of putting the young fellow under your protection.

To the Duke of Ormond:

Whitehall, June 11, 1712

My Lord,

I dispatch this messenger in haste to Your Grace, with some additions to, or rather explanations of, the last orders which I had the honour to transmit to you. On the supposition that Your Grace will receive, from the court of France, an acceptance of the conditions proposed by Her Majesty for a suspension of arms, the Queen directs that Your Grace should consider with yourself how to take possession of Dunkirk, in the safest and best manner, and this not only with respect to the enemy, but to the allies. Her Majesty thinks it proper and necessary that Your Grace should likewise know of Mareschal Villars, what facility he can give on his part to Your Grace in this matter and how you may best obviate such difficulties as Prince Eugene and the deputies may create.

What has passed lately here makes the Queen so absolutely mistress of her own conduct and cuts off to such a degree all hopes of breaking through her measures, that we hope to find, at the army and every where else, more ease and compliance than we have hitherto met with; but however, it is good to suppose the worst, and to omit no precaution in an affair so nice in its nature, of so great importance to the Queen's honour, and to the interest of her kingdoms.

Should the French not comply with the articles proposed by Her Majesty, Your Grace then understands yourself to be at liberty to act as if no restrictive orders had been ever sent you, and you will let the Mareschal know as much.

I have time to add no more but my assurance of being, with the utmost sincerity, My Lord, Your Grace's, &c.

To the Duke of Ormond:

Whitehall, June 14th, 1712

My Lord,

Though my letter is short, yet I thought the importance of it deserved to have a messenger dispatched on purpose.

Your Grace has seen what I writ by the Queen's order to France, on the subject of the cessation; the courier returned last night, and Her Majesty's demands are complied with to her satisfaction. If therefore, My Lord, Your Grace has any difficulties, as we foresee several which may arise, in taking possession of Dunkirk, you may keep your army entire, and our measures are ready here for sending over troops for that service.

Nothing can be more dreadful to the Dutch than this town in English hands. Consider, therefore, the temper they are in, and if you are likely to have the least disturbance on this account, keep the secret, send your accounts to the Queen, and, in the mean time, the troops shall be ready to enter the place from hence. We will find means of concerting things so that your declaration for a suspension shall be exactly timed with the evacuation of Dunkirk. We expect impatiently to hear from you. Monsieur de Torcy having sent me word that he dispatched copies to Your Grace of what he writ to me.

If you have taken possession, well; if you have not, we shall be able to do it from hence; and, perhaps, in the ferment you had better lie still and let Dunkirk be possessed first, and the clamour happen afterwards. On your next letters, we shall take our measures; I hope they may come tomorrow. I am ever, My Lord, &c.

To the Duke of Ormond:

Whitehall, June 20th, 1712

My Lord,

The instructions necessary, in this critical conjuncture, to be given to Your Grace are such as Her Majesty has thought to deserve sending the Earl of Strafford on purpose to the army. He will set out to-morrow, and make all possible haste to Your Grace, but in the mean time I thought it expedient to send Smith back to you with this notice, and the account of what has been done here upon your letters, and the dispatch received at the same time from the

Marquis de Torcy. Besides what you will find in my letter [dated June 20] to this minister, I told the gentlemen who were with me this morning that the Queen would look upon herself as acquitted from all obligations of arrears of subsidies or pay to that prince whose troops should refuse to obey your orders without hesitation, and that Your Grace would be directed on the receipt of my letter to declare as much to them and to require a positive answer from them. And as Your Grace will be more fully apprized of the measure you are to observe on the Earl of Strafford's arrival, and on the account you shall receive from France, so I believe the best use you can make of the intermediate time will be to continue vigilantly on your guard and to speak in the plainest and most resolute manner to the several generals of the foreign corps.

I inclose to Your Grace a state of the several troops, by which you will see which are in the entire pay, and which in the joint pay of the Queen and the States; those of the first sort must obey you in the whole, and those of the latter in the same proportion in which they are paid.

Your Grace will, I believe, think fit to give the Mareschal [de Villars] notice of the endeavours used by the Queen to subdue the obstinacy of those who refuse to obey; of the expectation you are in to hear from him on an express sent from hence to the court of France, and of the Earl of Strafford's coming to the army with fresh instructions from Her Majesty. Your Grace will farther observe by my letter to Monsieur de Torcy that the Queen has altered her intention concerning the manner of taking possession of Dunkirk. She thinks that sending the troops from hence will be a method liable to fewer accidents than making a detachment from Your Grace's army, or even marching with all the troops which will obey your orders to the sea. If, therefore, you receive an account from the court of France that Her Majesty's last proposals are agreed to, and orders are dispatched for the surrendry of Dunkirk, Your Grace will have no more to do than to declare the suspension between Great Britain and France, and to keep the whole body which shall obey your orders entire, and to withdraw in the best manner which the circumstances you shall be in will allow.

As to the troops in the town and castle of Ghent, I have no particular directions; neither is it easy, in the present conjuncture, to give any. Your Grace will advertise them to be upon their guard, and I hope we shall soon be able to bring not only them, but all the rest of the Queen's troops out of that country.

Your Grace will excuse me for using another hand than my own, but, in the present hurry of business, it is impossible to do otherwise; and I hope Your Grace will not stand on the ceremony of writing with your own hand to me. I am, &c.

[P.S.] I need not caution Your Grace that the inclosed to the Marquis de Torcy is fit to fall under the eyes of no person whatsoever but Your Grace. . . .

From Monsieur de Torcy

Marly, June 22nd, 1712

Sir,

Yesterday I received, through the courier whom you sent back to me, the letter which you did me the honor of writing me on the 6th of this month, O.S., and the memorandum containing the articles proposed by the Queen of Great Britain for a suspension of arms between the armies which are presently in the Low Countries.

I read this memorandum and your letter to the King, and I assure you, Sir, that all the esteem and all the respect which His Majesty has for the Queen's requests were needed in order to have the article concerning Dunkirk accepted, under the terms which you persist in calling for; but there is no way to refuse the entreaties of such a great princess, who declares so openly her feelings for the reestablishment of the general peace of Europe; and although you very rightly showed that there are cases in which prudence requires one to take the most careful precautions between the closest relatives and between the most intimate friends, this maxim—which is so wise and so true—weakens before the King's sincere desire to satisfy a queen whom His Majesty cannot yet treat publicly as a friend, although he already feels for this princess the sentiments which the closest friendship inspires, even more than blood ties. Thus, Sir, the King agrees to have his troops removed from the city and citadel of Dunkirk, and from the forts surrounding it, to allow the English troops of the Queen to enter in their stead on the day when the suspension of arms begins, and to leave Dunkirk in the Queen's hands, until the [Dutch] Estates General has agreed to give the King an equivalent to the demolition of this fortress which is satisfactory to His Majesty.

Lastly, he approves the remainder of article three, and the fourth of your memorandum concerning Dunkirk. He orders me only to add that the French officers entrusted with guarding his supplies, both for land and for sea, will remain in the city and will continue to carry out their work during the stay which the English troops are to make there. This clause results from the Queen's promise to leave everything in the same condition in which it now is, and from the safety which she promises the King's ships, and those of individuals and their belongings. His Majesty thus assumes that he is proposing nothing new in stretching this article a little.

Since he believes he can give the Queen no more obvious proof of his absolute trust, His Majesty declares to her that all the results of negotiations carried out successfully to the very point of concluding the agreement would be lost through insisting on the clause in the second article which states that the renunciation of the Crown of France by the King of Spain, for himself and for his descendants, shall be ratified by the Estates of the kingdom. The Estates of France do not meddle in matters concerning the succession to the Crown; they lack the power to do it or to rescind laws. When kings convoke them, it is stated in the letters [of convocation] that it is to hear the complaints of good and faithful subjects and to seek remedies for current ills.

The examples of previous centuries have shown that these sorts of assemblies have almost always created troubles in the realm, and the last Estates [General], which met in 1614, ended in a civil war; since the King feels certain of the Queen's true intentions, His Majesty is persuaded that this princess is simply seeking certitude as to the renunciation, and that it is sufficient, as a result, to provide [a guaranty] more in conformity to our customs, and which will not be subject to the inconveniences of an assembly of the Estates, which, not having been called for almost a century, has in a sense been abolished in the realm.

This guaranty shall be, Sir, to have published and registered, in all the parlements of the realm, the renunciation of the Crown of France made by the King of Spain for himself and his descendants. Edicts and declarations signed with these formalities have the force of law; the French are accustomed to this practice, it is used for treaties made with foreign powers; and the King's intention is at the same time to order that the letters-patent which His Majesty issued in favor of the King of Spain, preserving for him his birthright when he left France to go to Madrid, be removed and erased publicly from the registers of the Parlement; the revocation and annullation of these letters will be the result and a sort of confirmation of the renunciation which this prince has resolved to make of his rights to the Crown of France for himself and his descendants.

There, Sir, are the unique addition and the sole change which the King wishes made in your memorandum; the addition concerns the permission for the officers entrusted with guarding the land and sea supplies at Dunkirk, and I am convinced that it will create no difficulties. The change concerns the assembly of the Estates; permit me to say that it would also be contrary to the King's authority, to the peace of the realm, and even to the general peace for us to accept such a proposal involving a thousand inconveniences too detailed to explain here; and that there is reason to believe that when [the English] stipulated an assembly of the Estates, they knew neither the uselessness of this precaution nor the trouble which convoking them might create.

The King is sending, Sir, to Monsieur the Marshal of Villars, a copy of your memorandum and of the replies; and since His Majesty grants, in essence, everything the Queen requests, he does not doubt that the Duke of Ormond will carry out the orders he has received concerning the suspension [of arms]. He also assumes that this general, in declaring that he no longer has orders to fight against France, will not only keep the English from fighting, but also all the foreign troops under his command, and that steps will be taken to prevent the Dutch from being able, as they boast, to take into their pay the troops which are now in the pay of the Queen.

I hope, Sir, that, when you have received the letter I have had the honor of writing you, nothing will delay the departure of the Count of Strafford, and that you will give him the necessary instructions to join the King's plenipotentiaries, so that they can agree to impose the law upon those who shall refuse to accept the just and reasonable conditions of the peace. I beg you also to believe that I am, Sir, your &c.

DE TORCY

63. A Final Assessment by a Country Priest

Whether really written by a country priest or by some pamphleteer posing as a country priest, this assessment presents the stereotype of Louis XIV's reign which would survive in popular histories and even in textbooks. Not all the elements of the stereotype are there: the charges that he waged war too much, oppressed the French peasants to pay for Versailles, and was sexually immoral developed when bourgeois republican historians turned to writing French history. The Sun King's image as the persecutor of Protestants and burner of German villages had already entered popular lore before his death.

One thing is clear: there has never been any doubt about the importance of Louis' personality and individual impact on French and European political life, 1660–1715. Whether castigating or praising him, authors recognize the Sun King's own role in a mass of issues and decisions made over a fifty-year period. There were some decades, of course, in which Louis was more influenced by his ministers than in others, but still and all his effort to dominate the forces and circumstances which he faced has been recognized. Louis was never one to veil his personal role, and this recognition of his initiative is probably how he himself would have wished to be remembered. Acting, so he believed, according to God's will, Louis was greatly concerned about his public image during his lifetime and took steps to project the image of a great king into the future. The ancient maxim that to be respected and obeyed was preferable to being loved might be the Sun King's reply to the country priest.

In any final assessment of Louis XIV it is unfair to omit the problems which he faced, many of which were not of his own making. He and his ministers grappled with these problems; and even if they did not find solutions, the effort had been made in France at least. The internal reforms they attempted made France a leader among states in the process of political centralization. But these reforms were often thwarted or rendered ineffectual as much by the French themselves as by the international wars which undermined fiscal and judicial probity. Opposition to many reforms was so successful that the term "absolute" as used by the country priest in this document has little significance. Gov-

SOURCE: "Appréciation du règne de Louis XIV par un curé de campagne," a selection from the "Remarques" of the Curé of Saint-Sulpice, as quoted in *Archives Historiques, Artistiques et Littéraires* (Paris, 1889–90), Vol. I.

erning twenty million Frenchmen in the seventeenth century was anything but an easy task. An illiterate peasantry which felt threatened by any innovations, a military landlord class with great power, and merchants and manufacturers who were often content with the traditional ways of doing things suggest some "third-world" society in the twentieth century undergoing the painful process of modernization and industrialization.

Louis 14, King of France and of Navarre, died on September 1, of this year, little mourned by all his realm, because of the exorbitant sums and the very substantial taxes he levied upon all his subjects. They say that he died owing 1,700,000,000 livres. His debts were so substantial that the Regent could not remove the taxes which the aforesaid King had promised to remove three months after the peace [of Utrecht], that is the *capitation* and the tenth on the income from all possessions. It is not permitted to utter all the poems, all the songs, and all the discourteous speeches which have been said and written against his memory. During his life he was so absolute that he went above all the laws in order to do what he wished. The princes and the nobility had been crushed, the parlements had no more power; it [parlement] was obliged to receive and register all edicts, whatever they were, so powerful and absolute was the King. The clergy was shamefully servile to doing the King's will; scarcely did he ask it for help than it would grant him more than he had requested. The clergy had become horribly indebted; all the guilds were no less so. Only partisans [tax farmers] and swindlers were at peace and lived happily, having in their possession all the money in the realm. The King was borne to Saint-Denis [the royal necropolis outside Paris] on the 10th or 12th of the above month, and the funeral oration was given at Saint-Denis toward the end of the month of October.

GLOSSARY OF FRENCH TERMS

Aides Indirect taxes, particularly the excises on the sale of fish, meat, wood, wine, and so forth.

Bailliage A geographical-judicial unit in northern France which established royal justice at the local level. The equivalent of the *sénéchaussée* of the South.

Bourgeois In France, urban property owners who were inscribed on the electoral rolls of their town and were eligible for service in the militia and election to offices in the *bureau de la ville.* Almost invariably exempt from the *taille,* they nevertheless held *rôture* or common social status and were considered part of the third estate.

Capitation A "head tax" created in 1695–1698 during the War of the League of Augsburg, reimposed in 1701, and collected throughout the War of Spanish Succession. Applied to everyone, in principle, the twenty-two rates (from 2,000 livres to 1 livre) were intended to be proportionate to one's fortune rather than one's class.

Chambre des Comptes A group of sovereign courts having both administrative and judicial functions, including matters of the royal domain and titles of nobility.

Cinq grosses fermes A private tax farm authorized by the government to collect five royal customs taxes on trade between provinces over a large area of central France. In 1664, pursuant to a consolidation of the various tax farms, Colbert merged these farms with the *gabelles* and eliminated internal customs within the area encompassed by the "five great farms," creating a free-trade area. (See document 41.)

Consuls A court established in various towns to settle disputes between merchants up to the sum of 500 livres.

Cour des Aides Courts established for litigation arising from the assessment of excise and other taxes.

Dérogeance The loss of noble status by an individual whose primary function was to serve the king in war. A nobleman who engaged in retail trade or became a tenant farmer for another noble lost his privileged status and became subject to the *taille.*

Échevins Officials of the municipal governments of Paris and numerous other cities.

Écu A French coin, valued at three livres, or sixty sous.

Élection A geographical-administrative unit for the allocation of taxes. See *généralité.*

Ferme Indirect taxes such as the *aides* and *gabelles* were leased to groups of individuals who, in return for a guaranteed sum to be paid the Crown, received the right to enforce and collect royal taxes. The tax farmers often made immense profits through oppressive methods of collecting taxes. About one third of all royal taxes went as profits to the farmers.

Gabelle A salt tax which varied regionally depending partly on production of salt in that area. The privilege of the *franc-salé* exempted nobles, clergy, and certain royal councillors and magistrates from the *gabelle.* (See document 41.)

Généralité One of twenty-one geographical-administrative units for the assessment and administration of taxes, chiefly the *taille.* The *généralité* was composed of a number of *élections*, each with a *bureau des élus* which allocated the sums to be collected throughout the various parishes in the *élection*, to meet the total taxes fixed by the King's Council. The *receveur général* was the chief collector for the *généralité.* In five *généralités*, however, known as *pays d'États* in contrast to *pays d'élections*, the provincial estates voted the total sum to be paid.

Gentilhomme In France a nobleman whose privileged status in the second estate was either very old and therefore illustrious, or who was at least certain of the noble status of his father and grandfather. "A gentleman is born, not made," is a contemporary phrase reflecting the seventeenth-century tenet that kings by letter patent could grant nobility but not gentility to a subject whose ancestors, usually in the army, had exemplified personal bravery in service to the Crown.

Gloire Personal attainment, the realization of a gentleman's highest potential, as established by noble birth and courage; the basis for recognition, honor, and reputation while alive, and immortality after death.

Grands The dukes, peers of France, and princes of the blood; the most illustrious and powerful members of the second estate.

Laboureur Since the middle ages a distinction had existed between the *laboureur*, or peasant who owned and rented out teams of draft animals, and the poorer peasant who tilled with a hoe or rented a team and plow for his small plot. The *laboureur*, with his herds and numerous fields, often leased from noble or bourgeois landlords and was frequently wealthier than the proprietors.

Lettre de cachet One of the means by which the king exercized his personal justice. This sealed letter, usually directing the imprisonment or exile of a person named in it, was used primarily to confine persons whose conduct was likely to discredit their families.

Livre (*tournois*) Money of account, valued at twenty sous.

Marc d'or A fee paid to the Crown by a royal official upon taking office.

Noble In France, an individual having a privileged status in the society, including the right to bear arms. Eligible for service in the royal army if the *ban* or *arrière ban* lists included him, the nobleman was for this reason exempt from the *taille.* A member of the second estate, forbidden to engage in retail trade, and often possessed of honorific titles such as count or marquis, the nobleman might or might not simultaneously hold a venal royal office, be part of the royal household, or own manors (*seigneuries*) and fiefs in the country.

Parlements Highest or "sovereign" courts in the French judicial administration. Their decisions could be overruled by the king in council. The Parlement of Paris was the most powerful of these bodies, exercizing jurisdiction over half the realm.

Parties casuelles Payments for newly created or newly reverted offices; included *la Paulette* and the *marc d'or.*

Paulette An annual payment to the Crown, or *droit annuel,* by all holders of venal offices of one sixtieth of their purchase price. (See document 41.)

Pays d'État Some provinces, notably Provence and Brittany, had representative assemblies or estates which met to discuss provincial political matters and levy taxes. (See *généralité.*)

Peuple, menu peuple The most numerous, the poorest, and the least propertied inhabitants of a city or region.

Présidial (*présidiaux*) Created by Henry II ostensibly to handle minor legal matters which were slowing down the courts of the parlements, but also to gain revenue from the sale of offices. Certain more important *bailliages* or *sénéchaussées* were elevated to *présidiaux* to pass final judgment on cases being appealed in ordinary *bailliages* (for sums under 250 livres).

Prévôt des marchands Highest ranking official in the municipal governments of Paris and numerous other cities.

Receveur général The royal official charged with the collection of royal taxes in each *généralité.*

Sénéchaussée A geographical-judicial unit in southern France, equivalent to the *bailliage* of the North.

Tailles The greatest source of revenue for the Crown, and strictly speaking the only direct tax. The amount was assessed yearly for each *généralité* and was apportioned by *élection.* The *taille personnelle* was paid by the overwhelming majority of Frenchmen, excluding the privileged clergy, nobility, and many of the individuals heading the third estate. The *taille réelle,* confined to the South and Southwest, was a levy on landholdings and allowed fewer exemptions for social status. Some of the *pays d'États* voted an annual sum as equivalent of the *taille.*

Taillon An extra levy for the upkeep of soldiers to supplement the original *taille.* (See document 41.)

CHRONOLOGY

1635 France declares war against Spain
Founding of the French Academy
Chapel of the Sorbonne, by Lemercier
Charles I, by Van Dyck
Peace of Prague

1636 Capture of Corbie by the Spanish
Popular rebellions in much of southwestern France
Le Cid, by Corneille
Founding of Harvard College

1637 Death of Emperor Ferdinand II, succeeded by Ferdinand III, d. 1657
Discours de la Méthode, by Descartes
Croquant revolts in Languedoc and Provence
First *solitaires* enter Port-Royal
Solemn League and Covenant, Scotland

1638 Birth of Louis XIV
Saint-Cyran imprisoned
St. Vincent de Paul founds the *Enfants-Trouvés*

1639 Nu-pied revolts in Normandy
Revolts in Brittany, Provence, Languedoc, and Poitou

1640 Revolt of the Catalans
French troops occupy Savoy
Augustinus, by Jansen
Revolt of the Portuguese
Death of George William, succeeded by Frederick William, Elector of Brandenburg (the Great Elector), d. 1688
First session of the Long Parliament

1641 *Méditations*, by Descartes

1642 Death of Cardinal Richelieu
Olier founds Congregation of Saint-Sulpice
De Cive, by Hobbes
Nightwatch, by Rembrandt

1643 Death of Louis XIII
Battle of Rocroi
Popular revolts in Rouergue, Auvergne, Dauphiné, Normandy, Brittany, Touraine, and Provence
The Guards, by Le Nain
La Fréquente Communion, by Arnauld
Solemn League and Covenant, the English Parliament

1644 Peace negotiations begin at Münster and Osnabrück
Barometer, by Torricelli
Death of Pope Urban VIII; election of Pope Innocent X
Areopagitica, by Milton

1645 Battle of Naseby
Popular revolts in Provence, Guyenne, Dauphiné, Burgandy, and Paris
1646 Lully arrives in Paris
Turenne invades Bavaria
1648 Fronde (Parlementary)
Cromwell reestablishes English authority in Ireland
Treaties of Westphalia
Pilgrims of Emmaus, by Rembrandt
1649 Treaty of Rueil, ends parlementary Fronde
Charles I sentenced to death and beheaded
Traité des Passions, by Descartes
1650 Arrest of Condé, Mazarin's flight during princely Fronde
Death of William II of Orange
1651 Ormée in Bordeaux
Suppression of stadtholderate in United Provinces
Navigation Act
Leviathan, by Hobbes
1652 *Liberum veto* formally instituted in the Polish Diet
Anglo-Dutch War
Battle of Porte Saint-Antoine in Paris
Bernini completes the Ecstacy of St. Theresa
1653 Dissipation of princely Fronde; Mazarin returns to Paris
Innocent X condemns Jansenism–denouncing five propositions
Cromwell named Lord Protector
Pascal enters Port-Royal
John de Witt becomes Grand Pensionary
Le Grand Cyrus, by Scudéry
1654 Coronation of Louis XIV
Christina of Sweden abdicates; Charles X becomes king
Survey of Ireland, by Petty
1655 Assembly of the Clergy
Solitaires of Port-Royal dispersed
Charles X of Sweden attacks Poland
1656 Beginning of formal Franco-Spanish peace negotiations
The Provincial Letters, by Pascal and Arnaud
Founding of the Paris General Hospital
1657 Anglo-French cooperation in a war against Spain
The Annunciation, by Poussin
1658 Death of Cromwell
Battle of the Dunes
Dunkirk surrendered to the English
Leopold I formally elected Holy Roman Emperor
1659 Peace of the Pyrenees
Pepys begins to keep a diary
1660 Declaration of Breda; Charles II returns to England
Louis XIV marries Maria-Theresa of Spain

Death of Charles X of Sweden; accession of Charles XI
Death of Velásquez
1661 Death of Mazarin
Enactment of the so-called Clarendon Code
Founding of the Gobelins tapestry works
La Vau's first work at Versailles
Lully named superintendant of the king's music
1662 Charles II marries Catherine of Braganza
Founding of the Royal Society in London
1663 French armies occupy the Comtat Venaissin
Le Nôtre's first gardens at Versailles
1664 French armies occupy Lorraine
Trial and banishment of Fouquet
Creation of the Compagnie des Indes
English capture New Amsterdam
Reform of the *rentes*
Tartuffe, by Molière
1665 Colbert named Controller-General of Finances
Death of Philip IV of Spain, succeeded by Charles II, d. 1700
Grands Jours d'Auvergne
Bernini presents plans for the Louvre
Anglo-Dutch War
1666 Colbert named Secretary of State for the Navy
Founding of the Academy of Sciences
Death of Anne of Austria
Great fire of London
The Letter, by Vermeer
1667 French armies invade the Spanish Netherlands (War of Devolution)
La Reynie named Lieutenant General of Police
Paradise Lost, by Milton
De Statu imperii Germanici, by Pufendorf
1668 Triple Alliance of England, Holland, and Sweden (negotiated by Temple)
Peace of Aix-la-Chapelle
Creation of French maritime conscription
Conversion of Turenne to Catholicism
Fables, I, by La Fontaine
Guarini designs the Chapel of the Holy Shroud, Turin
1669 Publication of the *Code des Eaux et Forêts*
Fall of Candia (Crete) to the Turks
Death of Rembrandt
Death of Cortona
1670 Treaty of Dover
Publication of the French *Ordonnance criminelle*
Pensées, by Pascal
1671 Crimean Tartars sack Moscow

Cartesian philosophy forbidden at the Sorbonne
Moral Essays, by Nicole

1672 Franco-Dutch War (the Crossing of the Rhine)
Charles II issues a Declaration of Indulgence
Leibnitz visits France
Assassination of the de Witt brothers
De Jure Naturae et Gentium, by Pufendorf
William (III) of Orange becomes stadtholder
Capture of Utrecht

1673 Turenne invades Westphalia
Dutch-Imperal alliance against France
Test Act
General Ordonnance on Commerce
Malade Imaginaire, by Molière

1674 French armies invade the Franche-Comté
Temple's embassy to France
John Sobieski, King of Poland
Treaty of Westminster
Art Poétique, by Boileau

1675 Popular revolts in Brittany, Guyenne, Poitiers, Le Mans, and Bordeaux
Death of Turenne
Le Parfait Negociant, by Savary

1676 Benedetto Odescalchi becomes Pope Innocent XI

1677 Louis XIV takes up permanent residence at Versailles
Beginning of Franco-Dutch peace negotiations
Phèdre, by Racine
Ethics, by Spinoza

1678 Treaty of Nymwegen
The Popish Plot
Beginning of the quarrel over the *Régale*
Pilgrim's Progress, by Bunyon
Histoire Critique de Vieux Testament, by R. Simon
Princesse de Clèves, by La Fayette

1679 Popular revolt in Brittany
First fortifications built by Sébastien Vauban
Politique tirée de l'Ecriture Sainte, by Bossuet

1680 Beginning of the sessions of the courts of "reunion."
Kneller succeeds Lely as court painter

1681 Annexation of Strasbourg
Opening of the Canal du Midi
Absalom and Achitophel, by Dryden
De Re Diplomatica, by Mabillon
Discours sur l'Histoire Universelle, by Bossuet

1682 Peter I proclaimed Tsar of Russia (along with Ivan V)
Newton discovers law of universal gravity

1683 Siege of Vienna

Popular revolts in Nîmes and Le Puy
Death of Colbert
Death of Maria Theresa
Rye House Plot
Invasion of the Spanish Netherlands by French troops
Puget completes *Milo of Crotona*
1684 Locke expelled from Oxford
1685 Death of Charles II of England; succeeded by James II
Revocation of the Edict of Nantes
1686 League of Augsburg formed against France
Budapest taken from the Turks
1687 *Philosophiae Naturalis Principia Mathematica*, by Newton
Destruction of the Parthenon
1688 War of the League of Augsburg
Flight of James II from England
Invasion of England by William of Orange
Death of Frederick William (the Great Elector) of Brandenburg
Letter concerning Toleration, by Locke
1689 Burning of the Palatinate by French troops
1690 Spain joins the League of Augsburg against France
Treatises of Government, by Locke
Battle of Beachy Head
1691 Death of Louvois
Battle of Aughrim
Athalie, by Racine
1692 Capture of Namur
Massacre of Glencoe
Lloyd's of London begins marine insurance
1694 Creation of the Bank of England
First edition of the *Dictionnaire* by the French Academy
Te Deum and *Jubilate*, by Purcell
1695 *Dictionnaire Historique et Critique*, by Bayle
Capitation instituted
1697 Treaty of Ryswick
Peter the Great visits Western Europe
Death of Charles XI of Sweden; succeeded by Charles XII, d. 1718
Prince Eugene defeats the Turks at Zenta
Détail de la France, by Boisguilbert
1698 Stradivarius at the height of his fame
Télémaque, by Fénelon
1700 Death of Charles II of Spain, succeeded by Philip V, d. 1746
Battle of Narva
Founding of an Academy of Sciences in Berlin
French translation of Locke's *Essay Concerning Human Understanding*
1701 Frederick III crowns himself king in Prussia
1702 War of Spanish Succession

Death of William III of England, succeeded by Anne, d. 1714
Camisard revolt
Heinsius becomes Grand Pensionary of the Netherlands
History of the Rebellion, by Clarendon
1703 Methuen Treaty
Building of St. Petersburg
1704 Battle of Blenheim
Newcomen steam engine
1705 Death of Emperor Leopold I, succeeded by Joseph I, d. 1711
Vanbrugh begins the palace of Blenheim
1706 Battle of Ramillies
1707 Union of England and Scotland
Invasion of Provence
La Dîme Royale, by Vauban
1708 Battle of Oudenarde
1709 Battle of Poltava
Battle of Malplaquet
Turcaret, by Lesage
Pastorals, by Pope
1710 Destruction of Port-Royal-des-Champs
Birth of the future Louis XV
Trial of Dr. Sacheverell
Handel reaches London
Completion of St. Paul's Cathedral
1711 Senate created by Peter I
Charles VI becomes Holy Roman Emperor
Spectator, by Steele and Addison
1712 Beginning of peace negotiations
L'Embarquement pour Cythère, by Watteau
1713 Treaty of Utrecht
Bull *Unigenitus* condemns Jansenism
1714 Death of Queen Anne, succeeded by George I
Treaty of Rastadt
Return of Charles XII to Sweden
Monadologie, by Leibnitz
1715 Death of Louis XIV
Iliad, translated by Pope

Index